W9-BOA-949

Miss Manners'®

GUIDE TO

DOMESTIC

TRANQUILITY

Miss Manners'

GUIDE TO
DOMESTIC
TRANQUILITY

The Authoritative Manual for
Every Civilized Household, However Harried

JUDITH MARTIN

 CROWN PUBLISHERS / NEW YORK

Copyright © 1999 by Judith Martin
Miss Manners is a registered trademark of Judith Martin
Illustrations copyright © 1999 by Gloria Kamen

Published by Crown Publishers, Inc., 201 East 50th Street, New York, New York 10022. Member of the Crown Publishing Group.

Random House, Inc. New York, Toronto, London, Sydney, Auckland
www.randomhouse.com

CROWN is a trademark and the Crown colophon is a registered trademark of Random House, Inc.

Design by Barbara Sturman

Printed in the United States of America

Library of Congress Cataloging-in-Publication Data
Martin, Judith
     Miss Manners' guide to domestic tranquility : the authoritative manual for every civilized household, however harried / Judith Martin. — 1st ed.
     1. Etiquette.   2. Households.   I. Title.   II. Title: Guide to domestic tranquility.
BJ1854.M37   1999
395—dc21   99-22824
                                                                      CIP

ISBN 0-517-70165-0

10 9 8 7 6 5 4 3 2 1

First Edition

For

Rebecca

and

Nicholas

ACKNOWLEDGMENTS

Neither Miss Manners' cottage industry nor her cottage would run, let alone be livable, without David Hendin, Ann Patty and Kimberley Heatherington in the one and Eunice and Willie Riddick and R.G.M. in the other.

Contents

Miss Manners'

GUIDE TO

DOMESTIC

TRANQUILITY

Introduction

A blissful refuge, warm and cheery, serving as a buffer against the harsh world of commerce, competition and connivance—that was the Victorian notion of a household.

Never mind that we now know where Father was when he came home late and why Mother thought certain aspects of life not worth mentioning. Never mind that the children who grew up under such protection spent the rest of their lives sneering at those monstrous hypocrites, their parents, for being so ridiculously self-sacrificing and secretive. Providing that smug atmosphere only demonstrated how unrealistic, unimaginative and unadventurous they were, as their more sophisticated children kindly pointed out when they reached their majority.

Nowadays, the household is given greater importance than ever, but more as a source of material for social turmoil than as a refuge from it. Those peeking in the windows want to set terms for its composition, and those peeking out don't dispute the intrusion unless whatever arrangement they have—relatives, friends or strangers; the legally coupled or the extra-legally coupled; single people, single parents, single genders or the single-minded; adults with their children, his children, her children, no children or someone else's children—is criticized.

Inside, emotional heat is expended on declarations of individual rights and transgressions, debates involving gender and generation and discussions involving possessions and relationships. It makes a chilly atmosphere, seldom warmed by courtesy, cheerfulness and cooperation.

Miss Manners contends that the domestic oasis is still a good idea. To those who even now harbor the same feelings as those Edwardian ingrates (whose own children had the nerve to call *them* Victorian, as succeeding history-defying generations have continued to do in turn), she would like to point out that we have now tested the counter-measures they demanded. Modern families have done what rebellious generations have long prescribed as necessary for mental health: They have brought the fresh air of frankness, honesty and openness into the suffocating atmosphere of Victorian domesticity.

The real world not only came indoors, but made itself thoroughly at home. The hearth, now known as the entertainment center, is where the family loiters when the demands and the pleasures of the commercial world have been temporarily exhausted—in order to enjoy the company of images from the commercial world.

If parties are given at all, they are less likely to be for family merriment than for advancing someone's professional interests. The disappointments in parents' lives, especially in the matter of romance, are no secret from their children, any more than from the rest of the town. Nor are the compensations parents seek along these lines kept hypocritically hidden. Negative moods are frankly indulged, on the grounds that no one should have to put on a falsely happy demeanor at home. Articulating one's irritation with others in the household is encouraged, both because it frankly alerts those others to their shortcomings and because it clears the air.

The trouble with such policies is that they create the need for a cozy refuge. Those who don't want to move into the neighborhood bar might learn something from the policies they spurned.

Not everything, of course. Miss Manners opposes going mindlessly back to the past, if for no other reason than that re-creating the same conditions would lead to re-creating the same opposition. Nor is she insensible to the advances made in family happiness through the sharing of feelings and the relaxation of pressures.

Nevertheless, the traditional idea of a cheerful household is worth salvaging, even though it means passing up countless opportunities to make the other residents feel one's every dissatisfaction. Part of this is merely accepting the normal ups and downs of life rather than making scenes or pointing out everybody else's mistakes and foibles. Another part is shielding children from the more frightening or less savory aspects of adult life. The very hardest part is controlling large and small impulses that do damage to others in the household—and if not controlling them, at least veiling them from view. As the beneficiaries of this policy were quick to declare, it is hypocritical. It also makes things more pleasant around the house.

BUT WE'RE TOO BUSY

So many people wail that they would love to do what it takes to have a pleasant household—sit down to dinner together, extend hospitality, indulge in conversation, offer the children daily guidance in politeness—if only they weren't so harried, that Miss Manners came to believe that such was the condition of modern life. She was not willing to concede that an entire generation had to give up civilized domestic life, but she agonized about how they could achieve it.

Tragically, there are people who are just about forced to give up living life in order to make a living. Oddly enough, these are sometimes the very people who refuse to succumb. Basic family rituals and amenities are often most strictly maintained by someone working two jobs while rearing children, perhaps alone, and still finding time to assist the occasional needy relative or neighbor. Those are not the folks from whom Miss Manners hears about modern busyness.

It was only when she took a look at the schedules of those who are doing the complaining that her sympathies began to wane. They are also working around the clock, perhaps not at two jobs but at one divided among daytime, nighttime and weekend shifts, featuring not only the work itself but working lunches, employee birthdays, client entertainment, office parties, business trips, weekend retreats and attitude-training sessions. It barely leaves them discretionary time to watch television, surf the Internet, work out, follow courses of personal self-improvement and drive their children to equally rigorous schedules.

These are all respectable activities, and Miss Manners does not begrudge people any pleasures they may find within the bounds of work. She is willing to help them pack in as much as they want, while rigorously maintaining her defense of those who eschew pseudo-socializing on the job, and promising not to expect a working household to be a showcase for revived old crafts. Acknowledging that the structure of the modern working world does make it difficult to maintain a satisfactory domestic and community life, she devotes herself to teaching how it can nevertheless be achieved. In her small way, she labors to change the cruel system by which the normal duties and pleasures of personal life are treated as frills that working people have to squeeze in as best they can while surrendering all their waking hours to keep a roof over their head during their sleeping hours.

However, when people lament that time devoted to self-improvement forces them to shortchange their families and friends—when those who have no time to break bread with their families or share a crust with friends can find time to bake it and to go to a gym to work it off—she decides that they are taking up too much of her time.

Chapter One

THE PEOPLE

THE PROPER ATTITUDE

Why can't private life be organized on a businesslike basis? Miss Manners would have thought the answer to be: Because it's not a business. You can't fire the children, and you are not likely to make a profit from them. You wouldn't have hired them in the first place, if you had been aware of their skills and attitudes. That this does not discourage people from having children, Miss Manners understands. There is such a thing as Nature. Unfortunately, neither has it discouraged a great many people from approaching family and social life with the same techniques they apply to work. They compete with their spouses, they plot ways to entertain without incurring personal expense, they advertise for romance and they market what might otherwise be considered the sentimental occasions of their lives to extract cash and goods. If they can't fire their minor children, they keep giving them notice, and they sever connections with any other relative whom they deem unsatisfactory.

The results have not been encouraging. Private life is full of paradoxes that elude logic, not to mention business techniques. By letting it be known that you are avidly searching for romance, you render yourself unattractive. By requesting donations from friends, you stifle their generosity. By engaging in competition, you drive your spouse into the arms of competitors. When you fire relatives for poor performance, you suffer enormous financial losses.

True, there are areas of the household that do gain from business acumen. The family budget, for example. In organizing a household and keeping it supplied, a systematic approach works wonders. Miss Manners herself uses an inventory system (replacing household staples not when they are used up but when their replacement is used up) for which she understands the United States Navy also claims credit.

One can also contract out tasks that used to be performed at home. A household doesn't need to grow its own food; Miss Manners wouldn't dream of checking on whether it even cooked its own food, provided whatever is served makes a decent appearance on platters and plates. It can contract out any number of domestic chores, sometimes to astonishing new services, such as those that will nag the other services.

It is only when it comes to contracting out to commercial companies and professional counselors all the basic services that a family circle of relatives and intimate friends is supposed to supply—compassion, sympathy, companionship, advice-giving, emotional support, teaching morals and manners—that she becomes alarmed. When the personal aspects of family life are all supplied by outside professionals, the family is destroyed. Nor does it get its money's worth, no matter how esteemed and valuable these services may be. In family life, unlike in the business world, who does the job is even more important than how well it is done. Nepotism is a requirement.

Anyway, the premises on which family life are based would not be considered prudent in business. The family distributes its resources according to need, not merit, and values people without regard to how much money they make (which is why nonproductive children are given allowances). It considers pleasing people to be a better justification for the way things are done than logic or uniformity or speed. It puts extra work into caring for the helpless, instead of unloading them. It expects people to work free for the common good (which is why Miss Manners opposes offering the children money for chores).

All this is amazingly inefficient and not well focused on the bottom line. It is also the only way to live.

Getting Down to Business

DEAR MISS MANNERS—I know that in previous and more refined generations, my question would be unnecessary, but freedom to speak has taken a turn for the worse and I think other women of my generation (the Baby Boomers) and younger would find this an appropriate topic.

I am a single woman with a lively personality, educated, fun to be with, and with a pleasant physique. A number of times, I advertised myself in the personals columns of various publications as looking for a companion and husband. The ads are inviting and straightforward; they do not suggest I am looking for an affair. I have also responded to men's ads that seem to be age, interest, religion, etc., appropriate.

The problem is that in my initial conversation, on the telephone or when meeting a fellow in person, the man will sometimes say, "So how come you are not (or have ever been) married?" Many of these guys are divorced; perhaps they are envious or jealous of my freedom. My comeback is, "Well, that is a very personal question." There are reasons I've never been married but the reasons aren't important now, and the question is rude.

I am disappointed by this marriage question. Should I just rip up their letters and not go out with them? Or are they just having a lapse in proper etiquette?

GENTLE READER—The proper etiquette for what, exactly? You want these gentlemen to consider you as a marriage partner, but you don't want them to get personal?

Miss Manners acknowledges that proper etiquette prohibits strangers from asking such an intimate question. She believes it so very intimate a question that even your relatives should restrain themselves. About once a decade should be about right for your parents or grandparents to take you aside and ask you privately. Even then, you may point out how superfluous such probing is by replying politely, "When I have something to announce, you will be the first to hear it."

She also admires those who guard—and protect others from—their privacy. As a case in point, there is no conceivable reason that Miss Manners would need to know that you have a pleasant physique. Similarly, a gentleman who was courting you in the conventional fashion would have no claim to ask your reasons for not marrying until he was clearly thinking of marrying you himself.

Forgive Miss Manners for intruding, but isn't that exactly what you are petitioning those callers to do?

You may guess that Miss Manners does not care for this method of skipping the preliminaries, which she considers to be as unsafe as it is unattractive. She realizes that she, in turn, is considered to be quaint, if not callous, by those who are impatient of the traditional method of cultivating a wide acquaintanceship using social, rather than business, techniques. However, you differ. If you are going to advertise yourself as if marriage were a job, it seems only fair to discuss your qualifications with the applicants.

The (Sort of) Traditional Way of Acquiring Relatives

In the traditional, minimal standard of extended family etiquette—if you could call it that—the rule was that no one could directly insult someone who was not actually a member of the family. In order to be told to your face what was wrong with you, you had to be related.

Those who were tentatively allied to the family through courtship or engagement were not yet eligible for this privilege, and had to be satisfied with being criticized behind their backs. Until they became family, they were guests. Presumably, defending the candidates after they had left was thought to be practice in marital loyalty for their future spouses. Lackluster defenses were considered a sign that further attacks might succeed in blocking the entrance of that person into the family. If they got in anyway, they were in for good and thus eligible for family treatment, such as it is.

Notice the wording in which Miss Manners takes care to distance herself from all this. She considers the premise that it is perfectly all right to insult relatives as rude as it is dangerous. As far as she can make out, neither blood nor marriage contracts remove the sting from being evaluated and found wanting.

The old practice nevertheless contained a clause that is higher than the prevailing standard now: protection of the innocent. This is unfortunately no longer observed. Rather, the idea now seems to be that non-relatives may be slighted or openly insulted all the more easily, precisely because they are not "really" members of the family. The assaults are apt to be less on grounds of personal objectionableness, which just supplies the ammunition, than on the validity of their ties to the family.

This whole new form of rudeness in the family circle is possible because nobody knows, anymore, what defines a relative. Are non-marital partnerships excluded even if they have outlasted all the family marriages? If they are allowed, at what point does somebody's fond houseguest become part of the family? Are relatives' step-children also relatives? How much does blood count? How much does custody count? Short of disowning people, is it possible to demote them from full family status if one dislikes them or disapproves of their behavior?

All the above factors have been widely used to declare certain people not quite members of the family and to exclude them from family events or to let them attend in order to treat them shabbily. Miss Manners therefore finds it necessary to issue a new set of rules. Without condoning the way some families treat their undisputed members, she wants to make it clear that there can be no such thing as second-class family membership.

At ceremonial events, relatives are eligible through the relationship, not their personal appeal. For example, you can have a guest list cutoff at second cousins, but then you can't include the third cousin you like and exclude the first cousin you hate. Nor should there be first-class and coach treatment—presents for bloodline children but not step-children who are in attendance. It is objectionable to make the distinction of "blood" between children born to the family and those acquired by adoption—when it comes to that, the parents have no blood ties to each other. Marriage counts, regardless of whether everybody thinks the new partners are suitable or the old ones could have done better. Non-legal alliances are the call of the family member involved. It's a full partnership if that person says it is. If not, then the visitor is treated as a guest. If that means better treatment, so be it.

Defining the Modern Family

DEAR MISS MANNERS — My sister plans to make up a family tree for our parents' wedding anniversary, but she wants to omit all steps and list only biologicals, and she wants to change her part by omitting the date and place she and her second husband married.

A nephew had an operation so he wouldn't have children, but married a gal who was pregnant (not by him) and put his name as father on the birth certificate. My brother married a gal with six children, and they had two together. He wants to include those two plus two of hers that he helped raise. One sister doesn't want to name either of her husbands because they didn't contribute to child support. Another sister wants to omit her second husband (no children) but include her fourth husband (no children).

Needless to say, all this has created quite a rift in the family get-along ability. I am all for accepting anybody who wants to be put down, as I believe families have been adding and eliminating at whim throughout the ages. It just rubs me the wrong way for someone to say, "Oh, don't include him in the picture—he's not family."

GENTLE READER — What, pray, does your sister have in mind by drawing up a tree of this family? Binding everyone closer together? Ensuring that next year's anniversary party may be held in a very small place?

Miss Manners knows of no genealogical society, however strict, that counts only biological ties. Marriage and adoption are undisputed ways of joining a family, and even your relatives have not exhausted all the newer possibilities.

The currently popular idea that truth requires hurting people's feelings is bad enough; Miss Manners agrees with you that declarations of who is in the family and who is not are never kindly intended, and that the results are always disastrous for the future of the family. What your sister wants is not even defensible as scholarship—it is to paint a false picture, but of her own choosing.

This is a really terrible idea, and your parents will hardly be likely to appreciate her setting off family feuds. The nicest present she could give them is to abandon the project, and get them a rubber plant instead. If she insists on continuing, Miss Manners hopes that the family will agree that the only way to figure out who is in and who is out is to ask each branch of the family to submit its own list.

Reaching the Limit

DEAR MISS MANNERS — My sister, age 50 plus and divorced, has been seeing a married man for over six years. He is invited to family functions, birthdays, etc., and has been privy to a lot of the family problems. All these years, our family has never gotten to meet his grown children or any of his friends. He does not discuss them. His wife lives out of town and, according to my sister, he will never tell her if he's getting a divorce or what is happening with his personal situation. My sister keeps him around (I think) because he takes her out to eat a lot. They do not have a loving relationship.

I am getting tired of him being around all the family events, hearing about us and never sharing anything of a personal nature. My husband is tired of him also. I would like to exclude the man from certain events because I feel he's an intruder, but I don't want to hurt my sister. There have, however, been times that I have told her I just want to be with the family and not him. My husband's daughter, who is not well acquainted with him, is having an expensive wedding out of town and does not want him to come but will invite all the family. Is it polite to tell my sister that the invitation is for her and not her friend?

GENTLE READER — You have at your disposal two relevant etiquette rules:

1. Although it is not true that single people must be allowed to bring their own guests to weddings (presumably to provide themselves with more emotional sustenance than they could hope to get from witnessing the marriage and to relieve them from the tedium of socializing with the family's other guests) and dinner parties, it has become customary to invite established couples together.

2. It has always been obligatory, and still is, to invite married couples together, whether or not one knows or likes the spouse of a prospective wedding or dinner guest.

Miss Manners suggests that your husband's daughter invoke both rules. She should tell your sister that of course she would like to invite her companion, but that she wouldn't dream of doing so without inviting his wife.

Repeated Extensions

DEAR MISS MANNERS — We have a ticklish situation here. Our son, 41, twice divorced, now lives with his girlfriend (the survivor of three marriages) and claims that they have a commitment. He expects that we treat her like a member of the family, and that she be invited to all family gatherings. We try to keep peace, but it hurts us every time he insists on this. Who knows whom he will commit himself to next month? How should we act?

GENTLE READER—Miss Manners understands your exasperation, after presumably having twice been through welcoming a new daughter-in-law, telling her the family stories, giving her the family pearls or whatever. You may even have to go through it again, perhaps with this particular person.

What you need not do is to allow your weariness with making passersby into members of the family to exaggerate your son's present request. Surely you can have her at family gatherings, and treat her with the informality due an intimate, without putting her in your will. If you got the pearls back, you can hang on to them.

The Unrelated Family

Can friends fulfill the traditional functions of a family?

Without getting into unpleasant debates about the moral and/or insurance implications of reconfiguring the patterns by which people group themselves into household units, Miss Manners has a simple answer: Sure.

Families no longer routinely fulfill the traditional functions of families, so why shouldn't ad hoc groups be able to do just as little?

In theory, there is no reason why people unrelated by blood or marriage should not be able to supply one another with the emotional and practical support that society assigns to the family. In fact, there are numerous stunning examples of people who have nurtured the young and the elderly, taken in the abandoned, cared for the sick, educated the ignorant and otherwise opened their homes and lives to people to whom they had no more binding obligation than that of common humanity.

More commonly, romance provides a powerful incentive to behave like a family. For that matter, romance provides a powerful incentive to produce a traditional family. Increasingly, it has also produced an extra-legal version of it among people who cannot, or prefer not to, avail themselves of the legal prototype.

Another sort of romance has a long history of inspiring small groups or communities of like-minded people to set up housekeeping together: a vision of living in harmony through the simple method of rising above the more troublesome human traits. Such communes tend to be dramatically short-lived, but then so do a lot of marriages nowadays.

Milder sentiments than virtue, romance or vision have also motivated the establishment of joint households. Such as tax breaks. Or shared child care. Or the most powerful of all: not being able to afford the rent alone.

Whatever the circumstances, cooperation strikes Miss Manners as a fine idea—as does pooling resources among those who share a roof. The extent of community—how much they also share duties, possessions and leisure time, and supply one another with encouragement and assistance—naturally varies among these different types of groups according to the degree of commitment.

Or so one would think. Roommates thrown together by convenience should respect one another and respond to emergencies but are hardly expected to dip freely into one another's bank accounts. At the other end, those who consider their bonds to be as stable and strong as those of marriage or blood would be expected to hold jointly not only their goods but their emotional interests. Not anymore. Unrelated groups—taking for the rule the extraordinary exceptions among their kind—tout their ability to supply all the traditional family services. Meanwhile, families have started acting like roommates, with their separate stashes of food, their private schedules and their competing ambitions, so that the unfortunate exception is in danger of becoming the rule.

Setting Entrance Requirements

DEAR MISS MANNERS—I met a fellow from out of town without a proper introduction, and after three months of living with me, he adamantly refused to tell me what he did (or had done) for a living, attributing to Miss Manners that my asking was being rude. Two months later, I asked him to leave because he wasn't significantly contributing to the well-being of the household. When I moved to his state (I sent out moving announcements) half a year later, his concerned mother tracked me down looking for him. Among other things, she informed me this well-educated, upper-middle class fellow had been living in his car for five years. Was it incorrect to ask what he did?

GENTLE READER—Now have you learned the value of proper introductions? Good. The next lesson is not to take etiquette advice, even if it spuriously carries an impeccable name, from those to whom you have not been properly introduced. Intimate questions may be asked by those on intimate terms. In this case, even Miss Manners could have figured out the answer without asking.

THE IMMEDIATE FAMILY

Mothers

Without claiming that mothers have it harder than other people, Miss Manners does wish to point out that they are more generally picked on. Fathers have children too, and children endure the extreme hardship of being children. Family life surely does not spare them from hearing about their shortcomings.

But they don't spend nearly as much time on the receiving end of unsolicited advice and uncharitable criticism from the society at large. Fathers have to fail spectacularly, with crime or desertion, to come under attack. Children get to distribute blame without having to observe a statute of limitations or fear reprisal.

No complaint is too petty or too personal when its object is a mother. You don't have to be a mother to know better than they how they should live their lives, yet mothers have never even been able to count on professional courtesy from their own kind.

Miss Manners used to attribute this rudeness to a lethal combination of prejudice, busybodyness and childishness, and had hoped that social advances would be the cure. Now she is beginning to suspect that the problem actually is caused by faith in social science, which has given us the peculiar notion that we can discern cause and effect in regard to human behavior, and the habit of explaining in those terms the unpleasant human effects that keep appearing. As we can no longer talk about bad eggs and rotten kids (or was it the other way around?), much less shoulder responsibility for doing wrong in spite of knowing better, there is a greater need than ever for a scapegoat. Hi, Ma.

Miss Manners will restrain herself from marching into questions of moral responsibility and character. Not only does she leave that murky field to others who are wearing sturdier boots, but she considers the etiquette insults that sprout there to be more of a nuisance to society.

That the children—and the neighbors and everyone else, besides—can figure out better than Mother how to do Mother's job is an eternal delusion she cannot hope to change. What she can do is to point out that it is a violation of manners to let on to anyone that you know a great deal better than she what she should be doing. Furthermore, it is a requirement of manners to offer sympathy, gratitude and admiration to someone who is struggling to do a difficult job.

There are a number of ways to do this that children who wish to be good to their very own mothers have at their disposal.

They can refrain from pointing out that they will escape her jurisdiction because of age, financial independence, being out of sight, contrary instructions extracted from Father, teacher or peers, or the ability to be even more stubborn than she is. It is not tactful to call attention to the fact that people's skills are undesirable and their jobs futile.

They can graciously allow Mother to repeat herself. Although this does not require asking "And then what happened?" when she is reminiscing about the listener's bout with measles at the age of three, it does require an attentive look. The proper response is a prompting "Ummmm," rather than "Oh, not that again." It might help to understand that these stories are told for the sake of maintaining tradition, rather than conveying information, much less surprising or entertaining listeners.

They can forgo pointing out that her version of past events is not in keeping with their knowledge of the facts. An enormous percentage of family conversation time is taken up with this, when it's really annoying and nobody cares.

They can drop a teasing point that she doesn't like, such as how much she weighs or what color her hair used to be. Normally cessation of teasing is a matter of family negotiation—you stop telling about how I used to get carsick, and I'll forget about the time your blouse split—so a free turn is a generous present.

They can make friends with her friends. Failing that, they can make conversation with her friends.

They can say those words Mother needs to hear that are not flowery enough to be emblazoned on Mother's Day cards, mugs and pillows:

"You're really the best judge of that."
"I'm sure you have your reasons."
"There's only so much you can do."
"I wouldn't dream of telling you how to live your life."
"It's amazing what you manage to accomplish under the circumstances."
"It's not your fault; you did what you could."
"By the way, I've been meaning to tell you that you were right about . . ."
"Here, let me do that."

Finally, they can request advice from her, preferably with the preface "You know more about this than I do." This is such an easy and charming thing to do that Miss Manners wonders why children do not do it more often. Perhaps they confuse it with the more unpleasant task of following a mother's advice. As grown-up children and particularly children-in-law are notoriously slow to realize, advice may be requested and accepted graciously without a future intention of heeding it.

Fathers (Resident)

Did Father make a mistake in granting the children permission to question his opinions? To allow his issue to take issue with him?

The audacious practice of contradicting a parent having long since become the rule, Miss Manners hardly expects to find modern children who are aware of the traditional manner of accepting Father's pronouncements. She doesn't even expect them to hear about it without a hoot that is highly illustrative of the change. That guy? We were supposed to pretend we thought he knew what he was talking about?

Nevertheless, it was once standard family policy, in theory and occasionally in practice, that Father enjoyed the highest respect simply by virtue of his position, and nobody gave him any lip. Well, Mother did, of course, but she did it after the bed curtains were drawn, because it was also policy for parents to refrain from contradicting each other in front of their children. Mother was not supposed to be questioned by the children either, but in an unfair world, she sometimes had to resort to issuing that vague but thunderous threat "Just wait till your father gets home."

The change in family standing happened benignly enough, as a result of parental enlightenment rather than childish rebellion. Out of a kindly belief in developing the children's powers of reason and persuasion, fathers and mothers began to permit rebuttals to their wisdom. Among nice parents, affection, not power, was supposed to sustain filial respect, so they made it possible for anyone to win an argument simply through superior reasoning. Miss Manners admits to cherishing fondness for this presumption, even if it did have the effect of producing a generation of little lawyers.

A lot has happened to fatherhood since then: custody disputes, the defense of single motherhood by characterizing it as equal or superior to married motherhood, unfair competition in consumer goods from those with no responsibility, such as Mother's beaux, and the wide dissemination of horrific tales about some fathers that sadly cast suspicion upon the position itself. Suddenly it was no longer just the case that negligent or otherwise criminal fathers forfeited respect. Rather, a normal father was expected to prove that he had especially earned it. At the same time, non-custodial fathers with disposable income were setting a standard that no father-in-residence could meet. Even the most dutiful full-time father almost never whisks the children off for exciting weekend adventures—certainly not every, or every other, weekend. Vacations aren't exotic surprises but are tediously planned and discussed in advance. Allowances may appear regularly, but surprise checks do not. Presents arrive on the holidays when they are expected but rarely between; the occasional extras a residential father produces are chance novelties, not major items.

In sum, he is predictable. He never even has mystery houseguests for breakfast. Wheedle as they will, the children can never get him to give his permission when he knows that Mother has refused hers. Affectionate though he admittedly may be, he is thinking more about rearing the children than about impressing them.

Miss Manners thinks that to be quite enough of a job, and believes that it should entitle him to be restored to his previous status as a figure of respect. She doesn't feel that she has to restore his claim of infallibility for him to garner that respect.

Fathers (Non-Resident)

Quaint evidence indicates that Father's Day was invented to honor some comfortably rumpled old soul who was more or less permanently planted in a wing chair, reading the newspaper and smoking a pipe. You know this was a long time ago because every father was able to equip himself with an afternoon newspaper.

If such a person could be found nowadays, how would his family honor him?

By telling him how disgusting his pipe was and how it was likely to kill not only his weak-willed self, which would be no more than just, but everyone with the misfortune to live in his vicinity?

By demanding that he move himself out of that chair and pitch in with the housework?

Mind you, Miss Manners is not saying that the standard model of Father did not deserve some polite and loving guidance. But his situation does not shed much light on the modern question of how we should celebrate the paternal holiday.

The traditional method of celebrating Father's Day was for the children to busy themselves making touchingly lopsided ceramic ashtrays for those pipe ashes. Today's youth is much more likely to be engaged in the sad process of sizing Father up and finding him wanting. Instead of attending to the kiln, they are asking themselves whether Father really deserves to be honored, or even tolerated. Under what conditions should his claim to the paternal position be rejected?

Suppose he lives elsewhere, with a whole new family.

Suppose he arrived after the children's birth, on the unseconded invitation of Mother.

Suppose he was there at the crucial time before that birth but not in an official capacity.

Does his having left home disqualify him?

If not, does his having defaulted on child support payments disqualify him?

Suppose he sends birthday presents but doesn't visit.

Suppose he sends letters but no presents.

Does refusing to pay for the child's dream wedding oust him from the father position? How about not paying enough? How much is the cutoff?

This process of rating Father, which is born of bitterness, however much provoked, is not going to make for a happy life for either father or child. Miss Manners urges that these questions be settled on the generous side. Every child seems to consider generosity one of the most highly valued qualities of a father. But it is a quality that a child also needs to learn in assessing a father.

There are clear cases of child abuse and child neglect, and Miss Manners is not suggesting that such criminal matters be tolerated. Tragically, a child must sometimes be protected from—or worse, have to attempt to protect himself from—the person who ought to have been one of his or her chief protectors. But such charges against Father are sometimes glibly made. What a child calls abuse may turn out to be what an adult may consider legitimate, even well-advised, strictness. The label of neglect may be applied to what an adult would understand as an inability to do or give everything deemed fitting by a child.

The complicated circumstances of adult life are rarely understood by the next generation, and Miss Manners is afraid that there are instances in which decent fathers are damned by their children over matters which the child is not competent to judge. Choices involving the allocation of discretionary monies—that is to say, for luxuries beyond the basics of child support—are particularly easily condemned by those who do not feel sufficiently benefited. Conflicting duties are even less subject to understanding on the part of the claimants themselves.

Miss Manners does not want to hear how specific grievances against individual fathers justify denying them mercy. Rather, she wants to encourage a Father's Day present that might be even more affectionately constructed and more useful than the ashtray: the benefit of the doubt. At the very least, it may set Father a good example.

An Etiquette Test for Parents

DEAR MISS MANNERS — My wife and I are very recently separated. She said that she was unhappy and needed her "space." She moved into a very nice apartment with her 15-year-old daughter from a previous marriage and our eight-year-old daughter. We have been very civil to each other throughout this whole matter.

As it turns out, she has an out-of-state boyfriend who financed the whole move. I know that some day, I am going to meet this man, probably when I am picking up my daughter. I would like to know what would be a proper greeting and what I should say (if anything). I know what I want to do, but I wouldn't want to do the wrong thing in front of the children. I also don't want to give the impression that I am satisfied with the situation.

GENTLE READER — Oh, yes you do. Not only is that the proper thing to do, and one that will not be offensive in front of the children, but it is the only attitude that will truly give you satisfaction. Allow Miss Manners to explain.

Any nastiness you exhibit will be attributed by everyone who witnesses it to your devastation at losing your wife. That can only add to the triumph of the man who spirited her away from you, surely not the effect you hope to achieve. However, if you greet him not only politely, but enthusiastically, you will plant the idea that he has done you a favor.

Think about that. He is bound to do so.

A Family Etiquette Test

DEAR MISS MANNERS — In our small, sleepy town, a popular and respected couple is breaking up because of an affair the husband had with an old girlfriend. However, the wife insists she is not seeking a divorce because of the affair per se, but because her husband took their son to meet his lover under cover of a trip to the young man's college, and because the lover brought her daughter-in-law on one of their weekend trysts, as a "cover," so that her own husband would not suspect what she was doing.

The wife says that there are "rules of etiquette" for affairs; that she understands that her husband slipped because he was in the midst of a mid-life crisis, but that she could never again trust someone who could callously use young people by making them accomplices to their elders' cheating. Isn't this hair-splitting? Isn't the affair itself the real injury, as it is a moral transgression, and if the wife can forgive that, shouldn't she forgive the details? When the wife describes the details as "callous," isn't she actually making an ethical judgment, rather than talking about bad manners?

Her husband wants to save the marriage, and insists the son was not made an accomplice, since he did not suspect that the woman he met was his father's lover. He also maintains that the daughter-in-law is too old to be an "innocent," seemed delighted that her mother-in-law was having such a good time, and so the question of exploiting her was moot.

GENTLE READER—Yes, Miss Manners believes it possible to forgive a moral transgression without being able to stomach a transgression of manners. As our own dear moral philosopher Ralph Waldo Emerson put it in his essay "Manners": "I could better eat with one who did not respect the truth or the laws, than with a sloven and unpresentable person."

Your particular example is not a clear one, because the involvement of the child could be considered immoral rather than unmannerly. Miss Manners does not consider the august question of manners to be one of mere "details," but the husband's argument that the son was protected from knowing, and the daughter-in-law willingly complied, does get him off from an etiquette charge. Yet cannot you imagine, for example, a wife's being willing to forgive a husband for having a one-night-stand in a distant motel, but not being able to forgive him if it had taken place in their own house where he had allowed someone else to try on her clothes?

Step-Parents

It might be nice to say a kind word about step-parents. Well? Miss Manners is waiting for the step-children to speak up.

In the meantime, she hastens to assure birth parents who feel that they were displaced by these interlopers that they need not join in. They are only required to refrain from saying mean things, a rule designed as much for their own sakes as for the sake of politeness. Unpleasant comments have the effect of suggesting that similar unpleasantness, applied to other subjects or to life in general, speeded the departing spouse on his or her way. (An etiquette bonus in this difficult situation is that the person who speaks most generously of a successor is considered to be the winner, because the gracious one is presumed to have either happily acquired or happily unloaded the spouse in question. Miss Manners also believes that dissatisfied ex-wives should all have friends who report back, "She's put on a tremendous amount of weight," and dissatisfied ex-husbands, friends who report, "He's losing his hair." The correct reply to such remarks, pronounced sweetly and then allowed to hang in the air without elaboration, is "Oh, now, come on, that doesn't matter," or if they can't manage that, at least "I'm sure they're well suited for each other.")

It is step-children and other maritally acquired relatives in whom Miss Manners wishes to encourage active kindness towards step-parents. Some of the worst offenders are not small children in the throes of painful bewilderment about their parents' divorce, but grown-ups, sometimes those with families of their own.

The idea that step-parents need not be treated politely because they entered the family with some sort of second-class status violates a basic principle of manners. Relatives are relatives, and few of them were acquired on purpose; yet they must all be treated to consideration and loyalty, right up until a lucrative offer is received for one's autobiography. Etiquette does not engage in the futile task of trying to mandate emotions, any more than a less-than-eagerly welcomed step-parent should do. It does insist on good manners—and so should step-parents, and, even more vehemently, the parents responsible for bringing them into the family.

Miss Manners cannot be in each household—and what a relief that is for her—to point out the fine difference between distance and disrespect. Trying to soften the former while forbidding the latter, and being alert to nuances, is the least parents can do for those to whom they subject their ready-made children. It is her hope that being required to practice manners will encourage appreciation and, ultimately, compassion, both of which are needed in great quantities by anyone who enters a partially assembled family—rarely with a welcome but usually with the expectation of having to tread carefully and absorb slights and with the resolve to provide guidance and warmth.

Miss Manners doesn't doubt that terrible step-parents also exist but condemns etiquette's being used as the weapon of choice between closely linked enemies. Coldness is sometimes justified among adult step-relatives, although not towards children, but rudeness never is. There is such a thing as a dignified agreement to maintain distance between family members who do not get along, which is best expressed—if it cannot be mended—by letter-perfect formal correctness. Unfortunately, unhappy people do not seem to be able to leave it at that. To Miss Manners' dismay, they keep peppering the situation with slights—say omitted invitations or unpleasant presents—from the arsenal of etiquette violations. That she cannot permit.

Small children who are regrettably untutored should be used not as proof of one's predecessor's shortcomings but as an opportunity for true step-parental heroism. Miss Manners has heard from many a one who despairs at having to put up with children who were never required to practice good manners—not just towards them but in any situation. Rather than enter a doomed popularity contest to see who can neglect the children's education more, the step-parent can represent an alternative way of living. Children who are required to behave politely, even if only for weekends and holidays, will at least be aware of a higher standard than they would otherwise know. Pleas that standards are laxer in the other parent's household are irrelevant. The answer is noncritical but firm: "I'm sorry, dear, but I do things differently."

Here is the minimum honor one must do a step-parent if one wishes to honor a parent:

1. Recognize his or her existence. Miss Manners shouldn't have to say this, because the refusal to recognize the existence of a human being with whom one is thrown into contact is the highest insult there is and usually reserved for mass murderers. Nevertheless, she has heard of the technique's being used to indicate mere distaste. This establishes the shunner as being rude.

2. Recognize the position of a married couple. This means that step-parents are invited to ceremonial occasions such as graduations, weddings and funerals, along with their husbands or wives. However, anyone whose presence is known to create a hardship for a predecessor gets extra etiquette credit from Miss Manners for gracefully declining such invitations or staying in the background.

3. Recognize the authority of both people who preside over a household. After all, the children are expected to follow their beloved Granny's rules when they visit her, and not blast her out of her senses with noise, or appear in their underwear at the breakfast table, however reasonable this behavior may be considered under their own roof. Parents-in-residence should set their household customs together and support each other's authority, however much they may debate privately, and

the children must respect them, even in a household once shared by both parents but now under the jurisdiction of a step-parent. It may be of comfort to know that grown-up children returning to their own married parents' house to find that changes were made after they moved away feel something of the same resentment.

Step-Children's Parents: Confusion

DEAR MISS MANNERS — Due to many necessary forms for school, Brownies or church, we are always asked "Who is an emergency contact person?" and "What is the relationship to the child?" We always use my husband's daughter's mother (from a previous relationship, not by marriage), and state her relationship as "friend." "Step-Mom, -Dad, -child" is not usually used because our children (I have a daughter from a previous marriage) prefer to call us Mom and Dad. All parents involved (except my ex) are, and have been, on friendly terms.

Should we continue to use "friend" or leave it blank? Also, what would my relationship be to "previous relationship"? Obviously "husband's daughter's mother" is too complicated, and "friend" does not explain it thoroughly. I jokingly call our relationship "mothers-in-law."

GENTLE READER — "Mothers-in-law" is adorable, but Miss Manners suspects that if the other lady finds you have identified her as merely a "friend" to her own daughter, there is going to be another person no longer on friendly terms with you. That lady is the child's mother. That the girl addresses you as Mom and your daughter addresses your husband as Dad is fine, so long as this doesn't deprive others of their rightful titles.

Allow Miss Manners to say that it is a pity that you are perpetuating the prejudice against the term "step-mother," because that is what you are, and saying so on forms would eliminate the confusion of the children's having multiple parents. Although now that Miss Manners comes to think of it, no one is confused by anything of the sort these days.

Step-Children's Parents: Compassion

DEAR MISS MANNERS — What place, if any, does the mother of my step-daughter have in the events of my husband's family? I certainly welcome the presence of my stepdaughter, who is married and almost thirty years old, but both my husband and I are dismayed that her mother still tags along to funerals, weddings and other gatherings. The girl was a result of an affair and although my husband financially supported the girl, he never married the woman. This woman never married and hasn't had any involvement with my husband or his family for nearly 19 years.

GENTLE READER—Presuming that you acknowledge the mother's involvement in any family matter pertaining to her own daughter, Miss Manners will admit, as you wish her to do, that someone who never joined a family can hardly claim to be a part of it. She can also understand that this lady's presence is something of a nuisance to you and your husband. Still, she hopes you will allow for the pathos of the situation. Clinging to such an identification after all these years is so sad that Miss Manners finds herself hoping that you will put up gamely with the presence of someone who is, although not a relative, the relative of a relative.

CHILDREN IN PART-TIME RESIDENCE

A great many people have been eagerly looking forward to receiving summer visitors who will stay for weeks, disparage and quarrel with the rest of the family, make themselves at home in the sense of doing whatever they want but not in the sense of going along with the customs of the house, complain about household conditions and gather critical personal information about them to take back to the hosts' adversaries.

Why would anyone allow such guests in the door—especially since they are all people who have been there before—much less look forward to their visits?

Because these are their own children. Children who annually spend part of the summer in the homes of a non-custodial parent are not guests at all but members of the family who can legitimately consider that they have a claim to being at home wherever a parent lives. Theirs is not an easy situation, and Miss Manners does not mean to suggest that it is their fault that these visits are often hard on the full-time residents. They are likely to be even harder on the children.

What visitor would want to spend weeks away from home but not exactly on vacation, being expected to take part in the routines of a household in which he or she is neither treated as a guest nor successfully made to feel part of the family, subjected to unfamiliar rules and conditions and perhaps made to hear criticism of a parent and other relatives?

Who, then, is to blame for the unfortunate fact that so many of these joyously anticipated visits turn out to be disappointing for everyone concerned? Reluctant to blame each other, parents and children traditionally identify other villains: The non-custodial parent blames the custodial parent, and the child blames the non-custodial step-parent. Miss Manners does not think that this solves the problem.

Perhaps there are some parents who train their children to be disgruntled spies, and step-parents whose desire it is to make children feel tyrannized and unwanted, but Miss Manners tends to doubt that there are as many such monsters as she hears claimed. She is aware that the situation itself is capable of producing misery all around, totally without the assistance of ill will.

Polite guests stay for a short period of time, take care to show their gratitude for being entertained, and are on the lookout to fit in with their hosts' expectations, even if it means suspending their own wishes; while polite children-of-the-house can expect to be in a relaxing atmosphere where the customs are familiar and were, indeed, made with their needs in mind. Polite hosts devote themselves to amusing guests and adjusting the family routines in order to make them comfortable, while polite parents can expect to be in unquestioned charge without their devotion being questioned.

So what we have here is an etiquette crisis waiting to happen—a situation in which no one quite knows which form of behavior to follow. An etiquette conference is called for, in which the mixture of expectations and rules for such a hybrid situation is made explicit:

"We keep rather a neat household, so the best place to sprawl out is in your sleeping quarters, or on the porch. But the living room is fine too, if you just take things with you when you leave the room. We'll try to get out of the house quietly in the morning because you like to sleep in, but when we're home, please use the headphones when you're listening to music. Want to come along on the grocery shopping and help get things you like? Is there anything you particularly don't like? No, we don't have television on during dinner, but if there's a particular program you want to see, perhaps we could eat before or after . . ."

Miss Manners is giving the adult side of the dialogue because she does not mean to say that everything is negotiable; by virtue of their being parents and the heads of that particular household, the adults are in charge. She is assuming that they are also entertaining requests by the child, whenever possible.

What is meant to be missing here is any critical comparison of the two households where the child has parents. The etiquette rule against criticizing anyone else's home and relatives applies equally to adult and child, no matter how closely they may be related.

Welcoming a Step-Child

DEAR MISS MANNERS — We have an every-other-weekend visitation with my husband's ten-year-old son by a previous marriage, and I do everything I can to make the visits go well, including meal planning, grocery shopping and cleanup after the child leaves. My husband seems to think that I do not need any notice—or very little—regarding changes in the visitation schedule. I have asked for a week, or at least two days', notice—which I seldom get. He says the child should be able to go freely between homes.

I say if I'm going to play hostess, I need notice, otherwise things will not flow smoothly and I get stressed out and am expected to run to the store at the last minute, or spread our meal thinner. Am I being too uptight, or is he not using appropriate manners?

GENTLE READER — Your husband is using perfectly proper manners for members of the family. What you are asking him to do is to use the manners appropriate for guests, not his own child. Miss Manners suggests you think less about playing hostess and more about being a mother. She believes it is crucial for children to feel that any home in which a parent lives is also their home.

If you want to enlist Miss Manners in encouraging your husband to do chores when you are feeling stressed—or even when you're not—she would be more agreeable—provided you make the point that you need more cooperation in running the household, and refrain from suggesting that it is the child who has created the problem. It should be the child's household, too. If you get into the habit of being really welcoming, not to say motherly, Miss Manners will even allow you to throw in a reminder that notice, if possible, does help. The way you can put it is, "If you can possibly give me warning when Brian is coming, I'd appreciate it, because I'd like to run out and get him some of his favorite treats."

Demoting a Step-Child

DEAR MISS MANNERS — My fiancé and I began living together eight months ago. His 17 year old son lives with us also. He will be 18 in April. My step-son-to-be holds a full time job, but does not contribute to the household expenses. He does not seem to be concerned about the cost of utilities or food and does not make any effort to conserve or contribute. When and how would it be appropriate for us to approach him about contributing to his living expenses?

GENTLE READER — Forgive Miss Manners for saying this, but could this problem be stated another way? Perhaps "I moved in with my fiancé and his son and want to know how to make the son start paying his household expenses."

Moving into an existing family and attempting to demote one of its members to boarder status is a really bad idea. It raises unpleasant questions about who the outsider really is.

Presumably, you are on confidential terms with your fiancé, and he is on confidential terms with his son. So you need only worry about making the suggestion politely to him (Miss Manners advises something along the lines of "Don't you think it would be a good thing for Sean to have him learn financial responsibility?") and, if he agrees, allow him the pleasure of taking it up with his son.

Barring Step-Children

DEAR MISS MANNERS — May I limit my visits with my spouse's grown children to pre-arranged restaurant meals? He's agreeing that we should perhaps consider that alternative.

We met six months after his wife of 34 years and the mother of his three grown children left the family home to continue an affair with a co-worker. She wanted nothing to do with marriage counseling—only adjustments-to-divorce professional help. We live happily in the modest (middle-middle class) neighborhood home in which these three children spent their childhood and adolescence. The former wife and her co-worker also live in this city. Even though they misused this house as a trysting place during my spouse's out-of-state trips, we like the house's low maintenance and established yard features and so decided not to relocate. The children live out of state.

My efforts to be generous—not haughty—to the children on their yearly visits have been mixed. I have had difficulty with their opening drawer after drawer and exclaiming, "I can't find anything any more!" They fill our plastic bags full of trail snacks and remove fruit from a fruit bowl as they head out of our house for a hike with their mom and her co-worker. When I saw this fill 'em up activity, the wife of the older son told me with sardonic glee, "I don't ask—I just take!" When they left, she said, "It's been fun!" instead of any heartfelt thanks. They are medical doctors, teaching and doing research. My spouse has been extremely supportive and acknowledges that these children still have some growing up to do. He applauds me for steering clear of any unseemly contest with his former wife and her co-worker.

The bigger picture here is a comedy of manners. My wonderful spouse even laughed and said he felt complimented when he learned that at a convention, the cuckolding co-worker and the mother of these three children had arranged an impersonator for my spouse. We feel sure you'll dismiss that new euphemistic term, "blended families," as ironic at best.

GENTLE READER—Do not take offense when Miss Manners says that all those vivid and interesting details are irrelevant. She enjoyed hearing them, and naturally shares your admirable view of life as a comedy of manners. However, the problem here has nothing to do with co-workers and trysting places. It is simply that the children think of this house still as their home, in which you are a newcomer if not, in their view, an intruder; while you see them as your guests, who do not know how to behave as guests.

Miss Manners does not defend their behavior. Announcing that one "just takes" and never thanks is unpardonable. It's just that banning them from their father's house, which is also their own childhood home, is rather a drastic solution to what is, after all, a misunderstanding of manners.

Your husband sounds like a true and much tried gentleman. Perhaps he can explain to them that the house is your home now, not theirs; and to you, that they are family, not merely houseguests. Dissatisfied hosts and guests defer to each other during the visit and then resolve never to repeat it. Families have to work out compromises, and a compromise could be reached between their feeling free to ransack your drawers and your feeling that they should have to ask permission to take fruit from a fruit bowl.

What, after all, is the alternative to a blended family in these circumstances?

When Miss Manners' last kitchen blender died, it was replaced by a vicious weapon of a kitchen machine that approaches nearly everything with a mean chopping blade.

Retraining a Step-Child

DEAR MISS MANNERS — My husband's son, now 16, who has grown up in a cave surrounded by social idiots, moved in with us last summer. He has absolutely no knowledge of any of the social skills that I've always taken for granted. He has the table manners of a five-year-old: He does not know how to use basic utensils properly; he cuts up all of his meat prior to eating; he places used utensils directly on the tablecloth or placemat; he has terrible posture; he doesn't know how to put his napkin on his lap, etc. etc. The list goes on and on. He also thinks I'm crazy for making him take off his cap when he comes to the table.

It's driving me absolutely nuts! I grew up in a family that taught and practiced proper table manners. The same is obviously not true of him. Should I try to change 15 years of ill-mannered behavior? How can I convince him this isn't stuff I'm just dreaming up to torture him?

GENTLE READER — Perhaps by changing your attitude. One of the social skills Miss Manners would like to take for granted is that a lady does not speak of her husband's former home and that of the mother of her step-son as a cave of social idiots. This is especially necessary since the first person you should enlist to help you is a former resident of that establishment, or, as you might put it, an idiot from that cave, namely, your husband. Presuming that he did nothing previously to teach manners, you need to persuade him to insist upon them now.

Miss Manners recognizes it as a sufficient argument that this is the way you wish to live. She would throw in the fact that the boy will do better in life if he does not disgust those who might evaluate him even more coldly than his step-mother. Once the principle is established that good manners will be practiced in your home, your part will be to use good manners to enforce them. In other words, the approach to take daily is "Darling, do put your napkin on your lap—now what was it you were saying?" rather than "You're driving me absolutely nuts," which could be taken as encouragement to continue until the job is done.

The Grown-Up Child

If all you parents don't stop bad-mouthing the children, Miss Manners is going to have to send you to your own quarters. That, you have made it abundantly clear, is where you want to be. Alone.

Everywhere, one hears parents rejoicing that they no longer have to bear the company of their very own children in their very own houses. Mind you, those are children whom they were supposed to bring up to have enough manners so that when they did get out on their own, the rest of society would find them bearable.

"Thank goodness school has started," the parents of small children say. "It wouldn't have been possible to stand them another minute."

"Alone at last," say those whose children have gone off to college. "It's great to have the house back."

"Isn't it dreadful that so many children are moving back with their parents these days?" ask the parents of grown-up children who have returned home. "Just when we thought we were finally rid of them."

Is this a polite way to talk about one's relatives—publicly to express pleasure and relief at getting away from them? Suppose the children talked that way about the parents?

Many of them do. The little ones may not rejoice that school has started, but they learn early to trade complaints about their parents, and many of them never stop complaining about their parents to everyone they meet.

This doesn't make it right for the parents to do so. Parents are supposed to have a higher standard of behavior than the children have yet mastered. And they are supposed to teach family loyalty—for the sake of their own reputations, if not for the sake of good manners.

Why are they setting such a poor example?

Miss Manners, who had rather thought parental fondness was a natural instinct, suspects that some of it is bravado. The "empty-nest syndrome" having been popularized as the natural punishment for having devoted one's life to the nurturing of others, these people are trying not to sound pathetic.

Or they are trying to counter the bad manners of their children, who engage in teasing that unpleasantly suggests that the parents are emotionally absorbed by a tie that they find annoying or trivial. It may be true that parents enjoy visits from their grown-up children and grandchildren, who find the duty of visiting a drag, but it is rude to let on.

Miss Manners has even heard versions in which the object seems to be to make it clear that parental friskiness and intimacy have been renewed. People will use any excuse nowadays to make their private lives public.

But perhaps these people really are glad to be rid of their children. Given her belief that parents tend to be fond of their children, Miss Manners suspects an etiquette crisis. The children have not been taught to respect the parents or their privacy or their property. Or perhaps the parents have not imposed such requirements—because they didn't want the children to grow up inhibited, or because they no longer feel that they can set house rules now that the children have grown up. But every household will be unbearable if there are no regulations enforced. Ask any student who has lived with peers who borrow his belongings unasked, leave messes they refuse to clean, and run up bills to which they refuse to contribute.

Miss Manners suggests that it is never too late to insist that anybody living in one's house refrain from conduct that makes life unlivable for other residents. Failing that, however, there is still a rule of etiquette saying that if you don't like your relatives, you should at least not brag about it.

THE EXTENDED FAMILY

Some years ago, there was an outbreak of nostalgia in society—not only, as is customary, for the junk items of generations past but for their owners: the extended family. People were lamenting the isolation of what is not so gently called the nuclear family, and musing about how nice it would be to have grandparents and other relatives within easy reach if not actually in the same dwelling, as in societies they admired from a distance.

Miss Manners found this curious, considering that in this particular society, family attachments are considered to cease when the young become teenagers. "They'll hate you," well-wishers say to those parents who are not yet at the stage to receive either condolences for having the children around or congratulations on having gotten rid of them. The normal ambition of children is supposed to be to leave home as soon as possible, to the extent that those who tarry are considered damaged. Their destination is assumed to be chosen without regard to its distance from family of origin, unless it is to ensure their emotional welfare by being far enough to make visiting difficult.

Now that paradoxical wish for clan living has come true for many people, although perhaps not in the way they had envisioned. The thought—extremely appealing to Miss Manners, who was never willing to accept the idea of natural antagonism between the generations—was of a family where the old would share their wisdom (not to mention household and child care duties), while the young offered their more robust protection in reciprocation.

Here's what has happened instead:

Grandparents found themselves to be the primary guardians of the children of their divorced or never-married children, sometimes when the original children were still young enough to require parenting themselves, and sometimes in their total absence.

Grown children found themselves living with their parents, not for the satisfactions of continued family life but for the sort of landlord-boarder arrangement that both would frankly characterize as motivated only by financial necessity. Even more children found themselves to be the primary guardians of parents in need of nursing care.

Amid all the talk of burdens and mooching and separation-anxiety complexes, Miss Manners has also heard about extended families whose reasons for living together are love and compassion. However, she recognizes that even they are not immune to the special etiquette problem of having more than one grown-up generation in a household.

The difficulty is in redistributing the amount of autonomy, jurisdiction, responsibility and authority that exists between parents and minor children without altering the respect owed to all members of the family, and particularly to the elders. Adult children acquire more autonomy and responsibility, both of which may have to be lessened for the oldest members. Nevertheless, a family household is not a boardinghouse, where people are supposed to pretend they have no stake in one another's private lives, even while they are keeping careful and critical track.

Generally, the generation that established the household, parents or grandparents, has jurisdiction over how it is used, such as the distribution of space. They are not landlords who arrange things as they please, inviting anyone who doesn't like it to leave; they are supposed to check that they are acting in everyone's interest.

While the household rules may have been developed by the eldest generation in residence, the household is not a business controlled by those with the most stock. Among its grown-up members, the trick is to accommodate opinions through compromise, not through a dictatorship or majority rule. Each family must make its adjustments to take into account the others' preferences and requirements.

Miss Manners is not claiming that any of this is easy—psychologically or logistically. This does not prevent her from having vehement objections to the usual way of doing it, which is distributing power according to how much money each contributes. Families may pool their resources, but even those who are hard up are not supposed to offer for sale power and respect in the family hierarchy.

NEW RELATIVES

Some warnings are themselves dangerous. How do you alert people to the nature of a wrongdoing, supplying sufficient detail so that they will be able to recognize and avoid it—but without inadvertently providing instructions for people who would like to commit it?

This is the problem that confronts Miss Manners when she wants to help people avoid treating in-laws and assorted family newcomers in ways that will accidentally make them feel criticized and excluded. There are some people, she is aware, who would be only too happy to learn techniques for alienating those with whom their relatives are inexplicably in love.

That is not only impolite but unwise. If you tell your daughter that the gentleman she brought home looks like an axe murderer to you, and he, in fact, turns out to have been an axe murderer, she will not say gratefully, "Father, dear, you were right, and I was wrong not to have listened to you." She will say huffily, "Well, maybe he is, but you were just awful to him. You always hate all my friends. You're just trying to ruin my life." So you might as well be nice to these people. Some may stay and others may depart, but at least you will not be considered at fault. As your rudeness will probably not drive them away, and has been known to cement an otherwise shaky relationship, you have nothing to gain by it.

The typical situation occurs after someone's serious interest is first brought home for inspection. That the initial encounter is a notoriously difficult situation for everyone concerned is often what saves it. When all participants are nervous and on their best behavior, there is a high tolerance level. It is after that that the real etiquette difficulties begin.

No matter how much good will is expended, the initiation period begins to be fraught with trouble—and not just any trouble, but etiquette trouble. To Miss

Manners' dismay, most such clashes are provoked by explicit or implicit differences of etiquette. The complaint is almost never "We don't want an addition to the family" or "This is a horrid person" but that he or she "just doesn't know how to behave."

Mind you, this does not occur because the family is etiquette-conscious. On the contrary, students of etiquette understand the idea that just as the surface rules of etiquette vary among societies, the habits governing intimacy vary among families, and therefore not understanding new ones is, well, understandable.

A family may be known to friends as being friendly, easygoing and warmhearted, and still strike a prospective or new member as hostile, exacting and cold. This is because family members refrain, in front of company, from speaking a language of inside jokes and memories, whereas they feel free to do this in the family circle, even if it includes candidates or members who do not yet know that language. The family does not expect even its friends to know all its routines and habits, but a new family member who doesn't—one, for example, who doesn't know whether help in the kitchen is expected or resented—is likely to be faulted for bad intentions.

The teasing level of a particular family is known only to its members. What might strike one family as insulting is the language of love to another. Conversely, what might seem innocuous to an outsider might be known in the family to be poisonous. Family lore gets abbreviated, so that an expression that sets off laughter or sentimentality might be incomprehensible to a newcomer. The question of how things are done comes to mean that not only the common etiquette of the society but the family customs carry so much weight of tradition that a family member who violates them seems ill-willed, rather than just uninformed.

One reason people dread in-law visits, from either generation, is that the household customs are so often violated by people who seem to be members of the inner circle but can't behave that way. The best-intentioned person in the world can mistake jokes for serious comment or help out in ways that irritate everyone and create more work. The family then resents it, and the newcomer feels like a fool. This is why polite people, confronted with an addition to the family circle, all join in providing an introduction with translations:

"That's a line from our favorite movie . . . We use the blue dishes for breakfast, not the white ones . . . Oh, he doesn't mean anything by that . . . Mamma likes to sit there when she reads the paper . . . They're talking about batty Uncle Oscar . . . It's a standing joke that Daddy can't carve the turkey . . . That's a reference to the time we went camping in the hurricane . . . No, there wasn't another sister—that was the name of our old car . . . Oops, I forgot to tell you that the hot water is on the right."

It is obligatory that this commentary be delivered in a tone of delight at sharing, not impatience at ignorance. The effect to aim at is "We know we're weird, but we're glad you put up with us." That's how you make someone feel welcome.

Giving as Well as Taking

DEAR MISS MANNERS — I am a 22-year-old gay man and I live with my lover, Tom, who is 26. We have been together for over a year and consider ourselves a "married" couple. Tom's family knows about our relationship and we attend many family dinners, birthday parties, barbecues and other social occasions together. Tom's family is not totally comfortable with our relationship, but they include me in invitations, knowing that Tom will not attend if I am not invited. They are polite to me.

I no longer feel it is appropriate to call his parents Mr. and Mrs., yet they have not told me to call them Bob and Jan. Should I take the initiative myself, or should I ask my lover to do so?

GENTLE READER — Miss Manners finds it interesting that you accept the graciousness of Tom's parents towards you although you know they are not totally comfortable with the relationship, and yet are unwilling to sustain your own discomfort in order to allow them to choose how they want to be addressed. Why should all the comfort be on your side? Having made the substantive point, cannot you allow them to decide a stylistic one?

The relevant factor for this etiquette rule is not any of the circumstances you have set out except one: Tom's parents are a generation older than you. They therefore get the choice about forms of address. Do not brood that their formality indicates disapproval. Among legally married couples, the question of what in-laws should be called is far from settled, and there are as many young people professing themselves uncomfortable with being asked to say Mom and Dad to a spouse's parents as there are ones who squirm at Mr. and Mrs. So Miss Manners suggests that all of them, and you too, learn a lesson in graciously sustained discomfort.

CONFLICTING EMOTIONS

Feeling Inferior

DEAR MISS MANNERS — I went to my daughter's house and stayed overnight. She had her in-laws there, and it ruined my day. This is not because they aren't great people. That's the problem. They are well read, musical and talented, and even though I am not a stupid woman, I felt so intimidated. They were talking about authors, etc., that I knew nothing about. I guess that comes from a lack of education. Also, I felt the gifts I gave, even though they were expensive, were not appropriate. Their son was happy with song books and art books, instead of the leaf blower I gave him.

I am widowed and decided if this happens again I will just stay for the day and not overnight. Perhaps I'm making too much of this. My friends say I am well read and have a good sense of humor and other qualities. I just feel that they have so much to offer our new grandson and I have so little that it depresses me.

GENTLE READER — It is not how much you are making of this, but what you are making: Trouble. Miss Manners is horrified that you seem to have declared a competition with your daughter's in-laws, and that you have worked yourself into a dreadful state because you feel you are losing.

People you yourself characterize as "great," who have many interests, are unlikely to count among them a passion for showing up a connection on the grounds that she has less education. Your grandson is probably not very interested in whether you know the same authors as his other grandparents. As appreciative as your son-in-law may be of getting song books, he probably doesn't want a double load of them any more than he wants two leaf blowers.

In other words, Miss Manners believes that it is you, not they, who have invented this unseemly and unpleasant situation. As a cure for your depression, Miss Manners recommends not withdrawal but the opposite. How about attempting to make friends with these people to whom you are so closely connected? If they are discussing something you don't know, ask them about it. They will be infinitely more charmed than if you had been able to attempt to top them. If they are making music, applaud, which will delight them.

What you have to offer your grandson is the same thing they have to offer him—love, attention and the sharing of your experiences and interests. You should be offering it, instead of attempting to divide the family. Miss Manners is sorry to be stern with you, but she is determined to wrest from you an attitude that has already caused you misery, which you apparently contemplate spreading.

Feeling Superior

DEAR MISS MANNERS—I am a lawyer who has married into a family of tradesmen. My wife is devoted to her family and enjoys their company during the summer and for most holidays. My problem is that I can't seem to carry on a conversation with my brothers-in-law. They enjoy talking to each other and to the other male in-laws, who are also tradesmen or factory workers, but they seem to feel uncomfortable with me, and we have little in common. No one reads the newspaper, and the topics of conversation are either their work or sports. I make attempts to strike up a conversation, but after a few minutes, they turn to each other and leave me standing. I then usually defer to the company of the ladies, supervise my children's play or sit quietly. This only makes me feel I look like a snob. These affairs last an eternity for me.

I would like to enjoy their company. They are really decent people. Curiously, I have a good time when I'm their host. That means that I may be the problem, not them.

Would it be proper to bring a trades magazine with me? I do a lot of building projects around the house, and I thought if I could delve into a book on a subject in which my in-laws are proficient, it would serve to bring me into the conversation by asking for their ideas. If it didn't, I'd at least have an excuse to read. However, it may make me out to be a worse snob to be reading and seeming to make a deliberate effort to separate myself.

If I have to live with this the way it is, I will. I've got 30 more years of this to look forward to, and I don't want to hurt anyone's feelings.

GENTLE READER—What do you mean that you don't have anything in common with these people? You have your wife, who is their sister. You have your children, who are their nieces and nephews, and their children, who are your nieces and nephews.

In other words, you have the well-being of the extended family in common, with the interest that ought to create in all the ups and downs of each relative. Miss Manners submits that that is a great deal more in common than you have with, say, a law partner whose only stake in your welfare is in connection with mutual business concerns.

The small talk of family life differs from that of ordinary social life, in which one must reach for such outside topics as are found in the news. Among relatives of good will, which you say these are, private successes can be shared without fear of bragging, and difficulties without fear of whining.

Because you have a good time when they visit you, Miss Manners suspects that your brothers-in-law may be more astute at picking up such clues for conversation—commenting on a building project in your house, for example, or a new possession, or a project of one of your children's. You might try doing that when you visit, by way of showing an interest in them. You don't have to confine your sociability to talking to the brothers-in-law. Talking to the ladies, playing with the children and asking the hosts if you can do something useful are all proper ways of participating in family parties. Reading is not.

Feeling Neglected

DEAR MISS MANNERS — My mother used to have a good job with a great deal of free time and a good salary, so she would write and buy gifts for her very large extended family. She lost her job and has less time to write and no money for gifts. This Christmas, many of these family members didn't even send a card! How can I suggest to my aunts, uncles and cousins that my mother would appreciate this attention?

GENTLE READER — Miss Manners was prepared to join your indignation at your relatives' cruelty in snubbing your mother in her misfortunes—until the slight suspicion arose that perhaps your mother had dropped them first. When she lost her job, your mother didn't just stop sending presents—she stopped writing as well. No matter how little time she has, this carries the unfortunate implication that wishing her relatives well was a pastime of leisure, rather than an act of love. This by no means excuses the relatives from having dropped her, but it should soften your blame to realize that for whatever reason, they merely acted as she did. That should enable you to tell them in a friendly way, "Mother's too proud to say so, but she really misses hearing from you."

Feeling Martyred

DEAR MISS MANNERS — My husband's sister lies by omission. It has happened again and again, and I have endured it for 40 years—she tells mutual acquaintances the worst stories about me, simply by omitting the final truth. The latest was a story (told with proper sighs and eyebrow raisings) that I did not attend her daughter's funeral—neglecting to add that I had been hospitalized just a few days prior, with multiple fractures due to a fall at a shopping mall. I do my best to be pleasant during the infrequent times we meet, and direct confrontation only leads to more of the same. My husband is too weak to handle this problem by correction.

GENTLE READER — Miss Manners congratulates you on having endured this horrid treatment for 40 years. Perhaps she can talk you back from the cracking point so you can put in a few more, rather than mar that excellent record.

The comfort she can offer you is the assurance that everybody who hears these stories is onto the person who tells them. It is impossible for anyone to go around telling nasty stories for 40 years without being found out—especially when she tips people off by exhibiting the rudeness of bad-mouthing a relative. You may be sure that no one who hears these stories believes that you are the person who has been behaving badly. So there is really no need for you to retaliate against someone who is doing so effective a job against herself.

AND ALL THOSE OTHER PEOPLE

Non-Member Residents

In a household of non-relatives, where each person pays a share of the rent and does a share of the chores, what do you call the person who stays for a prolonged period of time through a connection with one of the householders?

"Guest" is not exactly the term, because social visits are set for finite periods of time, and for recreational purposes in which it would be rude to consider the convenience of room and board to be a factor. As for the words the other householders begin to use after a week or two, Miss Manners does not care for them, no matter how severe the provocation.

"Non-member resident" is the term suggested by a gentleman of Miss Manners' acquaintance. He based it on the position of "non-resident member" at some college residences—the graduate student who provides tutoring and other services but has decided that a free room is not worth being known to be available in the middle of the night when messy, party-related illnesses strike the inmates.

To the householder involved, there is all the difference in the world between a non-member who is in residence because of a romantic bond, and a former college roommate or other friend who is passing through town, looking for a job, broke or otherwise eligible to be put up out of necessity. Other rent payers find the distinction increasingly hard to make as time moves on. Three days, or one shampoo while someone else wants to use the bathroom, will usually do it. Any such household should decide its etiquette rules in advance for non-member residents, beginning with the definition of how long it takes for a social visit to be declared a temporary residence—and therefore how long for the rules to shift from those appropriate to genuine guests, on whom all comforts should be freely showered even if they hog the shower.

The rules for non-member residents (conveyed via the inviting householder as "I hate to have to tell you this, but my roommates are really strict about how things are done around here") should certainly include cleaning up whatever mess they make, checking before using up any supplies and quickly replenishing them and taking messages. Staying out of the way of major traffic during a morning rush when everyone else has to go to work is not unreasonable.

The visitor who wishes to remain will take these as only a starting point. The idea, if you do not wish suddenly to find your clothes on the porch, is to assume neither the privileges of a guest, in consuming hospitality without the need for immediate repayment, nor those of the host, in voicing opinions about how the place ought to be run.

The obligations of a guest, in being agreeable to everyone and to all arrangements, are required, along with the obligation of a host in keeping things going. In lieu of rent, the visitor thinks of charming things to do: any stray cooking or cleaning that seems helpful; doing repairs or at least the tedious work of arranging to have them done; being home when deliveries are expected.

Miss Manners is aware that it is difficult to have the manners of both host and guest simultaneously—to be useful without having a say in how things should be done. That's the etiquette toll for free rent. Besides, it is useful training should one ever seek political asylum in an embassy.

De Facto Residents

DEAR MISS MANNERS — My roommate wants to have his girlfriend stay the night about five nights a week, and I've objected. He and I have been friends for ten years, and this is putting a real strain on our friendship. She comes over in the evening, stays the night and leaves rather early.

She has not been a nuisance other than that I don't enjoy having to share my evenings with someone. I have said I could tolerate her being over three nights per week or, if he wanted her to stay more often, that they contribute $50 to the rent (about 10% of the rent). Have I stepped out of line to set limitations on visitors?

GENTLE READER — What you have there is not a visitor but a third roommate. What you badly need is a retroactive agreement with your original roommate about who else can move in and what the responsibilities will be.

Every living arrangement needs to have its terms spelled out to the mutual satisfaction of everyone participating, although if that sounds as if children should have an equal voice with their parents in the household rules, Miss Manners apologizes because she means no such thing.

In the case of roommates, it is a good idea to discuss a third-party contingency ahead of time, although understandable that the need for this may not appear important until it suddenly strikes. People of good will ought to be able to reach an agreement that recognizes the comfort of both, and does not insist that love trumps all previous considerations.

Love does sometimes require new living arrangements, but as you do not dislike the lady, yours seems salvageable. You and your roommate are in urgent need of a private session in which you can work out a compromise (in terms of how much time the new resident spends with you, and how much she or her host contributes to the rent) that both of you would consider pleasant and equitable.

Non-Residents' Guests

DEAR MISS MANNERS — My boyfriend has keys to my apartment. He is welcome to come and go as he pleases, eat whatever is in the refrigerator (he's the cook), use my art supplies, and wear my jeans (even skirts, if he so desires). I walk home from work for lunch every day, and enjoy his company when he's around.

Today at noon, I arrived just as a mutual friend did, who was dropping something off for Boyfriend and then taking him for a spin. Boyfriend had invited her in to see our holiday craft projects. My place was a mess of glitter and junk and yesterday's clothes, so I voice my objection as she parks her car, but say, "Too late, you invited her in, she comes in, anyway."

Now he's angry, tells her I don't want her in, please wait outside, but she boldly enters and makes jokes. (Glad she did.) Even if my apartment hadn't been so ugly, I object to such intrusions on my lunch at home without prior consultation. I don't have keys to Boyfriend's place. Was I justifiably disgruntled?

GENTLE READER — It is a bit hard to slap house rules on someone who has been invited to go through your closets and wear your skirts. Having done everything you can to make your boyfriend feel at home in your apartment (hospitality that has conspicuously not been reciprocated), you now wish to claim that he is merely a guest who is not allowed to let anyone in in your absence. You could, of course, take your apartment back, but Miss Manners believes that had you wanted to throw him out, you would have done so without her help. Well, then, let us consider the alternative. How about saying "If you're going to have anyone over, please clean up first"? That should ensure you a quiet lunch hour.

Chapter Two

THE PLACE

SPACE

A comfortable place to live has as many bathrooms as there are people in residence, plus one for guests. It is like the formula for making tea—one for everyone there and one extra for the pot. (This is a comparison Miss Manners suddenly realizes she does not care to continue.) It also has twice as many closets, a gymnasium and an indoor parking lot. Such houses actually exist, although not exactly at all price levels. What astonishes Miss Manners even more than their cost is the other amenities that dream houses now require to accommodate the way the people who can afford to buy them choose to live.

It has become obligatory to have an enormous eating area in the kitchen so that nobody has to eat in the dining room and (when we are talking high luxury) a facility for storing and heating food near the bedrooms so no one has to eat in the kitchen, either. The kitchen is used to entertain guests so they don't have to use the living room. This entertainment now consists of letting the guests watch what used to be the preparations for entertaining guests.

The family doesn't want to use the living room, either. Nobody does. It's considered a nice place to have and to furnish, but not a place to live in. Miss Manners suspects that living rooms are now so often done all in white out of some dim memory of bridal white as a symbol of the untouched state. Now there must be a family room to take over the living function of the living room, but that is no longer where you might find the family. Another room has done to the family room what the family room did to the living room. This one is known as the entertainment center or media room; before that, it was called the computer room or the television room. The name keeps changing because the room's purpose is to house electronic equipment the family must share—first it was the only upstairs telephone, then the television set, then the computer. When the object is no longer a novelty and each inhabitant gets one in his or her bedroom, the family moves on to the next luxury. Right now, this room might have the only movie-theater-sized television screen in the house, so it is where the children do their studying.

There are at least two other rooms properly fitted up as studies, but those are maintained as separate retreats for the only adults who have to share a bedroom, which is no longer a bedroom but a master suite. Couples used to achieve privacy from each other and the children by going into the bathroom and locking the door until forced to respond to desperate pleas, and Miss Manners might have thought that the affluent would be all the more easily able to do this because they have more bathrooms. No such luck. The huge modern his-and-hers bathrooms have double sinks, such as Miss Manners remembers from her dormitory days, implying that other people are expected to drop in.

Far be it from Miss Manners to suggest that people should eat in their dining rooms, live in their living rooms and be alone in their bathrooms. If the rich want to show their solidarity with the less fortunate by huddling into a few small rooms above lobbylike spaces they never use, that is surely their privilege. What does concern her is what the system says about the attitudes of the inhabitants and their guests towards themselves and one another. Much as she likes the old plan, she would have thought that the modernization of the old-style formal house would result in less wasted space and a warmer atmosphere. Instead, there seems to be more space than ever devoted to pure show. Once, it was just the front parlor that might be saved for company and grand occasions; now it's the dining room as well, and the company has been banished along with the family.

The old plan for a luxury house recognized the need for privacy with a lady's boudoir, a gentleman's study and a children's playroom. The presumption was that these provided retreats from a robust communal life, rather than a way for the family to lead solitary lives under the same roof. Miss Manners hears a lot about the new casual ways of living, and how much less stiff they are than the old ways. If anyone wants to debate this with her, she'll be sitting in the pristine living room, hoping to see a friendly face.

The True Luxury

DEAR MISS MANNERS — My husband and I reside in a modest, older home. Whenever one of his sisters comes to visit, she freely criticizes our home, comparing it to her new, lavish residence in another part of town.

On her last visit, she said, "This is such a little house. It's hard to believe people actually live in such tiny homes." I was so stunned by her remark that I could not think of a reply. I couldn't decide if she was just ignorant, or if she was deliberately trying to hurt me. No matter her intent, I was hurt and angry. What could I have said to educate her and perhaps prevent such comments in the future?

GENTLE READER — Miss Manners recommends not wasting time on imagining a motivation for such awful remarks. Rather, she would suggest that you produce a sweetly pitying smile, and such kindly words as "Yet little houses can be full of happiness, as ours is. Perhaps that's why we have never found it hard to believe that people would want to visit us in our little house."

Open Spaces

DEAR MISS MANNERS — The dining room and library of our home are on the ground floor and when we entertain, we often put several small tables in each. At the foot of the stairway opposite the library door is what is politely called the powder room. It is in full view of all coming down the stairs—and those seated in the library.

My wife feels it is "middle class morality" to keep the bathroom door closed when the room is not in use. While I agree that those on the bedroom level should be open, I think, as a matter of aesthetics, the fixtures on the dining level might best not be always in view. I advocate, in this case, leaving the door about four inches ajar to indicate availability in a less obvious way than if it were flung wide open. Will you comment on this disagreement?

GENTLE READER— Middle class morality? Oh, no. Anything but that! Miss Manners is aware that an accusation of practicing middle class morality is the deadliest of insults, but she has never understood why. Don't all people identify themselves as being middle class, the rich to avoid arrogance and the poor to avoid pathos? Why would people be terrified of being caught practicing morality? Because it might ruin their reputations? Anyway, how does the bathroom door get to be a moral issue?

Miss Manners dearly hopes you are going to spare her the argument that privacy constitutes hypocrisy, but if that's it, then you upper and lower class disdainers of morality should just take those bathroom doors off the hinges and watch one another. We hypocrites prefer other entertainment, and we especially do not enjoy dwelling on the connection between eating food and eliminating it. Furthermore, we are also resourceful enough to ask for a bathroom when we need one, and to knock on closed doors before entering.

Closing Off Spaces

DEAR MISS MANNERS— I have relatives with young children who come to our home fairly often, and as soon as they arrive, they immediately scamper off to play in every room in the house. They feel as if it is their playground and their parents don't say anything. After they leave, I find different things moved around. My husband and I have also had several people ask how much we paid for our new home. I think it is rude, but I do not want to lie, so for lack of a better answer, I tell them the truth. I don't want to seem mean but I know I was not allowed such freedoms at ages 5 to 11. I do feel that at least our bedroom should be a private area and my only thought was to lock our bedroom door when they come over. Am I being too picky?

GENTLE READER — Too easily picked on, Miss Manners would say. You are allowing everybody to rummage at will through your house and mind, ceding territory as fast as anybody thoughtlessly claims it.

True, your friends could be more reticent, and it would be attractive for their children to hang back shyly in the absence of instructions. That may be out of your control, but if you could learn to reply to questions with a cheerful "Oh, I'm not going to tell," and to announce to young guests "Let me show you the family room, where you can play," you would find that all but outright louts will accept the boundaries you set. You don't want those hanging around your nice new house, anyway.

Fencing Off Spaces

DEAR MISS MANNERS — We would like to know how to handle an annoyance we are having with a friend. This woman will not allow anyone in her living room/dining room for any entertaining, to the point of having a fence in the doorways. These are not rooms with priceless antiques, although we are not dealing with unruly people or messy children. It has become such an insult to my husband that I think he will probably scale the fence and sit in the room alone, just as a matter of principle.

We are met at the front door, walked down the hallway to the kitchen, ushered to the family room. This has happened for weddings, funerals, Christmas, graduations, showers or any other occasion that may occur. The gates are explained as being barriers for the dogs, but the animals are usually kenneled at the time of company.

Is there some polite way we can make her aware of her rudeness? We realize she has the standard white carpet, but no one has manure on their feet or bib overalls from the barn.

GENTLE READER — Were you the only people banned from these sacred parlors, Miss Manners could understand how you could take offense. She would not permit you to occupy the territory by force, but she would acknowledge that you might not care to be entertained by someone who did not consider you worthy of her best.

What you have here is—how can Miss Manners put it politely?—a nut case. None of this lady's friends seem to be worthy enough to use her best rooms, and no occasions—weddings, funerals—important enough. What is she waiting for?

Miss Manners recalls reading a short story about a similarly afflicted lady who was saving her best for an occasion so special that it never arrived in her lifetime. That lady was guarding the bed linens from her trousseau for a sufficiently important occasion, her own wedding apparently not qualifying. Finally, she was no longer able to protect the now-crumbling sheets, and they were used—as her shroud. There seems to be a moral here about enjoying things while you can, and sharing them with people you care about. There is no way for you to "handle" someone else's peculiarity, except to share Miss Manners' hope that your friend allows herself to tiptoe into the rooms when no one else is around and to eke what pleasure she can out of having white rugs.

Ceding Space

DEAR MISS MANNERS—I once returned from college to find my old bedroom painted pink and my sister's things firmly planted in it. I turned and opened the door to the guest room—there were my things, in much better order than I had left them. I felt kind of bad, but I certainly didn't argue. It wasn't my house.

My sister is gone again, married now, and I've made my return as she did, except with my husband. Domestic issues are not a problem as long as we remember who owns the house and give respect and deference where it is due. (No, we didn't get my old room back.)

GENTLE READER—Miss Manners hopes that you realize that you have seriously violated a tradition of family life. When parents so much as replace a chair in the room of a child who has moved away, even if it was years ago and the child has his or her own house twice the size, custom requires that it set off an emotional rampage.

Not having a permanent shrine is considered the basis for fruitful family discussions, such as "I bet you were glad to get rid of me" and "You always did love her more." Miss Manners congratulates you on forgoing this opportunity. By conceding that your family should enjoy the extra room, you have also made room in your psyche for more interesting topics.

Guarded Space

DEAR MISS MANNERS—I live in a security building which contains eight apartments. When guests arrive, they must first ring my apartment from the front door. I may then use the intercom system to allow the guests to announce themselves, and then electronically unlock the entrance from my apartment. This seems to be somewhat inhospitable, as the guests must then see their way up a flight of stairs and through a series of doors. Should I be greeting them at the door, and saving the intercom for package deliveries?

GENTLE READER—While appreciating your hospitable intentions, Miss Manners believes it superfluous for you to greet your guests in the lobby. (It is even considered a politeness, for those who have the luxury of a household employee to open the door, to allow guests to collect themselves and smooth the ravages of the weather before being greeted by their hosts.)

This is not to say that you want them stumbling about the building. You have an intercommunications system, so use it to say a pleasant word of greeting and give your guests instructions. In these circumstances, it would be a hospitable gesture to be waiting at your open apartment door when they arrive.

COMMUNAL SPACE

For Private Conversation

DEAR MISS MANNERS — In the communal parts of the house (kitchen, living room, dining room, family room), when is it proper to initiate a private conversation between two people when three or more are in the room? If it's not, why not? What is the polite way to arrange or initiate a private conversation? If one walks in on a private conversation, what is the proper way to proceed?

GENTLE READER — Technically, one never holds a conversation that excludes one or more persons within conversational range. That said, Miss Manners is as aware as you that a household in which every exchange had to be broadened to include everyone who happens to be in the room would be seething with enough unexpressed tensions to cook the roast without benefit of microwave.

The polite method of securing privacy for a two-person conversation in a three or more person household, other than waiting for the unwanted people to walk the dog, is to change the venue. Three people are in the living room, and one says to another, "I need to talk to you," whereupon they repair to the kitchen.

Should someone walk in on a private conversation already taking place, the people holding it may indicate what is going on by saying "Would you excuse us? We'll come join you in a minute." It is not rude to admit to the need for privacy, although a polite excuse, such as "This is not something that you would be interested in" or "We're having a father-daughter talk," takes the edge off its exclusionary nature.

Miss Manners recognizes that there are times, such as family dinner, when a brief private exchange can't wait, and yet leaving would disrupt the occasion. Two people exchanging significant glances do so at their own risk. Two children rolling their eyes as a commentary on their parents' remarks should make sure they are not caught.

Parents, on the other hand, have a privilege not politely available to children. If they speak a foreign language that the children do not know, they are permitted to exchange a few words in that language. The excuse is educational: Many a child has been encouraged to study with the motivation of finding out what the adults are saying.

This privilege does not apply to children, especially if the language is pig Latin. Miss Manners has never bought the argument that parents are allowed no privileges they don't democratically share with the children.

For Private Parties

DEAR MISS MANNERS — We are four graduate students of both sexes sharing a large house in a university town. One of us owns the house, but other than collecting the rent, does not claim any special privileges. Each of us has a private bedroom, but the kitchen, living room, and dining room are shared equally.

One of us hosted a stand-around-and-chat sort of a party—with music and snacks, vaguely like a cocktail party, except that no alcohol was served; dress very casual—without inviting any of the residents of the house. One, in particular, was miffed. They are members of the same organization and consequently have many of the same friends, although she does not belong to the sub-group that was being entertained. She did not like the idea of being compelled to leave the house for the evening, or lock herself in her room, so that a group of her friends could gather in her living room, but—believing that there is no proper way to complain to a hostess for failing to invite one to a party—has not discussed this. Their relationship has cooled to a point which can only be described as arctic.

The following week, the same housemate had a potluck dinner party in the house, not inviting any of the other residents but chattering on about the special delicacy she was going to contribute which we would have the opportunity to try because there probably would be leftovers. Other residents of the house probably would have declined if invited, but perhaps should have been invited anyway.

Left unanswered is the question of whether the one who knew them was excluded to allow the groups privacy in which to reminisce, or to keep her from feeling left out while listening to their conversation. If the latter, I think she should have been invited and allowed to decide for herself whether she would feel so uncomfortable that it would be better to decline the invitation. If the former, I think the groups should have found other places for their parties.

I have on occasion "invited" housemates by saying "I would love to have you, but I am afraid you might be bored." This often results in the housemate declining without feeling slighted. Of course, sometimes the housemate accepts. The keys to making this work are being (or seeming) sincere in wanting the housemate's company if s/he is willing to sacrifice an evening to attend the potentially boring event, and treating the housemate as a welcome participant in the activity if the invitation is accepted.

Personally, I would never dream of giving any sort of a party in any private home without inviting everyone who lived there, whether permanently or as a house guest. I can't think of a polite way to state or imply the message: "I would like to have a party in your home, but I think the party would be improved by your absence, so find somewhere else to go that evening." I know my practice is acceptable, but is it required?

GENTLE READER — Is this a rooming group or a group marriage?

Wait. Miss Manners would like to withdraw that question—but not because it sounds like a more interesting inquiry than she intended. It is the wrong question because even members of a happy family should occasionally be able to entertain their own guests at home without including the entire household. No one is supposed to sulk if not invited to be a fifth at bridge, so to speak.

By definition, people who live together already like one another (Miss Manners is tactfully ignoring those who are plotting escape), and therefore the issue is one of using rooms rather than misusing feelings. Although your bit about improving the party through someone's absence is indeed an unfortunate one, Miss Manners can think of a way of saying the same thing politely: "Does anyone mind if I use the downstairs on Tuesday to have some people over?"

The Communal Laundry

DEAR MISS MANNERS — Is there a rule to follow regarding the use of washers and dryers in apartment building laundry rooms? If someone else has left clothes in the washer and the cycle is completed, is it permissible to remove the clothes? Or must you wait until that person comes to retrieve them? What about the dryer? If it is OK to remove the clothes, should you fold them?

Sometimes people leave things in machines a long time, and it is extremely difficult to keep coming back to check (not to mention the fact that someone else may cut in ahead of you then). At the same time, I feel uncomfortable about unloading people's clothes, much less folding them. I don't mind doing it, but I feel like I'm invading their privacy, if you know what I mean.

Personally, if I am delayed, I am glad if the next person goes ahead and takes the clothes out, because I am not intending to inconvenience them. But needless to say, not everyone may feel the way I do.

GENTLE READER — Miss Manners prefers not to pursue the avenue of inquiry suggesting what inroads one makes into another person's privacy by folding that person's laundry. For the sake of convention, polite people consider other people's wash to be invisible, whether it is hanging on a line or sitting in a puddle in the machine. However, this should not prevent other people from using the machines. Provided the laundry is handled in such a way as not to make doing it again necessary, it may be put aside by anyone wanting to use the machine.

The Communal Shower

DEAR MISS MANNERS — Following a shower, does a person step out of the tub to dry, or stay in? For the second, less water ends up on the floor, yet it seems like bathroom floors are built to take water. Please clear this up for my brother and me by giving us the correct bathing etiquette.

GENTLE READER — The correct bathing etiquette is that you do not invite Miss Manners to join you in the shower. Manners require that you leave the bathroom floor dry for the next person. How you manage this is up to you. Acts performed alone are outside the jurisdiction of etiquette, which ought to make you as grateful as it does Miss Manners.

The Communal Facilities

DEAR MISS MANNERS — My boyfriend and I went to visit some friends for the weekend, and upon our arrival, we both had to use the facilities. Having had more coffee than I, my boyfriend used the washroom ahead of me. Later that evening, I took him aside and reminded him to be careful not to leave the toilet seat up, as he had earlier. I told him that I thought it rude. Not wanting to be an ignorant guest, he made a conscious effort to put the lid down for the rest of the weekend. Subject dropped.

But whenever he is in my apartment, he leaves the lid up and it irritates me. He knows this bothers me and we argued over whether a guy should put the lid back or not. He says that he does half the work by raising it, and I should do my share by lowering it. I guess I'd really be overworking him if I asked him to put both lids down!

What is the etiquette of the toilet? Does it matter whose house you are in, a male's or a female's? I can live with this idiosyncrasy if I'm just being overly picky, but need to know what is right.

GENTLE READER — Miss Manners hopes you are not thinking of marrying this gentleman. Aside from the fact that he tires so easily, he has a peculiar sense of etiquette. It is not toilet etiquette to which she is referring, although both toilet lids do belong down. (That way, to enter your unappetizing argument, you both have lifting and lowering to do, although he will be dealing with the double weight of two lids.) What about the etiquette of intimacy? Don't you wonder why he continues a practice that—regardless of any arguments about fairness—he knows annoys you, when he is willing to be considerate of others?

The Communal Pool

DEAR MISS MANNERS — I live in a housing development with a communal pool—a very large lap pool, although no ropes are provided to mark off individual lanes. The pool is seldom crowded, so lap swimmers (I swim laps nearly every day) and casual bathers seldom have problems sharing. However, during school vacations, the pool becomes very popular with children and teenagers who frequently get in my way and sometimes crash right into me. I take great pains to avoid them, but to no avail.

Even when the pool is far from crowded, if I start to swim in a vacant section, within minutes there will be roughhousing youngsters blocking my lane. Since most of these children are old enough to swim without adult supervision, there is no parental authority to which I can appeal. My polite requests that they try to be more courteous of other swimmers are seldom heeded. Outright scolding sometimes works, but seems awfully harsh. After all, I do not want to spoil their fun or squelch their high spirits. I just want to swim in peace.

GENTLE READER — Miss Manners is glad that you recognize that full-scale naval battles do not fit into swimming pools. As you point out, the children are not purposely annoying you, but merely enjoying a different kind of fun in the pool.

What they need is not scolding but rules, and reminders about rules. In a communal pool, you cannot make rules unilaterally, but you can appeal to managers and other tenants to draw up rules that will allow everyone to enjoy the pool. If separating the lanes does not work, perhaps regulating the hours by activities will.

Communal Property

Technically, newspapers, magazines and books may be the individually owned property of the person who ordered them. This does not alter Miss Manners' belief that any collection of people—be they roommates or family—who share the same living quarters and yet have no desire constantly to share what they have learned from reading is doomed.

A gentleman of her acquaintance once complained to her that he was sinking under the number of his lady's favorite books that had arrived following his declaration of love. "Have you ever heard of a romance that had a reading list?" he demanded. Miss Manners replied that she had never heard of one that hadn't.

Nevertheless, a household where people cannot find their own reading material in readable condition is also doomed. In practical terms, this means:

First rights over a household newspaper belong to the person who gets up first, and then makes the supreme effort of fetching it. Reasonable generosity is nevertheless mandated. A considerate early riser would, for example, hand over any sections not immediately being read. A clever early riser would quickly read the sections not of great interest before the first footsteps are heard, and reserve the most satisfactory ones. Miss Manners has had to agree that the first reader may also reserve any sections which contain the continuation of any story in the section he or she is actually reading. She only notes that this necessity has led her to the suspicion that newspapers with the policy of jumping stories from one section to the next must be anti-family.

The advantage of early rising is not confined to first choice. It allows the privilege of announcing the news—but that privilege also carries its etiquette obligations. Frightening exclamations ("Oh, no!" "Guess what?" "You won't believe this!") are strictly rationed. Using them as an excuse to read off all the headlines is an irritating habit, leading to domestic mayhem. But then, so is whistling or laughing provocatively, and then not saying anything until the other person is forced to ask "What? What? What?" Indeed, there is a responsibility to alert others to items that may be presumed to be of interest to them, without skimming off the pleasure of reading them. It is a service to summarize information that others should know but that no one enjoys reading. This is a delicate balance, but no one ever said that sharing a household was easy.

Readable condition means that the first reader of the paper—indeed, all but the last reader—may not tear articles out, spill coffee, trail it in the bathwater or, without prior agreement, do puzzles. It also means refolding the paper the way it came.

Magazines differ in that the pleasure of first reading (not to mention that of tearing off the plastic wrapper and disposing of the little subscription cards among the pages) belongs to the subscriber, not the first person to spot an issue in the mail. The subscriber also gets first choice at clipping, sniffing perfume advertisements and filling out reader surveys, but is otherwise expected to share.

New books are at the disposal of their owners or prospective owners (meaning that you can't leave fingerprints in a book you plan to give as a present); a household book remains in the domain of the person who is reading it—even when that person has gone off temporarily and left it.

Of all reading skills, the greatest of all is the ability to interest another person in the book one is reading oneself, without inciting hostility—from either boredom or the hope of snatching the book away.

Communal Property in Communal Space

DEAR MISS MANNERS — Please advise if there are guidelines regarding reading while occupying the bathroom.

GENTLE READER — Well, let's see. Miss Manners hadn't thought about it, but there must be some.

> Don't drop a library book into the bathtub.
> Don't pretend to be so engrossed that you can't hear another member of the household delicately inquiring whether you are going to be in there all day.
> Don't use dental floss as a bookmark if anyone else is ever going to read the book.

Communal Entertainment

DEAR MISS MANNERS — I live in a house with three roommates. We are all good friends and all college students. Three of the four have televisions in our own rooms. Recently, two of us decided to get cable television installed; the other two did not. The two of us split the cable bill.

In the beginning, when there was a good movie on, my room turned into a movie theater, and it was a lot of fun to get together like that. But now when I come home from classes, one of the two without cable is always in my room watching. I see them getting ready to jump into my room when I go out to study. The inconvenience is not their being in my room—it's that neither of them has had the courtesy to offer to pitch in a little each month. Were I in a better financial situation, it would be no problem. I'm not even asking that we all split the cost equally, but a few dollars would help. The problem is that I don't know how to ask. If I did, I'm sure they would respond, "I don't watch that much." And believe me, they do.

GENTLE READER — It is a basic requirement of roommatehood to be able to talk frankly about splitting costs, chores and privileges. It seems to Miss Manners that the proper way of asking is to say "Hey, I don't mind your being in my room so much, but could you help with the cable costs since you like to watch?" Considering the answer you anticipate, the time to do this is at the end of a long session of television watching.

Communal Lives

DEAR MISS MANNERS — After realizing that there is no right time to tell your parents that their child is gay, I finally did it, and somehow we've all managed to survive. They don't fully understand, but we're at least communicating. I have also informed siblings, relatives and close friends about my sexual orientation, because I didn't want them to hear about it from a third party. As a result of all this "sharing," I've found most people to be supportive and many of my relationships have grown even closer.

What this is all leading to is that I've recently moved into an apartment with several other people whom I've known for a couple of years, but not really well. Should I sit each person down as I did with family and close friends, or leave a gay newspaper on the coffee table and see what happens? Am I setting things up for an explosive situation, or am I over-reacting?

If they do ask, I plan to say yes, I'm gay, and ask if they want to talk about it. If they're not thrilled with this, I plan to tell them that I don't have time to deal with their sexual insecurities and walk away. The worst thing that could happen is they would ask me to move, and honestly, that wouldn't be the end of the world. I just want to live in a situation in which I can be fully open about my sexuality.

GENTLE READER — To allow people to find out that you are gay, even to make sure they find out by the newspaper ploy you suggest, is one thing. Roommates generally know what one another's social lives are like, and you don't want to have to hide yours. But to invite people to talk it over is to invite them to offer opinions on a matter which is none of their concern. Their approval would be as patronizing as their disapproval would be distressing.

Communal Messages

DEAR MISS MANNERS — As the resident of a large condo building, I have often wondered as to the correctness of sticking notes and/or cards in doorjambs. Some notes I can understand—"Alice, call me when you return"—although I feel they should be in an envelope, not just hanging out for all to read. But what about cards, and thank you notes, and invitations? Does propriety dictate that they be mailed?

We have a woman living here who will write on anything and tape it to a door. I once came home to find a paper plate taped to my door, and another time, a shoe box lid.

GENTLE READER— Propriety does not get a cut from the Post Office; a hand-delivered letter may be every bit as formal as one that is mailed. As a matter of fact, sending your footman around with a letter is even more formal than posting it, even if today's footman wears nothing but jogging shorts and works for a bicycle delivery service.

So the issues here are what the letter is written on, and where it is left. Shoe box lids and paper plates are not what you would call formal. You should not write your wedding invitations on them. In fact, Miss Manners is hard pressed to think of anything that is sufficiently informal for their proper use.

And while it has become commonplace for college students to hang message boards on their dormitory room doors, for the convenience of people making appointments or delivering witticisms, open communication is not quite proper in a grown-up apartment building. It may also be dangerous, as it alerts strangers to the fact that the occupant is not at home. How much extra effort does it take merely to slip a note under the door, rather than to tape it up?

Posting the Instructions

Some people now want to practice etiquette in the original sense of the word, and Miss Manners is alarmed. She remembers those dear old days at the 17th-century court of Versailles, and she doesn't want them back. Codes of civilized behavior are far older than that, of course; by definition, they date back to the beginning of civilization. Miss Manners would be only too glad to see ours put back into practice. She is happy to explain its rules upon request, and to amend or prod them now and then, so that they keep up with the times.

Louis XIV went too far with his habit of continually posting arbitrary new written rules of behavior—not just for soldiers, as had been customary, but for everyone else within his purview. Hence we are stuck with that odd word "etiquette," a version of the French word for those pesky stickers. And stuck with the idea that one can keep making up new rules, posting them on the walls and expecting everyone else to jump to obey.

A lot has happened since this practice was introduced, such as the French Revolution and the Enlightenment, and now citizens are doing this in their own homes. Above a typical "Welcome" mat, the front door may announce "Wipe Your Feet"; inside, the living room may bark "No Smoking"; and the bathroom admonish you to "Clean Up After Yourself." The television room might have one sign about putting the remote control back and another about rewinding videotapes. Various doors may be marked "Quiet," "Sleeping," "Please Knock" and "Keep Out." Some signs are written in pleading tones ("Please Think of Others") and some in hostile ones ("I Am Not Your Maid"). The only sign missing is "Post No Bills."

Miss Manners has been wondering what is going on here, apart from the habit of snitching public signs and bringing them home for souvenirs. It seems to her that it is something more than the peculiar inclination people now have for displaying their sentiments, witticisms, affiliations and brand loyalties on their bodies.

These are instructions, and they are seriously meant. The motivation seems to be the same as that at the French court: to get people to follow the rules. But Louis XIV was not what we call a great role model. It's not just that he thought it was funny to plant hairs in a lady's food because she was so affected that she ate with a fork instead of with fingers, as he did. He kept setting and changing rules as a power play, which is not a proper function of etiquette, even if he did give that noble concept its name.

Miss Manners understands that the citizens who are now imitating him have more benign motives. They want to be able to set the rules in their own houses—but not because they are tyrants who like to keep everyone frightened of doing something wrong. The rules they post are, with few exceptions, reasonable ones that every civilized person would agree upon to maintain a pleasant atmosphere for all. However, in order to do this, they sacrifice the atmosphere with stern and unsightly signs. Why would a society that considers billboards to be eyesores want to live among them?

All of this is an argument for the teaching of etiquette, so that everyone in the society knows that it is not nice to leave a mess in the sink or make a racket when someone is trying to sleep. Meanwhile, however, the house is full of people who don't know what to do without explicit commands. If they are your children, you teach them, by example, word of mouth and as much nagging as you can get in until they leave home. If they are roommates, you work out an agreement about the rules. If it is someone who professes to love you, you say "I know it doesn't seem important to you, but it is to me, so would you, darling, please, for my sake?" If they are guests, you use symbols (the absence of ashtrays means "No Smoking"; closed doors mean privacy) or requests disguised as apologies or helpfulness ("Oh, dear, I'm afraid it's so messy out; just stay there a second while you wipe your feet and I'll get you a towel"). The stubbornly rude guest doesn't need a sign, because he won't obey it. All he needs is one stroke of the pen—through his name in your address book.

S T U F F

Good Taste

To go into someone's home and then roll your eyes, whisper comments on the decor or report afterwards to others that it is in terrible taste is rude. So much for the spring house tour.

Miss Manners admires the selflessness of those whose charitable impulses lead them to open their premises to uncharitable remarks. For every "Isn't this lovely!" there is always a full chorus repeating "I'd go crazy if I lived here," "That couldn't possibly be real" and "Will you look at that?" Taste being taste, nothing is going to meet everyone's standard.

So we have a strict (and unenforceable) rule against guests' talking about their hosts' possessions. "Commenting on one's things," it is witheringly called by those who maintain the old-fashioned sniffiness of believing compliments to be as impertinent as insults. The thinking is that hospitality does not confer the right of appraisal, so even approval is out. Also that in the natural course of events, people live in an accumulation of stuff from previous generations, not to mention that awful stuff introduced by the subsequent generation in residence, so they should receive neither credit nor blame for the effect.

Modern hosts have suspended at least half of the evaluation rule. If they put a lot of work and/or money into their surroundings, they are eager to produce a burst of admiration. Sometimes they stimulate this by pointing out new possessions or offering tours.

Perhaps it seems hard on guests to be required to produce compliments, as indeed they are if prodded, and still to be barred from divulging any other opinions once they are safely outside. Miss Manners expects them to manage it anyway. She sets an example by unswervingly believing that everybody who wants to live in a place characterized by quiet good taste does. As far as she knows, that notion, or perhaps delusion, applies to just everyone who doesn't live in a fraternity house.

It is possible that more than kindness is involved in her reluctance to issue edicts declaring what is good taste in the way of household furnishings and what is not. Many of her distinguished predecessors unfortunately went on record declaring that everything Victorian—the very adorable look so warmly cherished now—was horrible beyond belief. Dear Edith Wharton loathed the style for

THE HOUSEHOLD SHRINE: *The urge to celebrate oneself is best indulged at home, but even there it must yield to the rule against boring others senseless. Souvenirs of triumph should therefore be confined to bedroom, bathroom or study, with tours and explanations offered only upon request and with occasional pauses in the narrative to allow escape.*

which her name is now admiringly invoked, jammed with her once-distinctive preferences into the trunk of history.

Still, Miss Manners thinks it useful to mention a few checkpoints associated with household taste. One might consider them when judging one's own house, since she has forbidden judging anyone else's.

> Shrines to oneself should be displayed discreetly. Award statues may be used as doorstops, plaques and diplomas can be hung in the kitchen or bathroom, but your wedding portrait goes in the bedroom, the mounted fish you caught goes in the study and photographs taken with the Vice President or a movie star must be placed in shelved albums—not even albums left on coffee tables.
>
> Nothing should seem permanently roped off. You may tell the children to play where there is less to break, and you may refrain from using your grandmother's china to feed those louts who constitute the immediate family, but everything should be used sometime. It is insulting to maintain rooms or objects that you consider too good for anyone you know to use.
>
> Things should either be what they are supposed to be or miss by so much that there is no possibility of confusion. This is why real flowers are fine, china flowers are fine, but artfully done plastic or cloth ones are not.
>
> Objects left visible in a bathroom should not be surprising or distasteful to anyone else, housemate or guest, who may need to use that bathroom.
>
> Table space and chairs must be provided for anyone who is asked to eat anything more serious than a cucumber sandwich.
>
> Finally, it is in bad taste to have a house in perfect taste. It screams of having excluded all sentiment in the form of leavings or offerings from others.

Over-Tasting

DEAR MISS MANNERS — I want to know if one must have just one theme in a room and/or house to be correct? I have nautical bathrooms, blue and white dishes in kitchen and library, and the living room is decorated mainly with florals, sea/ship/lighthouse pictures, but I just got two Egyptian drawings I want to put in there. I know it should reflect our interests but don't want to do anything too drastic.

GENTLE READER — Miss Manners trusts that you understand that she is not the decorator. There is indeed an etiquette aspect to the question you ask, but it has nothing to do with helping you achieve a fashionable look. On the contrary, etiquette is wary of anything too fashionable or too consistently anything.

In the matter of household decor, it just doesn't consider aesthetic pleasure to be worth the price of banning things of emotional value—discoveries, legacies, children's art, presents and such—because they don't fit in. Presumably what you have there is a house, not a ship or a theme restaurant.

Getting Good Stuff

Modern couples have no trouble explaining, in a tone of high morality, why they consider it important to live together before deciding whether to marry: They get an idea of how they feel about each other apart from the artificial circumstances of going out; they see what the other person is like when not on his or her best behavior; they see if their daily moods and habits are compatible—and so on. Anyone with children past the dinosaur stage is familiar with this argument. As most parents do not wish to be considered in the dinosaur stage themselves, they pretend to agree, and say nothing about what people who live together before marriage miss out on when they marry:

The trousseau.

Didn't think of that, did you, you impetuous young things, you?

Don't tell Miss Manners that love is more important than dry goods. If you feel that way, why do you spend your official engagement period hysterically evaluating every known pattern of china, silver and trash compactor? (Come to think of it, why do you go after all that good stuff at all—and forever afterwards entertain your friends using paper plates and drinks in their original bottles and cans?)

Even the most tolerant parents could not keep a straight face if a modern bride attempted the traditional announcement that she really must have a fortune's worth of intimate lace because she would be embarrassed to have the bridegroom see her in her old things. He has probably been seeing her wearing his old things.

However, bridal couples do get away with asking for a trousseau of silver, china and crystal usually, Miss Manners regrets to say, from their wedding guests—and with the cheeky excuse that they are only anticipating what agonies these people would otherwise suffer in not knowing how to please them.

However such goods are now acquired, here is a traditional starter set of household goods.

Every new couple needs fine china in order to feed the traditional marital argument about whether or not it may safely be washed in the dishwasher. There should be at least one extra of each item, so as to soften the agony (and the instinct to cast blame) at the first sign of a chip. Otherwise, only as many dinner plates are needed as there are dining room chairs—presuming that when bridge chairs and other improvised seating is needed, there will be plates in two patterns, one of them borrowed. When dinner plates are asked to do extra duty—for example, in place of a cake stand—they do it with bad grace and drip icing over the side, so some platters are needed. The real workers are eight-inch plates, which are used alone for breakfast, luncheon and tea, and at dinner for first courses, salad and dessert, so there should be either a lot of them or a fast hand with the suds in the kitchen. One also needs five- or six-inch plates for bread and butter and fruit, and to serve as underliners; and bowls, which get up early to do cereal and stay up late for informal soups (grand soups are served in rimmed plates at dinner, or double-handled cups for lunch) and runny desserts.

Specialized glasses for each type of drink hardly exist any longer. It must have been that last earthquake that made people who used to have special glasses for hock, claret and Rhine wine decide, Oh, the heck with it. Just about everybody is down to two sizes of wine glasses (for red and white, or for sippers and guzzlers), with stemmed water glasses and tulip champagne glasses for the festive table (Miss Manners misses sherry glasses to go with the soup course) and unstemmed large glasses (short for whiskey or juice, long for cocktails, diet soda or milk).

Don't get Miss Manners started on silver. Confirming everyone's worst fears about etiquette as a trap for the unwary, she goes in for all the excesses of the Victorian imagination—terrapin forks, breakfast knives, berry spoons, asparagus tongs, strawberry forks, orange knives, marrow spoons, ramekin forks, chocolate muddlers, pastry forks, sherbet spoons and so on. What a normal person needs are dinner knives, forks and large oval spoons (not teaspoons) for soup and dessert; a smaller-sized knife and fork for salad, fish and breakfast; a teaspoon for tea or a demitasse spoon for after-dinner coffee.

There also used to be a linen department to the trousseau, consisting of white damask tablecloths with flag-sized napkins and mats with smaller napkins for daytime meals only, six complete changes for every bed and dainty guest towels for the guests to ignore while looking for the family towels to wipe their hands on. The presumption was that no decent person used paper napkins, put bedsheets on a table or considered a bed to be made when covered with something huge and lumpy, other than the family dog. Also that people made their beds before they slept in them. So you see that the trousseau really is an old-fashioned idea.

Giving Stuff Back

DEAR MISS MANNERS — My sister and I are having a war over borrowing and lending and desperately need your insight to settle our disagreement.

I believe that when someone borrows something it is their responsibility to:

1. Pick it up
2. Take good care of it
3. Only keep it for a reasonable length of time
4. Arrange for its return

Well here's the story: My sister asked to borrow a VCR tape that I had recently purchased. Since I'm at her house frequently, I delivered it. About two weeks later, I asked her if she had watched it, which she had, and might I have it returned to me.

At that point she told me that she had allowed her next door neighbor to borrow it and that she would get it back as soon as possible. Another week passed when I asked again for the return of my property at which time she had a fit.

Her fit isn't important, but am I correct in saying that she is in violation of good manners in that she loaned something that wasn't hers (without my knowledge) and she kept it far too long. My video store considers one night long enough for its newest releases and five nights for the next level. My sister was way past that point!

GENTLE READER — Your sister has lower standards than your video store? My, you do have trouble.

Miss Manners doesn't condone your sister's behavior, but she doesn't understand yours, either. Surely you have a long history of your sister's claiming your sweaters, books, lipsticks, scissors, perhaps even beaux, and returning them late and damaged, if she returned them at all.

One should never again lend one's belongings to someone who has violated the rules you listed, and certainly not to someone who then produces rude fits (which may not matter to you, but which matter more to Miss Manners than all your rules put together). What you should offer her is a polite refusal—"No, I'm sorry, I'm going to need it"—without leaving yourself open to argument.

Getting Stuff Back

DEAR MISS MANNERS — How can I tactfully get friends to return books that I have loaned them?

GENTLE READER — By continuing to do what you intended when you lent those books to friends—urging them to read them. Every chance you get, you should ask whether your friend has read that wonderful book yet. It shouldn't take more than two or three times before the friend starts telling you how terribly busy he is—overworked, with a lot of other reading to do, and so on. At that point you say, "Why don't I take it back, then, and lend it to you again when you have time?" Miss Manners promises that your friend will be as happy to be rid of it as ever he was to borrow it.

Throwing Stuff Out

If rampant consumerism is vulgar, as everyone at the mall agrees it is, there remains a respectable way to have fun with dry goods. The basic idea is the same, but in the opposite direction: Instead of acquiring things, you get rid of them.

Unless this involves leaving refrigerators on the sidewalk or piling empty bottles in the neighbors' trash, you can get a lot of moral credit for disposal, Miss Manners has noticed. If you give things away, you are an angel of charity; if you throw them away, you are at least a good housekeeper. Also, it costs less than shopping.

One might think it would cost nothing at all, but that is not quite the case. Those who get into the spirit, merrily pitching anything they can get their hands on, occasionally find themselves shamefacedly obliged to run out and replace what they may have pitched prematurely. Such as sections of the morning newspaper that other people haven't finished reading, even though breakfast is almost over.

This brings up the sad fact that there is also a moral onus on getting rid of things. One might expect it to be directed towards those who preach the joys of being free of materialistic ties, especially while heavily dependent on the generosity of those to whom they are bragging. What astonishes Miss Manners is that even modest folk are attacked if they confess to enjoying a good sweep.

Aside from unpleasant personal comments, they will be challenged on allegedly practical grounds:

1. I haven't finished with that yet.

This may be perfectly true, in so far as it goes. What is left unsaid is that it is clear when something is never going to be finished—the jigsaw puzzle that has been occupying the dining room table since Christmas, the tools on the floor near where there has been talk of building a shelf, the magazine that has been on the bathtub ledge for a week.

2. I might need it for reference.

But you won't be able to find it, anyway. That's why we have libraries and all that information on the Internet.

3. You can't throw out books!

No, but you can donate the duplicates of good books to schools and the terrible ones to neighborhood book sales. Hard as it is to believe that anyone will ever want to read another book about how to love oneself or lose weight without feeling deprived, someone always does.

4. We need the box in case we have to send it back.

But you won't be able to find the warranty, and by the time you do, it will have run out. The thrift involved in saving containers has to be weighed against the extravagance of allowing them large portions of living space, sometimes enough to sublet.

5. If anything breaks, we'll be glad to have a spare.

The traditional way to refurnish was to wait until a piece of furniture fell apart and then go foraging around for replacements kindly left by ancestors, but this presumed a castle with infinite storage, in which good furniture had the grace to turn itself quietly into antiques. That you will want to cannibalize the defunct electric toothbrush for parts if the newer one breaks is not a likely scenario.

6. We don't want it, but we're keeping it in case someone else in the family might.

You might ask them. Otherwise, this holds only for people with children who can be expected to set up residence elsewhere (from their parents or present spouses) within the next few years. Even then, they often prefer to buy other people's cast-off furniture from the same place to which you could donate yours.

7. Those things are going to be worth a fortune someday.

Whoever created the market for old comic books has a lot to answer for. The formula that junk plus patience equals a fortune is believed only by those who haven't been around long enough to observe otherwise.

8. It's bound to come back into style.

Here, Miss Manners weakens, because indeed it might. This is justification for keeping things one truly loves, although not what is perfectly good because it has never been worn.

9. It would break my heart to part with it.

Here, she really breaks down. Yes, you should keep dolls, stuffed animals, wedding dresses and letters. There are a lot of superfluous things in every household, but a heart is not one of them.

Not Throwing Stuff Out Yet

DEAR MISS MANNERS — Recently a friend of mine gave me an olive green lamp with a tasseled shade as a house warming gift. I tried putting it in numerous places in my house, but wherever it is, it sticks out terribly. I value her friendship and I don't want to insult her, but I can't stand the sight of this lamp. What should I do?

GENTLE READER — Flag your friend's name in your appointment book with the note "Green lamp," reminding you to get the awful thing out of the closet before she visits. Miss Manners promises you that you don't have to do this forever.

Once given, a present goes out of the jurisdiction of the donor, who is not supposed to notice, let alone inquire about, what happened to it. Nevertheless, it would be kind to have it around for a while before disposing of it. The only strict requirement of etiquette on your part is to make sure that you do that in a manner not likely to come to your friend's attention. No lawn sales if she lives in your neighborhood.

Stealing Stuff

"The napkins quickly became the event's treasured stuff-in-your-purse souvenir," stated the glossy report of a swish gala taking place in what is now defined as society. That is to say, the event was a dinner dance given to honor a designer of the sort of clothes one needs to have if one attends dinner dances in honor of designers of the sort of clothes one needs to have, and so on. Miss Manners has always been in awe of this world as a perfectly self-contained economic system.

She admits to being startled that public commentary, written in an unmistakably admiring tone, noted that the guests were stealing the napkins. An accompanying photograph showed an untouched place setting, still with its fine cloth napkin, especially embroidered with the theme of the occasion.

Is this how people are furnishing their houses? No doubt it is an economical way of doing so, but people who try to justify it actually do so in terms of sentiment.

In this case, the napkin was identified in the caption as a "hot dinner item," and Miss Manners has always understood hot items to be goods offered for sale from the back of trucks by suspicious-looking characters who seem to be in a pressing hurry to complete the transaction. She was startled by its referring to items swiped by expensively costumed people out to do honor to someone they admire. If pilfering were, indeed, the activity of the evening, doesn't the information belong in a police report, rather than in society news?

Not that Miss Manners means to quibble about what is or is not society. Surely the commercial world has a larger interest in prosecuting shoplifting than the world of mere play. Is it possible that this is what its distinguished members do to one another on their stylish outings? If not, or at least if everybody present was not involved, haven't any innocents among the smiling people pictured been insulted, if not libeled?

What shocks Miss Manners most is that she suffers all this debilitating shock alone. Helping oneself to the fixtures now seems to be considered respectable, provided it can be classified as collecting souvenirs.

There is another word that has had to be redefined for Miss Manners in its modern sense: "souvenirs." She used to think it meant objects that travelers bought when driven to distraction by airport boredom and the realization of being short one present. She could think of no other way of accounting for the idea that snow scenes of state capitols make coveted paperweights. "Souvenir" has now gone back to its earlier meaning of being a keepsake to stimulate the memory. What's more, memories are in dire need of help, judging from the photographing, recording and grabbing that goes on all the time now. It seems to Miss Manners that most fancy occasions now suffer from the Heisenberg Effect: The festivities themselves are significantly altered, not to mention obliterated, by the rush to record them.

She understands that there is also a tremendous interest in owning artifacts that will remind people of the hotel rooms in which they have stayed. Once that meant lifting ashtrays. Now television sets and lamps are the souvenirs of choice, but the problem of packing them has led travelers to settle for the paltry toiletries that

ACQUIRED TASTE: *Although off-the-budget décor is a popular method of suggesting worldliness, stealing is not an approved method of furnishing a household. Those not impressed by the moral angle might consider that their children and guests may be sufficiently in agreement to take up the implied offer.*

canny hotels offer as a lure to keep them away from larger heists. Miss Manners once made a laughingstock of herself by confessing that she thought these goods were just to be used while occupying the room, and was insulted by the notion that they were there to satisfy her presumed appetite for theft. Still, she cannot imagine that all ball-goers feel that they have been invited to steal the tableware.

Come to think of it, the honest ones may have been the ones who took the napkins—to put over their faces so as not to be mistaken for anyone who might have taken the forks instead.

Coveting Stuff

DEAR MISS MANNERS — My grandparents have a desk that I would like. I do not want to hurt their feelings or be pushy or rude. Is it all right to ask for the desk now while they're alive, or ask if they put it in their will that the desk be given to me?

I do not want to embarrass my mother—or myself. My mother is an only child, so she will probably be in charge of their estate, but I do not want to ask her for fear of hurting her feelings.

If this is totally out of line, please tell me so. My grandparents are in their early 90's. I have admired this desk ever since I was a little girl.

GENTLE READER — Yes, this is totally out of line. There is no polite way to make cheerful plans with people that, in order to be realized, involve their being dead.

What you can do, if you promise Miss Manners not to be obvious about it, is to admire the desk. You can tell your grandparents and your mother that you have loved it since you were a child, and hope that this will encourage them to think that you should inherit it. When your grandparents actually are dead and their property is being dispersed, you may ask your mother, as executrix, if she would be willing to let you have the desk, which you would cherish in their memory. Miss Manners hopes this will be a long time from now, as grandparents are harder to come by than desks.

Showing Off

Showing off is bad manners, as every child knows. "Oh, you're just showing off," even the littlest ones will say scornfully as a way of refusing to concede defeat when they have been shown up. So how do we get people to admire our stuff?

Within the ranks of show-offs, there is special condemnation for those who show off with their possessions. While it is true that pride in having skills or receiving honors is supposed to be masked with humility, kindly disposed people (a category in which Miss Manners oddly places herself) have a certain amount of sympathy for those who occasionally peek out gleefully from under the mask. Achievements are presumably the result of dedication and work, which we do admire openly.

Pride in owning things is not appealing. Although the argument can certainly be made that skill goes into the selection and placement of what one owns, and having paid for it suggests a direct link to working, the sentiment still comes off as crass. What inevitably springs to mind when objects are flaunted is the monetary value they represent, and flaunting money is just not respectable. In spite of our ancestors' efforts to link wealth with virtue on the grounds that God gives merit raises, anyone who still believes that the rich and poor deserve their respective states is advised not to say so.

Yet charitable people occasionally get excited about having new toys and want to show them off. Miss Manners cannot see a great deal of harm in this, provided they don't—show off. Perhaps that little distinction is not clear. Perhaps the whole problem is puzzling to a society of crazed consumers. With everyone going around offering critical evaluations of everyone else's clothes, cars, furniture and groceries, demanding to know where it was all bought and for how much, it may seem unnecessary to worry about how to draw an object of pride to anyone's attention.

In spite of provocation and temptation, Miss Manners expects polite people to refrain from behaving like shopkeepers and customers in their social lives. She doesn't care for the attitudes and comments that displaying and examining one another's wares provokes and tempts them to reveal. To point out every new pair of socks you are wearing, even with the sly approach of asking for an opinion, or to greet everybody who walks through your door with a house tour instead of a drink, is to ask for trouble. There has to be a presumption of particular interest on the part of one's targeted audience. It's not nice to go around shouting, "Look what I got!"

Nor do such tactics unfailingly produce admiration. People who can safely be presumed to take a kindly interest are: those who take an interest in every move you make, or lovingly pretend to—in other words, people who love you; shopping pals, for whom the rules about comparing bargains and finds are suspended; collectors or fanciers of the particular item you want to show off; prospective or recent purchasers of the same sort of thing; and those who express enthusiastic interest.

Miss Manners is not saying you cannot stimulate this interest—but only if you recognize that you are honor-bound to listen to advice you solicit, issue house-warming invitations only to people you plan to entertain again, and find occasions to reciprocate the admiration. The last is particularly valuable, as it proves to them that you have good taste.

Displaying the Good Stuff

DEAR MISS MANNERS — Our daughters, who enjoy a very casual approach to entertaining—jeans, BBQs, beer from cans and milling around the kitchen, yard or deck—asked my opinion about the display we saw during a gathering at a friend's house. On the dining room table were china, crystal and silver, along with flowers and candles. No place mats (that's considered formal), but fancily folded napkins were stuck into the goblets. This was not set for that evening, but as daily decor, as are pillows on the sofa.

The lady of the house received no family training in the social graces, but was led by TV and/or advertisements to believe this "proper" and socially acceptable. My belief is that you display your acquisitions by inviting your guests to your house to use them. Also, since your home is not a restaurant, napkins are not displayed across the dinner plate nor stuffed into goblets. I still think that a bare table is not proper. I can understand that place mats have replaced the old-fashioned tablecloth, but recognize that some place mats are more "formal" than others.

GENTLE READER — Mothers are higher authorities on propriety than television, as Miss Manners trusts your fortunate daughters realize. While she feels sorry for people who don't learn the common customs of their own society at home, she does expect them to think over what they are seeing elsewhere before copying it.

Surely it takes only common sense to realize that although it is reasonable for advertisers to show off their wares, it is just plain show-offy to display privately owned dinner equipment to people without inviting them to dinner. While she's at it, this lady might as well show off her cooking by bringing out platters of food without offering her guests any to eat.

Miss Manners could quibble with you about the details of table setting, as two people who know the customs but recognize that they change. She actually doesn't mind a bare table if the wood is interesting, yet she clings to that "old-fashioned tablecloth" (although not so tenaciously that she pulls the dishes onto the floor), considers place mats to be informal at dinnertime even if they are made from spun gold, and shares your aversion to the silly fad of stuffing napkins in glasses.

The creepy idea of setting up a phantom dinner party goes much deeper, making a mockery of the sacred concept of hospitality. The respectable alternative to formality is informality, such as your daughters practice, not pretentiousness.

Giving House Tours

DEAR MISS MANNERS — When friends visit your home for the first time, is it impolite not to show them through your home? I was brought up believing it was almost impolite to do so.

GENTLE READER — Far from being a required part of hospitality, house tours, while not actually forbidden, must be accompanied by an excellent excuse from the host and a whole chorus of requests and protests from the guests.

Miss Manners understands perfectly well what you mean by their being "almost impolite." A house tour, being an invitation to admire a whole range of possessions that may not interest or amuse the tourists, is presumptuous of the host to offer. Yet requesting one seems to demand that people who have extended hospitality in their communal rooms also present their private rooms for inspection.

Suppose you have a host who would love showing off and a guest dying of curiosity? How can they manage to get together?

The host can initiate the idea by saying that he or she has just finished moving in, or redecorating, or mentions some point of historic or other interest in the house, or offers to show an object located elsewhere in the house that has come up in the conversation.

A guest can only bring the subject up by discussing how interesting the house is, and saying brightly "I'd love to see it sometime, if you don't mind," the "sometime" allowing the host to smile blandly and agree to that indefinite future, or to jump up and begin at once. If there is such a tour, however, guests must remember to pronounce everything charming. The tediousness of this for either or both parties if there is no genuine interest explains why the tour must be deliberately and mutually negotiated.

Tourist Attractions

DEAR MISS MANNERS — I am a working woman who is fortunate enough to own a horse farm just outside the metropolitan area where I work. The farm is most frequently described as a "showplace," and there, frankly, lies my problem.

My profession is stressful, and I look forward to weekends as a chance to recharge my batteries. I forget about make-up and pantyhose, and spend hours puttering around in my "grubbies" and playing with the Dachshunds, gloriously alone and blissfully relaxed.

Hardly a weekend goes by, however, without the quiet being shattered by the doorbell. There stands a friend or acquaintance—somewhat sheepishly—usually with several complete strangers in tow. The recital nearly always goes, "I know we should have called, but we were driving by and I knew how much my friends would enjoy seeing your beautiful farm and the horses." I smile weakly and am trapped into what usually amounts to an hour's tour, followed by the obligatory glass of iced tea or cup of coffee.

Short of putting up locked gates at the farm entry, which I would resist, how can I discourage these people? What would you think of a sign by the courtyard gate that says, "The best friends are those who are expected." Or, more bluntly, "Please, no unexpected guests." Seems a little brutal to me, but then, I'm getting desperate. I should add that I am not a recluse and love entertaining, but at times I select!

GENTLE READER — How about issuing megaphones to the dachshunds and then training them to run out and hide in the front bushes? Failing that, you might set up a speaker system with the house, which asks all visitors to identify themselves at the gate, along with a recording that always responds that Madam is not receiving visitors today.

Miss Manners makes these suggestions only to save you from having to appear in your grubbies and enact the following perfectly polite scene:

Open the door only part of the way, and respond to their requests by saying, "Oh, dear, I'm so sorry, this just isn't a good time for me to show them around. Do drop me a note when you're planning to be in the neighborhood again, so I can be sure to save some time for you." Then, with a regretful smile, shut the door.

With a showplace or a hovel, the rules are the same: You do not have to let uninvited people inside your house. The only difference is that when one owns a renowned tourist attraction, it is considered gracious to make a special effort to allow people to see it on one's own terms. For example, you might volunteer the grounds for a picnic for a worthy organization, now and then. Then you could add to your doorway regrets, "But we're having a benefit for the county here next week, and I do hope you'll come."

Using the Good Stuff

The well-appointed house is stocked with things that are much too good for anyone in it.

Miss Manners isn't making this snobbish judgment. The people who live there are. The same people who bought all that stuff in the first place. The same people who are responsible, through marriage, birth or invitation, for the presence of all those other unworthy people. Everything they own is, in their opinion, too good for their children to go anywhere near, too good for regular family use, and much too much trouble to take out for company.

The concepts of "best" and "everyday" are of long standing, and the distinction was made even in the humblest households with the idea of providing a sense of occasion now and then. The difference between then and now is that such occasions actually did occur. The best things were taken out for guests, but also for the family to use, if not to lend dignity to family dinner every night, then at least on Sundays and holidays, even if no one else was there.

In our times, Miss Manners has observed a downgrading of the worth of the people involved, and a corresponding upgrading of respect for the worth of things. These unpleasant judgments now cover everyone ever likely to cross the threshold and everything in the house that can possibly be put away or placed off limits. Once, it was only the dog who was required to keep his paws off the sofa. Now the guests are being told to keep their shoes off the rug.

It started with the china and the silver, which were so obviously too good for the family that they had to be supplemented by duplicate sets of second-string items—also called "nice," but less expensive and fragile—made of earthenware and stainless steel. In many households, those, too, are now considered to be too good for any entertaining that is done. Surely paper and plastic are good enough for the kind of people who come for parties, holidays, meetings or weekends. The table linens also went rapidly to paper, obliterating the distinction between the good damask for company and the family's plain cloth napkins.

Rugs and upholstery soon followed. The vogue for white rugs overcame the illogic of using them to furnish houses in which walking took place. To this day,

Miss Manners receives bitter letters from rug owners who have no qualms about exposing their priorities when they complain about guests who balk at taking off their shoes.

Another method of protecting things from people is to place entire rooms off limits. The front parlor was in its glory for visiting clergy and dead relatives—the former to take tea and the latter to be laid out—but was also available for guests. While that concept survives in the modern living room, this room is left empty while guests are entertained in the kitchen, which has been enlarged for the purpose.

Miss Manners can only suppose that the quality of guests has gone down. Even they seem to agree that they are not good enough to use the guest towels.

Even without watching daytime television, Miss Manners has heard enough people talk about their families as to have no illusions about what they think their relatives deserve. She remains puzzled about why, then, it is still customary to stockpile all that good stuff. Surely it would make sense to shop around for better people—or worse stuff.

The Unused and the Unwashed

DEAR MISS MANNERS—Either I know more uneducated slobs than the average person, or they just find their way to my home by themselves. I have two guest baths, one up, one down. These baths also can be used with corresponding bedrooms (but rarely are) so there are towel bars. I have very expensive decorator towels on these bars, which I replace with nice towels if the bathroom is to be used by a staying guest.

The problem is that visiting people use these towels after they have used the guest bath. I have guest towels laid out on the sink, but they don't use them—they walk across the floor, dripping water, and use the decorator towel, which necessitates washing it (do they think I can't tell?) and shortly ruins the beauty of the towel. I've even tried the paper towel route, but nothing helps. I've considered making a sign stating "USE THESE," but that seems crass. I've considered taking down my decorative towels, but that leaves a bare towel bar staring you in the face.

GENTLE READER—Miss Manners was all set to sympathize with you when she thought you were plagued with guests who ignored the guest towels for the family towels, out of heaven knows what sense that they were saving you trouble. You lost her with the horrid idea of "decorator towels," especially "expensive decorator towels." Miss Manners does not know what decorator towels are, and she doesn't want to know. No doubt they are all the rage with what you would call educated slobs. She will tell you that anything that hangs in the bathroom and looks like a towel is going to be mistaken for a towel. What belongs on the towel rack of the guest bathroom are guest towels.

Child-Proofing

DEAR MISS MANNERS — I have company coming for two days with a two-year-old, and I have just received a letter saying, "You may want to pack up all the knickknacks from the living room to child-proof the place, or else our son may get into things you don't want him to." I have four children of my own, and I always watch them whenever I visit. And I have a large family room where the little boy can play. Instead of packing things away, I am thinking of putting a "child's security gate" in my living room.

GENTLE READER — Miss Manners has the feeling you may want to pack up all the knickknacks from the living room to child-proof the place, or else their son will most certainly get into things you don't want him to. His parents have served notice that they are not going to stop him.

As you and Miss Manners both know from having children around, it is possible for parents to tell even toddlers that certain objects or areas—Miss Manners does not know whether we are talking about an ordinary adult household, or one in which a collection of priceless china figurines is displayed in open cases just off the floor—are off limits, and to enforce this through parental vigilance. This is nearly impossible for the hosts to do, both because they do not have the authority, and because it violates the hospitable impulse. As these parents have brought the subject up themselves, however, you could ask whether it wouldn't be better to tell the child where he might (and might not) play freely.

Preventing Accidents

DEAR MISS MANNERS — At a party we had, with several round tables and chairs for our guests, one gentleman was in a family antique Windsor, leaning back on two legs of the chair. He is quite large. I was across the room, and would have had to maneuver to speak to him quietly or get his attention. I decided to let it go, but ended up with a damaged chair. It didn't break, but the spindles are now quite weak. I have had this happen before, where someone leans back and rocks on a chair. I am saddened about my chair, but I didn't want to embarrass my guest, either. Should one politely ask a guest not to lean back on a chair? If my children do it, I always ask them not to.

GENTLE READER — One difference between one's own children and guests is that the latter may not be instructed in proper behavior. However, a gracious hostess always worries about the welfare of her guests. You need only say "Oh, dear, I'm afraid you might get hurt in that chair—let me get you one you'll be more comfortable in" as an excuse for substituting a nondescript but indestructible chair for your valuable but fragile one.

Accepting Accidents

DEAR MISS MANNERS — It may be correct etiquette but I think the idea that a guest should replace a broken dish or glass is ridiculous. Now if they drink too much or somehow act negligently, that would be different.

It is the host/hostess who decides the price of the dishes that they will use for their guests. A guest is not given the opportunity to say they don't want to use expensive dishes or glassware. Expensive dishes and glassware certainly don't make the food or wine taste any better. Therefore, if the host/hostess chooses to use expensive table settings, it is purely for their own personal expression of taste and decoration. If they choose to do it expensively, then they should bear the cost of normal accidents. I would be happy to eat and drink out of disposables or inexpensive dishes. I don't want to be responsible for their expensive pieces.

I use inexpensive table settings and if something gets broken (which it has), I can simply say, "Oh, don't worry about it." I figure it is the cost of entertaining. So, unless the host/hostess is willing to let everyone know that they are assuming an expensive replacement liability, he/she should replace it themselves.

GENTLE READER — Miss Manners doesn't disagree with your conclusion, but she has to confess that she hates the way you arrived at it.

Indeed, occasional breakage is the risk of entertaining. While guests should try to replace what they break, hosts should try just as hard to prevent them from doing so. However, food does taste better when it is nicely served. That is because this is done to honor guests, even possibly clumsy guests. The argument that being gracious to guests is some sort of ego exercise on the part of the hosts can be made about any attempt to please other people—but not to Miss Manners, it can't.

A Lesson in Gracious Acceptance

DEAR MISS MANNERS — When a group of some 30 French children and their teachers visited our children's school for two and a half weeks, we welcomed a lovely 12-year-old into our home and spent considerable time and money making sure she had a good experience on her first stay in America. At the end of her visit, it became apparent that she had broken our plumbing. (Although I had talked discreetly to her about sanitary supplies and she seemed to understand, she had flushed some. Also, I know that she was using a lot of toilet paper but it did not occur to me that she was not flushing enough to push it through.) By the time the plumber was gone for good (it took three trips and replacement of some sewer line in the backyard), our guest was back in Paris and we had a large bill, which we were able to pay but not without some negative feelings.

Hoping for insurance, we have talked to the umbrella organization which sponsored this trip, but they said they would pursue reimbursement from the French family. The teacher and parent coordinators from our own school also say that the French family should pay. But we had talked to this family by phone several times and feel a personal relationship, sight unseen. We feel awkward having a third party deal with the situation and ungracious pursuing it ourselves.

While the bill was within our means, it was more than we are spending to send our own child to camp this summer.

We know that this girl is from a wealthy family and that her parents sent her with an international phone card so she would not have to run up our phone bill in case of emergency. Should the other family's finances even be a factor? What are the rules of hospitality in a case like this?

GENTLE READER — Are you sure you want the rules of hospitality? Even if they require pretending that you are more interested in sparing the child's feelings than in recouping your expense?

The host's only concern when a guest breaks something is supposed to be in dispelling the guest's embarrassment. That is not to say that a guest should not offer to replace what is broken, and the protesting host may fold after a strong argument, and only to relieve an obviously distressed guest.

In this case, the child may have been unaware of what happened, or unwilling to confess it to her parents. Their wealth has nothing to do with the issue, but their providing a telephone card is a sign of their wanting her to be a good guest.

You have probably already succeeded in teaching this child (and her family and everyone they know) that Americans are a warm and generous people. Now you have a chance to undo this by sending them another stunning lesson: that Americans see everything in terms of money. (This is an outrageous slur, of course, but Miss Manners notices that it seems to apply to your advisers.) Consider, also, the lesson that it would teach your own child. Dear as it may cost you, an example of graciousness in spite of personal loss is of inestimable value in child-rearing.

Chapter Three

THE RULES

HOUSE RULES

The way to keep romance alive, according to the conventional wisdom, is to practice the etiquette of courtship at home. Fill every day with imaginative treats and calls and notes and a thousand other little ways to say "I love you." Miss Manners supposes this is all very well for those who have no objection to that sort of thing. She also knows sensible people, for whom endless courtship would take the fun out of settling down. They can be perfectly devoted to their mates without being able to face a daily barrage of romantic surprises. They consider part of the joy of marriage to be a sense of relief at never again having to play emotional guessing games. In spite of her affection for gallantry, Miss Manners sympathizes. Having one's ear nibbled while one is trying to work, or being kidnapped for an exciting outing when one was looking forward to taking off one's shoes, is more of a nuisance than a pleasure.

However, there is a risk in defending such people against the world's dreariest charge: "You don't really love me." Many who are eager to drop courtship etiquette never take up any other kind. They think that being on their very best behavior during courtship is the only etiquette that couples practice, and consider that after a courtship's successful conclusion, no etiquette is necessary. In other words, they feel justified in being rude at home. They don't call it rudeness; they call it relaxation. What they mean is abandoning etiquette. The justification is that what they do at home does not concern society at large, which is true as far as it goes. They skip the question of whether it concerns anybody else at home. This is a fatal idea.

While a household can establish whatever manners it wants within its own domain, it is a poor idea to stray far from the general standard. (Picking up bones and gnawing on them—perhaps; picking up spaghetti—no.) People who get used to behavior that is unacceptable to society have a hard time remembering not to practice it out there. People who get used to behavior that is unattractive to their spouses may soon find themselves out there.

What is needed to replace—or augment—courtship etiquette is household etiquette. Miss Manners thought of being cute and calling it Happily-Ever-After Etiquette, but it also applies to never-romantic household alliances.

When there is a conflict in negotiating household rules, whatever is nearest to the outside standard prevails (you can't eat with abandon if it disgusts others at the table) and whatever is intrusive (noise, smoke, strewing things all over the place) must yield to objections—or at least be reasonably contained.

Now here comes the good part: After settling that sort of conflict, nobody should have to argue to justify whims and preferences.

If "happily ever after" means anything, it means living with someone who knows and indulges your favorite little routines—which chair you claim, in what order you read the newspaper, how often you talk on the telephone—without asking whether they are right or even reasonable.

Negotiating Rules

DEAR MISS MANNERS — Am I being a fuddy-duddy, uncharitable grandfather because my 22-year-old granddaughter has come to live with me (I'm almost 70) to get a start in business? She did not bring her own toilet articles, uses my shampoo and comb, washes in kitchen sink, dishes there or not. Says I'm a very negative person and like things too neat. Sleeps wherever she plunks herself, is hungry when nothing is prepared and full when a decent meal comes off the stove.

I have arthritis very bad and heart problems. Why is she antagonizing her grandfather in everything she does? Am I just set in my ways, a senile man using bad manners? Are my manners out of line when I attempt to correct her and expect her to pay for her own things? (She found a job within two weeks and bought a car.)

GENTLE READER — Now, now. You two roommates have got to figure out a way to get along. Living together could be a very nice thing for you both, emotionally as well as practically, but you must first agree on how.

Preparing such an agreement should be the first step of forming any new household, from bridal couples to computer-matched groups. (The exception is that when someone enters a household through birth, its parents have to speak for the new arrival as well as themselves—as in, "All right, I'll provide the meals, but if I give you a few weeks' grace period, you have to promise to learn to sleep through the night.") Each person makes a good faith effort to provide a maximal list of what he or she would be willing to contribute, and a minimal list of what he or she really can't bear. Chores don't necessarily have to be divided evenly, and requests may be idiosyncratic rather than strictly reasonable. The terms must be settled to everyone's satisfaction.

If this turns out to be impossible, the arrangement cannot be made to work through daily quarrels. In your case, the first rule Miss Manners would set is to ban all generational insults. (Not that there is another category of insults Miss Manners likes better. There is nothing like "You're a negative person" for poisoning a household—unless it is "Why are you doing everything you can to antagonize me?") If you are getting that senile fuddy-duddy stuff from your granddaughter, you had best ask her to stop, possibly in exchange for refraining from talking about "young people today." If you are volunteering it in anticipation—well, then, please stop. Miss Manners can't bear to live with it.

In setting other rules, please try to explain politely what you can tolerate and what you cannot. Your granddaughter's combing her hair in the sink over the dishes, if Miss Manners understands you properly, would be high on your annoyance list. No doubt the young lady has some requests of you.

Because you are the grandfather, and because it is your household she has entered, you do get certain extra privileges. Child-rearing—attempting to impose routines, such as mealtimes, to which she has not agreed, or offering regular doses of unsolicited advice—is not among them. Perhaps you could leave her a nice little snack for when she feels like eating, rather than preparing an entire meal she doesn't want and being hurt when she doesn't eat it. Then she might take you for a nice little spin in that new car—perhaps stopping off so that you can pick up the present of her very own bottle of shampoo.

Rules About Rules

DEAR MISS MANNERS—I have been with my partner now for 14 months, and every time we have an argument he tells me that I am not at all the person I first made out to be. He usually always insists on sorting out a conflict as soon as possible, rather than to let it drag on. I, to start off with, thought this was a good quality he had; however now I find it annoying as he always comes out with the same "Shit" each time, and nothing ever changes. I prefer to just go to bed and forget about the whole thing. I know I am in the wrong, please help me to learn how to respond to his behavior and get something out of it at the same time.

GENTLE READER—Miss Manners is shocked that anyone should think of establishing a household without first establishing household etiquette rules. Yours seems badly in need of them.

How about: he gets to make a rule that you have to settle an argument immediately, but you get to make a rule that past transgressions may not be brought up during the settlement. Miss Manners gets to make the rule that you must phrase etiquette questions in polite language.

Readjusting Rules

It strikes Miss Manners that a surefire way to get perfect housemates would be: Approach them when they are helpless and impressionable. Administer detailed daily lessons in whatever you consider to be the right way to live. Supervise them for years to make sure they get it right. Surely by then, they should get the idea. So why do parents complain that their household peace is shattered when their adult children continue, or return, to live at home?

Miss Manners figures that some parental groans about having their children at home are purely conventional. Too modest to brag that people who know them only too well actually want to live with them, they claim that the attraction must be free or cheap board and services. Others may be saying this to protect their children from worse outside attacks. Few people hesitate, when they hear of such a situation, to express the modern assumption that adults who live with their parents are financial, romantic and psychological failures—unable to get decent jobs, stingy, emotionally stunted, lazy, irresponsible, bad marriage prospects, self-indulgent and afraid to face the world.

Putting aside such rude welcomes, the fact remains that these people have already lived together satisfactorily enough to make them all willing to try again. So what really could go wrong?

Everyone involved agrees that the difficulty lies in an inability to adjust properly from the behavior appropriate to parents and minor children now that the children are major. They just differ as to whether a change should involve increased freedom for the children while the responsibilities remain the same for the parents, or increased responsibility for the children while the parents' restrictions on their freedom remain the same. They use the wrong paradigms. An adult child living at home is neither a guest, who is waited upon, nor a tenant, who is charged rent. The parent is neither a host, who must put up with whatever behavior the guest chooses to inflict, nor a landlord, with no intrusive interest in the tenant's health and happiness. Rather, the grown-up child is a full member of the household, which means not creating burdens for others and pitching in with work and money that is needed. (Just as Miss Manners has never believed in paying one's own small children for doing chores, she doesn't believe in charging them for accommodations.)

Adult children are likely to have different ideas, tastes and habits from their parents, but such is also true of husbands and wives, of the many near-equivalents of such that we seem to have among us, and of less exciting arrangements for shared housing.

Adults who live together are expected to work out compromises that don't unduly annoy, worry or outrage one another—not only in regulating questions of noise, food and cleanliness, but by declaring more or less when they expect to be home, obtaining agreement for houseguests and borrowing one another's belongings only with permission. If they are able to do this, they may find that they are together for the most bizarre of reasons: They enjoy one another.

Compromising

DEAR MISS MANNERS — My mother is a non-stop smoker, and I am concerned with her health and have told her so. But after smoking for 40 years, she appears to have no intention of quitting. We see each other almost once a week, and I obligingly put up with it when in her house or car, while she reluctantly agrees not to smoke in my house.

Conflict arises whenever we are in "neutral" places, like restaurants or someone else's house or car. She tells me I should "rise above" my discomfort with the smoke, as if the problem is mine, not hers. Well, I do have a problem with her smoking. How can I get her to—if not quit, at least hold off while we are together? If not all of the time, at least some of the time?

GENTLE READER — When there is an irresolvable conflict, etiquette implores compromise. This conflict is not only between your comfort and your mother's, but between the evils of smoking and the evils of distancing oneself from one's mother.

Miss Manners is delighted to see that both of you have already accepted the notion of compromise, even if you place territorial limitations on it. What remains is only to realize that compromise must take place not only on your territory and hers but wherever the two of you may be.

Not Making Trouble

DEAR MISS MANNERS — At her daughter's home, my sister was upset and offended because she wasn't offered a drink before me, a more recent arrival. She stated she "wasn't given respect." I maintain that she should have asked for a drink if it was her desire, as I did. I felt boorish. Who's being too sensitive here? How might this have been turned around? If we accept the offer of hospitality from our hosts, don't we, as guests and reasonable people (and especially among family) have the happy (one hopes) duty of making ourselves agreeable in return?

GENTLE READER — Miss Manners is not opposed to sensitivity, but she does wish that people wouldn't be so quick to classify every transgression as a lack of respect. You'd think we were all 18th-century aristocrats, ready to pounce on the merest flicker of a hint as an intolerable insult to be avenged with the sword.

What your sister failed to be given was not respect so much as a drink. She is perfectly right that guests should not have to ask for drinks, but perfectly wrong that a mother must be served before an aunt and that there was any intention of insult. The omission should be classified as a misdemeanor against hospitality, rather than a felony against parental respect. Her making an issue of it should be classified as an etiquette crime.

Acknowledging Defeat

DEAR MISS MANNERS — My oldest daughter, who is 25, still never married, has decided to have her third child. Although this is most intrinsically against my morals and lifelong value system, I kept the peace. Previously, I had said nothing to her or her live-in boyfriend (the parent of all three). When I was advised of the inception of the third sibling, I could no longer tolerate further indulgences and phoned her mother, from whom I have been divorced for many years. She confirmed any of my previous doubts of being gleefully parted from her, and endorsed my daughter's maternity with vigor. There has been no subsequent communication with my daughter, save a sincere attempt on my part when I was told "to lose the number and also lose any ideas of grandparental aspirations" and then stared at a silent receiver.

I just cannot endorse this behavior. This is a blatant breach of all Christian values abided in her through what time I was able to be a full time parent. I am totally bewildered how my daughter can embrace this immorality, and show complete disregard for sensible responsibilities—worse, flaunt them, while living on public funds.

I have been made to feel as though it is I who is the guilty party. I have never seen the new addition, and only recently learned that it is another male. I fervently miss my daughter and her children. This is a heart-rending situation for me, particularly since she is my oldest, and we did share a rather close relationship in her primary years.

GENTLE READER — That was the time to attempt to teach her your values. You had all those years, divorce or no divorce, before she did something irrevocable, which in this case was when she had her first baby. The arrival of the third child strikes Miss Manners as an odd time to take a stand. Even if she had suddenly taken your point, what on earth could you have expected her to do about it now?

Miss Manners is all for parents teaching their children how to behave, certainly the major task of child-rearing after providing for the child's physical welfare. She sympathizes with the fact that the effort does not always produce the intended results. What she cannot countenance is your approach of teaching them retroactively, when the fact of those children makes the lesson as useless as it is offensive.

There comes a time when one must move from the abstract idea to the particular reality. At that point, you can either disown your child for not living up to your standards—which, in effect, is what you have done, to your own regret—or ignore that and love them as individuals. To do so now will mean pleading with your daughter that you miss her and her children and want to be taken back. You will then be honor-bound not to bring your disapproval into their household. That should not prevent you from participating, as a loving grandfather, in the moral education of your grandchildren, as long as you can do so without using their own parents as examples.

NON-NEGOTIABLE AMENITIES

Acknowledging Existence (Surface)

DEAR MISS MANNERS—What is the big deal about saying "goodnight" before going to bed? My parents insist on it and I obey them, but it makes me angry. The whole "Good-bye," "Good morning," "Hello" and "Good night" routine seems a little childish to me. I have a friend whose parents don't say "Good night" to each other and don't expect it of him, either.

At home, quite a few formalities are relaxed, but when it comes to "Good night" my parents are unyielding. Isn't there some point where I can stop having to go through this unnecessary routine every night? What is its point?

GENTLE READER—You can stop going through this when you grow up and go to live by yourself. You will see the point when you start saying good night to the television set.

The point of greeting and taking leave of people is to acknowledge their existence; the greatest insult one can give someone is to fail to do so, which is called cutting or shunning. Why it should be a big deal to human beings to have others know we exist, Miss Manners cannot tell you. For that matter, why should we want others to respect us or love us? She can only assure you that you are no exception. Should you have the experience of being ignored by people whom you take less for granted than you now do your parents, you will understand.

Acknowledging Existence (Deep)

DEAR MISS MANNERS — I visited my good friend Chris and his family, and observed something that made me very sad. Chris's aunt sent a box of gifts for his family—nice presents for Chris's mother, his father, his two little sisters, and even for a family friend. She didn't send anything for Chris except (I still can't believe this) a couple of packages of almost stale rolls. One of Chris's cousins also sent a box of gifts, including something for everyone except Chris. I watched his face as the gifts were handed to everyone but him.

What could Chris have done to be ignored like this by his family? Was he a wild teenager? Did he drink, use drugs, commit crimes? No, he was an excellent student and is now a contributing member of society. Is he an unpleasant person, making enemies with his terrible personality? No, he is bright, charming and funny. All the people I've ever introduced him to have told me how much they like him. What, then has he done?

More than 20 years ago, at the age of 16, he had a terrible accident (not his fault) which left him paralyzed, in a wheelchair, with only very limited use of his arms and one hand. (Yes, he completed both high school and college after his accident.) Since then, most members of his extended family have behaved as though he no longer exists. Only one thoughtful aunt, who always remembers him with notes and little gifts, is a shining exception.

I don't understand why people would behave like this. I also don't understand why Chris's parents (really wonderful people, who've never given up on him) would accept gifts for themselves from people who are so thoughtless and cruel (even if unintentionally) to their son. Chris had told me that he wanted nothing to do with them, but the one time I met them, several months ago, they seemed nice people. Now if I ever saw them, I would find it difficult to be pleasant. I certainly would be strongly tempted to tell them how bad they made him feel.

GENTLE READER — Thoughtlessness is not exactly the word to be used here: It is not as though Chris's existence had merely slipped their minds momentarily.

Miss Manners would consider this cruelty unintentional only in the sense that criminal negligence is.

She is appalled to have to tell you that it is not uncommon behavior. Explanations of why otherwise apparently polite people are so monstrous always have to do with the fear resulting from contemplating a fate that could strike them at any moment. That may be, but so what? Miss Manners has no sympathy whatsoever for anyone who would allow such fears—or anything else—to dictate rude and ugly behavior. To her, this seems proof that God sent us etiquette with which to improve upon natural behavior, and that we cannot have a civilized society if people do not govern their nasty impulses.

Feigning Interest

DEAR MISS MANNERS — Years ago, my wife and I agreed that we would not read at the table during meals, in what I thought was an attempt to eliminate a bad habit developed during our single lives. So when my wife recently started reading at the table during meals, I objected. She asserted, I think accurately, that she can read and take part in conversation. Thus she reasons that it is not improper for her to read. I, on the other hand, tend to get absorbed in what I am reading to the point where I frequently do not respond to comments addressed to me. Therefore, my wife asserts, it is not okay for me to read at the table. She can read, I can't.

Actually, I don't think this is about manners. I frequently do not respond to my wife's comments when they are not in the form of a question or I do not have a ready response. My wife complains that when I do not say anything, she does not know if I have heard her. I understand her point and try to do better, but I am not perfect. I think each failure adds to a heap of disappointments in a marriage that may have had more than its fair share of stress. A counselor's office would be a better place to resolve this issue than in your column, but she won't see a counselor and I am not yet prepared to threaten to end our marriage to get her to one. As we are trying to teach our children good manners, I would appreciate your thoughts on reading at the table during meals.

GENTLE READER — Miss Manners does think this is about manners, which is to say that she considers the situation more serious, not less, than ordinary marital strain—even a large share of ordinary marital strain. So you have come to the right counselor.

First she will deal with the etiquette rules involved.

1. It is rude to read at the table when someone else is present, and being able to converse as well doesn't make it any less rude. The insult consists of saying symbolically, "I'm bringing my own entertainment because I sure don't expect much from you."

2. It is rude to greet another person's remarks with silence, even if no question has been asked. The insult consists of saying symbolically, "What you say is not interesting enough to warrant any acknowledgment."

At this point, Miss Manners hastens to disabuse you of any notion that she has slyly led you to what a different sort of counselor would say right off—that the solution lies in better communication. On the contrary. She knows perfectly well that there are times when the newest George Eliot novel has a great deal more to say than even the most beloved of husbands, and that the most interesting wife in the world is, like everyone else over the course of a lifetime, bound to deliver a great many unremarkable remarks. So communication—especially honest communication—would only compound the insults you are already exchanging by putting them on the table, so to speak. What you need is politeness, which is to say the respectful pretense of interest in each other. Your wife should arrive at the table as if she expected you to be interesting, and you should respond to whatever she says with an encouraging noise, if only "Oh, really?" or "Hmmm." The deeper manners issue here is that neither of you is willing to make the effort to be polite to the other. The only solution would be to make that effort and hope that the show of interest and respect will rekindle the real thing.

Miss Manners' approach of dealing with the surface, rather than whatever lurks beneath it, will seem less eccentric if you think of how you want to teach manners to your children. As parents, you probably know that they love you—and yet you also know that they are often bored senseless by much of what both you and your wife wish to say to them. If you allow them to express the boredom, it will make the whole household unpleasant. If they are not taught to feign interest in other people, no one else will want to establish a household with them.

Losing Interest

DEAR MISS MANNERS — My roommate and friend, who has many wonderful qualities, makes a lot of demands on my attention. She loves to talk, and during the evenings after work, she tells story after story, many of them quite amusing. The trouble is, I'm starting to feel as if I am spending each evening listening to her ramblings. I participate, too, and she is quite engaging, but there are times when I just don't want to talk, when I'd like to read or watch television or stare at the wall.

Sometimes I'll say, "Well, I'm going to balance my checkbook now," or "I think I'm going to go for a walk," but I'm tired of always having to have a reason not to talk to her—especially since then I actually have to go and do it, when what I want to do is nothing. Once in a while, I'll slip in a general comment that I don't like talking as much as she does, but that hasn't helped. I realize that the best solution would be for me to get my own apartment, but I live in an expensive city, and make a low salary, so that's not really an option.

GENTLE READER — Not only to relieve such polite people as yourself, but in the hope of avoiding household mayhem among the less restrained, etiquette provides somewhat looser rules for domestic conversation than for social. This by no means legitimizes rudeness; Miss Manners does not allow anyone to say "Am I not to have a moment's peace and quiet around here?"

It does allow one to mention one's habits, as a general principle for establishing certain periods of quiet: "I'm not up to conversation in the morning," or "I do a lot of my thinking when I'm just sitting around—I'd rather we talked at dinner." For times when you are nevertheless caught, Miss Manners suggests cultivating an absent look and saying, after a pause "Did you say something? I'm sorry—I was working something out in my head. Let me just finish so I can concentrate on what you're saying."

Repressing Interest

As everyone knows, etiquette rules about whose business is whose are different for relatives than for people to whom one is less permanently and closely connected. Or perhaps everyone doesn't know that. An awful lot of families seem to run into trouble by assuming that there are no rules at all among intimates. Isn't that what intimacy is? Not having to worry about making a difference between what crosses your mind and what comes out of your mouth? Then why do you dread gathering around the family table for another frank session?

Miss Manners' job, in regulating the querying and nagging permissible between one generation and another, has been made easier in the last few years by a phenomenon that has made life harder on everyone else. She apologizes for that.

The change is that it used to be only parents who fussed over children, probing to find out what their children who were too old to be supervised in person were doing, and advising them to stop. Or to start doing what they were neglecting. Nowadays, it is only too likely that children are equally active in nagging and scolding their parents. The tone and fervor are the same; it is the choice of topics that is slightly different. Miss Manners has noticed that the parents' usual agenda is sex, and the children's is health. The fact that school systems have long used the latter as a euphemism for the former only adds to the confusion.

Favorite adult conversation openers at family gatherings include:

"When are you going to get married?"
"When are you going to get rid of that no-good so-and-so and find someone decent?"
"Don't you realize that you ought to be having children while you're still young?"
"Look at yourself—no wonder you haven't found anyone to settle down with."

Whereas the children would rather open with this sort of thing:

"How can you eat that stuff? Don't you know it's killing you?"
"How can you eat that stuff? Don't you realize it's immoral?"
"When are you going to stop smoking? It's not only disgusting, but it's endangering the rest of us."
"Look at yourself—no wonder you're out of breath all the time."

Ask people on each side about their own remarks, and you will be told that these are prompted by loving concern and care. Ask them about the other's remarks, and they will say that they are made out of spiteful nosiness. Miss Manners is not going to step into the middle of that one. You should know better than she which areas drive your relatives crazy when probed, and what approaches are more or less successful with them. It would be sad if a stranger could tell you more about your own relatives' sensitivities than you have discovered by living with them.

So Miss Manners prefers merely to offer some guideline techniques for being on the giving and receiving end of personal advice:

Unanswerable questions should be banned. "Why don't you get married?" and "Why are you eating that?" are never going to produce illuminating answers.

People should be allowed to declare topics off limits. "Look, I know I need to exercise, but I don't want to discuss it," or "I promise to let you know when we are going to have a baby, so there's no need to ask" are statements that should be honored.

Finally, Miss Manners suggests that everyone going to a family gathering keep repeating to himself or herself: "If they didn't love me, they wouldn't be interested. If they didn't love me, they wouldn't be interested. If they didn't love me . . ."

Suppressing Information

DEAR MISS MANNERS — I desperately need to know how to deal at holiday gatherings with one family whom I shall call The Materialistics. The moment their children embark from the car, they can hardly wait to tell you how much money they have and what they have recently bought. Then they begin asking such questions as, "How much money do you have?" and "What did you pay for that?" These are not young children, mind you. During the last visit, the son asked our daughter how much rent she pays for her apartment. She was so caught off guard that she told him. His reply: "What a rip-off!"

It never occurs to Mr. and Mrs. Materialistic to correct their children; in fact, they ask such pointed questions as, "How much insurance do you carry on your home?" and "What percentage of the market does your employer control?" Of course, they never volunteer such information about themselves.

The Materialistics do not respond well to politely vague replies, but only consider that a green light to dig deeper. If we say, "Oh, I really don't know," they act surprised at our ignorance. Since they are family, we want to enjoy their visits, but we dread them. Each visit leaves our family emotionally drained. Any hints on how to deal lovingly with such people?

GENTLE READER — One of Miss Manners' basic techniques for the preservation of family life is for common victims to share secret amusement over the distasteful practices of their relatives. Thus, the most important time to deal with these people is after they have left. Rather than lying around emotionally drained, you should be merrily exchanging stories—"He told me he bought a state-of-the-art paper shredder!" "Yes—well, she asked me how much I'd paid for my umbrella!"

As for avoiding interrogation at the time, you might try some playful teasing: "Oh, Sean, you're amazing! Do you remember all these figures? Last year, you made me tell you what I paid for my shoes—do you remember how much they were?"

Child-Rearing

An innovative theory of child-rearing is upon us. Parents are gobbling up popular new books and lectures stating that children need to be given limits and discipline, that they should be taught to respect their elders and that they really must learn some manners. Far be it from Miss Manners to question a trend that promises to lighten her workload, but what was the previous theory? That it was a good idea to have children first, and then, a decade or so later, to stumble upon the basic idea of child-rearing?

All these years, Miss Manners has been doing remedial work for children and recent-children who come to her when they discover the flaw in their etiquette-free upbringing. They report that they were taught that what was important was to express their feelings and opinions openly and honestly. This is an easy assignment, and things are fine with them until they find that other people do not necessarily consider all their feelings and opinions attractive.

Their parents' reply is that they should not worry about what other people think—apparently on the theory that there is something principled about ignoring any annoyance you cause. Yet as they get older, the children notice that they find some of those other people awfully attractive, and wouldn't mind pleasing them if only they knew how. This is when they show up for etiquette instruction, and Miss Manners obliges by introducing them to the concepts and rules that make people pleasant and civilized life possible. She does her best, but the language of behavior, like other languages, is most easily learned when one is too young to think about it. It is better to get it from one's parents.

So why are the parents only now thinking of teaching it? Miss Manners is talking not about neglectful parents, but about reasonably advantaged people who may feel harried but have no major sociological excuse for not doing their duty by their children. If they don't feel obliged to teach them to behave in the community, don't they at least have a stake in teaching them to be bearable around the house?

Miss Manners suspects it has to do with a belief in what we shall have to call original innocence. This is the charming idea, launched every two hundred years or so, that people are born good but then are corrupted by civilization, so that the best thing one can do is to protect their natural virtue from the evil of artificially learned behavior. It is beyond Miss Manners' understanding how such an idea survives the first month of parenthood, when it is vividly demonstrated that infants are miraculously born adorable, gurgly and cuddly but with no interest whatsoever in the exhaustion they cause those who wait upon their every demand.

Nevertheless, original innocence accounts for the idea that the child is actually wiser than the parents. This, in turn, has led to some strange parental notions:

That a good parent acts as the child's lawyer. This means not only helping the child get what he or she wants but forcefully defending the child against teachers, coaches or other people who impose duties or penalties for misbehavior.

That our belief in democracy requires abandoning the traditional benevolent rule derived from the authority of age and experience, and giving children an equal vote, if not their own dictatorships.

That the forces of peer pressure and television are so widely accepted that it is not only useless to compete with them but unfair, as children need to share the culture of their generation.

That as no individual is perfect, and cultures vary and change, it is useless and false for parents to believe that they can define what behavior is right and what is wrong.

That happiness and self-esteem are the natural results of receiving a constant stream of compliments, uninterrupted by guidance and instruction.

Finally, there is the saddest delusion of all:

That never crossing a child not only makes a child feel loved but increases the child's love for the parent.

Now that these notions have met with less than rousing success, parents are taking up child-rearing again. This is a great boon to Miss Manners, teachers, coaches, social workers and others who were trying to do the job. It is an even greater boon to their children.

Retroactive Child-Rearing

DEAR MISS MANNERS — What would be a correct way to prompt my husband's married children to write thank you letters or notes for gifts? I was trying to convince my husband to stop sending gifts altogether and they will get the message. He complains and feels that the girls don't care, but still sends the gifts. If it means hurt feelings, I'm not too sure I would bring it to their attention. But I would just like to know if it's proper etiquette to stop sending the gifts or write them and let them know what is happening.

GENTLE READER — Are you asking Miss Manners if it is polite to send out written punishments on holidays? Well, no. And that goes double for step-parents.

Here's how to do it: You send them greetings with your fondest love and a lot of warm family chitchat. Only at the end of the letter do you say you haven't sent the usual presents because you gather from their silence that previous attempts to find something to please them have not been a success.

Miss Manners insists that only your husband can authorize such a letter, as they are his children. It would be best sent by him, but you could write if you make it clear that it is on his behalf, not your own. If he refuses, Miss Manners suggests that you prompt the daughters with a call in which you humbly ask if the presents were all right, thus eliciting some kind of thanks. Your object, after all, is to salvage his feelings rather than to rough up theirs.

Resisting Being Outcharmed

DEAR MISS MANNERS — Our 14-year-old son is very bright and fairly polite. Children that age think they have the world completely figured out, but Sam is certain that he understands everything better than anyone else. He frequently expounds at length in a manner which would be pretentious even from a world-renowned expert.

Sam is like a two-year-old with new words, using a vocabulary which is admirable, but often a little too fancy for what he is trying to communicate. How can we guide Sam into a more pleasant mode of communication without discouraging him from using others as a sounding board for his ideas?

GENTLE READER — You don't mind if Miss Manners is charmed with Sam, do you? It will in no way interfere with her approval of your wise realization that he is an unfinished product in need of gentle guidance before he turns into a bore. It's just that she happens to be wild about that sort of child. So are the proud parents of such children. Unfortunately, their delight usually takes the form of unquestioning admiration, which soon turns those curious and articulate children into perfect pests.

The way to make Sam's conversation bearable without dampening his enthusiasm is to treat it seriously—by questioning his information and opinions in the polite manner you might use during a discussion with an adult:

"Really? Why do you think that?"
"Funny, that's not the way I heard it. Where did you get your information?"
"I don't quite follow—would you try explaining that again?"

This shows a respectful interest in what he says while making him responsible for supporting and defending it. It also gets him used to the fact that conversation consists of give and take, not of lectures. Done properly, it shouldn't discourage him from talking—only from being glib.

THE NICETIES AND NOT-SO-NICETIES

Nice Teasing

The difference between teasing and taunting is like the difference between kissing and spitting. The ingredients are the same; it is the emotion that determines whether it is pleasing or repellent.

Teasing is based on love or affection, and taunting is based on—perhaps not hate, but at least annoyance and often worse. Therefore, teasing is not rude by definition, but taunting is.

Miss Manners is the last person to suggest that anyone's behavior in this or any other matter be guided by instinct. She has seen what etiquette-free instinct prompts people to do to their families, not to mention to the rest of us who are only trying to cross the street. Yet teasing is based on such intimate knowledge of the other person—not only that individual's foibles but the particular sensitivities, humor and mood at the time—that she would have expected some help. Those who are authorized to tease certain people ought surely to have some feeling for how. Silly Miss Manners.

So here is the way it works:

Both teasing and taunting depend for their subject matter on special observation of the person being teased. This is what gives them their power. Everyone wants to feel that his or her unique combination of qualities has not passed unnoticed in this world. What makes this foolhardy is that everyone also expects, against all evidence and reason, that the natural outcome of close and accurate observation will be approval. This is why people who get into trouble are quick to say that they have been misunderstood. We all feel that anyone who really understood us would be crazy with admiration. Make that adoration.

Nevertheless a steady diet of straight compliments doesn't quite satisfy. We are awfully picky, for people who expect to be worshipped, and want the admiration we excite to be laced with proof that we have been fully observed.

"You don't really know me!" is the way people respond to premature avowals of love, finding them more laughable than flattering. Taunts that miss the mark aren't deeply hurtful. Only ones that target weaknesses that are known to the person being taunted do that.

However, Miss Manners does not feel obliged to instruct unsuccessful taunters how to be effective. She prefers to save her counsel for helping teasers avoid delivering taunts. Proper teasing says, in effect, "I know all your little oddities and faults, but, as they are part of what makes you special, I find them charming." Taunting, in contrast, makes only the harsh statement "I have noticed what is wrong with you."

Therefore, the rules are:

Teasing can only be about characteristics that are not a source of worry or shame. You might tease a young person about being absent-minded, but you would not tease an old person about memory loss.

A cheerful and affectionate tone is required, to make it clear that there is no serious complaint involved. You don't tease someone about knuckle-cracking or leaving dishes in the sink if it makes you homicidal. You just ask or beg that it stop.

The desired effect is a look of pleasurable embarrassment, as if you had administered a compliment. Anyone who doesn't stop teasing immediately upon producing real embarrassment, anger or tears is not really teasing.

Rough Teasing

DEAR MISS MANNERS — My husband's family thinks it's fun to gang up on one person and make jokes about them. Unless the victim is me, he or she has lots of snappy come-backs and knows how to put everyone in their place.

I have no idea how to defend myself without insulting someone. It is only a game to them, and I don't want to be impolite. My only solution has been to keep my mouth shut at all times, but I cannot be silent forever. These are people who have done a lot for me, and I respect the way they raised their son. I would like to remain in good graces and avoid hurt feelings. What can I say?

GENTLE READER — Teasing is fun, but picking on people is cruel. The trick is in telling which one it is. In this case, Miss Manners is convinced that you have merely wandered, unprepared, into some benign family teasing. The evidence for this is that you testify to the general niceness of the family, that you have been welcomed by them and that the practice is enjoyed by the rest of the family.

They are still guilty of failing to observe that you don't like it, although even that probably happened out of the assumption that you are so much a part of the family that they forget you have not acquired its habits. The way to draw this to their attention is to admit your inability to handle their teasing, without condemning the family tradition. Miss Manners suggests declaring cheerfully that you are appointing your husband, or perhaps a favorite in-law, as your defense attorney.

Offensive Teasing

DEAR MISS MANNERS — This is a second marriage, and I came into it with more or less the same amount of money as my husband. However, whenever we go out, he is always making some derisive comments in front of other people about me spending his money (which isn't true) or that I have more money than I know what to do with. I have worked all my life and earned every penny, and have only just retired at 65. I find this embarrassing, and I pretend to ignore it as I don't want an argument in front of my friends.

GENTLE READER — Although discussing a spouse's spending habits was never anything but hideously rude and disloyal, your husband is not the only one of his generation to make the mistake of assuming this to be cute and funny. However, all couples starting out are entitled, regardless of age, to a few rancor-free requests about how they are to be discussed. The simple statement that any mention of finances in front of friends embarrasses you ought to be enough to put a stop to public comments. Your actual financial arrangements are beside the point, although Miss Manners would heavily suggest putting some extra restraint on complaints by keeping separate accounts.

Inadvertent Transgressions

DEAR MISS MANNERS — My roommate and I advertised for a third room-mate. The one we chose appeared to be the best fit but now that he's moved in I find that I wake up to his LOUD snoring every night and can't get back to sleep. Our doors are closed but his snoring comes right through the walls. This lack of sleep among other things has caused me to seriously reconsider this arrangement. How can I talk to him about this without creating an extremely tense situation?

GENTLE READER — By remembering that people do not snore on purpose. This is apparently an extremely difficult thing to do. Miss Manners has heard of otherwise devoted and trusting spouses working themselves into furies of suspicion and defensiveness because the non-snorer holds the deep conviction that the snorer is doing it out of spite.

Whether the best solution is for your roommate to get medical assistance, you to get a white noise machine or for you both to make different living arrangements is something you can discuss civilly—but only if you are able to conquer the idea that if he had any consideration for you he wouldn't snore.

Conflicting Cultures

Now that everyone finally understands how vile and rude it is to insult people on the basis of their race, religion or ethnicity, is it safe to insult them individually by using your own race, religion or ethnicity? A lot of people seem to think so. Miss Manners hears people brag about doing nasty things on the grounds that they are expressing their culture. They talk dirty and call it the language of their people; they practice extortion on their friends and claim it is an ancient custom; they jeer at other people's success and announce that their failure is more authentic. Then they pause to be congratulated for having thus honored their ancestors.

Culture is also the current instrument of choice for making other people feel socially forlorn. Families will make a special effort, when newly acquired relatives are present, to speak a language they don't understand. Acquaintances will make a point of telling others that they are forever excluded by their origins from understanding their point of view or their jokes.

Here poor old Miss Manners had thought we had made etiquette progress on the cultural front. Whenever people start deploring the deterioration of manners in modern times, Miss Manners (who is not immune to this morose habit herself) pops up optimistically with the reminder that there have also been dramatic improvements in manners in modern times.

It is not so many years ago that the open expression of prejudice was considered acceptable, not to mention amusing. Miss Manners stoutly maintains that expressing prejudice was always horribly rude, but it is unfortunately true that there were seldom adverse social consequences. The very people who most wanted to court widespread public favor—politicians—not infrequently laced their beliefs and jokes with derogatory assumptions about one group or another. Then, painfully for those who failed to catch on (right as this may have served them), the standard changed. People may not have suddenly become enlightened about their fellow human beings, but the smart ones have learned that they get in trouble if they air unpleasant generalizations.

Offenders still trot out the excuse of ignorance, although it is now more than a generation since the change was made. Their punishment, social ostracism, is often now commuted to serving time in retraining sessions, because many people believe, in the face of overwhelming evidence, that hostility automatically evaporates upon exposure to its targets. Miss Manners never understood how this was supposed to explain bigotry against those whom one had ample opportunity to get to know and may even—as in the cases of mothers, sisters, wives and daughters—profess to love.

She is also distressed at how energetically people who never bestirred themselves to discourage bigotry decry the excesses of condemning it. The examples they cite always turn out to be ludicrous incidents where the foolish or the vicious take innocently intended remarks or gestures as slurs. Still, Miss Manners—who is sadly familiar with the bizarre use of false alarms claiming violations of etiquette in order to violate the spirit of manners by making trouble—does not believe that these add up to a reign of terror. On the contrary, it is an enormous achievement that bigotry is now socially condemned.

Now this needs to be expanded to include the self-inflicted insult of claiming that one has a cultural duty to behave badly. Virtually all cultures maintain the ideals of honesty, hospitality and kindness even if they don't practice them, and these exclude using one's culture to humiliate others.

It is also true that there are traditions that condone institutionalized viciousness—many people immigrated to America to avoid them—but they are no more acceptable for being old. Miss Manners is very fond of tradition, but she is not so enamored of it that she can't see the difference between right and wrong.

Conflicting Beliefs

DEAR MISS MANNERS — I am a practicing Christian, and although my wife is Jewish, she has always agreed to help celebrate Christmas in our home. However, whenever our two little girls visit my wife's parents, their grandmother tells them that since their mother is Jewish, they are, too, and shouldn't be celebrating Christian holidays. Although my wife and I have objected to this, we can't seem to get her to stop doing it. Any suggestions?

GENTLE READER — The chief suggestion is that you protect your children from slipping into theological debates with your mother-in-law, which would make it a long winter, because nobody is ever going to win. All Miss Manners' supplementary suggestions have to do with teaching them to avoid this while showing understanding and respect toward their grandmother.

However much your wife's parents may have objected to her marrying a Christian, their concern now is likely to be that their grandchildren not turn away from the Jewish part of their heritage. However, as your wife's mother undoubtedly knows, many Jews do follow at least some Christmas customs without considering themselves the less Jewish for that.

No—that's not the argument the girls should make. Didn't Miss Manners say to avoid theological debate? That should be only a throwaway line ("But Amy gets Christmas presents, and she's Jewish" "But the Sterns have a tree and they're Jewish") before your girls switch the conversation by showing a positive interest in Judaism. When they engage her in instructing them, through asking questions or showing off what they know about Jewish holidays, she is not likely to cut it off by returning to the Christmas issue.

Conflicting Practices

DEAR MISS MANNERS — My husband and I are trying to bring up our young children to be devoted Christians, and this includes the habit of giving thanks before meals. The children's grandparents, with whom they get along well, are hostile to any display of a belief in God, especially my mother-in-law. I have a cordial relationship with her, avoiding religious discussions, even though she has a strong tendency to bring the subject up. When visiting, we usually sneak our family grace together in the bathroom while we help the children wash their hands.

Other times, we instruct the children to silently give thanks on their own. On some occasions, such as Thanksgiving, we will have a more elaborate prayer in the car on the way there. However, there are times when one of the children will sit down at the table and blurt out, "They don't say grace in this house! Right, Mom?" It is an awkward situation.

When we have meals with other families who do not say grace, no one is ever ill at ease if we circumspectly remind our children to say a simple blessing. However, their grandparents were barely able to conceal their discomfort when we said an ever-so-brief blessing last Thanksgiving in our own home. I'm afraid things might get more complicated as the children get older. How should we best explain this sort of etiquette to the children?

GENTLE READER — Don't worry about this getting any more complicated. Miss Manners assures you that the etiquette you need to teach right now is about as complicated as it ever gets. Furthermore, it is not only the children whom you need to teach. Everybody involved here needs to learn about the meaning and practice of respect and tolerance. Even you, who are making such an extraordinary effort to accommodate your in-laws.

The children are already learning that people of good will may differ strongly on matters of religion, and that one gets along with them best by refraining from comment as well as discussion. You have to learn that this does not require giving up one's religious practices. Much as she values family harmony, Miss Manners can't stand the thought of your saying mealtime grace in the bathroom or separating the thanks from Thanksgiving.

Etiquette requires those who do not say grace to sit in silence while others do so. Provided you are not praying aloud that your in-laws be saved, or that you be saved from them, they have no cause to take offense. Miss Manners understands that they have not learned this, presumably because they have not accepted the fact that their son's beliefs are different from theirs. He is therefore the one to make the gentle point that he has made an adult choice for which he wants the same loving respect that his family accords to them.

Conflicting Customs

DEAR MISS MANNERS — At Christmas time, my husband and I enjoy receiving gifts for our daughter, but my in-laws insist on giving my husband and me a gift, which really embarrasses me. In my family everyone older than 16 was "too grown" for a holiday gift, and taught to enjoy the spirit of the season, not the material. I've tried to explain how uneasy this is for me, but it has made matters much worse. They now quite literally shower my husband and daughter with gifts. Isn't there some age when this nonsense should stop? Or am I being a Scrooge, like my husband tells me.

GENTLE READER — Miss Manners is not sure it isn't Mr. Scrooge who needs defending in this comparison. He was bad enough, but you seem to have carried his idea further by labeling as "nonsense" the obviously kind intentions of your husband's family toward you, and by suggesting that they are materialistic because their family custom differs from your family custom.

Limiting the present-giving to children is a fine idea, but it is less common than the presents-for-all tradition. That your family knows and practices this is not an excuse for you to sneer at people who don't. This goes double when they are your very own husband's family, and triple when their offense is giving you presents.

What they are doing now by showering presents on their blood relatives— your husband and your daughter—is trying to make up to them for your meanness. Miss Manners suggests that you make up for it yourself by apologizing for trying to foist your family's practice on them. When they understand what that is, they may or may not want to adopt it for themselves. They will surely continue to respect your desire not to receive presents, and Miss Manners hopes that you will respect their desire to continue their custom with the rest of the family.

Conflicting Views

DEAR MISS MANNERS — My Uncle Bill is the chief family letter writer, often offering, along with family news and copies of letters to and from others, his sometimes vitriolic political views. He doesn't state these as personal attacks, but as observations, and he only does so in the letters he sends my mother (which he knows she shares with my brother, sister and me and our children) and never in the letters he writes to us. These remarks about cheating welfare mothers, idiotic Democratic officials, etc., really bother us. We love Uncle Bill and have never responded to his comments; nor has our mother. We simply leave politics out of our family letters.

Does etiquette allow us a response that will maintain family harmony? We appreciate Uncle Bill's efforts to stay in touch, but wish he would stop his attacks on our beliefs and political party.

GENTLE READER—Yes, there is a response, and you should all learn it—mother, brother, sister, children and you. You just shouldn't write it to Uncle Bill. The response is "That's Uncle Bill for you." Said with a smiling shrug, it means "We know he's impossible, but we love him." This is an even better family lesson for the children than the one you would love to teach Uncle Bill, but would never succeed in doing.

THE FAMILY AS SUPPORT SYSTEM

Public Support

You know that the institution of marriage is in trouble when perfectly respectable couples with apparently stable marriages won't let go of each other in public. Not only do many husbands and wives now join hands to face the world, but even when they need their hands free and are among friends, they still can't bear the pain of being separated. One hears them waxing indignant if expected to sit apart for the entire length of a dinner party and expressing shock at the idea of dancing with anyone else.

This is what Miss Manners calls the Ondine Marriage, after the water sprite in dear Jean Giraudoux's play by that name. Extravagantly in love with the plodding chevalier, Ritter Hans von Wittenstein zü Wittenstein, and seeking to guard against future abandonment, Ondine rhapsodizes that they two should be like creatures of the sea who, once coupled, are never parted for an instant but go through the rest of their lives forever side by side. Hans is in love too, but he remains unenraptured by Ondine's description of bliss. When he is able to get in a word, he shamefacedly admits that every now and then he would like to go off to visit his horse.

Lacy-hearted though she may be, Miss Manners sympathizes with Hans. People who are in love nevertheless want to go off to visit their horses once in a while. What's more, those who live under the same roof have ample opportunity to walk around their own houses holding hands. Most people no longer believe that dancing leads directly to sin. Couples with a lot to say to each other develop a shorthand way of talking that isn't easily shared, and fanning out socially gives them twice as much material to talk over later.

So although Miss Manners is charmed by evidence of marital happiness and loyalty, she is troubled that the current methods of showing it suggest the opposite. It may be true that it is difficult to establish a flirtation with anyone else while clasping the spousal hand, but—as we know from centuries of chaperonage and worse—vigilance can be more of a challenge than a deterrent. Besides, there are better ways for couples and other family members to display their love and loyalty. Considering how many people have taken up the Ondine posture, Miss Manners is amazed at how rarely the same couples avail themselves of the traditional methods.

Basking in each other's glory is an attitude that has fallen into disuse. Perhaps political wives killed that one, gazing so adoringly at their husbands and laughing so uproariously at their repeated jokes as to frighten off civilian couples from any betrayal of fondness or pleasure. Miss Manners also suspects that an unpleasant sense of individual competition has created an unwillingness to assume a supporting role—even temporarily, with the understanding that this will be reciprocated in turn.

When she first heard people asking successful ladies if their husbands and children weren't resentful—as if one naturally wished one's dearest ones failure—she was amazed at how casually such terrible insults to their families were delivered and received. When she also heard husbands, wives and even parents using their relatives' moments of glory to make the point that they were important too, she realized that the assumption of resentment—although still rude—could be warranted.

Even quainter than beaming with family pride is the forgotten habit of keeping family secrets. When Miss Manners has mildly suggested that a proclivity to complain about one's near relatives to anyone who will listen is not quite nice, she hears that bad-mouthing the family is good for one's health. The distinction between reporting in-house crimes for one's protection and exposing family foibles for amusement seems to have been lost. Perhaps she should not be surprised that modern spouses should want to keep a firm grip on the people most likely to upstage their achievements and betray their weaknesses.

Logistic Support

DEAR MISS MANNERS—I am a 15-year-old aspiring actor with a reasonable amount of talent. I have invested a lot of time and hard work over the last seven or eight years, and I've done quite well. My parents have been wonderfully supportive, but they've always made it clear that my participating in productions is a privilege. I know that if my grades fall, my room becomes a disaster or I choose to ignore the proper way to behave that I've been so carefully taught, I'll have to take time off from my practice to "catch up" on these things.

My high school productions are fun, but I'd like to broaden my horizons. Acting is such a hard business, I'd like all the experience I can get. The problem is that all of the local theatrical groups are headquartered at least thirty-five miles away. My parents both work outside the home, and I'm sure they have better things to do with their copious free time than chauffeuring me into town nightly and then waiting to take me back home. I cannot drive, and I know no one in this immediate area who belongs to one of these groups.

I need to know how I can politely ask them to allow me to join one of these groups, showing that I can earn the privilege of being taken back and forth. I have quite a convincing case for how it will benefit me, but I need to show that I can do something to make up for their trouble, making a reasonably fair exchange.

GENTLE READER—By the time she finished reading your letter, Miss Manners had her car keys out. It wouldn't be the first time she fell for a young person with your serious approach to both life and art.

She is also charmed by your parents, for having successfully taught you that schoolwork is your primary business and proper behavior a lifetime requirement, so neither may be neglected for your other interests. By continuing to demonstrate your acquiescence, you have done more for them than you perhaps realize. All you need to do in addition is to tell them that Miss Manners promises that they will have a lot of very pleasant and quiet reading time, because the good stage parent needn't—probably shouldn't—keep too critical an eye on the rehearsal. Oh, and to promise that when you win a Tony, the first words out of your mouth will be "I owe it all to my dear parents."

Intergenerational Support

Whenever the subject of parents and their grown children being thrown together for short or long periods comes up, even otherwise mannerly people feel free to assume that this arrangement will make both parties miserable. What's more, everybody feels free to voice that assumption to the faces of the very people involved.

Miss Manners is not talking about offering sympathy or consolation to those who have confessed to unfortunate family relationships. She is talking about cheerfully volunteering poisoned hypotheses to relatives of different generations who seem to be perfectly happy—so happy, in fact, that they seek one another's company. That they are doing so is what prompts people to offer mean interpretations as if they were commonplace civilities.

For example, a child mentions going home for a visit.

Does anybody say, "Have a good time"?

No, they all say, "Why? Did they do a guilt trip on you?"

A parent or child announces that they will be vacationing together.

Does anybody say, "Great—have fun!"?

No, the grown-up child's friends say, "Well, I guess it's one way to get a free trip." Astonishingly enough, the parent's friends say more or less the same thing: "Well, I guess they figure they can put up with you for the sake of a free trip."

A parent tells friends that the child will be coming home to live after graduation.

Does anyone say, "How nice—you must have missed her when she was away at school"?

No, they all say, "Oh, boy, and just when you thought you were rid of her forever."

Mind you, these well-wishers, as they think of themselves, are not people who intend to be rude. They would be shocked to hear that they are insulting friends and instigating them to be rude to those whom they ought most to protect.

On the contrary, they believe they are speaking from shared assumptions, and they astonishingly succeed in forcing these assumptions on those whose experience is otherwise.

The result is an unseemly display of family disloyalty, exactly because parents and children feel it would be rude to challenge what is so widely believed. If there is anything ugly to be said, they will say it; and if there isn't, they will fake it. So we have the curious phenomenon of innocent people claiming to be mercenary or psychologically intimidated in order to avoid defending those they love.

Even if you did want to escape your relatives at the first opportunity, and to restrict all future dealings unless there is financial gain or an emotional power struggle in question, it would be rude of outsiders to say so and appalling for you to admit it. Miss Manners does not favor reviving the duel, in which only death would avenge attacks on family honor. But she would at least like to revive the spirit that made protecting family honor a matter of pride rather than embarrassment.

Working Support

DEAR MISS MANNERS — During the day, while my husband attended meetings at a professional convention in a delightful mountain city, I discovered the charm of the locale and food. All was pleasant until the last evening, when we joined a couple of my husband's former colleagues for dinner. I had known these persons briefly, and realized that there would be a certain amount of reminiscing of old times and acquaintances, but the whole evening consisted of this, with myself feeling more and more excluded, despite several attempts to join the conversation. I was tempted to make a biting remark and leave the table, but I held onto my feelings and tried to appear courteous. Afterwards, I expressed my feelings to my husband, who answered that as an adult, I had the responsibility to offer my own conversational direction. With that remark, I really blew up, and turned on my heel, feeling doubly angry. I believe all three of my companions were terribly rude and completely unconscious of the group dynamics, which is strange, considering they are psychoanalysts. How would Miss Manners deal with the situation?

GENTLE READER — By leaving you at home.

Oh—you mean how should you deal with the situation? By realizing that it is a solemn obligation of marriage to put up with the occasional position of gracious listener while a spouse and his or her old pals, colleagues or other unshared ties chatter happily on about matters of mutual interest. This is especially true when a husband or wife tags along at an event not as a participant but merely as an accompanying spouse, taking advantage of the travel and opportunity to share the other spouse's interests.

This is not to be taken as Miss Manners' generally condoning conversations that exclude anyone present. However, to go along at a convention, invite out people who want to reminisce about their joint past, and then turn surly—and threaten to insult them publicly—because they do so is what strikes Miss Manners as rude.

Besides, your husband's reminiscences and old associations are supposed to be of interest to you. The only aspect of such a situation that Miss Manners would accept as a legitimate complaint would be your husband's refusing to be gracious to old friends or colleagues of yours when the occasion presents itself.

Ego Support

At the family gathering, those expected include:

Cousin Miranda, who had seemed finally to have a prospect in tow, but advance word (from her younger sister) is that the announcement, if it is made, will be that the prospect has become engaged to marry the student who walks Miranda's dogs.

Grandma, who asked if she could bring her fiancé, and has been warning everyone that he is just a tad younger than she is.

Uncle Al, who was asked to leave junior college under a cloud, after 14 years there, and who has now published his unfinished notes for an inspirational book under his publisher's brilliant title change, "The World's Dumbest Ideas," currently on the best-seller list (How-To Paperback Division), with the sequel scheduled for spring.

Aunt Genevieve, who used to tell everyone that all you have to know to succeed in high finance is how to keep your eyes open and your nose clean; who advised everyone to take up her hobby, collecting antique cars, because it is so relaxing; and who has now spent every penny she had on lawyers who are telling her to plea-bargain.

Cousin Harold, who told his wife that he wouldn't stand in her way, that she could take whatever she wanted with her, and she did.

These people are all your relatives, so presumably you wish them well. What are you going to tell them at the cozy family occasion?

Most people would tell Cousin Miranda that no wonder she's lonely, it's her fault for being so accommodating that she gets treated like a doormat; and if she doesn't learn to dress and get a job where she can meet eligible men, she's never going to get married.

They would tell Grandma that she should act her age and not be taken in by fortune hunters (counting her Social Security check as the fortune).

They would tell Uncle Al that his success was a fluke, unlikely to be repeatable, and that he still had to get his act together and learn a real trade before the family will take him seriously.

They would tell Aunt Genevieve that she got what she deserved for living high off the hog.

And they would tell Cousin Harold that he was a sucker.

No wonder people hate going to family events. At least among strangers, one can be reasonably sure of not being called unattractive, decrepit, undeservedly lucky, justly punished and stupid. Well, maybe not all that sure—these are mighty cruel times we live in—but it wouldn't hurt as much. Also, they could walk away.

Miss Manners has noticed that (1) unhappy family gatherings are painful because people put off their company manners and speak more freely than they would with outsiders; and (2) happy family gatherings are satisfying because people put off their company manners and speak more freely than they would with outsiders. Oddly enough, the same standard of behavior makes one family look forward to times when they can let down their guard and makes another family have to call in the National Guard. The difference is in what they use that freedom to express. In all families, there is more knowledge available about everyone else than there is in ordinary society. Thus, all those people might manage, with luck, to squeak through a party of mere friends without having to tell their full stories.

Among family, however, speaking more freely should mean relief in having everything known. They should be able to announce their triumphs without fear of bragging or boring and to admit their defeats without fear of censure. Thus proper family manners dictate telling Cousin Miranda that she has had rotten luck in gentlemen and is better off without that bounder, which she will soon realize when you have her over to meet some truly interesting people worthy of her attention; Grandma, that she is too charming to have remained a widow; Uncle Al, that his cleverness has been recognized at last; Aunt Genevieve, that she has been framed by the unscrupulous and doubtless will be vindicated; and Cousin Harold, that he is a gentleman.

What? Lie to them?

No, Miss Manners is merely suggesting that family may be treated as an extension of oneself. You may be sure that the other relatives, were they in the same positions they are so quick to criticize, would accord themselves the more charitable explanations given here. In offering soothing consolation and enthusiastic support to relatives, you do no more than you would do for your very own self. That is the guide to proper family manners.

Feigned Support

DEAR MISS MANNERS — My sister-in-law was not able to conceive a child after many years of trying, and always said she would not adopt. However, I finally got pregnant after eight years of infertility and when she found out, she became very angry and, with her husband's insistence, they finally adopted a child.

I have regretfully resented her hostility toward my pregnancy ever since they told us they adopted because I got pregnant, and I can't seem to resolve my feelings. We were close before, and are courteous now, but no warmth remains. We live in the same town, and family functions are almost unbearable for me. Should I avoid her? Or just remain noticeably polite and cordial?

GENTLE READER — Regrettable as this situation is, Miss Manners is at least relieved to hear that the tone maintained on both sides is polite and cordial. Might she encourage you to persevere and make your own behavior even more artificial? Pretending to warmth and forgiveness, as you two begin motherhood together, may actually encourage you to put your hurt behind you and resume an affection that should never have been tested by such brutal frankness.

Natural behavior is not so wonderful as to be so indulged, as your own justified complaint illustrates. It may well be a natural reaction to begrudge someone else —even someone to whom one has close ties of relationship and affection—a happiness one has been denied, but it is an ugly one. Your sister-in-law never should have confessed this to you; she should have disguised it with the proper show of delight at your happiness that your pregnancy deserved from her. Such false behavior would have saved you grief. It might also have raised her own feelings.

Qualified Support

DEAR MISS MANNERS — I would like everything to go as smoothly as possible at my wedding, but the problem I foresee is that my sister-in-law had an affair a few months ago, and she and my brother split up for a while but are now back together. I have not spoken to her since this unfortunate incident came to pass but would like to avoid any embarrassment to either one of them.

Do I act like nothing happened, not mention it, and greet her warmly? Or hope that no one in my family puts their foot in their collective mouths and says something untoward to her? Before all this happened, I really liked her, but I am in a quandary. Please understand that I am not worried about the wedding being ruined—I just want to avoid any incidences of temper or confrontation.

GENTLE READER—Let's start with "not mention it." If you did mention it, what would you say? There you are, in your bridal finery, your bridegroom at your side, both of you surrounded by a flurry of bridesmaids, relatives and other well-wishers, and your sister-in-law approaches.

"Caitlin," you say—

Then what?

"How could you?"

"Don't you dare ever do such a thing again!"

"I hope you were listening to the marriage vows this time."

Miss Manners trusts that you see the problem. The solution is that as long as your brother has taken his wife back, you must treat her as a family member in good standing. Miss Manners is not saying you have to approve of his doing so, much less that you have to approve of what she did, only that you must respect his right to deal with the situation.

You need not be as demonstrative as you might have been before this occurred, but you have to be cordial enough so that no one observing the scene will be able to detect something amiss. If there is any danger of other relatives acting differently, perhaps one of your prenuptial events ought to be a very secret briefing session with the family, to articulate this policy.

The Insupportable

DEAR MISS MANNERS—My brother visits me stoned. I have told him he is not welcome when he is doing drugs. He agreed not to bring his habit into my life; however, he does. I do not stop him at the door, as I do not become aware that he is stoned until he has been here a short time.

Then what? His wife, and my husband are present. I do not want to embarrass everyone, however, I cannot let this disrespect go on either, never mind the fact I am worried sick that he will have an accident on his way home.

GENTLE READER—Heaven knows that Miss Manners is prone to defining everything wrong in the world as being an etiquette problem, but she is having trouble doing so here. It seems to her that what your brother has is not so much an etiquette problem as a drug problem. It is true that showing disrespect to you would be an etiquette problem, but this would require intent, and Miss Manners doubts that your brother's motive in getting stoned is to annoy you. While your fear of embarrassing him would be an etiquette problem, she also doubts that your brother's wife and your husband are unaware of the situation or even that he thinks they are.

She suggests that the family take whatever steps it can to get your brother cured of his habit. Etiquette's contribution is to supply euphemisms (having to do with vague sicknesses and problems) to protect your brother's, and indeed the whole family's, privacy from unwarranted curiosity.

Unending Support

DEAR MISS MANNERS — My brother is married to someone from, as they say, a dysfunctional family. At most family get-togethers, she is in a bad mood. But for 20 years, we have always cut her a lot of slack for the above reason, and because we didn't want to alienate our brother and his children.

Now we are wondering if being gracious and solicitous of her and humoring her behavior has been the best course. By our silence, we have kept her from knowing the truth, i.e., that her behavior has been unacceptable. Now, in her children, we are seeing similar actions. I suppose in a private moment, one of us could have said something, but frankly, she cannot accept even the slightest criticism. Sometimes we feel like the enablers one hears about in connection with addicted people. We keep on accepting boorish behavior and there are no unpleasant consequences for the one who ruins every holiday.

GENTLE READER—Oh, dear. Miss Manners has terrible trouble getting used to the idea that nowadays people write in to an etiquette columnist because they are distressed that they have been polite, and worried that perhaps it was their duty to be rude.

As Miss Manners understands it, you have, for 20 years, refused to allow one boorish relative to push the rest of you into retaliation. Out of love for your brother, you have heroically refrained from starting a feud with his wife. Now you are musing about what you may have missed.

Somewhere in your minds, there seems to be lurking a scenario in which an ill-tempered and inconsiderate person has a sudden change of heart brought on by a chastising from her in-laws, and she reforms. Perhaps in the last scene, you see her offering humble thanks for having brought her to her senses. Miss Manners would not advise you to count on it. The less pleasant scenario you envisioned when you decided to refrain from criticism—the one in which your already long-suffering brother would find himself forced into alienation from his family—is a great deal more likely. What is not likely is that such a person as your sister-in-law has otherwise enjoyed general popularity, and is thus blissfully unaware that any-one is less than charmed by her bad behavior.

Chapter Four

THE SYSTEM

THE TO-DO LIST

Life's basic To-Do List isn't all that long. On it, typically, are:

Earn a living.

Attend to personal and household needs.

Look after relatives.

Spend time with friends.

Spend time alone.

Enjoy the arts.

Keep up with what's going on in the world.

Improve the world.

That's only eight tasks, and the same ones that people have been more or less managing since civilization began. So why is everyone suddenly complaining about not having enough time? What has changed besides the shorter workweek, the horseless airplane, the air-conditioned summer, the no-iron fabric and ever more ways of receiving news and entertainment without having to get dressed?

All Miss Manners ever hears is how busy people are. Some of them are just bragging, now that having to work all the time has achieved the status once enjoyed by never having to work. Others are practically weeping from exhaustion. Miss Manners hates to add to their burden by asking them to take the time to reschedule their lives, but the present approach clearly isn't working. All those categories remain essential, but some of them have been seriously neglected because others have developed too many subcategories.

Earning a living now includes so much faked friendship, what with oxymoronic workplace partying and business entertaining, that it all but obliterates spending time with friends. Any social time left has, with the assistance of computer games and chat rooms, disappeared into time spent with invisible friends or, as we used to say, alone.

Attending to personal needs has come to require so much devotion to food and exercise that there is hardly time for looking after relatives. What leftover time there is for that has been shifted into agonizing about whether one is doing the right thing by one's young children, aged parents or mate; this leads to therapy that brings it back, full cycle, to looking after oneself.

Enjoying the arts and keeping up with the world have come to require so many joyless hours of watching television that the more one learns about what needs improving, the less time there is to do anything about it.

Miss Manners would never suggest that anyone eliminate any of the basic tasks. Still, something has to change when everybody has time for files of old jokes circulated by E-mail and nobody has time for dinner at home. She suggests getting rid of those frills that are either no fun or don't work:

1. Feeling guilty.

Miss Manners never has to feel guilty because she never does anything wrong, but those who are human should substitute doing the best they can and correcting what is wrong. Fretting doesn't help anyone.

2. Hanging out with people you don't like but think might be of use to you.

They probably won't (unless it was in their own interests anyway, in which case it isn't necessary) and even if they will, you'll get to feeling bitterly that no one loves you for yourself and, having neglected disinterested family and friends, you'll be right.

3. Saying yes when you mean no, because it takes longer to get out of something than it does not to get into it. Saying yes for family members without checking, because it takes even more elaborate excuses to explain.

4. Keeping up with the latest in any field other than your work or a beloved hobby, especially when it's something in which change is the main point, such as fashionable restaurants or teenage slang. Miss Manners is a hopeless newspaper addict, but even she realizes that there are only so many significant changes in the world.

5. Remembering to stay mad.

6. Improving the world by means of lavish social events for good causes, instead of giving your services or money to those who need it.

7. Goofing off when you should be working, and working when you should be goofing off, so that both activities are ruined by the feeling that you are supposed to be doing something else.

8. Ironing the newspapers.

Ironed newspapers were once considered an essential detail of the properly run establishment, and a self-respecting butler would no more have tolerated the appearance of a newspaper in its natural state than that of a parlormaid in hers. However, since we really must streamline our lives (now that Sunday is no longer a mandated day of rest and there is so much more shopping that has to be done, and now that we have dishwashers and computers and therefore must spend the time our ancestors had at leisure in waiting for repairs to be done on them), Miss Manners will set an example and make that one humble sacrifice as a concession to the pace of life.

Girl Jobs

DEAR MISS MANNERS — Is it acceptable in this day and age to expect one's husband to lend a hand with thank you notes? I know that traditionally, the wife is designated as the social coordinator; however, I come from a large family (and incidentally a very generous family) and I am fortunate enough to be able to acknowledge many thoughtful gifts around the holidays, birthdays and our anniversary. I do not think it would be unreasonable to ask my husband to write thank you notes to his family while I am writing them to mine.

My case is further strengthened by the fact that most of his family lives in Germany and does not speak much English. I do not speak any German, while my husband is fluent. It seems to me that it is a nastier violation of etiquette to expect the entire family to learn English in order to decipher my note than to ask my husband to put pen to paper.

GENTLE READER — Miss Manners has long since abolished the silly custom of dividing household duties by gender. It seems to her that two adults who supposedly love each other should be more interested in reaching a division that is satisfactory to each. Ordinarily, that would mean that each can write some letters or the person who is best at writing letters, or who least dislikes it (nobody except Miss Manners seems actually to enjoy writing letters) is the person to do it, and the other takes on something that person is good at or doesn't mind. As the job in this case is to write letters in German and you do not speak German, you cannot do this at all, so it is unreasonable of your husband, who can, not to do it.

Boy Jobs

DEAR MISS MANNERS — In our marriage, my wife "owns" the checkbook. She has a tendency, though, to pay the full amount of every bill the day it arrives and then agonize over being on a tight budget until the next paycheck arrives. How can I politely convince her that she needs to create a budget and take a longer-term view, without sounding condescending?

GENTLE READER — By volunteering to save your wife a great deal of worry by taking over the administration of the checkbook. Or by thanking her for going to the trouble of taking care of these matters without your having to worry and leaving it at that.

Miss Manners has observed that there are people whose idea of financial prudence is to put off paying bills so as to hold on to the money as long as possible, and people whose idea of financial prudence is to pay all bills immediately so as not to risk incurring a finance charge for any delay. A problem arises only when, as in your case, such people are married to each other. Which method prevails is not something on which Miss Manners has a position. She does know that putting one spouse in charge and having the other criticize is not a compromise likely to lead to household peace.

To Do: The List of Lists

1. Find out where everybody—spouse, children, parents, coworkers, boss, support service people—is supposed to be when and make master calendar with copies for home, work and pocket. Requires system to get their input and put out changes to everyone concerned. Should contain birthdays, anniversaries, vacation times; also location, filed by date, of tickets, invitations, notifications of meetings and numbers for confirming reservations.

2. Update home, work and portable address books with
   ✓ telephone numbers—home, work, car, cell, fax, pager, private lines, children's line
   ✓ addresses—E-mail, permanent and vacation homes, work
   ✓ numbers for emergency and regular services
   ✓ addresses for holiday cards
   ✓ separate portable books for travel keyed to locations.

3. Set up financial records of every penny owed and spent in such a way that it is possible not only to tell where the money is going and when it might be coming, but to prove it with receipts for tax purposes, insurance, charge accounts, expense accounts and donations.

4. Keep up reading, sorting, answering and/or trashing incoming mail, invitations answered immediately, bills in due time, letters in proper time.

5. Make shopping list forms for food, clothing and other supplies, so that anyone who uses something up can note that replacement is needed, anyone going out can grab a copy to take shopping, and it is always possible to justify temptation with retroactive entries.

6. Keep inventory of household possessions, noting where each item was acquired, its price, current value, schedules for maintenance and location of instructions and warranties; lists of books and other items lent with date and name of borrower; wills, secret codes and pin numbers, and other important papers.

7. Keep track of presents given and due, menus served to guests and hosts owed return invitations; everybody's allergies, taboos and preferences; master guest list for major occasions such as weddings or death notification; index of successful recipes by chief ingredient with cookbook page numbers.

8. Duplicate all personal necessities in miniature versions and keep in ready-to-go bag in case of travel, fire, flood or childbirth.

9. Organize the past for future biographer, court-required alibis, and embarrassing children to their future spouses; verified engagement calendars; albums of labeled and dated photographs; file of children's report cards, drawings, evidence of cuteness; attic closet of outmoded clothing for recurring trends, dress-up, costume parties and school plays.

10. Make master copies of all this on paper for when power (or brain) goes off and erases electronically stored data.

Scheduling Children

Many devoted parents make sacrifices so that their children can have the enriching experiences provided by after-school athletic and cultural activities. They sacrifice time, energy and money, ferrying the children around, buying them equipment, encouraging them, practicing with them and standing around waiting for them—all so that the children will grow and learn. Some of them also sacrifice their manners and morals. This enables the children to learn irresponsibility and grow into menaces.

Miss Manners has always been the sole defender of stage mothers and Little League fathers, and, as they came along, soccer moms and backstage fathers. She never understood why it is presumed reprehensible to allow children to develop and pursue activities requiring skill, discipline, work, accountability and fairness. She has also noticed that, far from pushing their children, most of these parents are being mightily pulled into these worlds. With or without prompting, their children oddly consider such activities more exciting than what are considered to be the normal young people's sports (watching television) and art (strolling malls looking at merchandise).

Unfortunately, competitive parenting has now turned too aggressive for Miss Manners to ignore. It is no longer a question of overly rambunctious cheering or sympathetic partisanship; rather, it is one of teaching the kind of behavior that gets champions fined and divas fired—fighting authority, flouting rules, not showing up when expected and, not infrequently, using violence. So if the objective was to give the child professional training, the effect would be counterproductive. Anyway, that is not often a reasonable objective. Few children will be offered opportunities that will allow their parents to turn professional with their coaching. If they are willing to sacrifice that possibility, they can teach the children skills that really will help them become stars of any field in which they have sufficient ability.

Miss Manners admits that the ability to organize one's time in order to accomplish what one wants, and the responsibility to live up to commitments, ought not to give people an advantage in the working world. Without everybody's having them, that world doesn't work very well. As you may have noticed when trying to find reliable workers at any level—and as a result of which these simple attributes are prized.

So parents can help their children most by sacrificing less. Extra activities should be returned to the realm of privilege, requiring the children to wheedle and promise. Let them plan the schedule and do whatever reminding it takes to execute it. Let them learn the rules and take any consequences for breaking them. It is a parent's job to see that a child meets all the requirements of school and family obligations, but extras should be earned.

Miss Manners realizes that it takes practice for a parent to develop the callousness to say "I'm not surprised you got kicked out—you're always late for rehearsal" and "It doesn't matter what you or I thought—if the umpire says you're out, you're out." This sacrifice is worth making. If you can't turn your children into artists or athletes, you can at least turn them into champion planners.

Scheduling Around Children

DEAR MISS MANNERS—I have found my social plans changed more and more often by close friends who are also well-meaning parents, to suit the schedule or temperament of their children. They are in effect putting the young ones' needs above all the adults concerned, even when we, the childless couple, are the hosts or organizers.

These are not formal occasions or adult-only gatherings where a sitter would be hired, but casual get-togethers such as picnics, cookouts, etc. or short meals in family-style restaurants. The children are no longer infants but 4- or 5-year-olds, usually without siblings.

I have suggested a time or place to meet, only to find out that the food or dinner hour doesn't suit Junior's schedule. Then I find myself bending over backwards just to come up with something that agrees with everyone or suggesting diversions for the little one.

I truly enjoy both the parents and the children's company, but the logistics are exhausting! On the other hand, I often find myself excluded from such things as luncheons where the moms do gather with the children!

I am very aware that children have different needs than adults, shorter attention spans, etc., which is why I limit my invitations to casual occasions. However, when I was young, my parents took us lots of places where we were expected to behave (the old "seen and not heard" theory) even if we were bored, unhappy, restless, etc. My personal belief is that today's children will never learn to cope with these unpleasantries if they never have to learn to handle them while young.

Of course, my more immediate problem is how to handle my own social life:

Should I make new friends that are also childless? Forget my parenting friends for the next 10 years? Stop trying to have a social life unless I hire a playmate for their child or an on-site sitter? Or is this an etiquette concern at all? And another observation: When did it become acceptable social conversation to discuss in great detail Junior's potty training efforts?

GENTLE READER — People who talk potty should be seen and not heard; Miss Manners doesn't care how old they are.

Still, this is only a stage that your friends are going through. Surely you think them worth hanging on to, and your desire to include their children is admirable. The children of friends eventually make excellent friends themselves, if you stick with them.

Meanwhile, although your friends should not be making plans they have to change, you, as host, should be suggesting plans that you think will be agreeable to all your guests, regardless of age. Please don't invoke that seen-and-not-heard business—parents go ballistic when they hear that, just as if they thought it could work or ever really did. If, instead, you ask their help in fashioning plans that would please everyone, you would be entitled to insist that they not be frivolously changed.

P.S. Don't fret about being excluded from the mother-and-child luncheons; you don't want to know what they're discussing.

Scheduling Parents

DEAR MISS MANNERS — Picture this: The radio or TV "speaks" in the background. Daughter engages Dad in conversation. In the middle of a meaningful sentence, Dad raises his finger in the air, signaling her to stop instantly, while he listens to sports scores. Daughter is told to hold the thought until after the report. Daughter, who is 11, challenges this behavior, claiming it is a demeaning interruption and poor manners. Dad says she's oversensitive and unreasonable, because her thought can be said any time and the scores can only be heard once a day.

I am certain that the finger method of stopping conversation is rude, but I wonder if even the sweetest, most humble "Excuse me, could you hold that thought for just a minute?" is not also demeaning. Is stopping a person in midsentence for anything but emergencies rude? My husband says you'd answer differently if it were war news, rather than sports scores. I think we should learn together the self-discipline of truly listening to one thing or person at a time, and cease dividing our attention.

GENTLE READER — Miss Manners is with you on the issue of divided attention, and trusts that you have not allowed this daughter to do homework while listening to music and have never, never, never permitted any canned entertainment during dinner. But your husband may be surprised to hear that she has a point to make in his favor, as well. It's not because she considers war news (which often qualifies for emergency status) more important than sports scores. If the scores are given only once a day, both father and daughter should be aware when that is. It is no time to begin a conversation. If your daughter opened with "Is this a good time to talk to you?" she would be right to expect his full attention if he says yes. That means the television should be turned off.

Defending the Schedule from Strangers

DEAR MISS MANNERS — I am a hard-working patriotic, productive citizen who works two jobs to raise my family. When I am home, I treasure the time with my wife and three young kids, and I try to guard our privacy carefully. What I don't understand is how strangers could bang on my door, ring my telephone or send me junk mail with no regards to our valuable time.

Is it rude not to answer the door if I know it is some kind of religious group, charity organization or people who take surveys? Is it rude to hang up the phone once I found out the person is trying to sell me something? Is it rude (and a waste of paper) to throw away junk mail without opening it? If your answers are yes, is there a better way to deal with these situations?

GENTLE READER — If productive citizens were required to be open to all offers they receive, they would not be productive very long. Or respectable, for that matter.

Politeness does not require you to open your door or your telephone line to, or your mail from, strangers. It does not permit you to hang up on them or slam the door in their faces, but it permits you to ring off or close up (Miss Manners trusts that you understand the difference) immediately after saying "I'm sorry but I'm not interested." The reason these people importune you is that there are people whom they do manage to interest. So your declining to waste their time is as considerate of them as it is of your family life.

Defending the Schedule from Neighbors

DEAR MISS MANNERS — My neighbors feel free to stop by our house for a chat whenever the mood strikes them. Much as I like these people, I work long days and so look forward to private evenings at home with my family. How can I get the message across that unannounced visits are unwelcome? It's especially hard to get them to leave once they're in the door, though I act tired and distracted and eager to get on with, say, making dinner or giving my daughter a bath. If I go upstairs, they stay and talk with my husband!

GENTLE READER — How do these undesirable visitors get in the door? Do they pick the lock with hairpins? Do they claim to be delivering a lottery prize? Or do you open the door and say "Oh, hi; well, come on in," and step back to let them pass? Miss Manners suspects the last. Although she knows you do this out of a sense of politeness, bless your heart, she has to teach you to stop. She will even teach you to stop politely.

Dropping in used to be a neighborly thing to do, but that was before the invention of the telephone. Even when it was polite to call on people without advance notice, it was also polite to be unable to receive them. The two go together.

It helped to have someone to announce that you weren't at home, which is difficult to do on your own behalf, although peepholes and answering machines make excellent guards. If caught, you must do the next best thing, which is to say that you are not available. The polite way is to pour out expressions of anguished regret while barring the door: "Oh, dear, I wish I'd known you were coming, because I would love to have had a chance to visit with you. Give me a call another day and we'll find a convenient time for all of us."

Defending the Schedule from Friends

DEAR MISS MANNERS — A friend who knows I am an early riser phoned me to chat at 6:40 A.M. I must admit to being less than receptive to social conversation at this hour. I always thought social calls were properly made between 8 A.M. and 10 P.M. Care to comment?

GENTLE READER — Not at this hour. Of course, you don't know which hour this is. Miss Manners is afraid that although your friend knows that you are an early riser—and therefore considerately called you early—the fact that you are not an early converser is something you don't seem to have mentioned.

The standard polite hours for social telephoning are 9 A.M. to 9 P.M., but not during working hours, which are roughly between 9 and 5:30, or between 12 and 2 because it might be lunchtime, and not from 5:30 to 9 because it might be time for preparing or eating dinner.

Perhaps you begin to see why it is a good idea to let one's friends know when you like to chat—and for the friends to inquire, when they do call, whether it, in fact, is a good time on that particular day.

Over-Defending the Schedule

DEAR MISS MANNERS — My husband works over 70 hours a week, so I cherish the time before he leaves for work for conversation, and the weekends taking turns sharing him with the three children.

Neighbors pop in on me uninvited and, when I politely ask them to come back later, make me feel terrible with comments like "Oh, I'm *sorry* we bothered you" or "I didn't know we would be *intruding*." Another thing—when I say politely to come back later, they certainly do! What I really want to say is "Leave me alone until I invite you to barbecue or play cards. I don't have time for friends with three kids and a husband."

GENTLE READER — No, you don't want to say that. Trust Miss Manners. You don't even want to think that. This isn't only a question of its being rude to insult people who offer you friendship, even those who go about it with no manners and less charm. What worries her is your illusion that having a family means that you don't need friends and you don't need to be on mildly friendly terms with your neighbors.

Miss Manners agrees that it is rude to drop in without warning—it has been since the invention of the telephone. And centuries before that, human society became possible only because of a tacit pact to suppress skepticism about other people's pleas of being busy. Nevertheless, a family that walls itself off is going to run into trouble. As your children grow, both they and you will increasingly need the society of friends, and even now, in the midst of such a busy time, you all need the protection of having neighbors who, if not full-fledged friends, are at least not enemies.

The better way to ward off intrusions would be to offer your own terms. If you and your family made just one effort to entertain the neighbors, your plea that your family schedule unfortunately prevents you from enjoying spontaneous visits would be more sympathetically accepted.

THE CENTRAL EVENT: DINNER

Most households, whatever their size, have a room or an alcove dominated by a large table surrounded by chairs. Why? Some of the people who live there think it is storage space. Others think of it as a communal desk or the home for the 500-piece puzzle (or so it claims on the box, although actually there are only 497 pieces). But you can also eat there. Miss Manners knows that sounds silly.

There are so many rooms in which to eat: the kitchen, of course; every room that has a television set; every room that has a computer; every bedroom, even if they don't have both; the bathrooms if they have Jacuzzis or at least tubs with ledges for trays; and the front hall on the way out the door. Why mess up another room?

Miss Manners will tell you why: because a household where the members do not sit down at dinner together nearly every night is a convenience store, not a home. A home is a place where the residents, whatever their relationship to one another, perform the nightly ritual of breaking their bread and news together.

Now she probably also has to tell you how. Restaurant manners used to be taught as a variation on family table manners, but that was back when going out to dinner was a rarer occurrence than sitting down to dinner at home. It has become necessary to point out that the strange ritual of eating at home does not include deciding whether one wants to do so or not, ordering what one likes regardless of what other people are eating, complaining about what one doesn't like or starting to eat at the first sight of food and quitting the table when full or bored, although others are still eating. On the plus side, tipping isn't required.

It does require fixing a time when everyone can be home, even if that means the break between someone's day shift and someone else's night shift, and learning to say "Sorry, have to go; I'm expected home for dinner." Then one has to dress for dinner—an expression that is less likely to mean evening clothes, as it once did, as to mean clothes. Exercise outfits are not clothes. There is work involved, because actual plates, flatware and napkins are used, and yes, Miss Manners knows that means they must be put in a dishwasher or soapy sink instead of in the trash. Just don't use the poverty argument on her, because reusing things is cheaper.

It even requires table manners.

Family Dinner

DAILY DINNER: *The family dinner table is where civilization is taught—not only table manners but the art of conversation and the principle of consideration for others—and this one has a long way to go. The table has been properly set for an informal meal, with main course, bread-and-butter (to go on the small plates), dessert (to be eaten with the spoon above each plate) and, miraculously, real napkins, identified by napkin rings so they don't get one another's food stains while awaiting laundry day, and no television set anywhere in sight. However, Mother is in a stupor of exhaustion from earning the grocery money and mopping up after the baby, and it would be nice if the grandparents, instead of eating piggishly and rudely reading, were helping her explain the impropriety of showing up in underwear, bare feet, slippers or baseball cap, and of grabbing a knife by its blade and inhaling the pasta.*

Family dinner allows a certain leeway—it is lax enough to permit reasonable bone gnawing and sauce mopping but not commercial cartons on tables. Everyone must learn to sit (as opposed to supporting the body by resting the left arm on the table and wrapping it around the plate) and to operate that mysterious instrument that terrorizes everyone—the fork.

Because there is no background music, no recitals of today's specials, no looking up to watch the game, no getting up to answer the telephone, family dinner requires being able to talk. This skill should not be confused with what one hears on talk shows. You do get to complain and to brag, because it's family, but you have to fill in with conversation. Rather than being a series of pronouncements, confessions and fights, this involves building on what other people are saying, rather than waiting (or not waiting) for them to finish.

If all this sounds like less fun than the food court, it is because the rewards may be cumulative. By teaching eating and social skills, the family dinner dissolves the terror people claim to feel when they are required to seem civilized, if not charming, for social or business reasons. Therefore it precludes the necessity of having to confide in strangers in cyberspace because no one else will stop to listen.

The Crash Course

Presuming that you are both aware and observant of the rule of etiquette that forbids throwing food, which Miss Manners realizes may be taking a wildly optimistic leap, what can you do to shock people nowadays at the dinner table?

You certainly can't say anything to shock them. Whatever confession you can make, no matter how far removed from normal human behavior, they are going to yawn. They already heard your nasty habit discussed on television, and are in the grips of the deadening certainty that you are about to tell them all about your boring support group.

Miss Manners doesn't know that she has to supply shock material. There are enough people open-mouthed at the dinner table as it is, in violation of the rule against behavior that rivals food throwing on the Disgust Scale. (Actually, you can sometimes throw food: You can play toss outdoors with an apple or a pumpkin, depending on your weight class. Not so much fun? Well, you can spit watermelon seeds in a watermelon-seed-spitting contest, or in preparation for the Watermelon-Seed-Spitting Olympics, provided you do it outdoors and face away from the crowd.)

The fact is that it is fun to shock people at the dinner table, and one can do it effectively with proper table manners that are startling to those who are not familiar with them. We are not going to stoop to retrieve manners that have been stricken from the books. Yes, there was a time when picking the teeth at the table was acceptable, more centuries ago than Miss Manners cares to remember, but it was also a time when drinking cups were shared, and one washed out one's mouth by spitting into bowls provided for the purpose. But many perfectly good rules that are still on the books are unknown to most people, whose parents considered themselves lucky if they could get across the basics, and didn't even attempt the oddities and the exceptions. These fall into three general categories:

1. Setting the Table Funny.

Four was the minimum number for which a table used to be set, and to set it that way for two or three people is guaranteed to keep those people looking over their shoulders all evening.

Old European silver is engraved on the back, and intended to be placed on the table facing the tablecloth as if it were in disgrace. This, too, makes guests very, very nervous as they imagine you set the table upside down, and are worried about what you might do next.

Everyone knows what an entrée is, only everybody is wrong. Properly speaking, the entrée is not the main course but a light course, such as an egg dish or risotto or a light meat, that comes between the fish course and the meat course. You get a delayed reaction if you serve a true entrée, because the shock comes after they filled up and are then faced with the main event.

2. Picking Up Things That People Think You're Not Supposed to Pick Up.

Everyone knows you are supposed to eat your vegetables with your fork, but asparagus can be properly eaten with the fingers. (Stalks and all. A lady of Miss Manners' acquaintance sent her a report of dear Jonathan Swift's admonishing a guest for asking for seconds in asparagus tips: "Sir, first finish what you have on your plate." "What, Sir," was the reply, "eat my stalks!" "Ay, Sir! King William always ate his stalks!" Yes, Miss Manners knows it isn't polite to notice what your guests are eating, let alone to boss them around. But she doesn't feel up to taking on Jonathan Swift today.)

Everyone knows you are supposed to remove the inedible by putting it quietly back on the fork in which it arrived. But although fish goes in the mouth on a fork (unless you are a diver), the bones are taken out with the hands.

Everyone knows that soup must be eaten with the spoon, in a direction away from one's own dry cleaning. But bouillon cups with two handles may be picked up and the soup may be drunk. (So may be the guests, but that is not on Miss Manners' list of what is proper.)

3. Attacking Food with Strange Implements.

Everyone knows that you use a knife to spread butter, except that a potato is properly buttered with the fork.

Everyone knows that you can't eat fish with a meat knife or warts will grow on the back of your hand, but it is proper to eat fish with two forks.

Any idiot knows that you eat ice cream with your tongue, or with a spoon, but in the absence of an ice cream fork or an ice cream shovel, ice cream is properly eaten with both a fork and a spoon.

Doesn't that all sound like fun? Then why are you sitting there blowing bubbles in your milk?

The Civility Course

DEAR MISS MANNERS — With all the relaxed meals we have nowadays, take-out meals and order-ins, my family's table manners are deteriorating. My thirteen-year-old son thinks nothing of dipping and dunking the most unimaginable sets of food groups with each other, not to mention my husband forgetting that there are actually utensils to get the food from serving dish to plate, as well as the constant reminder to the entire family that elbows really don't belong on the table. How can I bring some civility back to dining in the home?

GENTLE READER — By dining, instead of grazing. Where you get your food is of no concern to Miss Manners, but if you allow fast-food manners in the household, she is surprised that your child has enough manners to be described as deteriorating.

The crisis in eating manners is widespread, but it astonishes Miss Manners. It is not as though these were esoteric routines that people rarely have a chance to practice. A culture's eating customs are supposed to be routinely taught by parents to children and practiced daily under their supervision.

You must, of course, enlist your husband's help. Unfortunately, habits are taught by example as well as nagging. Fortunately, once learned, they are no less "relaxing" than unauthorized eating methods.

A Refresher Course

DEAR MISS MANNERS — Several of us ladies at work all have the same complaint about our grown up children (mine are in college, the others are divorced, single adults of a second marriage or single, living on their own): They dine and dash. They never bring anything, offer to help clean up or invite us to dinner. When confronted, all of them said they are guests, and guests don't help. We would agree with that statement if they were occasional guests, but we're talking about several meals a week or every weekend. In actuality, we are subsidizing their meals, because they are struggling financially. None of us mind cooking family meals—in fact, we enjoy it. But we do mind being treated with such lack of consideration.

We, the parents, agree that children are never guests. This is a lame excuse for laziness. Children will always be part of the family and should contribute by bringing a dessert, helping clean up (which is more than taking their dish to the sink) or inviting us to dinner. These ladies are about to close their soup kitchens because of lack of respect. We raised our children with manners, but somewhere along the line, they lost them. We don't even get the token of a tip, like most good waitresses—just the mess to clean and a big insult from the ones we love.

GENTLE READER — Guests wait to be invited, write thank you letters afterwards and try to entertain their hosts as many times as they are entertained by them. If they are intimates of the household, they offer help when it seems to be needed. So Miss Manners believes that your grown-up children would be better off being relatives, even if they had a choice, but you shouldn't be giving them that bogus choice. You may have reared the children properly while they were at home, but your job is not finished. It is time to teach them the manners of grown-up children dining at their parents'.

HOUSEKEEPING

"Tidy" is a dear little word, and Miss Manners is sorry to see it pass out of use. Swept under the rug, as it were.

It is true that we have other ways of referring to people who enjoy keeping things neat, who pick up after themselves without being threatened and who maintain their homes nicely for themselves and other residents, instead of making desperate swipes at order only when guests are expected. Still, the modern terms for "tidy" don't have the same charm. Miss Manners doesn't care for either "anal-compulsive" or "control freak."

Even less does she care for the modern habit of redefining good habits as signs of bad character. It is clever to declare one's weakness a virtue and demand to be not just forgiven for one's lapses but admired. However, this ploy is at the expense of the dutiful, who are made to feel sheepish and apologetic about doing the right thing. Characterizing themselves as warm human beings (although Miss Manners does not quite understand how this automatically follows from an inability to put anything where it belongs), the unorganized routinely accuse the organized with whom they have supposedly warm relationships of petty larceny, petty tyranny and small-scale sabotage:

> "Did you take my glasses?"
> "I must have given you the tickets, because I don't have them."
> "No, it's not my fault; you're the one who forgot to remind me."
> "I would have put them in the dishwasher, but it was full, and I would have put the clean stuff away, but I don't know where you keep things and I knew you'd be upset if I didn't put everything away exactly where you think it should be."
> "Why didn't you tell me it was my mother's birthday?"
> "Of course I had to open another bottle—how was I to know that there were already two open in the refrigerator?"
> "I didn't stand you up. I just didn't look at my calendar."
> "Okay, what did you do with my keys this time?"

This is not warm human–type behavior. The justification, which is that no harm is done because anyone who keeps up with check-off lists more than three days after New Year's does not possess human feelings, is worse. How often topsy-turvy morality works when the suitors of young ladies argue that any resistance would mark them as cold and inhuman, Miss Manners cannot say. She does know that the notion that messiness is a warm and endearing trait, while orderliness is freakish, enjoys amazing success. Even people who truly love order commonly refer disparagingly to their own good habits.

None of this would be a problem if tidy and sloppy people didn't live together. Indeed, no self-respecting roommate referral system would pair people who see no point in making a bed—because they'll only sleep in it again—with those whose idea of a good point is hospital corners. It takes romance to make such volatile living arrangements. Love seems to be no respecter of personal habits, and people who can't tell the difference between a house and a hamper inexplicably manage to attract people who alphabetize everything they have, short of the children.

Incidentally, Miss Manners does not consider children the chief problem, and thank you, she does not care to view the state in which yours leave their rooms. Children are works in progress, and a surprising number turn out to want to live pleasantly the minute they leave home. The problem is between people of equal claim to running the house and unequal interest in maintaining it. Adults who live together cannot politely go around saying "Don't think you're going anywhere until you clean up this pigsty."

Miss Manners does not charge that the fact of being disorganized is rude— only that it often leads to rudeness in the way of inconveniencing and blaming others. She even acknowledges that the hopeless, if only they would stop bragging about their deficiencies, might also be human and therefore entitled to a reasonably peaceful life.

This is best accomplished by allowing them their own out-of-sight territory to keep as they wish. Miss Manners is a great believer in household zoning. In an ideal household, such a person would be assigned a separate bathroom, study and dressing room; in an average one, the free territory might only be inside a closet and a drawer.

Instead of receiving this gratefully, the mess-maker may notice that it implies that common territory must therefore be maintained at the higher standard, which is exactly what Miss Manners means. She brooks no nonsense about untidiness and tidiness being different systems of equal merit, nor about those who prefer the former having the same say as those who prefer the latter. A sloppy adult is not on the same august level as a tidy one.

She does not go so far as to assert that they have the same maintenance responsibilities. People who don't understand about order are never going to be able to manage it, so there is nothing to be gained by expecting it of them. What one can reasonably require of them is that they close what they open, put things back where they got them, replenish supplies that they use up, and not appropriate the pens and umbrellas of the tidy person on the grounds that they can't find their own.

Organizationally gifted or not, everybody has to take just enough responsibility for managing time, duty and space to keep from making havoc of responsible people's lives, inside the household and out. This means that everybody maintains a calendar of his or her own appointments, and participates in a master household calendar, although the disorganized must understand that they have no authority to accept invitations on behalf of others or perhaps even for themselves.

A central command post (and while electronic ones are admittedly seductive, nothing has replaced the refrigerator door, the one place everybody stops) not only enables the organized to spot conflicts and to issue reminders but it enables the disorganized to find them in case of emergency—having first agreed upon the definition of an emergency, and whether it includes "I can't find my skis!"

As long as they learn such basic household skills as leaving the newspaper intact and replacing the toilet paper instead of leaving unpleasant surprises, more complex duties can be assigned according to individual talents. Some people should never be asked to keep track of when Thanksgiving will occur, much less to connect this with the necessity of buying a turkey; they can compensate by performing tasks that they can master. Those who aren't sharp enough to be in charge of taking the car in for inspection while it is still legally possible to drive it can still be trained to take out the trash.

Even Miss Manners doesn't expect the disorganized to be able to figure out where their own scissors are or make a connection between running out of shampoo and buying more. That would be too much to expect. She does, however, expect them to resist the temptation to allow these shortcomings to lead them into a life of rudeness and thievery. In return, she expects the tidy person to keep a pleasant tone when revealing for the thousandth time where the spoons and dictionaries are kept. Noblesse oblige.

Name-Calling

DEAR MISS MANNERS — My boyfriend and I have different opinions when it comes to what is "done" and "not done," most recently on whether leaving one's underwear on the floor is rude or perfectly acceptable. I think it would be embarrassing for someone to walk in my room and see that intimate article of clothing strewn across the room. My boyfriend doesn't see what the big deal is.

I want to add that he leaves practically everything else lying around, too— cigarettes, food, half-empty glasses, and "half-clean clothes." Do I just have, as he claims, a silly social hang-up?

GENTLE READER — Apparently you have several: You are under the odd impression that a well kept house is better than a slovenly one. You think guests might not enjoy being forced to look at their hosts' underwear. You think you should have some say in how you live.

Miss Manners can understand that love is a powerful force and induces people to live with those whose personal habits are not as nice as their own. She fails to understand how anyone could bear to live with a person who strews around that meaningless but vaguely insulting word "hang-ups" to describe civilized living and/or your particular preferences.

Worse Name-Calling

DEAR MISS MANNERS—I leave dishes in my sink for days at a time. I know—I should be banished from civilized society, especially since I am about to add that I left dishes in my sink AND I invited a friend over. While I was upstairs, my friend decided to do me a favor and wash the dishes. It's not that I don't appreciate the help. At the time, I thanked him and felt relieved from an onerous task. It wasn't until later that I made the discovery that his idea of clean is the same as mine—only 25% less. He put dirty dishes back in the cupboard! Last night, he did it again. I thought it would be wrong to criticize an act performed as a gift, so I just told him I preferred he didn't do it at all, without explaining why. Now his feelings are hurt. He thinks I'm being inexplicably rigid and seems to be wondering what kind of psycho wife I might turn out to be.

GENTLE READER—Now just a minute here; please slow down and let Miss Manners figure out what you are actually saying. This is not just a friend, is it? By mentioning your concern with his opinion of you as a wife, you do plant that little thought that you might be considering him as a husband. In any case, he is eager to help around the house. Specifically, he has been eager to perform a task you hate and avoid to the point of preferring—Miss Manners is only echoing your own judgment—a degree of slovenliness. Yet this gentleman does not wash dishes to your satisfaction. Miss Manners has a hard time figuring out how his standards could be 25% lower than yours, since you don't wash them at all, but so be it.

Now—your solution to all this is that he should be discouraged from washing your dishes. Are you mad? If he were a casual acquaintance, certainly. One could say that his helpfulness crossed the border of intrusiveness, since he decided to clean up from a meal he did not share. But do you really think you must persuade a possible husband not to do any housework because he doesn't do it to the satisfaction of a possible wife who doesn't want to do it either?

Why don't you exert yourself, instead, in making the task easier for him? If you must leave your dishes in the sink, leave them soaking in soapy water. Not only will this suggest to him that you are at least trying, but the dishes will be easier for him to clean satisfactorily.

Calling a Truce

DEAR MISS MANNERS — I live with my fiancé and we are planning to marry next summer. We have already co-habitated for the past three years. I love him dearly and cannot imagine life without him. My problem is that he is a slob. Nothing I have done can remedy the problem. I have tried threats, thrown tantrums, joked about it, even thrown quantities of dirty dishes and clothes away, much to his surprise. My question to you is . . . is there anything I haven't tried? Leaving him over such a problem is not an option I would ever entertain . . . but it's driving me crazy!!

GENTLE READER — Miss Manners is pretty sure you haven't tried picking up after him. Any self-respecting lady would consider this far too degrading, not to mention sexist.

One of the nice things about marriage (Miss Manners needn't list others as you have already discovered them) is that you can make any sort of deal that suits you both. And the pleasantest work-sharing deal is not necessarily the one that would strike outsiders as fair, but one in which each of you does tasks you don't mind, while not having to do ones you dislike.

Surely there must be jobs that you hate to do that your fiancé would be willing to take on if you do the neatening up. In return for taking care of the dirty dishes and clothes, you ought to bargain to saddle him with quite a large load of work.

Respecting the Housewife

If the farmer and the cowboy should be friends, what about the housewife and the businesswoman? Miss Manners would put it to music if that would help, but she's too busy. Actually, she isn't. Miss Manners' idea of being busy is having to use her own dimpled knees to get the porch swing going because there is no one around to push it for her.

Meanwhile, all the other ladies are locked into a fierce competition over who is busiest, and she doesn't want to feel left out. Why this should be such an issue between housewives and businesswomen that they spend their time scorning one another, Miss Manners cannot imagine. Don't they have anything better to do?

Housewives are asked to give their occupations when out socially and are then roundly snubbed. Other ladies who talk to them at all go in for such conversation openers as "What on earth do you do with yourself all day?" and "Aren't you bored?" As a result, many housewives have been driven to the unseemly defense of declaring how much money they would get if they sold their personal services to their families instead of giving them away.

Miss Manners faints dead away when she hears this. That argument is horrid enough when it comes from divorcing husbands who, having once agreed to split the work of earning the family living and that of sustaining family life, turn around and claim that the latter obviously wasn't worth anything much because they didn't pay for it. Ladies don't need to encourage them.

Although housewives now assume that the attack on them is unprecedented, Miss Manners is old enough to remember how ladies who were doing paid work were charged to their faces with being selfish and worse. Salaries—such as they were—were considered to be a factor only in the lives of those who had improvident husbands or none at all (the latter condition being viewed as a matter of choice only in the sense that no one must have chosen them). Therefore, the only attraction of working had to be the opportunities and alibis it provided for promiscuity.

The workplace is no longer thought to be that exciting, but there has been a recurrence of slurs nevertheless. Housewives may routinely get the worst of it now that the society has adopted the counter-historical idea that people who work for wages are of higher status than those who preside over their own domains, but they also cast blame.

Whenever a tragedy occurs involving a child who was not under the immediate supervision of his or her mother because of that lady's job, it is open season on the mother in question and, by extension, every other such mother. Never mind who actually perpetrated the particular accident or crime. Never mind the shocking number of children being hurt by their own parents. Never mind that a mother who was with her child every hour of the day or night might inspire matricide.

Therefore, many ladies with jobs have been driven to the unseemly defense of pleading how deprived their families would be if they did not sell their services in the marketplace. Miss Manners doesn't like that version any better than the other one. She would like to see some sympathy among ladies, who all share the problem of balancing their contributions to their families and in the outside world, however different their solutions. If sympathy is not possible, Miss Manners would settle for some decorum.

Polite people show other adults the respect of acknowledging—or pretending—that they must know best how to run their own lives. They do not ask insulting questions, make accusations, draw unpleasant morals or offer unsolicited advice. If they haven't yet learned that people who talk about their jobs are among the world's great bores, they at least follow the social custom of addressing people as individuals, not job descriptions. They certainly do not discuss their own or anyone else's personal life in terms of its market value. People who sell their personal attentions do not belong in polite society.

Offensiveness

DEAR MISS MANNERS—A young woman said that I, as a wife "who doesn't work," am "the Cadillac of the 90s." Since I have three young children, surely she did not mean that I don't work. Perhaps she was saying I don't get paid and my husband is rich enough to keep me.

Because I do not have an income, we, as a family, manage without a lot of things that many Americans think are necessities. Far from being a luxurious commodity, I am incredibly versatile and indispensable to my family. Should I attempt to enlighten this person about how insensitive her comment was, or merely accept that she is a social clod?

GENTLE READER—Before you take insult, you might want to check what kind of car this lady has. No, maybe you'd better not. You would also have to know how well it's running. You're already devoting too much thought to a thoughtless remark.

Miss Manners doesn't care to defend people who make impertinent assumptions about other people's lives and resources, but she guesses this was a wistful remark that had more to do with the speaker's feelings about herself than with her estimation of you. It was certainly cloddish, but probably not meant to be demeaning.

Nobody knows better than Miss Manners that cloddishness is a social menace, but apparently no one else knows that the cure for it is not the cloddishness of going around "enlightening" people about how unpleasant one finds their pleasantries. If you were directly queried about your finances or criticized, you might have registered your displeasure with a freezingly polite "How kind of you to take an interest in my personal life." Here, a cold "Thank you" would have been enough to suggest that you are satisfied enough with your life to assume that any comment upon it would consist of admiration.

Defensiveness

DEAR MISS MANNERS—What is the ideal relationship between secretary and wife of the executive? The secretary sees him more hours during the day, knows his business associates, and takes part in what seems to be the most important part of his life—therefore, sometimes creating resentment on the wife's part. The wife's role is usually to do the things no one else wants to do, i.e., care of the young and the elderly (all of which America seems to warehouse) and spends many years inundated with diapers and bottles.

The husband spends all his years bettering himself as an executive and officer of a company and acquiring power, while the wife receives very little recognition and little time for mental stimulation spending her life being a wife, mother and homemaker.

A whole week for secretaries? There is only one day for mothers, and no day for wives. There should be some other way to reward secretaries for a job well done other than a social lunch with several drinks before. I have been both. As a secretary, I kept a very businesslike relationship and my president or vice president boss never took me to lunch; however, I planned many for him. I was not a wallflower, having spent some time as a model and I have a degree from a prominent university. I knew their wives and had great respect for them. I don't find myself in a similar situation, and feel that secretaries are going too far.

GENTLE READER—Miss Manners tries not to get personal with the etiquette questions but feels obliged to point out that your problem is not with secretaries—your husband's or anyone else's. Your problem is with your own present occupation. Nowadays, ladies who can afford to stay at home with their children generally do so because they find this satisfying. Such a person would not, however, refer to domestic life in the loaded terms you use. As you are a trained secretary, Miss Manners suggests you might want to return to being one, rather than blaming your husband's for your dissatisfaction with your share of his attention.

Respecting the Office Worker

DEAR MISS MANNERS — I am writing on behalf of myself and another female colleague *d'un certain age,* in regard to certain assumptions our husbands *d'un certain era* make in regard to their right to intrude in the professional lives of spouses. Most particularly we wonder if calling one's wife at the office to tell her what is desired for the evening meal or asking that she leave a meeting to be informed about a plumbing malfunction in the home is acceptable. In addition, we would like to know if it is proper for a spouse to complain to an administrator at his wife's place of business about the fact that his wife, on occasion, must toil past the time that her contract states that she is expected to be on duty.

GENTLE READER — At *un certain age,* you may have forgotten *un certain routine* you once used to teach the children manners. This was called How Would You Feel If? Miss Manners suggests you learn to play it again.

Typically, this went "Don't take away the toy your brother is playing with. How would you feel if he took away a toy you were playing with? Don't shove your sister. How would you feel if she shoved you?" and so on. It wasn't sparkling dialogue, but a certain primitive understanding eventually developed.

Now is the time to trot it out again: "Please don't interrupt me at work. How would you feel if I interrupted you at work? How would you feel if I complained to your boss about your hours?"

Miss Manners recognizes that it is barely possible a husband may be slightly quicker at this sort of thing than a small child, and may arrive earlier at the traditional crisis point. This occurs when, lulled into that way of talking, you say something like "Don't pull the cat's tail. How would you feel if she pulled your tail?" and the child proudly announces, "I don't care—I don't have a tail!" So perhaps the husband, with a smirk only too similar to his child's long ago, replies "I don't care if you call my boss—I am the boss!" or "Go ahead and interrupt me at work—I'm retired!"

The reply to the tail-less child, if you recall, was to pull a bit of hair and say "Well, that's what it feels like." With the husband, too, you may have to find something equivalent. If he is the boss, you complain to his deputy (in front of him) that he must be sent home on time, and discouraged from believing that he is indispensable. If he is retired, you have him paged on the golf course and ask him to do an errand on the way home. Miss Manners has a feeling this may not actually be necessary. Husbands tend to be more experienced than children, and have probably learned to accept the mere mention of retaliation in place of the deed.

HOME OFFICE-KEEPING

The many people who now do office or other professional work from their homes are decidedly testy about it, Miss Manners has noticed. Having no such wonderful buffer as a secretary, who can filter the outside world to them in useful and bearable doses, they have taken to snarling "CAN'T YOU SEE I'M WORKING?"

Neighbors drop by uninvited. Computers call to make unsolicited solicitations. Strangers appear at the door to spread religion or pitch politics. Friends telephone to chat. Children come and go at will. Housemates deplete the office supplies and play games with the office equipment. People who seem to have nothing to do look to them for companionship. People who are busy ask them to do their errands and household tasks.

The polite ones, bless their hearts, feel an obligation to let others consume their time. So they let them natter on with the mistaken idea that it would be impolite to cut them off. The rude ones are no better off. By blasting would-be consumers of their time, they leave the way open for counterattacks, which take up more time, and they get themselves into emotional states that interfere with work more than interruptions. Spoken or unspoken, however, the bitter response is always "CAN'T YOU SEE I'M WORKING?"

Miss Manners doesn't condone interrupting people at work, but she doesn't care for all that shouting, either. There is an underlying problem for both sides here that she would like to point out: "NO, THEY CAN'T SEE THAT YOU'RE WORKING." (Please excuse Miss Manners. What she meant to say over the din, in her wee, ladylike voice, was "No, they can't see that you're working.")

Any lady who has worked around the clock to run a household, rear children and serve her community could have told them that work done at home never really registers as being work. Furthermore, boundaries of time and space that once protected the sanctity of the home have now disappeared. The place has been so thoroughly invaded by those who bring in non-domestic work—from the burdened soul who has to bring work home to get everything done, to the sly one who hopes to soften up associates by turning them into guests—that it is impossible to tell who, among those at home, is working and who is not. They're home, aren't they?

The home office may also do duty as a sitting or dining room. The home worker may take time off during the day and put in extra hours in the evening. People who work at home have also been known to do their thinking in ways not traditionally associated with office work: while straightening the closets, watching the news or standing in front of an open refrigerator. These people are especially indignant when others assume that what they are doing is goofing off or puttering and that they may therefore be interrupted.

Miss Manners is not disputing that one may be doing urgent work while apparently relaxing, just as the computer has enabled the office worker to relax with games and interoffice chatter while apparently working. She is only suggesting that the worker need not assume a lack of respect for his or her work when others are confused about where and when it is being done. Someone who appears at the door in a bathrobe at noon, or who tries to beg off from chatting after dinnertime, doesn't look convincing when making the excuse of being in the middle of work, truthful as it may be.

All one has to do is to tell them. Nicely. Patterns of work should be announced to anyone likely to trespass:

> "When my study door is shut, please don't interrupt unless it's an
>   emergency."
> "Call me in the evening—I can't talk during the day."
> "I'm sorry I can't talk now; I'm in the middle of a work project."
> "This is not a good time to visit—I work during the day."

Anybody who works and lives in the same place should take control of all means of ingress, deciding whom to let in and when. The answering machine and the door peephole are the poor person's receptionist. Self-secretarial service consists of putting the telephone on an answering machine and ignoring the doorbell or telling those who ring it that you are not interested (if you don't know them) or not free until later (if you do).

It is not rude to say pleasantly (but with an air of preoccupation to illustrate the point) "I'm terribly sorry but I'm busy, so I must ask you to excuse me; good-bye" without providing an opportunity for the intruder to argue the point. No one need feel apologetic about not being available to everyone all the time—not even someone who is indulging in the office-sanctioned task of woolgathering.

Resisting External Pressure

DEAR MISS MANNERS — When I try working from home the phone seems to ring every 15 minutes so I have taken to turning the ringer down and returning all calls at the end of the day. So many people hang up without leaving a message, or hang up and call right back to try to get me to pick up, or leave a loud message saying "HOW COME YOU NEVER PICK UP THE PHONE?" Do callers have any right to be so hostile, and to try to fool me into picking up? How do you ask a couple of chatters, obviously cyberflirting big time, to chill out?

GENTLE READER — That wasn't your boss calling, was it? Or the person waiting for the report you promised to turn in three days ago?

Presuming that your work does not involve taking telephone calls—don't take them. Don't take bullying on the subject, either. People who turn hostile when you don't jump to do their bidding are exactly the sort you should be screening out— probably out of your life, Miss Manners would guess, as well as your workday.

Resisting Internal Pressure

DEAR MISS MANNERS — I feel like a prisoner in my own home. I am a teacher, and I often have work to do after school hours, such as grading papers, preparing assignments and tests, recording grades, writing progress reports, contacting parents on the telephone, and similar tasks. I often have to stay home to carry out this work while my family goes to a movie or some other family activity.

Today is one such day. Someone rang the doorbell and I decided not to answer. Apparently the caller waited a while or went around the block, because the bell rang again about ten minutes later. Just as I picked up the thread of my work, it rang again. Can't people realize that if nobody answers, it has to be due to one of two reasons: No one is home (and the caller is therefore wasting his time), or someone is home but must have a good reason for not answering, which should be respected.

Twice in the last few months, I did answer the door and although I explained politely that I had these school deadlines to meet and that was why I had stayed home, the callers stayed on while insisting they would only take a few minutes of my time. One was actually still here four hours later! My family returned from their outing tired and hungry, and I had not even had the chance to put some food together, let alone complete my work. So now I don't open the door, but I feel angry, guilty, imposed upon; in one word, unhappy. A friend of mine tells me it is bad manners not to answer the door or the telephone if I am at home. I say the unannounced caller should accept the fact that the time is not right and then leave or hang up after a few rings and no more than two tries.

GENTLE READER— Modern guilt is a wonderful thing. Here you were, home, minding your own business as it were, sacrificing your recreation to do your admirable work, hoping to get done in time to feed your little family, and some unlicensed judge of manners has made you feel that you did something wrong. Why? Why would you even consider the idea that you do not have a right to dispose of your own time in your own house?

Miss Manners suggests you learn to ignore or unplug the telephone or put it on an answering machine, and that you ignore or tape over the doorbell. Should you weaken and answer the door, learn to say politely that you are working—while standing firmly in the doorway and blocking the way in. She also suggests you stop taking illicit etiquette advice from interested parties.

Obligations to Self-Respect

It's not that Miss Manners doesn't know how you eat when you are standing there with the refrigerator door open, and what your idea of grooming, let alone proper dress, is when you're not planning to go anywhere. She hasn't a word to say about it because she considers it none of her business.

Etiquette is social behavior, and the sure way to get safely away from its demands is to stay home alone, shut the door and pull down the shades. There is really no such thing as being rude to oneself, and even Miss Manners doesn't do etiquette for hermits. It would be rude to intrude.

If anyone else is present, it is a different matter. Miss Manners does not care for the popular idea that being related and/or in love means you don't have to worry about the other person's sensibilities, a concept that has done so much to promote the broken home. Or, as those who advocate the etiquette-free home environment put it with an amazing zest for self-condemnation, "I just like to be myself at home." Oh, so that's who that awful person is.

But if it doesn't affect anyone else, and your wallowing self doesn't bother your critical self, why should Miss Manners care? She gets the day off too, knowing you are safely isolated, where you are not going to inspire etiquette complaints.

Suppose, however, it does bother your own self? As Miss Manners is aware, more people are working at home now by the flickering light of friendly computers. They still have, of course, etiquette obligations to those on the receiving end of their telephones, telephone modems, E-mail and bulletin boards.

Interrupters—the definition of people who call at the one moment of the day when the home worker didn't happen to be wondering whom to call for a little chat to while away the time before inspiration struck—may be dealt with briefly and firmly, but not rudely.

What no one else can see, hear or read doesn't count. That is the great advantage that manners has over morals. If you're not caught, there is no reason to register fault even on your conscience. Nevertheless, Miss Manners also knows that the thrill of an occasional release from social expectations can turn ugly when it becomes a way of life. So while she promises not to peek to see how anyone is doing, she offers, with uncharacteristic timidity, a few suggestions for optional etiquette as a courtesy to oneself.

As everyone knows, the proper dress for working at home is as close to nightwear as possible—soft, fuzzy and requiring little in the way of a support system. It is still dress, though, in the sense that it requires changing. With that goes a modicum of what may laughingly be termed grooming. This may be only a way of thinking about what goes undone: An unshaven gentleman should think of himself as "considering growing a beard," and a lady who leaves off whatever customary makeup she wears classifies this as "letting the skin rest." (Miss Manners doesn't even want to think about people who postpone brushing their teeth.)

By the same reasoning, beds should be made upon arising unless they are decently covered with the thought that one will be working like crazy for a short time and then taking a refreshing nap. Meals should be—meals. Miss Manners did promise she wouldn't look, out of concern for her own equanimity as much as for anyone else's privacy. She also promises that the person who sets a nice table will be happier than the person who doesn't use a saucer under every cup and bowl. All right—who doesn't actually sit down to eat. All right—who doesn't actually use eating tools.

Miss Manners would consider it a sensible precaution never to go more than two days without getting physically out of the house. This is not the health tips department, so it's not that. The purpose is to remind oneself that one is actually visible, in a world where other people exist. Frightening as this may be, it serves as a valuable warning not to let etiquette skills rust away. She hopes these few rules do not seem unnecessarily strict, and she has been told that no one who works at home follows them to the letter. She wouldn't dream of prying to find out.

Obligations to Visitors

DEAR MISS MANNERS — Long-time friends who both work out of their home invited us to spend the following day with them, suggesting a time. When we called ahead in the morning, however, we were advised, along with several reasons why, that one of the couple would be working while the rest of us ate and visited. Our attempt at canceling was sharply countered with a question as to whether this person's not working was to be "a prerequisite" for our attendance. This scenario, with the exception of our bowing out and the resultant unpleasant confrontation, has been oft repeated.

What are we to think? Either the person is truly busy and doesn't need the additional task of entertaining guests—or could this be a way of "politely" avoiding us?

GENTLE READER — One of the peculiarities of our time is the blur between work time and leisure. As Miss Manners understands it, the office is the place where showers and birthday parties are held, while the home is where mere socializing is a disturbance to serious people. Of course, it should be a prerequisite for accepting an invitation to be assured that your hosts were free to entertain you. No considerate person would intrude on someone's working hours. No considerate person would invite guests with no intention of entertaining them.

Obligations Towards Those Left at Home

Having just returned from a short business trip, a lady of Miss Manners' acquaintance embraced her husband at the airport and opened the sort of conversation that cozy couples have when they are reunited.

"Did you mail those packages I left?" she asked. "I hope you remembered to send them insured. I don't have any cash left, but I figured you'd have gone to the bank. Did you finally fix the porch light? I keep telling you it's dangerous not to have that working. I left you a message about picking up the dry cleaning—it's important because there's a dress I really need for tomorrow. Did you call my parents? I didn't have time, and I don't want them to worry about me. I skipped dinner on the plane, so I hope you have something we can have as soon as we get home because I'm starving. You did pick up the groceries on the list I left you, didn't you? Oh, don't tell me we have to stop for gas—I'm exhausted. Why didn't you get it on the way here?"

After a while, the lady noticed that she had not been receiving replies to her questions, so she stopped to give her husband a chance. Besides, although she was still keyed up from the trip, she was beginning to run out of breath.

"My dear," said her husband as he navigated through airport traffic, "the sight of a 747 soaring through the air is a wonderful thing. It's amazing to see it up there looking so powerful and free. But do you have any idea of the size of the ground crew it takes to keep it up there?"

Fortunately, that was all the gentleman needed to say. Even normally considerate people need an occasional reminder that they are not the only ones tearing around trying to get a lot of things done. Life on the road seems so much more disjointed than life at home that it is especially apt to give the traveler the delusion those left behind are at leisure. Furthermore, several days of doing nothing but business encourages the businesslike attitude of issuing instructions and expecting them to be followed.

This is not, however, a polite approach to take to family life. Miss Manners does not subscribe to the fantasy that business travel is a life of hotel and restaurant luxury, for which penance is expected in the way of compensatory duty at home. But since a family member who is subject to business trips heavily depends on extra help from the ground crew at home, it is wise, as well as polite and kind, to express appreciation for what is done and sympathetic tolerance for what was not done.

That this etiquette was only sketchily observed in the era when the traveler was nearly always the gentleman of the family and the support service was supplied by the lady does not make it less true. It does mean that spouses will have to develop dexterity in switching from making extra claims while away to doing double work when at home. It also means that—as with any other relative or friend who pitches in to compensate for travel absences—massive doses of appreciation will have to fly around in all directions.

False Obligations Towards Those Left at Home

Is Miss Manners the only person who is repulsed by that poster of a child—usually leering out of a resort gift shop window—captioned "What did you bring me?"

"Nothing, kid," any sensible person should be prompted to reply, "and what's more, I'm suddenly awfully sorry I came to see you." One can't actually say that— Miss Manners cares for rudeness towards children even less than she does for rudeness from children. Nevertheless, any person so attacked should make sure to teach the lesson that rudeness, amounting in this case to emotional blackmail, doesn't work. Grandparents—the poster is sometimes targeted to them, in the charming hope of convincing the aged that they can expect no unpurchased affection—may simply have to become forgetful on the matter of bringing presents at all. "Why, I hoped you'd be pleased simply to see me," they should say in astonishment; "I'm certainly happy just to see you."

Parents, especially those who have kindly sought to sweeten their absences for business trips by returning laden with gifts, will find that they, too, encounter this unpleasant welcome if they have not taught etiquette rules to the contrary. Relying on the fact that the child will, indeed, be happy to have the parent back, and having had this feeling bolstered by the child's protests against the parent's leaving for the trip, one can easily neglect to teach the rule about going for the open arms before going for the luggage.

One homecoming in which it appears that the primary interest is anticipation of material gain should be cruel enough to convince a parent that something is wrong. Those who go in for psychological complications may prattle of hidden resentments associated with fears of desertion. Miss Manners believes it to be a simple matter of etiquette.

One can love a person to distraction, with no reservations whatsoever, and still focus first on the glittering object in that person's hand. Ladies who receive romantic proposals often have to remind themselves to look deeply into the beloved's eyes before examining the diamond in the ring.

If gratitude toward the giver, much less the clear expression of it, were a natural instinct, nobody would ever have to be prodded to write a thank you letter. Also, not all presents are successful. Expressing love for the impulse of present-giving nevertheless is a refinement of civilization that must be taught.

Therefore, the child-rearing system of leaving children to express all their emotions uninhibited by the requirements of etiquette is a mistake. Parents who have depended on their children always to harbor and to express acceptable emotions are always going to encounter trouble. One must teach the artificial habit of associating the pleasure in a present with the generosity of the giver.

This is done by careful instruction in the proper welcome, along with an explanation of how wonderful it feels for a homecoming parent or a visitor to see smiles and happy faces. It also helps if the practice of bringing presents is somewhat irregular, not always expected as the child's due. It is the child who does not demand to know what was brought who should be given the pleasure of a genuine surprise.

Chapter Five

THE HELP

THE PROPER STAFF

The properly run household, as Miss Manners knows any proper person will be grateful to hear, has a minimum of five indoor departments: The pantry, which is the special province of the butler—who actually presides over the whole household, as his demeanor plainly shows; he runs it with a staff of footmen whose minds are on the housemaids. The kitchen, run by Cook with the help of the scullery maids and the cooking sherry. The public and private rooms, run by the housekeeper with a staff of parlormaids, chambermaids and their assistants, all of whose minds are on the footmen. The laundry, with at least one sweaty laundress doing the linens under the querulous supervision of the housekeeper; and the family wardrobes at the finicky direction of the lady's maid and the valet.

The nursery, if there are small children, ruled by the iron hand of the governess or nanny; or, if there is an elderly person, a nurse and companion of decayed gentility, run by the iron hand of the elderly person.

It has two outdoor departments:

The grounds, run by the head gardener.

Transportation, under the direction of the head chauffeur.

One of these two, but seldom both, are observed to be much too confidential with the lady of the house.

Even back in the days when everybody who didn't have a servant probably was one, it was acknowledged that households could run more or less properly with fewer people. Over the course of the twentieth century, Miss Manners has noticed, the number of people deemed necessary keeps decreasing. In the early decades, it was thought that perhaps one could make do with either a butler or a housekeeper indoors, a combination driver and gardener outdoors, and a depleted cast of assistants. By the time of the Depression, one maid-of-all-work was thought to be able to do it all if she weren't so shiftless. By midcentury, it was widely believed that a housewife ought to be able to manage the indoor departments with a weekly cleaning woman, while the gentleman of the house managed the outdoor departments. Then it was a housewife who, unless she was shiftless, would not really need to employ a weekly cleaning woman or bother the gentleman of the house. Now it is the lady and gentleman of the house who are supposed to be able to perform these tasks in their spare time after work, while a single mother ought to be able to manage it alone if she weren't so shiftless.

What has remained pretty much constant, Miss Manners notices—besides the excessively rude custom of insulting hard-working women—is the amount of work. Since the promise that electric appliances would replace human effort was not made good, and the prediction of perfect robot servants keeps being pushed into the future, here is the way a proper modern house is staffed:

The pantry, run by the lady and/or gentleman of the house, assisted by petulant children, answering machine or voice mail to mind the telephone, kindly neighbor to take in deliveries and bring in repair people.

The kitchen, run by the pizza delivery person, assisted by the microwave, the carryout and, for special occasions, the catering service.

The public and private rooms, intermittently run by the cleaning service who run by the vacuum.

The laundry, run by the dry cleaners.

The nursery, run by the day care center, the au pair girl whose mind is on the equivalent of footmen, or the foreign nanny whose ideas of children-rearing differ from the parents'; or the nursing home, for care of the elderly.

The grounds, under the care of the lawn tractor and leaf blower.

Transportation, run by the carpool and public transportation.

Miss Manners does not see much progress here, or even much of a bargain. All these years, she has been saying that everyone would be better off if household work were treated with respect and respectable working conditions. Perhaps it is time people listened.

The Servant Problem and the Employer Problem

DEAR MISS MANNERS — Regarding one's servants: How much should they be paid? Should any be paid more than another? What, if any, benefits should they receive? Should any receive more or better benefits? How many days vacation should they have? How many hours a day and how many days a week should one's servants work? Should they be expected to work day and/or night, weekends, and/or holidays?

Should one's servants be expected to work during their or their family's or their friends' special occasions, such as birthday, anniversary, graduation, play, recital? Should they be allowed extra days off to travel for holidays and special occasions? Should one ever treat one's servants as friends or as family?

GENTLE READER — Miss Manners remembers you. You're the one who made the so-called "servant problem" the staple of female conversation for all those boring generations. How did you get a modern postmark on your letter?

We now realize that what we had there was an employer problem. Domestic work, not being treated with the dignity and the humane measures demanded of other employment, is not what you would call a major job attraction. Those who undertake it should be cherished. By that, Miss Manners does not mean that they are to be treated as family or friends. People who are willing to clean your house might not be as eager to be your friend. Socializing with the employer should not be a part of any respectable job.

What is wanted here are the decent job conditions associated with any honest work: agreement on job requirements, higher than minimum wages for higher-than-minimum labor, such benefits as sick leave, paid vacation and reasonable leave for family duties and personal emergencies, a regular five day, one-shift schedule, holidays, extra pay for overtime, merit raises, retirement, and so on. These are what Miss Manners (who comes from a family of labor economists) considers to be a basic minimum. Miss Manners does not suggest your approaching any prospective employee with your ideas until they have been adjusted accordingly.

Job Limits

When Miss Manners first bravely set out into the workaday world, a mere slip of a girl timidly hoping to earn her bread and to be of use to society, the young had certain obligations to their professional elders. Such as waiting on them hand and foot. The indenture system had already been abolished, although it was sometimes hard to tell, but both respect for the senior members of the workforce and education for the junior members were still supposed to be furthered by such service.

Naturally, Miss Manners had aspired to a respectable occupation, so in her youthful wisdom, she chose journalism. There she soon found that the chief tasks of newcomers were maintaining the sacred tools of the profession (sharpening pencils) and the equally sacred welfare of its notable practitioners (fetching sandwiches). Indeed, this labor did produce wisdom, although the entire education, along with a hint about the degree of respect to be accorded, was passed down within the junior ranks by means of a single sentence:

"Be sure to collect all the money before you go out and get the sandwiches."

In due course, Miss Manners attained a modest amount of seniority of her own. When the day came that she would have liked to conjure up a sandwich, the system had changed. "They're not your servants, you know," she was informed about her immediate successors. What's more, she could jolly well sharpen her own pencils.

Miss Manners actually agrees with the idea that labor's bottom ranks should have more clearly defined limits than the most exalted positions, so that the most vulnerable workers are protected from exploitation. She just didn't care for the timing.

"They're not your servants" is an excellent thought to keep in mind when dealing with all employees, and never more so than with those who work in one's house. It was on the home front that the fantasy of devotion and personal attention between employee and employer most dramatically failed. The ideal was that of a loyal worker who had the same sense of responsibility for the employer's household as she had for her own, coupled with empathy that made her understand her employer's special needs and preferences. She would be loyal and flexible enough not just to get the job done as stated but also to pitch in when that was needed. The employer, in turn, was supposed to be appreciative enough to supply voluntarily the working conditions and benefits of workers with more bargaining power, along with a more general sense of responsibility and empathy for the employee's welfare.

Such employees and employers did actually exist, but not dependably, and seldom were they paired with those of equal commitment. So—whether it was that the help turned ornery or just wised up—the old personal service business has been put on a less personal basis. Some of the abuses of the old system are now gone, along with its advantages.

Household help is increasingly likely to consist of contractors—not only a cleaning service, delivery service, car service, catering service and so on, but services that supply such formerly lady-of-the-house services as sending letters and presents. The truly personal aspect, the devotion and continuity that produces that increased understanding and therefore even more pleasant service, is a rarity.

The job requirements and limits are as articulated as in an office, and no one in either kind of workplace should be able to sustain the illusion that catering to extra whims is sufficiently compensated by the education or emotional satisfaction that gives the employee. Not even those who grumble because they got caught in the change.

Limiting the Job

DEAR MISS MANNERS—We have a wonderful cleaning woman who has worked for us several years. We value her highly, thank her sincerely, and pay her handsomely. But she wants more. She wants to be friends. Miss Manners, I do not want to be her friend, any more than I would want to be friends with the pediatrician, the auto mechanic, the accountant or the mail carrier. I do not wish to appear heartless or rude, but I expect such people to solve their own problems and to look for companionship elsewhere. How does one politely convey such a message without coming across as mean-spirited?

GENTLE READER—The etiquette between household employer and employee has always been muddled in America, where the euphemism "help" was invented out of our belief in social egalitarianism. We expect more compassionate and dignified behavior than in the harsh, class-bound master-servant relationships of less democratically rooted societies.

We just can't figure out what it is. Miss Manners' own dear aunt was startled to find that her excellent cleaning lady had taken to greeting and taking leave of her with a social kiss, but was at a loss for an objection that wouldn't sound demeaning. Making friends, or pretending to do so, is hardly the solution. If your friends are so good as to clean up after you, you would insult them by offering to pay, but would be obliged to look for opportunities to clean up after them.

Did your cleaning lady but realize it, she would be worse off as your friend. You probably wouldn't be able to give her the quality of help she gives you. She also doesn't really want you messing in her love life or her spiritual life, as old-fashioned employers and modern friends are wont to do. You certainly don't want her messing in yours, considering that she has the run of your house and is of necessity privy to many of your private habits.

What is required (but almost never found nowadays) in a cordial business relationship is not forced friendship but pleasant professionalism. Someone who works in your home cannot be treated as formally as someone with whom transactions are transient, brief and public, but you can stop personal conversation at the first sign with such regretful statements as "I'm sorry, but I'm busy," "I really don't know anything about that," "I wouldn't presume to advise you" and "I won't keep you from your work."

Language Limits

DEAR MISS MANNERS — Several months ago, I hired a friendly, hard working, reliable woman to help clean my house. She speaks only Spanish, and normally this is only a minor inconvenience, since I speak tolerable Spanish and she is very forgiving of my grammatical mistakes.

However, I've noticed that when other people are in the house, the situation is a little awkward. When her name is mentioned in conversation, it seems obvious that I should include her by explaining the comment. On the other hand, when my daughter and I are huddled over her math paper, there seems no need to translate everything into Spanish. When I make a pot of coffee and offer a cup to a friend, do I translate that it's half decaf and the cream and sugar are on the table? When my friend and I burst into laughter over some joke, do I try and explain in Spanish? I realize that ours is a business relationship, but I don't want her to feel excluded.

GENTLE READER—Miss Manners dares say that your housekeeper would prefer to get on with her work so that she can enjoy her free time as she chooses, rather than delaying it by listening to your and your friend's translated jokes. Privacy works both ways: Surely you would not intrude yourself if she had a visitor.

The point about translating anything in which her name is mentioned is an excellent one, however. You should not be discussing your employee in front of her, but if her name comes up—as for example if you are mentioning that she will soon be picking up your daughter from school—it is tactful to let her know what was said.

The Uniform

DEAR MISS MANNERS—What should a housekeeper wear as there are so many different duties from formal serving to sweaty work?

GENTLE READER—Where did you find this gem? Miss Manners knows people who do formal service and she knows people who do sweat-producing housework. But the only people she knows who do both also have to pay the rent or mortgage on the house.

The evening uniform for a waitress is a plain short black dress, which is also what all the female dinner guests are wearing these days. The waitress at least gets to dress hers up with white apron, collar and cuffs. The uniform for anyone who does sweaty work is whatever that person feels like wearing. Inevitably, this means a T-shirt, jeans and sneakers, which is unfortunately also what all the brunch guests are wearing these days.

The Gentleman of the House

DEAR MISS MANNERS—When I had friends from my office to my home, a woman guest complimented me on how clean and neat my house was. I explained that my husband deserves all the credit; he's my full-time housekeeper. He's totally comfortable in his role, and I'm satisfied with our lifestyle and work arrangements. A few of my female friends didn't quite understand and were rather disturbed by having a husband as a housekeeper. Do you feel I handled the situation correctly? What would be the correct name for a male housekeeper?

GENTLE READER — Unlike your friends, Miss Manners believes that most ladies would call him a treasure. You are right to be proud of him, and are not responsible for their negative nosiness.

You are responsible for your own, however, and you are not doing much for your husband's pride by calling him "my" housekeeper. Households belong to all those who live there, and whatever division of chores is agreed upon, the responsibility is also shared. Speaking of him as if you presided over the household, and had merely contracted with him to do the cleaning, is rude. The fact that many ladies have been so spoken of by their husbands for maintaining the family hearth does not make it excusable.

The Lady of the House

DEAR MISS MANNERS — When I was a child and invited to friends' homes to play, my parents did not permit me to go if they didn't know their parents and were not offered opportunities to know them. At the time, I felt that they were hurting my social life, and I resented it.

Now my five-year-old daughter is receiving invitations from the parents of her classmates for her to come to their homes for a visit. I have chatted with these women at school, and felt that potential friendships were developing. However, the invitations don't often include me. I resent this practice. I know I am feeling rejected by these women. I am a stay-at-home mom and I'm fairly new in the area. My only social contacts are other moms. I can handle that, I think. My real concern is my reluctance to send my daughter into a home I've never visited with people I don't really know, at an age when she is not yet ready to take care of herself. There is so much in the media these days about children dying in shooting accidents in a friend's home, and children being molested in situations where their parents are not there. I am genuinely scared.

How do I handle these invitations without hurting my social chances, or hers, and without inadvertently sending her into a situation she is not yet ready to handle?

GENTLE READER — Miss Manners is afraid you are trying to deal at once with two different problems—your daughter's social life and your own. Protecting her, which is certainly your duty, can be done without requiring that all her friendships be two-generational.

There is no offense in the wisdom of asking who will be supervising the children while they are at play. If it is not a parent but some other caretaker, you are justified in chatting with the mother or father about that person. They are apt to be quite frank, the virtues and drawbacks of such employees being a major interest of working parents. Such a talk may very well lead to friendships. But since you do have the advantage of being at home, Miss Manners doesn't see why you don't solve both problems by inviting the parents and children to your house, where you can observe them at leisure for signs of trustworthiness to supervise your daughter.

The Nanny

It used to be said that you could always tell an upper class background from a person's manners, especially the table manners. They would be simply frightful.

The premise was that people who were rich enough to have nothing to do with their own children wouldn't. So while the parents displayed their fine manners at grand dinners and goodness knows where else, the children ate with the servants, picking up their manners and goodness knows what else.

Miss Manners has noticed a few things wrong with this offensive little formula. To begin with, where were those upper class parents supposed to have learned their own manners? Then there is the odd idea that manners are related to the circumstances of birth, rather than training. It's best not to get Miss Manners started on that mean triumph of snobbery over experience. Suffice it to say that the servants of an aristocratic household would be excellently versed in etiquette.

Mostly, it is a slur on the traditional nanny, who devoted her life to the noble, if doomed, task of teaching children to behave better than their parents. If it is difficult to learn the lesson that one must love and respect one's parents while they set bad examples, it is even harder to teach.

"Yes, I know Mummy likes to smash her champagne glass when she gets hilarious," Nanny would say with a straight face. "You, however, will drink your milk properly and take care where you put your glass."

The modern nanny (or au pair, or housekeeper, or day care provider) has a different situation. The children still don't eat meals with their parents, but that's because neither parents nor children actually sit down and eat meals; they're too much on the run. Far from wanting to get away from their children, the parents cherish their time together so much that they don't want to dampen it by giving instructions and corrections.

The result is not as different as it should be between aloof, frivolous parents and those who are devoted and overburdened. They all expect an employee to set their children a higher standard of behavior than they are willing to enforce. Miss Manners is afraid that this is never going to work. The parents may be angels and the employee may be a Godsend, but unless they make a team effort, the children are going to be neither.

Working parents are familiar with the orientation session between employee and supervisor, but something funny happens to them on the home front. Maybe this is the sixth nanny they've had, and if she doesn't work out, the family is going to split up fighting over who can more easily take off from work. Perhaps cultural differences make them afraid they might unknowingly offend. Or they think it all goes without saying. So they often slur over explanations of what they expect— rather a startling omission, considering that this is the most complicated, delicate and important job they will ever hire anyone to do. Child care inevitably deals not only with feeding, clothing and scheduling but with guidance in morals and manners, so it should not be offensive to go over this in detail with someone who is expected to do a good share of the teaching. It becomes offensive when this is done without leaving an opening in which the nanny can explain her own ideas and requirements. Anyone competent to do such a job will have opinions about how it should be done, and will know that it cannot be done if the employer engages in sabotage. Even such tender sabotage as allowing the children lower standards of behavior when Nanny isn't on duty, and calling it relaxation or quality time.

The Au Pair

DEAR MISS MANNERS— What does "au pair" really mean? Do we not have an English word that means the same, or is this just another attempt to distinguish the "wealthy" from the "lower classes"? Although I know the difference between housekeeper and nanny (another recent term being used in the U.S.), I have seen housekeepers, nannies and au pairs all doing the same job—taking care of children and cleaning house.

GENTLE READER— Miss Manners has seen lots of people doing what you describe, who are called mothers, fathers and grandparents. As she understands the usage, it is not the job that is being described, so much as the commitment of the person who performs it.

We don't really have an English equivalent of "au pair," which seems to mean "young foreigner who wants to come here to have a good time, which her employers hope won't be in conflict with the reason they brought her over, but don't want to squelch so much that she gets teary and homesick."

"Nanny" is understood to be a more serious person, trained and motivated more by an interest in children than the opportunity to have a rent-free social life.

"Housekeeper" is what people used to call a maid. Someone finally realized that there was something wrong in assigning a dismissive title to someone who did the same job that her employer would be honored for doing.

Attributing snobbishness is dangerous, because these terms are less likely to be chosen by the employers than the employees themselves, whose wishes polite employers respect. Besides, Miss Manners is reluctant to pick on people while they're trying to make their households function. They look far too desperate.

The Companion

DEAR MISS MANNERS — When a formerly active person finds herself— because of age or permanent disability—no longer able to live alone and hires a live-in companion/sitter, how is this person to be considered—as an attendant or maid? Or is she to be considered as a friend of her employer and therefore a friend of her employer's friends?

For instance, when Mrs. Employer (let's call her Mrs. E) is invited to her grandson's wedding, does her companion/sitter/attendant (let's call her C) sit with the family? When E is invited to a luncheon in a restaurant, is C expected to attend? If so, who should pay for her—E or her hostess? When E is invited to a birthday dinner in her honor in someone's home, is C one of the guests? When E herself entertains, is C a guest?

Please explain the difference between a paid companion, a sitter and an attendant. I realize that this sounds rather crass, but C is, after all, a paid employee, not someone living with E because of family relationship, friendship or love.

GENTLE READER — As Miss Manners understands it, a sitter is someone who comes in temporarily to administer small comforts and generally keep an eye on the employer's (or the employer's relative's) welfare; an attendant is someone in a permanent position, perhaps with some nursing skills; and a paid companion is an impoverished relative struggling mightily with the moral temptation of doing the employer in, with the simultaneous objectives of being relieved of a nuisance and remembered in the will. Perhaps Miss Manners has been reading too many turn-of-the-century novels.

The question of how that person should be treated in the employer's household is a difficult one, as the old etiquette conventions of such relationships have been confused by the admirable modern prohibition against treating anyone as an inferior. Generally, the best arrangement for both parties is that a companion is treated as a member of the household, while an attendant or sitter keeps a private social life, even if needed to convey E to her own social engagements.

Whatever E and C work out, it should be done openly at the time the employment begins, to avoid such disappointed expectations as C's thinking of herself as a member of the family only to find that she seems to be a servant, or, conversely, feeling that she has taken on the round-the-clock obligations of a family member, rather than the limited employment and personal privacy she had wanted.

When E is invited out, C may welcome a few hours away while E's friends are around her to tend to her needs. If C must remain professionally in attendance, she is offered a seat near her charge, and whatever food is served is provided by the hosts, and she is engaged in enough small talk so she does not seem snubbed, without its being so much that she seems expected to perform. If, however, E and C live on terms of friendship, above the necessities of the case, and go about socially together, then C becomes a full member of the social circle, with the guest's standard obligation of making herself charming to her hosts and the other guests. The difference is conveyed to other members of the alphabet who have no other way of knowing, by E's saying either "C and I go everywhere together; I'm sure you'll enjoy getting to know her" or "C will bring me, but don't worry about her; she has things to do if you can find her a quiet place."

The Sitter

All householders believe that it should be the ambition of every adolescent in the neighborhood to earn a dollar by devoting his or her free time to baby-sitting, raking leaves, walking dogs and shoveling snow.

Not only would this teach the young generation the value of money, but (Miss Manners is given to understand) it would build their characters. If they can manage to do all of these activities at once—without letting the dogs and the babies torment one another, or allowing the snow removal to interfere with the leaf raking—they might stand half a chance of growing into responsible citizens. Especially if they stay out of the refrigerator and throw in a free car wash.

It is a sign of teenage truculence that this labor supply claims to have other things to do. Miss Manners has been scornfully told that the alternative activities they claim to have, questionably grouped under the general name "homework," are only listening to loud noises and lurking idly.

In an even more indignant tone, it has been reported to her that nowadays teenagers expect to earn more money. Never mind the fact that they can command fortunes because they were born with the ability to understand computers—doesn't that just go to show you how seriously their characters are in need of construction?

Everybody knows that the cost of living has risen over the years, but we all also know that there are certain items that should be exempt from price changes. That candy bars cost a nickel is the firm belief of every middle-aged person, and the reality is a fresh shock no matter how many trips are made to the vending machine. A bookseller of Miss Manners' acquaintance has so wearied of customers' remarking bitterly "Why, I remember when paperbacks used to cost thirty-five cents," that he has taken to replying, "So do I, and I also remember that you earned three thousand dollars a year then."

Teenagers know nothing of those innocent days, as Miss Manners feels obliged to remind their would-be employers. So it is only kind to offer them the reasonable employment conditions of the era in which they live because they have no halcyon memories to compensate them for modern life.

These include not only reasonable current wages, but reliable working conditions. Agreement must be reached on the exact working duties, as in any job, but with the added realization that it cannot be taken for granted that relatively inexperienced workers know what to do, much less how an individual employer wants it done. If on-the-job amenities are negotiated—refreshment and the use of electronic equipment being the most common—those, too, should be specific.

Furthermore, the employers should be fair. If a job turns out to be significantly different from what was contracted—if the snow turns to ice in midjob, or the child had to be tended through an emergency—compensation should be adjusted.

When Miss Manners hears of grown-ups who don't meet their payrolls promptly, making the excuse that they forgot to go to the bank, or who don't come home when they promised and therefore force conscientious baby-sitters to disobey their own parents' instructions, she wonders what that generation is coming to. And she tries to think of some form of hard labor that might help build their characters.

The Music Teacher

DEAR MISS MANNERS — My son's trombone teacher comes to our house every Friday evening for an hour. I love the convenience, but I don't want to get as personal as she seems to want.

First, she wants to chat, for example, about what went on at my doctor's appointment (the reason I had to move our normal time). At that time of day I am exhausted, and hungry, and need to start dinner. Do I owe her conversation? I'd rather she just taught music and got it done with. Second, she seemed to want me to wait on her. The first appointment, she asked for a cup of coffee. Then milk. Then a second teaspoon, then a refill, then could I take it away.

I suppose I should mention that she is wheelchair-bound, so helping herself is really not an option. But instead of relaxing, I was hopping almost the whole hour. And I paid her for the privilege! I was infuriated, but didn't say so. However, the next two weeks, I made myself very busy doing laundry in the basement. She hasn't asked for tea since. Was I out of line? Do I need to treat a music teacher as an honored guest, with treats and attention?

GENTLE READER — As you know from 19th-century novels, a teacher who gives lessons in the household is accorded quasi-social status. This leads to all sorts of complications, such as the noble widowed father's marrying the poor governess and the impetuous daughter's running off with the French dancing master.

Miss Manners trusts that this puts your problem into perspective. All you need do is to greet the trombone teacher pleasantly, quickly announce "Well, I'll leave you two to your music," as if you knew they were eager to have you out of the way so they could start, and leave the room.

The Advantages of Being in Service

DEAR MISS MANNERS — Our mother, 58, still beautiful, witty, bright, a published writer, and recently widowed, is job hunting. But she is looking in the want ads for a position as housekeeper, cook or personal maid! We are in distress, all seven of us. Our father left our mother with two houses, a houseful of furniture, two cars, and $1600 per month. No bills except for taxes and living expenses.

Our mother feels service is not demeaning. She loves to cook and run a house. She could make up to $1800 per month, plus room and board. She would just like to immerse herself into a cozy home for a couple of years and save her salary.

We are not looking forward to introducing our mother to friends as "The cook for ———" or "———'s housekeeper." She might even end up working for the parents of friends in our social circle! Is this a supreme folly on our mother's part, or are we being stuffy?

GENTLE READER — Stuffy? No, that's not quite the word that comes to Miss Manners' mind. Could it be "insufferable"?

In contrast, your mother sounds splendid. Miss Manners doesn't need a housekeeper (and warns the millions of people who do not to write in, because she doesn't have your mother's name or address), but she would like to have such a wise and gallant lady as a friend. Your mother's pluck in turning bereavement into a chance to be of service to others, in the way she happens to choose, is as fortunate for her own happiness as it will be for the lucky recipients.

Miss Manners does not understand what you mean in your cracks about "service." She dares to say that you did not consider it demeaning when your mother cooked and cared for you. She does, however, understand your fear of having your mother find employment in your own social circle. With your attitudes, you may well suffer by comparison when your friends get to know her. Surely that is more than compensated by the pride you will have in being able to introduce such a lady as your mother.

The Disadvantages

DEAR MISS MANNERS — I have no doubt that the expression "You can't find good help" is a valid complaint but I have some suggestions for keeping a good one once you've found one. I have a house cleaning service which for the most part is problem free. Even the problems that do come up are easily solved. Simply put, there is enough business that I don't have to work for rude inconsiderate people.

This is a job. I know it looks like fun but this is my means of making a living. A time is reserved for your house to be cleaned and you need to honor that arrangement. Sure there will be last minute cancellations due to sickness and other valid reasons (on both sides), but last minute cancellations should be rare. "I was in the mood and cleaned myself," "My house isn't very messy this week" or "My mother stopped over for a visit and it's not a good time" just don't cut it.

Then there are those who don't cancel but make it nearly impossible to clean. Yes, I understand that you should take your turn for the neighborhood preschool playgroup but having them over when I'm due to clean is not a good idea. Having groups of friends or relatives over makes it very difficult. Some things can't be avoided but if your home is like Grand Central Station you may be cleaning it yourself.

Though most people just give me a key there are those who are uncomfortable doing that. If you forget to leave your door unlocked, I lose income. These things happen—but don't just shrug it off with "Oh, well, we'll see you next time." You'd better at least pretend you're sorry and give assurance it won't happen again. Because I understand doesn't mean it's ok to do—be prepared to pay anyway. I overlook the first time only.

You plan ahead weeks or even months for a vacation; wouldn't it be nice if I knew ahead of time, so I could use that time for appointments or doing extra work for those I already work for? I provide a flexibility to make room for special occasions and needs of those I work for. I do practically any job and am good at it. I'm honest and reasonable. I provide the services because I WANT TO not because I can't say no.

While it's true some may behave as they do because of a mistaken view that "she's just the cleaning lady" most start out considerate enough and after a period of time feel they can get away with being rude and inconsiderate. People often mistake my good-naturedness and easy-going way for an indication that I am a door mat and a pushover just waiting to be used and abused. When they are forced to see their mistake they seem so offended. I'd just love to know the reasoning involved in their attempts to blame and otherwise turn the tables making the user and abuser a victim of unkind or unfair treatment.

If the only thing preventing one from taking advantage of me is opportunity— they'll get it but once you make it known you're that sort of person I'll be your ex-cleaning lady!

P.S. I won't even get into the piggishness of some.

GENTLE READER—Miss Manners would say you already have. In whatever state they keep their sties, people who treat their household employees callously have certainly attained a state of piggishness. Miss Manners found your rules eminently fair and she admires both your flexibility and your firmness. The only thing that made her stop short was your suggestion that a reason that the employers don't treat housecleaning as a serious job may be that it looks like fun. It is surely easy for them—easier than they might think, as you point out—to dispense with your services and keep all the fun for themselves.

Honest Mistakes

DEAR MISS MANNERS—I hired a woman I know who lives down the street from us to clean house. She came down the evening before she started and we went over what to clean and what to leave. The following day, she cleaned and did an excellent job, or so we felt at the time.

The next morning, my husband was having a shower and noticed that our shower door was all streaky. It seems that she cleaned the door, which is especially treated, with some kind of new cleaner that ate away the frosted stripes on the inside. I was devastated. That was our new bathroom which we had just completed. She had indicated to me that she cleaned two other bathrooms with the same shower unit, so I trusted that she knew what she was doing.

I called and explained the problem, and she was nice about it and said she would pay to have a new piece of glass put in. She wanted to pay for all of it, but knowing that it would probably be around $80, I decided to pay half, even though I don't feel it was my fault. Her fee for the day was $35, and she insisted that I put it toward the piece of glass. Should I send her the $35? Should I expect her to pay half, or foot the bill myself?

My husband was upset with me, as he didn't feel I should have told her. Her husband won't let her clean for me any more. To complicate things, her mother is my dressmaker (and one I treasure) and I am afraid there will be hard feelings.

GENTLE READER—If someone offered you a responsible cleaning woman, a dressmaker and an approving husband, all for an $80 finder's fee, would you accept? That is the offer Miss Manners is making you, provided you turn over your fee to the cleaning woman, along with a note of appreciation for her offer and for the work she did.

One of the trials of domestic employment is that employers do not have the perspective common in other businesses, where the possibility of a reasonable mistake, especially in a new employee, is built into the situation. You do not want a slapdash cleaning person who treats breakage lightly. A competent person such as you describe should graciously be allowed a mistake or two.

Accusations of Dishonesty

DEAR MISS MANNERS — I clean houses. I don't work for a service, I clean on my own. I have for five years. Many a time, someone has called me to ask where something was. They have always found it. I guess what I am getting at is that a lot of people misplace things, and when they do find them, do you think they would even say "I'm sorry"? Most people that clean other people's homes for a living can't afford to steal. It would cost them their job. I just had to get this off my chest.

GENTLE READER — Miss Manners will be your best ally in fiercely challenging any employer who slurs your honor by hinting that you may have stolen something that is missing. The impulse to blame someone else for one's own lapses is rampant, but decency forbids it.

However, Miss Manners would also like to point out to you that "misplacing things" is not necessarily a euphemism. Lots of people do misplace things. (Time out while Miss Manners finds her glasses, so she can continue this.) Asking help from a housecleaner—who would have been going over the house quite thoroughly—is not an unreasonable idea. What such a person then owes you is not an apology but an expression of thanks.

Dishonorable Intentions

DEAR MISS MANNERS — A guest at my party interrupted my hired help (while serving guests and passing food) to ask if she would work at her home at a specified future date. I feel it would be more discreet to ask me for the telephone number or approach her at another time. Interrupting a festive cocktail party to solicit help for a party of her own was, to me, socially incorrect. Am I too strong in my judgment or a bit behind in the current social graces? Or doesn't it matter at all?

GENTLE READER — Why is it that every time Miss Manners is asked if etiquette has changed, it is in connection with a change that would be for the worse?

What has changed here is that poaching the help is not quite the crime it was when people had full time help and were in fear of competing employers. Presumably, your help could help your guest on another day.

What has not changed is the necessity for discretion in soliciting such help. These people are not only interrupting your party, they are mentioning another party within earshot of people whom they are not inviting, which will never qualify as a social grace.

THE HOUSEHOLD SUPPORT SYSTEM

Emergency Help

Help is on the way. Just stay put, don't panic, and a repairman will be right over, sometime between eight A.M. and five P.M. tomorrow, unless they're running behind, in which case they can't always call, but it will be the next day, for sure, except, wait, that's the weekend, so take it easy, someone will try to get over on Monday, can't say what time, somewhere between eight and five, and there better be someone there to let him in.

Thus, an etiquette crisis is grafted onto a household crisis. A hitherto gentle soul, who had just managed to remain calm in a kitchen full of water, or in a house no longer compensating for the weather outside, or without means to communicate from home to the outside world, begins to exhibit panic-fueled anger in uncharacteristic and decidedly unseemly ways. Miss Manners does not justify the ensuing behavior which, at any rate, carries its own punishment. If the householder doesn't high-handedly cancel the help he sought, thus having to begin the grim process over again with someone else, he has still alerted the rescuer that this is not a safe time to appear. But she does sympathize.

Surely one of the great trials of retaining control over oneself is to encounter the You-Need-Us-More-Than-We-Need-You Support System. Here are its rules:

You understand that we will help you in an emergency, but we will have to work you in then as best we can, because we also have to take care of our regular clients.

If you are one of our regular clients, you stand a better chance of getting help in an emergency, and you are less likely to have emergencies, because we will check things periodically.

Your appointment for periodic checks will be canceled if you are not there at our convenience.

If you are there at our convenience, you will probably have to wait because we are, by virtue of the service we offer, subject to emergency calls that take precedence.

If you don't like this, you can go elsewhere, although you will soon find that anyone else who may help you also operates this way.

The medical profession is credited with having invented this system, but a wide range of service professions have adopted it. Those that do not include emergency duty substitute the personal emergencies of the service givers, rather than those of the clients, in order to explain why they cannot meet a predictable schedule. Now all of life contains such vicissitudes. Surely professionals in any field develop a sense of how long it takes to deal with each kind of problem, how much leeway to leave between appointments and more or less when it is possible to be where. So why don't they tell their clients? Can't the plumber say whether he'll be in that part of town at the beginning, middle or end of the day? Can't the doctor's office call and say she's running late and all appointments must be set back an hour? Can't they apologize when they mess up other people's schedules? It is enough to send ordinary people screaming for and at help.

That is just what Miss Manners is asking them not to do. The way to deal with institutionalized rudeness is persistently enough to convince the offenders that you are not going to let the matter drop, but calmly enough not to allow them to do so on the grounds that they needn't deal with crazies.

Miss Manners understands that this doesn't always work. That is because the set-up is rude. She is trying to shame it into changing, and to suggest that someone could compete successfully in these fields by doing business in a polite and reasonable way. She is amazed at how often it does work to appeal politely to pity, honor and greed, in just that peculiar order. Some individuals can be seduced away from rote devotion to a rude system by sobbing tales of hardship, provided they are phrased to excite sympathy rather than to confer blame. A few will rally to re-establish the honor of their company, provided accounts of its failing are phrased in terms of disillusionment rather than insult. Even the usual methods of threatening to cut off payment or to sue are more effective when they are made with measured politeness than in a fit of unfocused madness.

Those who lack the control to try these methods are free to hire a contractor—who doesn't exactly come free but will promise to be on the spot to deal with all other services households require. The householder then only has to deal with waiting around for the contractor.

Fighting Back

DEAR MISS MANNERS — The new home we purchased has needed constant repairs since the day we moved in. I never receive calls from the service technicians stating when they will come—they merely show up unannounced. I refuse to answer the door unless I received a prior call to inform me of their arrival. I have been branded rude because of this, when I feel I am the one who is put upon by their behavior. My husband states he is happy they even show up!

GENTLE READER — Much as Miss Manners admires you, she knows just how your husband feels. One should not put up with blatant lack of consideration, but one also wants to get the toilet fixed.

Principle is rarely the first concern of people with plumbing problems in their houses, and the power to be inconsiderate goes unchecked. As this is a service contract, the easiest way to deal with it—switching your business to a polite company, if one can be found—is probably not practical. The next steps—appealing reasonably and politely to a manager's good will and getting other customers to make a joint complaint—take time. It is time well spent on behalf of a beleaguered public, as Miss Manners hopes your husband will understand.

Making Nice

DEAR MISS MANNERS — If someone comes over to do a job such as painting the inside of your house or putting in a new rug, is it rude to eat lunch or dinner in front of them? My mom says nobody should eat or drink in front of workers unless you ask them to have something, too. I disagree. If it's in my house, I don't feel it's necessary, as they are not my personal friends.

GENTLE READER — While Miss Manners always admires the hospitable impulse, she fears that your mother is setting an exaggerated standard. People who are having work done in their houses must be allowed to carry on with their normal lives, rather than behaving as if they have a household full of guests.

This does not mean that the obvious needs of workers should be ignored. Lunch is generally provided to regular domestic workers, while those who come in for a limited job are merely given a lunch break. In both cases, employer and employee dine separately so as not to create a social burden for either one of them. Miss Manners assumes that you understand this does not preclude a humane gesture, such as offering water or soft drinks on a hot day.

TIPPING

Who is this person and how much do you have to give him to make him go away for another year? What about that one, whom you consider as much a friend as an employee—if you don't give her what she expects, is she going to be hurt and perhaps slightly vindictive?

Is it any wonder that Miss Manners hates the tipping system? Almost everybody else does—those who give and worry that they don't give enough or give too much, and those who receive, or don't receive, or feel they should receive more.

Nor is Miss Manners fond of the people who keep this system alive—the businesses that appear to charge less and yet save on wages by extracting an added payment from customers; the service people who use this source of income to avoid paying taxes, or who increase it by complaining, soliciting or retaliating against customers; the customers who relish the power of dispensing rewards and punishments but who wouldn't last long themselves if they had jobs where they were docked every time they made an error.

She also has a special reason for wishing that America (where tipping was historically disdained as undignified—until a modern citizenry decided that money was worth more than dignity) would now follow the European lead and build a service charge into the cost of doing business. To Miss Manners' dismay, tipping guidance is considered a duty of the etiquette business. If she doesn't do it, people turn for guidance to the very establishments and individuals who are on the receiving end—as if it were prudent to ask people with extended hands to rule how much should be put into those hands.

Yet the kind of guidance people want is impossible to give. Miss Manners could easily give them principles: 15 to 20 percent, depending on the poshness of the establishment and the unusualness of the task; bills, not change, which is to say not less than $1, even for such services as carrying your briefcase from just outside the hotel door to just inside the hotel door.

But people don't want principles. They want figures.

"How much should I give my doorman at Christmas?" they demand, as if this were a universal problem, and not one that can be better solved by asking a neighbor what the custom is in the particular building. These are the same people who expect Miss Manners to select "the perfect present" for people they know well and she has never laid eyes on. ("What should I get my wife and my secretary?" they ask Miss Manners as the shops are closing on Christmas Eve. She advises them to get the wife a secretary and the secretary a wife.)

Another useless question is why one should have to tip certain people, such as taxi drivers, waiters and hairdressers and not others who perform similar functions, such as bus drivers, airline stewards and psychoanalysts. The answer is "Because." Because this silly system grew up haphazardly, and so now certain jobs depend on tips to round out the wages, while in others the compensation comes complete in the paycheck.

Well, maybe not complete. There is still that extra something at Christmas for people who are not customarily tipped but should get something because they give such good service and might sulk if they're not. It's called a bonus.

Year-End Funds

DEAR MISS MANNERS — Each year, my condominium association sends a letter to all unit owners requesting a "voluntary contribution" to the Employee Christmas Fund. This tradition, as they call it, allows us to show (in an anonymous way) our appreciation to those individuals "who work so hard for us all year long." I receive a similar letter from the management of a private club to which I belong.

Although I contribute to these funds because I do not wish to seem ungrateful or Scrooge-like, these requests strike me as inappropriate and, indeed, tacky. One would not expect a letter from the general manager of the law firm one employs, seeking a holiday fund contribution for the lawyers "who worked so hard on your account all year long." Is it unreasonable to think that it should be the condominium association's responsibility to provide Christmas bonuses for its employees? I realize, of course, that the unit owners pay for it either way, but slightly higher assessments seem more gracious than these brazen appeals for cash.

GENTLE READER — This is just a wild guess on Miss Manners' part, but if you check the year's accounts, you may find that you pay your lawyer more than you pay your janitor. Your comparison is therefore irrelevant: Tipping is a means of supplementing ill-paid work (even though custom has so much influenced which jobs it applies to and which not, as to make this distinction unreliable).

Mind you, Miss Manners abhors the practice of tipping, which she finds unfair to the employee, because it puts too much arbitrary power in the not-always-fair hands of the client. She actually agrees with you that it would be better to charge the condominium owners more and use that money to increase salaries or provide bonuses. However, until such time as she manages to transform the system (over the loud protests of the employees of snob-oriented businesses, where outrageous tips are often offered and not always declared on income taxes), one must cooperate. It would be Scrooge-like, not to mention wrong, to deny these workers their expected income merely because one doesn't like the method by which this is provided.

Tipping Service Firms

DEAR MISS MANNERS—I engage a housecleaning service for a few hours one morning each week. My concern is about gratuities. The same young man has been cleaning my house for several months, but there were several different cleaners before that. At Christmas, do I tip only my most recent helper? In the event that there should be someone else just before, should I tip that person as well? I understand that I do not have to tip the owner of the business. I plan to give a gift certificate to an audio-visual sales and rental store. Is this appropriate?

GENTLE READER—Gift certificates are a pathetic compromise convenient to people who do not trust their judgment about selecting the right present for those whose tastes they ought to know. In the business world, employers and employees should not be expected to know one another's tastes, so cash is given, in the form of bonuses or tips. Why limit what the recipient can do with it?

A cleaning service is an attempt to get around the awkwardnesses and insecurities of the individual householder–cleaning person arrangement. While you could tip your most frequent helper directly, Miss Manners suggests you give a sum to the owner with the direction that he or she distribute it proportionately to all of those who have been employed in your house.

Not Tipping Owners

DEAR MISS MANNERS—My hair stylist of 10 years has, as of this week, opened her own salon. Quickly, do I continue to tip her even though it all goes into her pocket??

GENTLE READER — The rule to which you refer—that it is an insult to tip the owner of a business—is still in effect. The only thing that has changed is that an awful lot of people no longer mind being insulted by money.

Miss Manners would prefer to presume that your hair stylist is proud of her new status. To show that you are recognizing that, rather than stiffing her, you should accompany your tipless payment with a statement about your pleasure in her success and what a privilege you find it to be attended by the owner.

Tipping Individuals

DEAR MISS MANNERS — What is the correct way to tip the person who carries out your groceries at the grocery store?

GENTLE READER — With cash. Handing over a banana, or a can that rolled out of the bag, is not considered a tip.

THE VOLUNTEER SUPPORT SYSTEM

Job Proposals

Etiquette reports about visiting mothers-in-law may be neatly sorted into two even piles, Miss Manners has discovered. Half are complaints about mothers-in-law who invade kitchens and nurseries and simply start doing things their own way, presumably to express distaste for the way the tasks have been done or left undone. They seem to feel that they can take over the household. Miss Manners is asked to scold them for being arrogant. The other half are complaints about mothers-in-law who sit there and do nothing, seemingly oblivious to the cooking, cleaning or child care chores going on around them. They seem to feel they are there to be waited upon. Miss Manners is asked to scold them for being arrogant.

(Wait, there's one letter left over. It's from a daughter-in-law who wants to know how to persuade her mother-in-law to visit more often. Without actually throwing it aside as a crank letter, Miss Manners is forced to classify it as statistically insignificant.)

Before starting an in-law matching service, Miss Manners would like to clear up a few things that are puzzling her. Such as: Aren't these the same daughters-in-law that the mothers were complaining were incapable of writing letters? Failing an answer to that: Where are all the other relatives? An occasional sister-in-law is cited, but fathers-in-law and brothers-in-law are held responsible only for their own particular messes, not for any general housekeeping. Also, where are the husband-son people while all this controversy is raging? It doesn't take that long to pick up some milk and detergent.

So we may be talking about more than meets the eye. Even so, Miss Manners is determined not to uncover any nasty psychological stuff. The beauty of etiquette is that it is supposed to clear up conflicts at the surface level, without exposing all those ugly tangles underneath.

The proper question to which she will therefore address herself is: What, if anything, can a visiting relative do that will not be classified as either interfering or shirking? The general rules for all houseguests are to straighten up after themselves, and to offer to help with mealtime-related work, but also to accept refusals of help. The purpose is to make the mechanics of visiting as light as possible, without presuming that the work is really shared. The hosts are in charge, and reciprocal visits should even things out.

In the case of relatives, however, there are complicating factors. The ordinary host-guest relationship is skewed by the respect due to age and parenthood, the habit of instruction from parent to child and the overwhelming fact of not being able to say "Okay, that's it, these people are never setting foot here ever again." In addition, some individuals prefer the work-as-you-go system, by which the visitor takes an active part in the household, while others prefer the work-on-your-own-turf system, by which the sharing is done sequentially, depending on who is hostess. Attitudes are not necessarily paired in the same family.

Regardless of preference, a visiting relative must claim to be of the former persuasion while the hostess must claim to be of the latter. Thus, the proper opening dialogue is:

> VISITOR: "Darling, you would really be doing me a favor to tell me how I can help you. You do everything so beautifully it looks effortless, but I know how hard you work. Besides, idleness makes me restless."
>
> HOSTESS: "Oh, I won't hear of it. You just make yourself comfortable and don't worry about a thing. I have everything all planned, and I just want you to enjoy yourself."

This exchange cannot be skipped; those who either just start doing things or get out of the way are bound to guess wrong about what is really wanted. Neither statement is to be taken at face value. These are conventional openings from which negotiation can proceed.

Specific tasks (or non-tasks, such as "Would you be a dear and check to see if the baby's still sleeping?") can be suggested or offered ("Shall I run in and see what Nicole is fussing about?"). All such tasks must be limited and obvious. What gets helpful people into trouble in other people's houses is figuring things out for themselves.

All housekeepers—good and bad—believe that their systems for doing things are logical, and anyone else ought to be able to deduce them from first principles. Of course that's where the glasses go; no place else would make sense. How can anyone in her right mind think that the towels should be folded in thirds? However, it is beyond anyone's power to detect a system in anybody else's household. Miss Manners suspects that half those poor vilified mothers-in-law decided it was best to go ahead and do what seemed to need doing, as well as they could; and the other half decided that it was best not to attempt things and do them wrong.

Compensation

DEAR MISS MANNERS—I am a new and single mom, and I don't know the polite thing to do when my family (or his) babysits for me. Should I offer to pay grandparents or godparents when they baby-sit?

GENTLE READER—People often ponder why we have to have etiquette rules, instead of just letting the well-intentioned, such as yourself, follow their generous instincts. It is in order to avoid having kindly impulses blow up in kind faces. Politeness has to follow well-known custom, to avoid lending itself to misinterpretation.

Your thought, Miss Manners assumes, is that the grandparents are going out of their way to accommodate you, and that you should therefore "pay them back." So you should, but not in money.

All parents (not just new and single, but even old and double) should do everything they can to make such occasions convenient and pleasant for the grandparents, to thank them profusely, and to do return favors for them. But the act of giving money for services dismisses their claim as grandparents and puts them into the category of hired help, which is highly likely to be interpreted as an insult.

The House Watcher

DEAR MISS MANNERS — What are the responsibilities of responders to home burglar alarm systems—the person who is on a notification list to be phoned by the security company if the alarm is sounded?

Typically, the police are summoned to drive by, and you're asked to go to the residence to reset the alarm. My sister had complained that a friend had given her name to the company without discussing it with her, which she only discovered when the friend's alarm went off and the company called. So you can imagine my surprise the following week, when my sister's home security company phoned me that her alarm had sounded. When I reached my sister that evening, after a day of trying to find her, she stated that I should "just ignore the company whenever they call."

This summer, a neighbor, whom I had invited for coffee a day prior to her vacation, handed me an extra set of house keys along with their security number and directions, "just in case our alarm goes off." Taken by surprise, I muttered, "Sure."

My in-laws move to their second home for six months every year, and we're told, "We were sure you wouldn't mind, so we left your name . . ." Sure enough, they left yesterday, and today we received a call. I estimate we get three to six calls from their firm per year, which isn't much, but timing can make the calls dreadful: Christmas Day; waking you up at 2 a.m.; during a dinner party; with a house full of guests, etc.

In addition to the imposition, what if I authorize a "police drive by" and decide to check the system first thing tomorrow morning, instead of immediately, and then find that a burglary has been committed? Am I responsible? Drive time to my in-laws is 20 minutes, so I like to think I wouldn't ever encounter a crime in progress, but what about my neighbor, who is only a two-minute walk away?

To date, we've been fortunate to only encounter false alarms. But no one has explained what they expect. Shouldn't this be discussed, and permission asked in advance to use your name and give out your phone number?

GENTLE READER — First, Miss Manners would like to congratulate you on identifying an entirely new area of manners, a subdivision, to be sure, of the ancient requirement of assisting others in emergencies, but a novel one. She hopes that it will be a comfort to you, when you are next awakened at two A.M., especially if your dinner guests are still there, to know that you have made a contribution to the field. (She also apologizes for gratuitously suggesting that you might nod off in front of your guests.)

That alarms are notoriously whimsical, given to bleating falsely just to see everybody scramble, does not alter the fact that they are there to warn of imminent danger. Who should spring in to help one in danger if not those near (such as the neighbors) and dear (as we politely designate all relatives and friends)? The designated person of trust is in the position of the executor of the will, except that the job is not done once and for all.

Miss Manners thoroughly agrees with you that they should neither be named without permission, nor have their services taken for granted. Because this is relatively new—at least in comparison with keeping an eye out for the milkman, feeding the cat or switching the lights off and on so someone appears to be at home—she suspects that offenders have not considered their obligations, but merely respond to their alarm companies' inquiry about whom they wish to trust, without considering the effect.

So here is a new ruling: One must ask permission to list such a person, and one must offer profuse thanks for acceptance (which can hardly be decently denied among those with such obvious claims on you) and for any services that are subsequently performed. One must also provide these people with a list of what to do and where to find them, or at least where to begin looking. "Run into the house and see if you can rabbit punch the burglar and snatch back my goods" cannot be the instruction. Checking that the police have paid proper attention is what is required until the owners can be located.

The House Sitter

DEAR MISS MANNERS — Some friends stayed in our house while we were away, and in a sincere attempt to be helpful, obviously spent many hours weeding our brick patio. Unfortunately, in so doing, they removed the beautiful mosses and other special plants I'd been cultivating there for many years, leaving a barren, weed-prone expanse.

What can I say to them? I feel I must say something and praise their good intentions, but "Thank you" is not what I feel! I certainly don't want to scold them, but as they may again be using our home, how can I tactfully let them know that if they want to be helpful, I'd like them to direct their efforts elsewhere?

GENTLE READER — If etiquette only required people to say "Thank you" when they were overflowing with gratitude, the polite life would be a lot easier. Especially

Miss Manners'. But it also requires people to give thanks for good intentions, however much the words stick in the craw, and however disastrous the results. Miss Manners has a good deal of trouble, for example, in persuading people that "This doesn't go with anything I have—please get me what I want" is not a correct response to an unwelcome present. So you must thank them for what cannot, after all, be undone. In the unlikely event that you again allow these people to be unsupervised in your house, you could say, without reference to the past, "By the way, please don't touch the grounds—we have complicated gardening plans for when we get back."

The House Sitter's Expenses

DEAR MISS MANNERS—A friend asked me to live in his house for about three months for security reasons. I am happy to house-sit gratis, as a favor, but do not feel that my service should end up costing me additional living expenses, since I have my own home and am not staying in my friend's house as a boarder. Should I ask him to reimburse me for expenses which I will incur while house-sitting, such as paper goods and food?

GENTLE READER—Additional living expenses for food and paper goods? How do you figure? Do you plan to double your eating, one set of meals at home and one at your friend's? And, ah, wipe up twice as many messes?

House-sitting does usually offer an advantage to the sitter, as well as the householder, but generally in the form of free rent or the chance to enjoy the location or quarters, none of which you need. It can also be done as a pure favor of course. Miss Manners has the impression that you are not as happy to do this as you declare, or you wouldn't be playing with the idea of double billing. Perhaps it would be better if you did not perform this particular favor and encouraged your friend to find someone who might be happier doing it. Even from his point of view, it is not a good idea to leave someone in charge of his house and possessions who is looking around for extra compensation.

The Carpool

Crime is not the only nasty possibility to be considered before offering or accepting a lift in an automobile. Miss Manners is the hapless recipient of evidence that this simple courtesy screeches into rudeness with frightening speed.

Drivers write to complain about the rudeness of people who ask them for lifts and even more bitterly about the rudeness of people whom they have voluntarily offered to drive. Passengers write to complain equally about the rudeness of drivers who don't offer to take them and those who do.

The charge all around is being inconsiderate of other people's convenience and money. These are not roadside hitchhikers and whatever comes down the road. These are people who start on friendly enough terms to know or share one another's travel plans. They are friends going out together, or friends of friends meeting under a host's roof, or neighbors with similar destinations, or members of the same congregation or organization going home in the same direction. Yet one way or another, they all end up feeling they have been taken for a ride.

Knowing something of the state of driving manners in general, Miss Manners was ready to put all this down to the popular belief that etiquette does not belong on the road because it might be a distraction from speeding, passing, darting, dodging, listening to music, grooming, making finger gestures and other traditional mobile pleasures. If people regularly leave etiquette behind as they pull out of their parking spaces, of course they will get on one another's nerves.

On closer examination, the complaints which these people are kindly passing on to her have to do less with the state of driving than with a problem that also underlies the equally deplorable states of hospitality and present-giving. These are the twin concepts of reciprocity and gratitude that are supposed to regulate social relationships. Failing to understand them results in viewing a social situation in terms of commerce or entitlement.

Passengers ignore the cost of running a car, drivers complain, and fail to contribute to the gas or upkeep. Drivers were going there anyway, passengers assert, so it doesn't actually cost them anything. Passengers think nothing of accepting rides all the time with hardly so much as thanks in return, the drivers report. Drivers think nothing of leaving people stranded, or canceling, or dropping them off short of their destinations, the passengers say, and have no sympathy for the danger and hardship of trying to get around when one is not fortunate enough to be able to drive. Miss Manners sees that all of them have a point, and that they all miss the main point.

In regular arrangements among acquaintances—carpools—the work and the cost should be discussed openly and divided in a way that seems fair to all concerned. Yet to treat an occasional favor as not a favor—as a service for sale, like public transportation, or as a duty that nondrivers owe to drivers—is insulting. Instead, we have gratitude, which recognizes that a favor has been received, and reciprocation, which keeps the burden distributed evenly.

Miss Manners agrees that offering lifts when one knows people who need them is a basic kindness. Obviously, the recipients cannot offer the exact kindness in return—they don't drive. Gracefully buying the gas is one partial solution, and picking up the lunch bills on joint excursions is another. It should be noted in addition that money is not the only point when a favor has been given and accepted. If they feel it is, the passengers should stick to taxis, and drivers who expect to be paid for rides should be studying for their taxi licenses.

People who offer favors should not be thinking of getting an immediate return in kind. People who accept favors should be thinking of favors—kind acts that are a convenience, as are offers of lifts—that they can do in return.

The Driver's Authority

DEAR MISS MANNERS — A friend whose children attend religious education classes where I teach one afternoon a week asked me if I could take her children back and forth. My friend has neither thanked me nor offered to reciprocate for other activities in which her and my children are involved. Each time I have the five children—my three, her two—in the car, there is bickering. There are also wrappers from their snacks left in my car. I have spoken to all five, but it hasn't helped. How can I stop transporting her children without severing our friendship?

GENTLE READER — You might invite your friend to sit in on class the day you teach the doing-unto-others rule, but Miss Manners supposes you want something more direct.

Invoke the captain-of-the-ship rule: "You know, when I'm the driver, I feel responsible for everyone's safety. I'm having trouble getting across to your children that when they're in my car, they must obey my rules. Perhaps you could make them understand that—or find someone to drive them who has laxer rules." If you say this firmly enough, your friend may not notice that candy wrappers do not constitute a safety hazard.

Donating Professional Service

DEAR MISS MANNERS — I have a daughter who is just getting started in her own catering business, and another daughter who lives a very comfortable life with her husband, and they enjoy entertaining. The married sister is preparing to give a dinner party for twenty, which will include many affluent guests. Should the daughter who is just getting started in catering prepare and serve the food in her sister's home?

GENTLE READER — Let us talk about the manners that would be required if she did, since it is not Miss Manners' place to tell grown sisters of their duties to each other, when their parent wisely refrains from doing so. (Still less does Miss Manners want to get into the question of whether or not the hostess's sister pays. She prefers an equal exchange of services among immediate family members, but is aware of the abuse of relatives expecting professional services to be abundantly available for free.)

The charming way to carry off such a party would be for the sister who is hostess to announce proudly that her sister is making the dinner, as if it were a favor to her, rather than a way of showcasing the new caterer's talents. You cannot invite people to dinner with the expectation that they will sign up to buy the services they enjoyed.

Both sisters should keep in mind that it is rude to make commercial overtures to guests. Rather, only after the guests begin to exclaim how good the food is should the admission be made she is now a professional, and it must be in the tone of family news. There should be no attempt whatsoever to suggest that the guests could hire her. Even enthusiasm should not be over-interpreted— politeness requires them to praise her, even if they hated the meal. At the most, one of the sisters can write down, upon request only, the caterer's telephone number so that serious interest can be shown by a business call after the social event. Not only is this polite to the guests, who will not feel pressured to patronize the business of their friend's sister, but it will put subsequent transactions on a businesslike basis. Miss Manners wouldn't imagine that your daughter wants possible clients to imagine that she goes around cooking dinners as a favor.

Conscription

DEAR MISS MANNERS — If a family member from out of state stays with us for two weeks, should they do dishes?

GENTLE READER — This question can only come up with one of two types of visiting relatives: those who do dishes when you don't want them to, and those who don't when you do want them to. Miss Manners gathers you have the latter.

One should also factor in that relatives come in three generations. If yours are a generation older than you, the most you can do is to say, "Oh, dear, I'm exhausted, but I hate to leave the dishes." If they are your own generation, you may say, "Do you want to wash or dry?" (Modern version: "Scrape or load?") If they are younger, i.e., your children, you should say (not ask) pleasantly, "How about giving me a hand," as you point at the kitchen on your way out of it.

Quitting

DEAR MISS MANNERS — Recently my dear brother graciously invited me to his home to celebrate my birthday, a dinner party which some of our mutual friends were also to attend. He suggested that I arrive early so that we would have a more personal visit, which of course I was most glad to do. We live over 100 miles apart, and seldom see each other. After about an hour of "catching up," as my brother and his room-mate began preparations for dinner, I asked if there was anything I could do to help. My hosts then produced the silver coffee service, a cleaning agent, and some soft cloths, therefore obliging me to fulfill the duties of "char-woman." May I add that the coffee service was not used at the gathering? While I personally am not above such menial labor, it does leave one's hygienic appearance compromised, and I did feel a bit embarrassed at the dinner table.

Is it acceptable, after offering assistance, to refuse a task that should not have remained until the last minute? Or at the next informal occasion, arrive with rubber gloves and knee pads in tow? Or do I sit by expecting to be catered to, appearing to be unappreciative of the efforts made to ensure an enjoyable, informal gathering?

GENTLE READER — Miss Manners is not in the habit of psychoanalyzing the childhood influences of people who come to her with etiquette problems, but she really does need the background to this problem. Did you grow up doing the domestic chores while your brother was excused? Do you assume, perhaps from ancient but painful experience, that it is dangerous to oppose his wishes?

Otherwise, this would be a relatively simple problem. If asked to polish the silver, you could say reasonably, "No, it's too messy a job, and I want to look nice for your guests" and offer to do something else. If you had done the polishing, you could affectionately have prompted him to use the pot by declaring, after dinner, "After all that polishing, we forgot the coffee!" As a matter of fact, you can start doing that now. Miss Manners doesn't accept psychological excuses for not improving one's behavior.

Chapter Six

THE VISITORS

THE WELCOME AND
THE UNWELCOME

When people complain to Miss Manners about their houses being overrun with critters, she feels sympathetic but helpless. These creatures are apparently arriving in hordes without warning, sometimes whole families of them, swarming all over the place until the people who live there can no longer stand it. Summer seems to bring them out, although year-round invasions are reported in warm climates. They eat everything in sight and much that isn't. They are quick to forage in cupboards, drawers and closets and so deft at this that nothing can be successfully sealed off. Everywhere they go, they leave a nasty mess. Domestic life becomes suddenly less comfortable and more expensive. There seems to be no protection from them. Nobody knows how they got in, or how to get rid of them. "Do something!" Miss Manners is implored. "We can't stand living like this!"

Miss Manners shares the victims' dismay but was initially at a loss to figure out what they expected her to do. She is not in the pest control business. Surely they should be approaching exterminators, instead. Then she found out they were talking about their friends and relatives. The pests were houseguests. So perhaps she *is* in the pest control business.

She will therefore go about that business in the proper way (as she does everything in the proper way because she can't help herself). Yes, yes, she will help you get your house back and keep it safe from subsequent invasion. But first a disclaimer:

Miss Manners is not an exterminator, not even a social exterminator. She will not allow you to treat your guests rudely, even when the guests are rude. Nor does she want to discourage anyone from having houseguests. On the contrary, her interest in the situation is in putting visiting on a polite level so that it can be enjoyed by both hosts and guests.

House visits among family and friends can be a lovely way to deepen an existing bond. The convenience to travelers who find a home base on their vacations should be equaled by the pleasure of stay-at-homes who can enjoy sociability without having to ruin their clothes by jamming them into carry-on bags. All it takes to make this pleasant is a bit of politeness on the part of the guests. But this is what Miss Manners is told is in short supply.

All right, now let's talk about pest control.

1. What is the point of entry for these pests?

In most cases, Miss Manners finds that it was an open-door invitation: "Anytime you're in town, you can stay with us" or "We have a great new vacation house, come on up whenever you like." Miss Manners, who believes in hospitality, does not want to nail this door shut. She only wants to add a screen door, so to speak. Charming as these invitations are, they are either too vague or not vague enough. The proper style is either "We'd love to have you come up for Labor Day weekend, Friday evening to Monday afternoon" or "We're up here all summer, and would be delighted to have you here for a few days or a week if we can get our schedules to mesh, so do give us a call."

2. Suppose we thought everything was plugged up, but they got in anyway?

Well, they got in someplace. Let's investigate the weak spots. If it was at the invitation of another member of the family, Miss Manners believes it is your job, not hers, to work out an acceptable policy. She asks you to bear in mind that all members of a household are entitled to keep it open to their intimates, although they may bear a special responsibility to keep them from annoying other household members. (Translation from the euphemistic: You can't ban your in-laws or your step-children, but you can ask their child or parent to get them to keep out of your study or turn down the CD player.)

3. What if nobody invited them? They just announced they were coming, or they actually showed up on the doorstep.

Then someone let down the guard, probably out of the goodness of not wanting to seem rude. There is a polite way to bar entry. One offers profuse apologies and regrets ("Oh, what a shame you'll be here then—ordinarily, we'd love to have you here, but that's a bad time for us") but no specific excuses that can be countered (with such blithe reassurances as "Oh, don't worry about that—we'll just entertain ourselves").

4. Okay, we shouldn't have let them in. But we did, and they overran the house—so how do we get rid of them now that they've taken possession?

Politely, of course. By thanking them for coming, and kindly offering them a ride to the station.

Taking Precautions

DEAR MISS MANNERS—We have some relatives who stop by our house every Friday night between 7 and 10 p.m. and stay for the weekend. Should our porch light be on before they arrive, or can we wait until we hear them drive up before turning it on?

GENTLE READER—Do you want them to find the house? Miss Manners is only asking. In that case, it would make sense to turn on the lights before they arrive. You might as well do that, anyway. It is difficult to conceal a whole house, even in darkness, and it will be no less trouble to you if your relatives miss and drive into a tree than if they can find their way.

Taking Control

DEAR MISS MANNERS — Throughout the years, our home has been the stopping-off place by many for fellowship, a bed, and food. Many summers, we have live-in company representing various "groups" (friends, relatives) for up to three months. On top of that, friends of mine have come to expect me to have an open-door to their college-career aged kids, as the parents in most cases have moved away or split. I have found there is no peace in our home, no time to have a private chat with our own four college students; the food budget is huge; the wet towels and dirty bed linens constant.

When I become "taken for granted" in this type of giving, I find it makes me angry and anxious for more free time myself. When I try to explain this to the "regulars," they feel hurt and "kicked out," no matter how I word it.

How would you find peace when for years, you've had relatively none, due to a constantly "used" home? All of the people I refer to are lovely people when here. I guess I'm tired from such hard work and constant interruption. My friends tell me I'm lucky people like it here. I love people, but where is the balance?

In this day of split homes and mobility, there are lots of single kids in their teens and twenties looking for a home-base. I used to think divorce was hardest on young children, but my observation is that it is also earth-shaking for the older kids. As a wife and mom whose blessings are innumerable, I'd like to share them without being taken for granted. Where do you draw the line, and how do you do it?

GENTLE READER — At the risk of sounding like your unhelpful friends, Miss Manners would like to say that your living arrangements sound ideal to her. A bustling household, where emotional sustenance is supplied to young people who are lovely in return, is surely a wonderful place in which to live, for you and your children, as well as for your guests.

You know that, or you wouldn't be doing this. You probably also know that you needn't worry about a too peaceful—which is to say, lonely—old age, because it will doubtless be full of requited love from the many people with whom you have shared your blessings. However, that doesn't help with the wet towels, does it?

Miss Manners must remind you that it is your household, and your immediate family's, and that you must set the rules for your guests. No fair-minded person could take personal offense if your needs, as well as theirs, are put forward. Until you do so, young people are likely to assume that you prefer running things as you do, with you doing all the work and not asking for privacy.

You must learn to reserve periods when you will not accept guests. "We'd love to see you in late June, but we always keep the first two weeks after our children come home from college, just to be together" is an acceptable response to a request to visit; or "No, the next few months are bad for us to have houseguests, but if you're going to be in town anyway, let's set up an evening when you can come to dinner."

Young guests can easily share in the household work. You can establish this with the invitation or when showing them around upon their arrival—"I'm afraid there's not much service around here. I hope you don't mind looking after yourself and your room, and taking a turn, along with the rest of us, at the cooking and cleaning."

A way to cut food expenses without seeming to charge for your hospitality is to include among the errands sending people out for the groceries they need for their turns at cooking. During long visits, you can also say, "I'm exhausted—would you mind making dinner?" or "Would you kids be angels and round up all the towels and throw them in the wash?" or "I'm going to be shut up in my room all day—would you people tend to whatever needs doing?"

This is not only a sensible way for you to make your life more manageable but a kindness to your guests. Miss Manners assures you that the lovely people you describe will be only too happy to learn how they can make you some return.

Taking Advantage

For the benefit of anyone who is spending vacation time staying with friends, Miss Manners would like to explain the difference between a private residence and a hotel.

That's right, bills. People you know who let you stay with them don't present bills. They don't even ask for an impression of your credit card. Hotels do. Therefore, staying with someone saves you money. You noticed that, did you?

Some of you are not above drawing this advantage to the attention of your hosts—as the hosts, in turn, have drawn your observation to Miss Manners' attention. They are not as delighted with your frank charm as you must suppose when you call up and say "We don't want to pay for a hotel, so we thought we'd stay with you."

Announcing that you want a room at the cheapest rate possible is not the only habit that goes over better at hotels than with friends. Hotel manners, even good hotel manners such as tipping for service and leaving the guest bathrobe lying around to make it clear you didn't pack it, do not apply to people's homes.

You're not supposed to volunteer your availability to relatives, let alone friends. In-laws and intimates can pose this as a question ("Would it be convenient for us to be there on the second weekend in August?"), but others can do no more than hint ("We'll be out your way in mid-August and would love to see you"). Even if this produces an invitation, they are required to be coy ("Do you mean it? Because we wouldn't want to put you to any trouble") before accepting. (There is nothing rude about a targeted host's replying instead "Oh, what a shame, we have plans for then" or "We'd love to see you too—where will you be staying?" The would-be guest is honor-bound to take this unflinchingly.)

An accepted guest is obliged to maintain throughout the visit the stance that his or her real interest is not in saving money but in gaining the host's company while avoiding being waited upon. In other words—those very words that bitter hosts inevitably use—they are not to treat the place like a hotel.

In a hotel, you don't need to make the bed, mop up the bathroom, put away incidental dishes you use and offer to help with the chores. As a houseguest, you do. In a hotel, you can announce in advance what you want, and complain if you don't get it. As a houseguest, you can only own up to preferences if the host makes repeated attempts to extract them, and whatever happens, you have to keep swearing that everything is just as you like it. In a hotel, you can come and go as you please. As a houseguest, you have to arrange your plans around your hosts' schedule and give them the opportunity to accompany you when you go elsewhere, without making it sound like their duty. In addition, you are expected to be alert enough to their wishes to avoid over-doing any of this, refraining from helping with chores they prefer to do alone or from appearing to want to be with them so much that they never have a minute to themselves.

All that is required as payment for their hospitality is an effusive letter, a thoughtful present and a reciprocal invitation (as well as an invitation to dine out in their own town). Some people might think it cheaper to pay bills. Miss Manners is afraid that some hosts, fed up with guests who do not follow the above rules, are threatening to present them.

Taking Worse Advantage

DEAR MISS MANNERS — Friends arrived for a six-day visit, bringing with them a case of wine which we assumed was our hostess gift. We provided breakfast, lunch and dinner, even taking them out for a meal. At no time did they take us out or bring any other gift into the house. Near the end of the visit, our guests presented us with a bill for the wine—of which they had drunk several bottles.

Since there was a possibility that they had thought we had asked for the wine, we paid for it. At the time, I wondered if there was something that needed to be said, perhaps along these lines: "Your total non-participation in supporting this joint social venture makes us feel taken advantage of." Nothing of the kind was said, and now we are struggling with feelings of resentment. Any suggestions?

GENTLE READER—You have already followed Miss Manners' suggestion, which would be to say nothing of the kind. However, that should not prevent either one of us from having the satisfaction of thinking what could be said if one were willing to be rude.

Since this is only a fantasy—because you were commendably incapable of being rude and Miss Manners certainly is—why settle for something so crude as a scolding? Why not dream of sending them a bill slightly larger than the one they sent you, but marked "corking fee"?

Not Taking Advantage

DEAR MISS MANNERS—Friends of ours who live in a distant city have business here, and when they do, they say they will visit us if convenient to us. It seems that their visits are more and more frequently to conduct business on his part, and less and less a friendly visit. I feel that I am used as a motel, because the two go off in the mornings, not inviting me, and she shops, they lunch together, sightsee, then come to our house for dinner and bed. Am I resentful needlessly? My husband says yes, but, then, he has no part in the entertainment other than his presence.

GENTLE READER—It is usually a good thing that hosts cannot overhear what their guests say to each other in private, but in this case, Miss Manners believes it would be useful for you to do some imaginary eavesdropping.

(Note: Real eavesdropping on houseguests is immoral, and carries its own punishment. You learn more about your house than any sensible person would want to know.)

HE: Why don't you sleep in, and I'll meet you back here when we break for lunch?

SHE: No, no, don't even think of it. I'd love to, but Arabella would feel she had to tiptoe around all morning, and then make lunch for us. I already feel that she's doing too much—we come so often, and she makes those wonderful dinners. I'll just go into town when you do, and do some shopping or something.

HE: Ask her to join us. The two of you could shop together, and then I'll meet you for lunch.

SHE: I'm afraid she'd feel she had to, when she has her own things to do. And she could probably stand a break from us.

HE: Okay, but let's head back here after lunch. We could help her cook dinner, or whatever.

SHE: I've asked, and she won't let me help. I don't like anyone else in my kitchen, either, so I know how she feels.

HE: So what are you suggesting?

SHE: Let's just stay in town and tell her we're doing some sightseeing so she has a breather. As long as we get back in time for dinner. That's the best time for socializing—which of course is why I came along on the trip in the first place.

HE: I know. It makes such a difference to me to have an evening with friends, and not just have to stay in some motel room feeling lonely.

Taking Liberties

DEAR MISS MANNERS — My husband and I have been married almost a year now. We have a get together every Friday night with his friend and his wife. I've always gotten along with them, but lately his friend has been rubbing my back, feeling my hair, and talking about obscene things around me. How do I nicely tell him to stop—I'm a married woman.

GENTLE READER — One need not be married to object to such behavior, but since you are, Miss Manners has a suggestion. Ask your husband the same question you asked Miss Manners.

THE POLITE REQUEST

With the prospect of pleasant weather and a bit of leisure, we have a resurgence of the charming custom of Looking People Up. People in resort areas. People in areas featuring tourist attractions. People with vacation houses. People with swimming pools. What nice people they all are, and wouldn't this be a good time to say hello—for, say, a week or two?

Miss Manners is always glad to hear of innocent sociability. She tries very hard not to assume any relationship between the seasonal popularity of these people and their living accommodations. So do they. This is why most of them have had their hospitable impulses severely strained. Frankness being in fashion, they have had it made only too clear to them that they are perceived as useful, more than desirable, by friends who don't scruple to conceal their interest in free accommodations or recreational facilities.

Their hostly hearts no longer leap with happy anticipation when they hear something like this:

"We've got some vacation coming, and we can't really afford to go anywhere great this year, so we thought we'd come down and spend a week or two with you. With what we'd save on hotels, we're going to fly, but don't you have a second car we can use if we need it? Anyway, the kids are excited about your pool, so they'll probably want to stick around. But maybe if there are any good shows in town, you could pick up some tickets for us."

The fact is that hosts, no matter how open-hearted, want to be in control of their invitations, which is to say, not unreasonably, of their living quarters. Trust Miss Manners that even the ones who have recklessly gone around saying "Come and see us anytime" feel this way—even if they have announced that they are too "casual" (a major term of self-congratulation these days) to expect any formalities.

A serious invitation has a date in it—not "Come anytime," but "Come on the 16th." If the prospective hosts have any sense, it will have two dates: "We'd love to have you come on the 16th, and stay till the 30th" or "Come down on a Thursday night, and stay until Sunday night, so we can have a long weekend."

This is not to say that generalized invitations are insincere. What the literal-minded overlook is that the term "anytime" in an invitation actually means "any time that is convenient for me, depending on what else I have to do then, how I feel at that moment about having guests, how much of a nuisance you are going to make of yourself and how many people you are thinking of bringing."

For anyone who hopes to turn a nonspecific invitation into a serious one, Miss Manners provides the following polite formula. Notice that it comes with two sets of responses from prospective hosts. Politeness is not a weapon that can be used to force people to take in guests they don't want.

> GUEST-CANDIDATE: "We're hoping to have a chance to see you. We're think-
> ing of spending a couple of weeks in your area, and we're hoping you'll be
> free to spend some time with us."
>
> EAGER HOSTS: "Great! We have some time off coming, and this would be a
> great way to spend it. But come and stay with us, so we'll really have
> some time together. We'd be insulted to hear of your going to a hotel
> when we have all this room."
>
> HORRIFIED HOSTS: "Great! Of course, we'll be working then, but be sure and
> save us an evening. Where are you staying?"

POLITE REFUSALS

Declining Rude Guests

DEAR MISS MANNERS — My husband and I bought a summer house by the shore, and after receiving guests since May, I was looking forward to having the place to ourselves in August. But we have friends who regard our hospitality as an indication that we want them to join us whenever they are not otherwise engaged.

I have grown to dread the question, "What are your plans for the weekend?" which is usually followed by, "I might come and see you on Saturday if the weather is nice," or "I'm dying for another visit! When are you going to invite me again?" I have tried, "We'll be at the shore for the weekend, but I haven't made any preparations for company." They come back with, "But I'm not company. You don't have to entertain me."

This is partly true—these people do not behave like company. Having extorted an invitation, they expect everything to be as it was on their last visit, in spite of my warning that I was not prepared for them. They felt at home enough to insult me with remarks like, "How could you forget the bagels? You know that's all I eat for breakfast," and "I froze last night. Don't you people believe in turning on the heat?"

Food was the main topic of conversation. Lunch came up for discussion at 10:30 a.m., and they weren't talking about the sandwiches and fruit I was prepared to offer: "I didn't let you drag me down here to eat sandwiches. I want a cookout."

My husband says we should go ahead and invite them, but take them literally at their word, not treat them like company, and go about our business as if they weren't in the house. Aside from being rude, this would mean we can't go about our business—having sex any time and any place we please—as if we were alone.

What I really need is a polite way to tell these people that my plans are my own business, and if I don't volunteer an invitation, it means that I don't want company or anything else for the weekend.

GENTLE READER—Your husband wants to teach these people a lesson by allowing them to treat your house as theirs, and you as the deficient house staff? Miss Manners has always admired saintliness, but this is ridiculous. You really must—as you recognize—learn how to say no.

The trick is not to make it seem negotiable. Granted that polite people wait to be invited, and even semipolite people who put themselves forward take the first hint of not being welcome, that still leaves a lot of people, such as your very own friends, who try to make the hosts seem rude to argue their way in. Do not allow them to bully you. You owe them no explanation, and to offer one only allows them an opening.

The polite answer to "What are you doing this weekend?" is "Oh, I'm so sorry, but we're busy" (no need to be as graphic as you were to Miss Manners about what you were busy doing). The answer to "When are you going to invite me again?" is a cheerful "Oh, you'll hear from me when we do."

As for complaints by guests who do get in, Miss Manners recommends taking them seriously.

"Bagels? You were cold? Oh, I'm so sorry, we really shouldn't have had you here when we were unprepared. We couldn't dream of allowing you to be uncomfortable—we feel awful about it. Here, I'll call a bed and breakfast for you. No, no, I insist. Don't stay just to be polite—we want you to be comfortable."

When they are then shamed into protesting that they were only kidding, you should look all the more stricken and confess "Well, I'm not. I want you to be happy here, and this is not the time; you really must come back another time, when we're ready."

Weighing Motives

DEAR MISS MANNERS — I am beginning to dread the Summer Olympics. During the Super Bowl, my house was used as a bed and breakfast for relatives attending the game. My brother and his family, and an aunt and uncle enjoyed my hospitality and then went to their game, leaving me to clean dishes and prepare a snack for their return. I would have loved to have gone to the game, but could not afford tickets. I will not be able to afford tickets for the Summer Olympics, either, and will resent being used again as a hotel. My family-guests do not visit me unless they are attending meetings, and just use my home as a stopping-off point.

GENTLE READER — There, there. If you really think they don't care to see you at all, but only find your house a convenience, you needn't have them stay with you. All you have to do is to respond "I'm afraid that's a bad time to have you here at the house, but I'd love to see you if you have some spare time. And I'd be glad to make a hotel reservation for you if you tell me what you want."

Miss Manners would rather not increase the estrangement you feel from such close relatives. Can't we assume that they are thoughtless, rather than uncaring? Don't you want to have a holiday at their houses, now and then? The way to check motives would be to say "I'd love to have you, but it's so tantalizing to have you here and not have a real visit with you. We so rarely see one another. I'd come to the Olympics with you, but it's really out of my reach. Why don't you save me an evening, and maybe we could go out and do something?"

If this brings them to their senses, they will either buy you a ticket or take you out to dinner—or maybe just come home to dinner with you, but at least stick around long enough for you to throw them a dish towel while you are washing up. If not, revert to Plan A with Miss Manners' blessings.

Making Reservations

DEAR MISS MANNERS — Friends from out-of-town are coming to town to visit us and do some sightseeing. How can I politely ask them to stay in a hotel? We have a very small house and they have a very active 3-year-old boy who doesn't like to wear his diapers around the house. These are good friends and I don't want to hurt them, but the anxiety of the large crowd in my tiny house is beginning to unnerve me. Please help me find a way to break the news. I am desperate for a quiet weekend but don't want to lose a good friend either.

GENTLE READER — Nobody who has a three-year-old is going to have a quiet weekend anyway, and nobody who has a three-year-old running around the house diaperless is going to have to worry about houseguests for long.

But you asked Miss Manners how to head them off. Originally, you should have responded to their announcement of arriving in town by saying, "How wonderful! We'll be so happy to see you. Please let us know your schedule so we can figure out when would be good. Where are you staying, by the way?"

Now that it's too late, what you should say is, "We were so looking forward to having you here, and I'm mortified that I haven't been able to arrange things so that you will be comfortable. We want to see as much of you as possible, but of course you'll want to be able to rest as well, so I think you'll be better off in a quiet hotel."

Sneaking Out

DEAR MISS MANNERS — I have received verbal invitations to about a dozen graduation parties from my graduating son's dearest friends. How can I balance my desire to attend those parties with the responsibility to the three relatives who will be staying at my home for that weekend?

GENTLE READER — By finding something more interesting for them to do. Not that Miss Manners imagines anything more interesting than celebrating your son's graduation. Neither do your relatives, which is why they will be there. But you can try offering them theater tickets, for example, or a friend to show them around. Unless you can persuade short-term houseguests that you are only being tactful by withdrawing for a short time so that they can do something they would prefer, you cannot run off and leave them.

You do have one last chance, though. When you decline those invitations, you can say that you are doing so because you have three houseguests—and then pause to see if your hosts choose to say "Well, bring them along."

COMPLICATIONS

Extracting Preferences

DEAR MISS MANNERS — When my husband and I entertain guests from out of town, we try to think of various activities in advance that the guests might enjoy, and to make preparations for meals according to their dietary needs. We often end up in a polite tug-of-war in which no one is willing to decide what we're going to do or what we're going to eat. The phrases "Anything is fine" or "I don't care" become well worn, and in the meantime, nothing happens!

Perhaps we are all hopelessly indecisive, but it is because we were all raised to be as unobtrusive with one's host or hostess as possible. As the hostess, I usually end up making the decision, but often feel uncomfortable in doing so.

GENTLE READER — What you describe is not so much a tug of war as a ritual, and you seem to have gotten stuck after correctly performing the opening step. The polite answer to "What would you like to do (or eat)?" is, indeed, "Anything is fine." (Miss Manners does not care for the modernism, "I don't care.") But then the next question should be "Would you like to go to see the Monet exhibit or go bowling?" or "Would you prefer chicken or sweetbreads?" These require a specific answer. If none is offered, you must prompt your guests by saying "Either one is just as easy and enjoyable for us—please do us a favor and make the choice."

Airing the Place

DEAR MISS MANNERS — My husband's parents are both smokers, and whenever we visit their home, I bring a small air purifier which I place in the bedroom where we sleep. Otherwise I feel extremely ill the entire time I am there. I also suffer from allergies which are aggravated by cigarette smoke.

My husband has told his parents that we are sensitive to cigarette smoke, me especially. They do their best to be considerate, but I am not sure that they understand how much it really bothers us, as cigarette smoke permeates everything. For example, they do not smoke in front of us. Instead, they smoke in the bathroom, their bedroom, or in any room which we are not in at the times they are. For instance, if we leave the house, we will smell the smoke in the kitchen when we return. They have also plugged in air fresheners and use air freshening sprays which mask the smell, but do not clean the air of smoke.

Would it be disrespectful of us to ask them if we could use air purifiers in other rooms of their house besides the bedroom? As it is their home and not mine, and I respect that I am in fact in someone else's space, I do not want to offend them. I do dread visiting them though, because I always end up feeling sick.

GENTLE READER — Miss Manners usually feels sick when the word "smoking" wafts her way, but your inquiry is like a breath of purified air.

Both you and your in-laws are making an effort to keep from being offensive. It isn't quite working yet, but bless your hearts anyway. Unlike the usual such clash—where the nonsmoker spreads disgust at the smokers, who react to protect their turf and their dignity—this has a chance of success.

Tell them how much you love to visit them, how appreciative you are of their inconveniencing themselves for you and how embarrassed you are at the extent of your problem. Then if you suggest that you put in air purifiers, it will sound like a solution, rather than a challenge.

Snooping

DEAR MISS MANNERS — I have a cousin who spent the night, and that evening she was going through my things and looking all through my closet. So the next morning I asked her would she pick up all the things she took out and she just sat there, so I asked her again and she looked at me and turned around so I told her that she couldn't spend the night any more. Do you think I did the right thing?

GENTLE READER — Almost. You should have resolved to do everything you could to prevent her from sharing your room again—but you should not have announced this to her. Miss Manners realizes that this is a subtle point. Going through the hostess's closet and leaving her things in a mess are both violations of etiquette that deserve banishment. But chastising guests and announcing they can't return are also violations of etiquette, however justly prompted.

Besides, there is the matter of making your decree of banishment stick. She is your cousin, and to bar her from spending the night in your room again (the relationship will undoubtedly allow her to get back through the front door) may require the sympathy and understanding of your parents. They are more likely to be on your side if you are able to show that you, at least, exercised mannerly restraint.

Sleeping Arrangements, Part I

DEAR MISS MANNERS — Our family of five—my husband and I and our three children—have company quite often. It is usually family. When they come and stay overnight, I feel I must offer our beds to them, which means that some or all of us are usually out of a bed and onto the floor. With as frequent as visitors are (we have a large family) we find that this is a bit uncomfortable as well as annoying. I absolutely love company, the more people the merrier, I say. But is there anything I can do about this situation without making my guests feel uncomfortable and unwelcome? Please help!!!

GENTLE READER — Futons? Sofa beds? Planks and nails for building an addition on the house? Miss Manners suspects these are not the solutions you want— but after all, you have made her guess your question. Annoyed hosts usually come to her for help in ridding themselves of perennial houseguests, but your saying that you love company suggests this is not the case.

You want to stay in your own beds and put the company on the floor; is that it? And you want Miss Manners to tell you that this is not rude. If they are frail and/or elderly, it is rude. If they are young and/or robust—or at least no less so than you—it isn't. So perhaps what you really need to know is how to tell people who previously occupied your beds that you would love to see them, but on the floor.

The answer is: by begging them to visit both immediately before and immediately after explaining the change. Something along the lines of, "Oh, you must come visit—we love having you here. I hope you don't mind if I put you in the living room this time, but I'll make sure you're comfortable. We'll all be so pleased to see you."

Sleeping Arrangements, Part II

DEAR MISS MANNERS — My mother-in-law, who is a widow, and her beau of several years plan to visit us this fall. They each live in their own houses. We have no idea what sleeping arrangements they would prefer for themselves. Could you please tell us whose responsibility it is (if there is a clear position on that) to inform us? Should she tell us, or should we ask? We feel it is their business, and only want them to feel comfortable with the arrangement. I think I am shy to ask, because I wouldn't try, for any other reason, to find out whether they sleep together. If they arrive here and we still don't know, could you please suggest a polite way to discover their preference without seeming to bias their answer?

GENTLE READER — Miss Manners, who admires your delicacy, does not know what guest facilities exist in your house. But presumably your mother-in-law does. "Where do you think you would be most comfortable?" can equally well elicit the reply "In the blue room, of course," or "I suppose I'll take the guest room as usual, and I'm sure Chester will be fine on the sofa."

In the unlikely event that you have moved to larger quarters since she last visited, the question could be "How many rooms will you need?" She can still say, "Well, let's see. I would dearly love to have a sitting room as well as my bedroom; I'm sure Chester will be fine on the sofa."

Questioning is best done in advance, but upon arrival, you could say, "You know the house, Mother—where would you like to be?"

Principled Behavior

DEAR MISS MANNERS — I have a friend who visits me in my apartment. After urinating in my toilet, he refuses to flush it. He says this is a waste of water and that one should wait for additional urinations before flushing. I have assured him that there is no water shortage here and that I consider his behavior unsanitary and disgusting. What can I do? I do not want him urinating off my balcony nor do I want to lose his friendship by having him evicted.

GENTLE READER — What a charming choice you offer Miss Manners. But then, you move in charming circles. What third solution you might conceive of, other than tolerating or evicting a defiant houseguest, she cannot imagine. She certainly hopes you don't think that she is going to march over there and make him flush the toilet or do it for him.

Telephone Calls

DEAR MISS MANNERS—I recently entertained houseguests who made a number of rather lengthy long-distance calls. I'd like to have them repay me, but at the same time, I've also been a houseguest of theirs on a number of occasions (but never made long-distance calls). How do I approach this gracefully?

GENTLE READER—Before the advent of the telephone credit card and other practical ways of billing oneself, this used to be a difficult problem. Polite guests were hesitant about repaying hosts for the cost of their calls, lest they be implying that the hosts were petty, and polite hosts could not bring themselves to send their departed houseguests bills. Now Miss Manners can simply classify houseguests who bill their hosts as being thoughtless to the point of rudeness.

But as you realize, it is still not simple for a polite host to collect. It remains unthinkable to send guests a bill as if you expected them to pay it, and they are certainly not going to pay it if they don't get the bill. So you should ask them to check it instead. An accompanying note could read, "I'm so sorry to trouble you with a matter of my household accounting, but I was about to dispute the telephone company about this bill, when I realized that this is about the time you were here and the bill might actually be correct. Would you be kind enough to let me know?" If the return note is unaccompanied by a check, you will at least have been forewarned before inviting these people again.

Doing the Dishes

DEAR MISS MANNERS—As a houseguest of friends or relatives, I feel an obligation to help clean up after meals. But everyone has quirks about how to prepare dishes for the dishwasher, load the washer, and even remove dishes from the washer to dry them again. Even offering to scrape and stack is complicated by what people will let go into the garbage disposal. In the days of sink washing, I always washed and let them dry and store. But what is one to do now? Should I ask where scrapings go, or what is done with dishes? I am not a rinser and I don't want someone to feel put down when I asked if that is how they do it—as rinsers and spongers do to me. Just removing items from table to counter seems inadequate—there you are afterwards, standing around while others (especially older relatives) are working away. It seems impolite to go into the parlor and read the paper.

GENTLE READER — You have identified an amusing nuance of modern behavior, for which Miss Manners is grateful to you. Now that she thinks of it, the variations are infinite—those who want the flatware pointed downwards in the dishwasher basket, for example, and those who want it pointing upwards—and views on them are ferociously held.

But the fact is that a helper in someone else's kitchen was always supposed to act as a helper, unempowered to make decisions. A polite offer of help is "What can I do?" followed by suggestions, and if necessary, "How would you prefer this done?" You must also be alive to the possibility that help is not really wanted. The last offer to be made then is "Well, should I stay here and chat, or would it be easier if I got out of the way?" It sometimes is, you know.

Shifting the Burden

DEAR MISS MANNERS — Each summer, my husband and I, who have a large cottage on a pristine lake, with lovely bedrooms and other comfortable sleeping quarters, host a week-long reunion for his family. Great amounts of preparation are required—at least one solid week of hard labor for each of us. We have small children, my husband works long hours, and I maintain two households.

My spouse and I function as virtual slaves during their vacation, beginning with numerous trips to the airport. The heavier burden falls on me in terms of endless cooking, cleaning, washing dishes and clothes, and dealing with relatives who would prefer a firmer bed, less noise at night, an opinion on a relative with whom they are feuding, etc. I try to be kind and fair to all and keep backbiting to a minimum. A few relatives help, but most sit like royalty, waiting to be served. I have tried asking firmly for help—with minimal and short-lived success.

Last year, we served 171 adult meals and 89 child meals (yes, I counted), and received donations of $100 on at least $600 worth of groceries. I don't want to sound mercenary, but this property costs us a great deal in mortgage, insurance, taxes and maintenance. My husband is loath to put any pressure on his family for fear of hurting their feelings or lowering attendance.

My questions are: How do I assure a more equitable distribution of chores? How do we solve the problem of financial contributions, including from those who have paid for airline flights? Do you have advice on dealing with accommodation complaints and gossip?

Or should I just be thankful they don't come for Christmas?

GENTLE READER—Miss Manners is not at all surprised that two people find it difficult to give a large-scale house party. Edwardians who gave similar entertainments on their country estates not only had batteries of servants to help, but expected their guests to bring their own servants to tend to their demands. Those hosts still complained of cost, bickering, gossip and the tendency of guests to behave like royalty, which some of them were.

Yet Miss Manners admires your husband for wanting to maintain this tradition, even while she seeks to relieve you both of the impossible burden you have gallantly borne. The solution is to redefine the event. Don't give a house party. Instead, offer your house as the base for a family reunion which is not "given" by yourselves but administered by a family reunion committee.

You will not offend people if you assemble them after a pleasant day and say how much their presence means to you, and how agonized you are by your inability to keep it up. Rather than abolishing an event that you cherish, and having to settle for inviting them individually (don't worry, Miss Manners is not holding you to this), you inquire if the family could form a group that would plan it so that the work and effort could be shared, without making it a hardship on anyone.

"We wouldn't want to miss any one of you at the next event," Miss Manners would advise you to say winningly, "even if we had to do everything ourselves. But if some of you could get together and figure out what would be feasible to everyone, so that we could continue to have the delight of gathering you here, we would be so very grateful." Miss Manners almost guarantees you that after the shocked silence, someone will come forward and say, on behalf of them all, how appreciative they are of your past efforts, and how much fun it would be to take an active part in putting on this wonderful event. But it might be well to have a particularly close and sympathetic relative briefed to say this, just in case.

The Guest Book

"Just a line or two—write whatever happens to come to mind," says a beaming friend, thrusting forward a nicely bound volume open to an alarmingly blank page.

"Anything—it doesn't matter. A thought. Make up a poem if you like. Or you could draw a picture. Whatever you feel like will be fine."

Whatever Miss Manners feels like doing at such a time is not fine. She feels like running away.

Surely she cannot be the only person terrorized by the guest book, the friend-ship book, the memory book, the collection of charming thoughts. If anything, she should expect to approach them with an advantage. Letters of thanks, which par-alyze many people, come naturally to her. Condolence letters, considered notori-ously difficult, overflow from her sympathetic heart. She has even been known to inflict 500-page books on a patient public. But a clever line that will gratify hosts and yet capture the interest of unknown guests to follow—perhaps inspire them as they flip back to see what is expected—is more daunting.

Everybody learns at an early age what to write in yearbooks: "Lots of luck," "Keep in touch," "Great knowing ya" (although how people get out of high school without the habit of spelling "you" properly remains as much of a mystery as who those people are, when viewed from the sophisticated perspective of a col-lege dormitory).

Books of comments at clubs and commercial guest houses easily inspire such comments as "Great time, lovely view" and "Please get the bottom step repaired before someone breaks a leg on it."

Masters of the genre are able to turn such simple observations into major pronouncements about civilization along the lines of: "Nobody seems to have complained that the bulb in the reading room is too dim for prolonged efforts, which says something about the state of literacy today, and indeed, about the val-ues of the modern world."

What is difficult about blank books is that they seem to be expecting some-thing original. The point of keeping one, after all, is to have a keepsake to read years later, on rainy evenings, to remember all that good fellowship (or quaint querulousness) from the past.

And there seem to be more of such books being offered around these days. "We're collecting notes from all our parents' old friends to put into a volume we'll give them as an anniversary present"—that sort of thing.

If Miss Manners could condemn this practice, she would—frankly, just to get out of it. But on what grounds?

She has no hesitation condemning those whose similarly worded suggestion is "We're collecting money from all our parents' old friends to give them an anniversary present," for example. She gets them on greed—or rather, since they are collecting other people's generosity so that they can provide a grand present without having to pay for it, greed once-removed.

Nor does Miss Manners hesitate to condemn the practice of thrusting a camcorder at guests and demanding that they say something about the occasion. She gets the interviewers on the charge of violating hospitality by causing embarrassment.

The book of mottoes, under whatever guise it is proffered, is a charming old custom that asks only for thoughts and tactfully offers time in which to compose them. About a minute and a half, while the book's owner stands there with an expectant smile, and the other guests look as if they are impatiently brimming with memorable thoughts.

To relieve the rattled guest, Miss Manners offers a verse found in an album in the Monhegan Museum in Maine above the name of Mrs. Angie Humphrey:

> *If scribbling in albums*
> *Remembrance secures*
> *With the greatest of pleasure*
> *I scribble in yours.*

This may not be original, Miss Manners admits. But as it was around in 1885, at least any copyright has run out.

Thank You Notes

DEAR MISS MANNERS — My teenage daughter spent a long weekend with a friend's family at their vacation home, bringing a hostess gift and homemade cookies with her. At the end, she thanked them "profusely," in her words. I asked her to follow up with a written thank you. She claims that nowadays, it is not necessary to write a thank you note. I believe thank you notes have never gone out of style. We are awaiting your reply for future reference. Meanwhile, she is writing a note.

GENTLE READER — Why is it that when people (other than Miss Manners) unilaterally declare rules of etiquette to be obsolete, it always turns out to be rules that would otherwise cost them a bit of trouble?

Why isn't your daughter arguing that in the 21st century, it is not necessary for other people to show her hospitality?

As long as such kindnesses are performed, showing gratitude for them will be necessary. And while she's at it, your daughter might reflect on how grateful she should be to have a mother who is teaching her courtesy.

Chapter Seven

ENTERTAINING: THE SOCIAL CONTRACT

Hermithood has its advantages, Miss Manners supposes, although it pains her to know that one of the chief advantages is that hermits don't have to bother with etiquette. They are not exempt from her injunction against being rude to other people, but if they never deal with other people, that's not likely to be a problem for them. However, most human beings like to surround themselves with family and friends. Not necessarily the family and friends they happen to have, of course, but somebody's. They love the idea, if not the individuals whom life has carelessly thrown their way. Miss Manners believes that a dwelling, no matter how lavish or humble, is not a home unless it welcomes guests. Not only is it a sacred obligation to share one's last crumb; but whatever else we may have in the way of amusement and comfort on cable or in the refrigerator, nothing beats people. So everyone but the hermit wants a social life, whether to enjoy family and friends or to search for better ones.

The catch is that no form of social life can exist without etiquette—and Miss Manners means specific etiquette rules, not only enough general niceness so that it isn't your particular family and friends who are out looking for a replacement. No social activity, from the most elaborate (which everybody believes to be bristling with etiquette rules) to the most casual (which they don't, but which are even more so), is possible without Host and Guest meeting their basic obligations.

Someone has to issue an invitation, and someone has to answer it. This sounds simple enough, but it is the subject of endless agonizing and accusations.

The host must know the targeted guest's name (a fine point young people tend to miss) and how to find out whether that person is part of a couple (a point adults who should know better tend to miss) and if so, the name of the other person. He or she has to state the date, time, style of formality and nature of the proposed activity and whether it involves a meal; and it is only decent to add a warning when planning something many people hope to avoid (which includes not only hot tubs and karaoke, but fund-raising, trolling for business favors and helping to pay for or cook the meal).

The guest is free to say yes or no, but not free enough to ignore the offer, and hedging is not nicer than declining—it's nastier. There is room for renegotiating the terms if the invitation is for a cooperative venture, but almost none if the invitation is to someone's home—maybe saying you got married last week and would like to bring your spouse, if you add that you would understand if that were not possible.

When the time comes, everybody who hasn't died in the meantime is expected to make good on the agreement—the guest to show up on time, dressed for the occasion, pleasantly open to socializing with everyone else there and pleasantly closed-mouthed about anything unsatisfactory. The host is required to introduce the guests to one another, shepherd strays together and shepherd guests apart at the first sign of argument. It is a nice touch to produce any promised meals before desperate guests start telephoning for pizza. Latecomers must grovel and their excuses cannot be based on their own tremendous importance. Hosts need not wait for them to start the meal but must offer the excuse "I knew you would want us to go ahead."

Afterwards, the host only has to clean up, while the guests must issue their thanks and plan the next round. If they don't do this—and if the other conditions of initiating and keeping appointments and being sociable aren't kept, whether the occasion is a wedding or a movie—the whole system breaks down, as any fed-up host or unfed guest can attest. Then we all get to be hermits, with only our invisible friends from cyberspace for company.

Enforcing the Contract

DEAR MISS MANNERS — For 20 years, my husband and I won a reputation as party givers, often hosting affairs with as many as 50 guests. What seemed strange to us was that our guests never reciprocated. Not one! Never! Still, we enjoyed the parties so much that we kept having them.

Two years ago, my husband died. I sold our large home and bought a smaller one nearby. I have not been a hostess since, although I do miss those happy times when we got together with people I still like to think of as friends. Now when I run into these people in church, in stores, or on the street, I am confronted with such remarks as "Oh, you must come for dinner . . . sometime." I've been tempted to respond, "Fine, I'll be there at six o'clock next Wednesday." But of course, I don't.

Instead of receiving invitations, I'm also getting a lot of "invitations to be invited." They say things like, "When are we going to see your new home? Why don't you start having small dinner parties? We'd really love to come." What did I do wrong? And what should I do now?

GENTLE READER — Only your second question needs answering. Miss Manners trusts that you know that not only did you do nothing wrong, but that you have 20 years of generous, as well as hospitable, behavior to your credit. Collecting on this debt will not be easy.

Of course, your guests should have been reciprocating all along. Now would be an especially appropriate time for them to take over the responsibility for continuing the socializing. Whatever reasons they have been giving themselves—that they are too busy to entertain, or don't know how to do so as well as you, or that you probably prefer to be the hostess—only serve to rationalize their failure to do their part, while profiting from your efforts.

When you receive one of those vague invitations, you can say, warmly and cheerfully, "You know, I really would love to. I don't quite feel up to entertaining as much now as I used to, but frankly, I have missed seeing you, and would adore to come to dinner whenever you say. When would be good?"

All these years, you have been big enough to overlook your friends' omissions in the interest of having a good social life. Now that you are widowed, they, with all their faults, are probably more important to you than ever. So Miss Manners urges you to continue your previous selfless policy, in whatever modified form you feel you can now manage—this time for your own sake.

BUT WHAT ABOUT SPONTANEITY?

Spontaneity is what adds sparkle to social life, Miss Manners has been told. Just think of all the splendid evenings you enjoy on the spur of the moment.

"Let's do something," you declare with an unpleasant emphasis on the "do." It may take a while for your chosen companions to register the fact that you have said anything, but eventually they turn towards you with a hopeless stare. The enterprising among them will finally inquire, "Like what?" Having taken the initiative, you are expected to urge them on by saying something helpful and encouraging, such as "Oh, I don't know. Something different. I'm bored out of my mind. We never do anything." Soon all those imaginative and adventuresome minds get busy, and out tumble the following suggestions:

Going to the movies
Sending out for pizza
Renting a video
Picking up some take-home food
Seeing what's on cable

It is difficult to choose among these treats, because as each proposal is thought through, there is someone to point out its disadvantages:

"There's nothing good to see."
"We'd have to get dressed."
"It's too cold (hot, rainy, late, crowded, expensive)."
"How're we going to get there?"
"Yuck."
"We did that last night."

But with any luck, the discussion keeps going until someone says, "If you can't make up your mind, I'm going to bed," and the evening is declared over.

Far be it from Miss Manners to spoil all this madcap fun. She would only like to raise the question of whether social spontaneity is so desirable as to make up for all the damage it causes. The victims are not those who are asked to join the spontaneity, as one might suppose, or even those who are left out. Rather they are people who have had the audacity to propose nonspontaneous entertainment in which they invite others to join.

These people are called hosts. They actually go to the trouble of preparing, for themselves and others, entertainment—parties, dinners, excursions—that requires making arrangements in advance. They cook food, buy tickets or think out who would enjoy whose company.

That is their mistake. The invited, in order to protect their limitless ability to enjoy spontaneous entertainment, refuse to accept the idea of a binding social engagement. How do they know, on the day it is issued, how they will feel on the day it will occur?

It is every person's privilege to decline an invitation. Miss Manners is far from suggesting that anyone is obligated to accept whatever is offered. If you don't go, you don't have to reciprocate, either, and you don't have to send a present if it is a present-bearing sort of occasion.

Oddly enough, those who want to preserve spontaneity rarely decline. They either hedge ("I'll try to make it"), or they accept outright but with the inner conviction that they remain uncommitted. No attempt is made to hide the insulting idea that the invitation will be weighed against whatever else is offered, and even against the opportunity to do nothing, and that the outcome is by no means assured. If something better comes along, the accepted guest simply takes it.

And so the errant guest acknowledges later—"My boyfriend came over," "I had some work to finish," "This friend of mine called." The assumption is made that the person who was stood up finds this understandable.

This is an unwarranted assumption. Hearing that one's activity was assigned a low priority always hurts. But even these paltry excuses are a cut above the explanations that assume a host doesn't mind hearing that he ranked below doing nothing: "I was tired," "I wasn't in the mood," "I just didn't feel like it." Although such behavior has become commonplace, it is not—repeat *not*—a new standard of manners. It is an absence of standards.

Young people who are used to casual engagements report being hurt when told that they are being dropped for a better offer. Older people who were brought up on the idea of binding engagements but have slipped into assuming that citing work cancels any social arrangements are wrong. The rule about engagements is that chronology is more important than convenience—the one you accepted first counts, not the one that attracts you most.

THE GUEST LIST

Qualms about entertaining at home are often expressed in terms of how perilous it is to have the boss over to dinner. So much can go fatally wrong, everyone agrees, even when you are trying your best.

It's not just that the food might burn or the children might turn obstreperous. Worse, the setting itself, or the way you do things at home, might fall short of the boss's standards. Instructions abound about how to deal with the myriad tasks involved in shaping things up, at least enough to pass muster by candlelight. Severe measures are deemed necessary to make a good impression on the boss—the last and hardest being the command to "relax and be yourself."

Miss Manners realizes that nobody has a home in quite the shape it should be, even (or especially) in the opinion of the people who live there. She would go so far as to argue that those who do must have either surrendered their lives to professionals who decorate, organize and scrub within an inch of the family's lives, or actually live somewhere else, say, in another state or hidden upstairs. Or both.

Still, any dwelling reveals things about its residents that they wouldn't want to be judged by a cold eye, especially if that eye is accompanied by the hand that controls their income. Fortunately, Miss Manners has a quick and easy solution:

Don't invite the boss to dinner.

That goes double if inviting the boss is the custom in your working place. Then it will not only prevent your boss from subjecting you to a home inspection but put the boss into your debt for inspiring gratitude in his or her spouse. If there is one thing more nerve-wracking than being host to someone whose judgment affects your livelihood, it is being that nervous person's guest.

Here is a revelation: Entertaining is supposed to be done purely for fun. This point has been lost even on those who mean to be selfless. They strain to put some sort of charitable angle onto their personal events, thus levying the expense of their philanthropy on wedding and birthday party guests. Miss Manners does want everybody to think of the less fortunate, but not by making their guests feel unfortunate.

Those who entertain for professional advancement are right to fear that much can go wrong. Even if the arrangements are flawless, the transparency of the motivation turns the guests cynical.

Everybody who crosses your threshold as a guest should feel obliged to regard you and yours with a warmer eye, however many critical opinions they feel obliged to deliver for your own good. These include relatives, friends, friends of relatives, relatives of friends, prospective friends who might prove interesting and (now and again, for sentiment's sake) old friends who have proven uninteresting.

Besides, entertaining such people is good for the career. Putting amusement, comfort, restfulness and perspective into your life offers a bigger boost towards success than you are ever likely to get from using the household butter for the purpose of buttering up the boss.

Updating the List

DEAR MISS MANNERS — My wife and I have been married for over two years, but my friends, singles and couples alike, are still addressing cards and invitations to me only. My wife has met most of them, and I constantly tell all of them how happy we are. I can't believe they still omit her.

Am I to assume that the invitation (from a longtime friend) that I am holding includes my darling wife? Should I inquire when I respond? This seems embarrassing to the host and hostess. (However, I feel they deserve it.) Should I have my wife respond, as is customary? My wife has said nothing, but I know that this hurts her. I've even offered to do a mass-mailing to those in my address book with her name and proof of existence, etc.

GENTLE READER — What you are describing is an increasing tendency—which Miss Manners deplores—to ignore the factor of the social couple and treat each person, attached or not, as a loner. This should not be taken personally by you or your wife, as it comes from general cynicism and laziness. One rationale is that it is too much trouble to figure out what constitutes a couple when divorce is so prevalent and there are so many sub-marital arrangements. Another is that social life is really an extension of one's work, anyway, where spouses are only present on sufferance. Thus while people may be lax about allowing their guests to bring along unknown dates, they are rigid about admitting anyone permanently, as marriage requires one's friends to do.

Miss Manners believes you must, indeed, make a point of this with your friends. Asking your wife to do so is not a good idea—she already feels hurt by your friends' callousness, and would seem to be pushing herself, rather than responding to your natural demand that she be accorded her proper place.

A mass mailing would have to be very lightly done, so as not to suggest that your wife was sulking. Miss Manners rather suggests that you respond to each invitation by calling the host and saying, "Is this a Mr. and Mrs. invitation? My wife and I don't lead separate social lives."

Submitting Substitutions

DEAR MISS MANNERS — If you and your spouse are invited to a function and you R.S.V.P. that you both will attend, is it permissible to take someone else if, at the last minute, your spouse cannot attend? Would it be the same if it is an invitation for a wedding, dinner party or just a party in general?

GENTLE READER — How can you be sure it wasn't your spouse whom they really wanted, and that they wouldn't be doubly disappointed if you showed up with someone else?

Now, now, Miss Manners isn't trying to be mean. She just wants to shock you into remembering that hosts make up their guest lists by selecting people they want to see—not (as guests seem to imagine) because they need a certain number of bodies to fill the space and don't much care who they are.

The idea of making substitutions is unthinkable for weddings—notwithstanding the fact that you and many others have thought of it. Then, of all occasions, the hosts especially want guests who mean something to them and have a genuine interest in the occasion—not strangers who naturally regard it simply as a chance to go to a party.

Miss Manners admits that on informal occasions there might be some leeway. If you accept an invitation for yourself and decline it for your husband, you could say, "But I'd love you to meet a dear friend of mine, whom I might be able to bring along, if that would be convenient." You might even suggest that for a dinner party, provided you know the hosts well enough to be sure they won't be embarrassed to say "We'd love to meet your friend some other time, but why don't you just come to this alone and we'll ask someone else we wanted to fit in."

That must be done at the time the invitation is issued. If your husband has accepted an invitation to a dinner party or a wedding, the only proper reason for him to find himself unable to go at the last minute would be sudden illness. In that case, you ought to be nursing him, instead of running around partying with someone else.

ISSUING AND ANSWERING

INVITATIONS

Sorting the Invitations

Two theories have sprung up about that elusive modern figure, The Guest:

1. People have so many demands made on their time, and they have to commit themselves so far ahead, that it isn't enough simply to invite them to something at the usual time. Weeks, even months, before an event, they should be sent "Save the Date" notices, so that they can plan around it, and so that anyone coming in from out of town can take advantage of advance-purchase airfare bargains.

2. People like to be spontaneous, and they can't really know ahead of time what they will be in the mood to do on a particular date, or what other demands may be made on them. They have to remain flexible, up to—and even on—the evening in question, when they want to see how one event is going before knowing whether they should move on to another.

So let's see: You are supposed to book these people up way in advance, acknowledging that they will not ever consider themselves firmly booked. While making it easier for guests to accept an offer of hospitality, you should recognize that it will be neither accepted nor rejected but held indefinitely as an option to be weighed against other possibilities.

Others may be pondering how to entertain such guests; Miss Manners is unkindly wondering why. The answer may be that there aren't any other people around. It seems to be a guest's market, in which anyone giving anything, from a child's birthday party to a grand ball, has to put up with this cavalier treatment of the generous offer of hospitality (and incidentally a manifestation of the precious offer of friendship) in order to have anyone there at all.

The results of such a humble approach, on the part of those who are opening their houses and hearts, are pathetic: parties whose sparse attendance attests to their having been spurned by the capricious, or parties overrun with strangers, there at the invitation of the guests themselves without regard to the host once-removed.

One of the things that has led to this state of affairs, other than the rapid decline of civilization itself, which Miss Manners believes she may have mentioned once or twice before, is the general confusion of the social invitation with the sales pitch. People who find that half their invitations consist of opportunities to drink while supporting business ventures, and the other half of opportunities to drink while supporting charities (including events in people's homes, where the object of charity is the host, who frankly requests specific presents or cash), may be forgiven for turning cynical. But not for turning rude.

Invitations to buy a ticket, inspect property that is for sale, welcome the appearance of a new product, or ones that otherwise cast a wide and indiscriminate net, are not real invitations. Therefore, throwing them in the trash is as proper a response as keeping them for last-minute consideration. Business or charity events connected with people one actually knows may be negotiated ("May I send my assistant?" "May I let you know when I see if I can fill a table?"), but they should be answered.

Social invitations, however, must be definitively answered, promptly—meaning, with a day's leeway to ask one's spouse if anything else is on the calendar, and three days, tops, to check if one is expected to work that weekend—and without any attempt to change the terms. It is considered unfair to issue them too far in advance—ten days being about right unless fancy clothes or airplane tickets will be required—because it makes excuses less plausible.

The escape clause is that invitations may always be rejected. Thanks, but no explanation, are necessary. The disappointed hosts will manage to get over it. What they will not get over is the strain and insult of being kept dangling.

Miss Manners just wishes they would stop responding to all that insulting hedging by begging. She considers it an unfortunate concession that hosts even need to state that they would like a response (in sensible times, guests could figure that out for themselves), and finds it distasteful that they feel they must provide the response themselves, in the form of prestamped cards or a voice-mail drop. Especially since such techniques don't work. People who are not polite enough to answer invitations are still not going to answer, even if you lie down in front of them and beg them to kick you once for yes and twice for no. It is far better to scale back one's entertaining to include only those who appreciate being invited.

Asking to have the date saved months ahead of time is flattering to intimate friends, convenient to those who must travel but oppressive to everyone else, as it seems to limit the ability to decline. It must therefore be done individually and informally.

All the host has to do is to state a clear invitation—take it or leave it. Refusals to reply should be treated as refusals to attend. You will save a great deal of anguish and leftover food by responding to the first "Well, I'm not sure if I'll be able to make it" (or even "I'll try to make it, but I'm not sure") with "Oh, I'm so sorry, I'll try you again another time." Only then, if you are still itching to do an extra mailing, can those who accepted with prompt enthusiasm be rewarded with a reminder card.

Requesting an Invitation

DEAR MISS MANNERS—What do you do when a dinner guest repeatedly asks you, the hostess, to invite someone they'd like to have attend your upcoming dinner party already planned for eight. Note that the dinner guest is already coming with a spouse.

GENTLE READER—Miss Manners has never countenanced the practice of treating people's houses like restaurants by assuming you can bring whomever you like, adjusting the time of arrival and stating your food preferences. But at least people understand that restaurants get booked up. Perhaps you can make your friend understand that you do, too, even if that person cannot master the concept that hostesses plan their own dinner parties.

All you need say is "I'm terribly sorry, but I have a full table." If this means that the original couple withdraws, so be it. You will have two more places to fill with friends, rather than non-paying customers.

Demanding a Reply

"Warning: This offer expires by . . ." Any day now, Miss Manners expects to see this engraved on formal invitations. The Shaded Modified Roman Lettering style might be considered tasteful for the apparently essential hostly task of threatening the guests.

Miss Manners knows that contemporary folk are going to have a hard time believing this, but there was once a time when people who received invitations were given no instructions at all about answering them. They just knew to do so, immediately upon receiving one. It took two minutes to check the social calendar and three additional minutes to have the traditional marital exchange:

"Must we? You know how deadly their parties are."

Long pause.

"Yes, dear, but perhaps it's best to go and get it over with."

Out went the answer—yes or no—five minutes later. That custom was common only back in the days when common sense was presumed. You need common sense to be able to reason that if you were entertaining people, you'd have to know in advance how many of them would be there, in order to know how much food to have and arrange the seating. Also, if some people declined right away, then you would have time to invite others in their places. This thought is too difficult for the modern mind.

So there has developed a series of increasingly desperate ways of begging guests to let their would-be hosts know if they planned to attend or not.

First it was the more or less discreet admonition in the corner of an invitation: "The favour of a reply is requested" or "R.s.v.p." Even aside from the necessity of remembering to put the useless "u" in "favor" and to refrain from uppercasing the abbreviation for "s'il vous plaît," this was an odd innovation. A sensitive guest would surely be insulted at the idea that he or she had to be nagged to perform an obvious social politeness.

Maybe there weren't so many sensitive guests. They still didn't answer. So newer forms developed to encourage guests to reply by making it easier. The ugly "Regrets only" appeared, not only relieving guests from answering in the negative, but already expressing on their behalf a polite regret at not attending.

Still worse is the "reply card," which seems to have gelled in the ghastly form "M ——— will/will not attend," requiring the guest to do no more than cross out one word or two and drop it in the mail. For those who find that too much trouble, telephone numbers are now supplied. Even the White House no longer expects its state dinner guests to be able to write an answer and still have enough energy left over to make it to dinner.

Yet the problem remains unsolved. Even guests who have been cornered by their hosts and asked point-blank for their decisions manage to escape. "We'll let you know" has replaced "We'd love to" or "We're so sorry, but that's the evening we wash the dog."

Miss Manners finds the necessity for pleading on the part of the hosts unseemly. They are, after all, only offering to be hospitable, not trying to force these ungrateful wretches to do what they want to avoid. So she is making a ruling that all social invitations must be answered within two days of being received. (Business invitations should be treated like requests for meetings, with varying degrees of attention, depending on the professional advantages; pseudo-social solicitations may be treated as junk mail.) She considers this quite generous. It allows plenty of time to consult spouse, boss, transportation schedules.

People who receive invitations need not worry that the possibility of their not attending would be so devastating to their hosts that dragging the matter out, in order to let their hopes down gently, is in order. The fact is that hosts are a lot less upset to receive polite refusals than their guests may believe. This only liberates them to invite someone more interesting.

The Polite Method

DEAR MISS MANNERS — When I periodically invite friends to join me for outings, dinners, etc., I frequently do not speak directly to the individuals I am inviting, but leave messages on their answering machines. At what time would I assume silence means "no" and invite someone else instead?

I want to be fair and give people time to respond after coordinating with their spouse, yet I don't like giving the next invitee no notice—i.e., "Do you want to go the ballet tonight?" Neither do I like letting tickets go to waste. Is it unreasonable to expect a reply indicating either yes or no? And what does one do about "friends" who repeatedly fail to return calls.

GENTLE READER — Miss Manners has a policy of giving people the benefit of the doubt, and doesn't in the least mind blaming innocent machines in order to do this. She always assumes that an ignored invitation is the result of a mechanical malfunction, rather than a manners one.

She has an increasingly hard time maintaining this fiction. Machines seem to be improving at the same rate that people are getting worse. Nevertheless, the polite assumption could be that the invitation was not received, so there is no harm in inviting someone else. Should you get a last-minute acceptance, you could protest, "But I hadn't heard from you, so I went ahead and made other plans," provided you use a tone of flustered apology, rather than a censorious one.

It might be less emotionally strenuous simply to make a second call. If you get the actual person, you can repeat the invitation and ask for an answer; if you get a machine, you can leave the benefit-of-the-doubt message: "I left a message before, but you must be away, so it's too late for getting together on the 17th—but do call me when you get back."

Questioning the Term

DEAR MISS MANNERS — After witnessing yet another complaint regarding the global misunderstanding of the simple meaning and social requirement of the "R.S.V.P." may I suggest that the term is now antiquated and needs replacing with a clear, English phrase that perhaps will assist all involved? It appears that the vast majority of people do not know what the acronym means, and even those that do often choose to ignore it, then feel free to answer "I thought that meant . . ." as an acceptable excuse to ignore the request.

Perhaps you could lead the effort—and make it totally proper—to use the simple phrase "Respond please to 555-5555 by January 1" or something similar.

The American love of acronyms could be satisfied perhaps with "C.A.L.U.K." (call and let us know) or the like. Obviously, in this modern time-conscious, get-to-the-point and get-the-job-done world we live in, expecting someone to interpret a foreign phrase then properly act upon it is no longer feasible. T.Y. (Thank You!)

GENTLE READER — Miss Manners is always happy to help make social duties clearer, to enlighten the befuddled and thwart the undutiful. But C.A.L.U.K.? N., T.

There has long existed an English alternative to "R.s.v.p." (the preferred abbreviation), "The favour of a reply is requested." You will notice that this, too, has a foreign flavour. Uh, flavor. In the interests of Americanization, Miss Manners is happy to do away with that "u."

She is also happy to go with the slightly less formal, but certainly-to-the-point, "Please respond." It is going to take her longer to reconcile herself to the new habit of setting deadlines. It has never been quite nice to threaten one's guests.

Misusing the Term

DEAR MISS MANNERS — Every year since the mid 1980's, we have planned a catered holiday Open House, always on a weekday night during the late afternoon/early evening hours, for the clients of the law firm where my husband is a partner. The number of invitations sent for the party has averaged between 375–400; most years, 150 clients have attended. At the bottom of each invitation, we add a "Please RSVP" notation, the date when we wish the clients to RSVP, and the law firm phone number. Although the clients have the invitations in their offices for either 4–5 weeks before we ask them to RSVP, only 20% make the effort.

Do you have any suggestions for us on encouraging our clients to RSVP? I always need to let the caterers know how many people are attending three days before the party. Why won't people be gracious enough to let you know if they're attending?

GENTLE READER — It's the "Please RSVP." The "SVP" stands for "s'il vous plaît," which, although literally "if you please," is the standard French way of saying "please," and why they should take three words to say what we say in one is another question. Perhaps your guests are so thrown by this double courtesy that they are speechless.

No, it isn't that. Please please forgive Miss Manners. She would never defend the rudeness of ignoring invitations, but she does believe that the underlying terms of your invitation indicate that it confers minimal social obligations on those who receive it.

It is not really a social party, but a little perk for clients; the term "open house" indicates more flexibility than expected at other parties; it is timed so guests can stop by for a drink after work, rather than making a special outing; and it's so large that they can reasonably assume that you may not even notice who is there, let alone have a chance to socialize with them. Miss Manners has no objection to these arrangements, which probably appeal more to your husband's clients than something requiring more from them. She is only pointing out that you have set it up to seem like an option, rather than a firm commitment. Even if you telephoned each person to force out an answer, she doubts they would feel their acceptances or refusals to be binding. Besides, if 150 people generally come, why don't you tell the caterer that? Miss Manners will save her indignation to use on your friends who refuse to answer your dinner invitations.

Questioning Oneself

DEAR MISS MANNERS — Through the years, I have become very angry at people who don't respond to my invitations, or respond at the last minute. Even when given an R.S.V.P. date, they often don't let you know by that date. However, recently I have realized that I quite honestly feel hurt when they don't call me upon receiving the invitation, and that may be my little hang-up. But it would be nice to know what is truly the correct way to handle this.

GENTLE READER—Oh, why don't we just redefine all expectations of basic manners to be neurotic, and Miss Manners will go take a nap. Probably in the river.

The way to handle an unanswered invitation is to telephone and inquire "Did you get my invitation? I hope I can expect you for dinner Saturday." You needn't say this too warmly, as your previous warmth, in issuing an invitation, was ignored. The long-run way to handle people who never answer invitations is to be righteously angry at them for being rude to you and to drop them from your invitation list.

SETTING THE TERMS

Issuing Warnings

When Miss Manners read a possibly apocryphal report that guests of the Roman emperor Nero had been known to feign death with the hope of being carried out while his private violin recitals were still going on, she was impressed. Amateur performances require accomplished manners. To risk premature burial in order to depart without protest from the artistic endeavors of the untalented struck her as a solution bordering on the heroic.

Yet Miss Manners is far from opposed to amateur entertainment. Given the choice between what passes daily for professional entertainment, and the enthusiastic, if not always perfect, efforts of friends, she prefers the latter. The days, or rather the evenings, when everyone was expected to be able to make a bit of music, read aloud, recite, participate in theatrics, dance, play parlor games or otherwise contribute to amusement in television-less drawing rooms were exciting.

Yes, there was suffering connected with being put on the spot and knowing that even in a concealed way, one was being judged and found wanting. Or ludicrous. Still, Miss Manners found those pink faces—flushed with embarrassment or triumph, and also with exertion—more alive than the bluish ones reflected in the dull glow of electronic entertainment.

She is always happy to see how much of that individual exertion takes place today. The fields of creativity have since been amplified, and not only by amplified musical instruments. Today's amateurs are more likely to be filmmakers than singers, piano players or violinists. However, as Nero's guests demonstrated by their sacrifices, amateur entertainment must be governed by an equal devotion to manners as to the arts, on the part of the performers and audience alike.

For performers, the chief rule is that one must provide fair warning. You can't invite people to an ostensibly innocent event and spring a performance on them. "Dinner and tapes from our vacation" or "We thought we'd have a sing-along after brunch" should appear on the invitations.

An essential artistic skill is to be able to judge how much a body can bear. Even a connoisseur of torturously long cultural events (Miss Manners has to her credit not only the eight-hour *Nicholas Nickleby* and several four-day *Ring* cycles but Kabuki sessions too numerous to mention; she will be the first in line when someone makes good on the threat of doing *Henry IV* parts one and two and *Henry V* with only meal breaks, perhaps with *The Merry Wives of Windsor* thrown in there somewhere) has limits. In her drama critic days, Miss Manners once offered to buy the local culture center a huge backstage clock measuring two-hour intervals, so that no matter what was playing, the curtain could be rung down at a merciful hour.

To entice people to buy tickets to an event, one must offer a party before or afterwards, but the guest's only obligation is to accept both or neither.

For amateur entertainment in connection with social events, half an hour is the uppermost limit, unless all present are part of the performance. This is a maximum time, not authority to ignore wandering eyes, drumming fingers, yawns and other signs of desperation short of the posture of death. Pleas for more should be taken in the same spirit that the host uses when urging people to stay on after they have finally shown signs of going.

Once cornered, guests are honor-bound to give a semblance of attention and enjoyment. Miss Manners mentions both, because bliss based on an unexpected nap opportunity doesn't count.

Perhaps the part many find hardest is the necessity for professing appreciation afterwards. Friends and critics are not the same thing; one can say they are opposites.

You do not offer a frank critique of such entertainment, any more than you would leave a dinner saying "The roast was over-done, and you really ought to provide more amusing companionship." Apparently sincere requests for impartial judgments are not that at all. You are safe in taking everything in the way of a question for a disguised plea for admiration, or at least the assurance—however counterfactual it may be—that the performer has not made a fool of himself.

Miss Manners understands that some are afraid that compliments might bring on encores. She assures them that there is a strict rule against amateurs providing encores, no matter how severely they are begged. Begging is merely the surest sign of good manners on the part of the guests.

Making a Counter-Offer

DEAR MISS MANNERS — My wife and I are dismayed by a perplexing phenomenon we have dubbed the "reverse invitation." This occurs when an invitation is proposed over the telephone by Party A to Party B—for example, "We'd like to have you and your family over for dinner." Missing the point entirely, Party B says, "Oh, great. But why don't you all come over to our place and we'll have a cookout?"

When we have invited a child to come and play with ours, the child, being a homebody, invariably says no—and then her mother comes back on the line with the reverse invitation: "Well, she doesn't want to come over, but could your little Margie come over here?" While it is polite and flexible of our friend to welcome our child, this thoughtless response effectively negates our invitation and puts us in the awkward position of pleading our case. Or we feel pressed to accept the reverse invitation, which forces us to completely change whatever plans we had in mind.

Chiefly, the reversing of invitations undermines our desire to be hosts. We are wondering if any of your readers have suffered this social irritation, and if you have any suggestions for averting it.

GENTLE READER — If Miss Manners ran a contest for identifying and naming new social phenomena, you would win a prize. She doesn't do so only because she has no desire to encourage innovations—they so often turn out to be for the worse. This one has some bumbling merit, in that it at least offers hospitality, normally a polite thing to do. But it also fails to respect the offer of hospitality, which isn't. The way to deal with it is to treat these two aspects separately, but in reverse order. Got that?

First, you accept the regrettable fact that your invitation was declined (even though it wasn't, exactly): "Oh, I'm so sorry you won't be able to make it; I'll call you again, another time." Only then do you (correctly) decline the invitation that was offered, "No; thank you for asking, but I'm afraid that doesn't work out."

Note that you have not offered excuses. These are always better omitted in a flood of regret at not being able to accept—but this point is especially important in the reverse invitation. There is no way you can plausibly claim to be busy at that time. Also, you don't want to set yourself up for continued negotiating, as that is what you find objectionable.

Charging

DEAR MISS MANNERS — Would you please enlighten me on the apparently new form of entertaining, the "no host bar"? I received an invitation to an anniversary party at a local club: "Join us on our anniversary. No host bar." The guests were kept waiting an hour for the host and hostess, who had been out to an expensive dinner and obviously had a few drinks. This rude tardiness could easily have caused their guests to run up quite a bar bill.

Now the same family is having their daughter's wedding. Invitation arrives: reception at the same club, "no host bar." I really hope this tacky way of entertaining does not catch on. Am I out of step?

GENTLE READER — You are if you call it "entertaining." Entertaining consists of hosts offering hospitality to guests. At a minimum, this means being there, as well as offering them some refreshment, however humble.

Miss Manners can hardly imagine how these people could make it clearer to you that they do not intend to be hosts. Why you should then pretend to be their guests, by awaiting their pleasure or by attending future occasions, is what she finds mystifying.

Subscribing

DEAR MISS MANNERS — I am a reference librarian with two patrons who wish to know the proper way to word an invitation to a luncheon held at a restaurant. Without sounding crass (BYOL, Buy Your Own Lunch, Cash Lunch), the invitations should indicate that those invited would be responsible for their own lunch tabs. I have been unable to find any information regarding this matter in our many etiquette books.

GENTLE READER — Like you, Miss Manners has enormous faith in research. Nevertheless, she can save you work: In your entire library, including everything to which you have computer access, you are never going to find a proper way to invite people to a luncheon on condition that they pay for their own food.

That is because there isn't one. You can invite people to subscribe to a charity event, you can notify people of a luncheon meeting, and you can dash off a note notifying people that some friends or colleagues are planning to go out to lunch together and you hope they will join you. If any of those are what your patrons had in mind, Miss Manners would be glad to tell them how to alert people to occasions at which they may buy themselves lunch. Please note, though, that those are not social invitations. You cannot issue invitations to a luncheon unless you are actually giving one—giving, not selling.

Splitting Costs

DEAR MISS MANNERS — When you invite a couple to go out to dinner, I contend that unless you state that you are paying or treating them, the inference is that we each pay for our own. My wife contends that it is appropriate, and maybe expected, that the couple doing the inviting should pay for everything.

GENTLE READER — The way the system of eating out works now is that the people issuing the invitation always assume that the others will pay for their own food, and the people accepting the invitation always assume that the inviters mean to pay for everybody's.

This is not working, folks. Unpleasant surprises at the end of the meal are not good for the digestion.

As long as some people use restaurants to entertain as they would at home, and others use them as meeting places to get together with friends without anyone's being a host, people will have to be extra clear about what they mean. Miss Manners' formula for the first case is "We would like to invite you out to dinner," naming a date, time and place as hosts do when they entertain at home. For the second, it is "We were thinking of going out to dinner—would you like to meet us somewhere?" A restaurant can be suggested, but when people are paying for themselves, they get a say in where they are going. She probably needs to work out a more severe warning. In the meantime, she urges all parties to such events to listen carefully.

Refunding Costs

DEAR MISS MANNERS — Cousin Maurice and his wife, Lulu, sent invitations to the family to celebrate, "Dutch treat," the 50th anniversary of Aunt Cornelia and Uncle Zachery at a local restaurant. At the affair, Cousin Maurice provided a cake and paid the tip, while each guest paid for his or her own meal.

A few days after the party, the guests duly received thank you notes from Aunt and Uncle with the postscript, "We are sorry for the misunderstanding" and a check for $15 per person. As we have never encountered such a situation before, we would appreciate your comments concerning the terms of the invitation and the subsequent reimbursement by Aunt and Uncle. The names have been changed to protect the parties involved.

GENTLE READER — Miss Manners was so disappointed when she got to the end of your story and found that these were not real names that she can hardly bear to answer your question. However, one must bear disappointments bravely.

Aunt Cornelia and Uncle Zachery, being well-bred people, were properly horrified to hear of guests being charged to go to a party, and have chosen the least awkward way they can imagine to erase such a blight from their anniversary celebration. Miss Manners congratulates them on their taste, as well as their anniversary.

Paying Off Hosts

Here's how many people pay their social debts:

Friend or relative gets married—buy and sign card, send check.
Colleague gets married—sign card and contribute to office fund.
Friend issues dinner invitation—bring bottle of wine.
Relative graduates from school—buy and sign card, send check.
Friend has baby—buy and sign card, make donation to baby's
    education fund.
Relative has birthday—slip cash into card with instructions to
    "get something for yourself."
Friends hold anniversary party—make donation to favorite charity.
Friends hold holiday party—show up with item of food, taking
    leftovers home afterwards.
Colleague retires—sign card and contribute to office fund.
Friend, relative or colleague dies—buy and sign card, make donation
    to favorite charity.

It's getting rather expensive to be sociable, isn't it? Not to mention all that strain of signing cards.

Well, that isn't the half of it. Even if someone faithfully makes all the above payments, Miss Manners will not consider those debts to be discharged. She is going to send around the social bill collector.

In the desire to simplify the pleasantries of life, so that no one has to waste time thinking about another person, and no one will be burdened with another's ideas, money is being used in the hope of replacing effort in human society. Almost every occasion seems to have its price. Scarcely is the milestone announced when the listener reaches for the checkbook. "Congratulations" and "I'm so sorry" have both been replaced by that charming reflection "How much is this going to cost me?"

Creativity seems to be represented by the selection of a preprinted card approximating appropriate sentiments.

It's getting so that the parade of guests who now each hand over a bottle of wine as entrance fees to a dinner party almost seem quaint for having gone out and bought something. Perhaps we will soon be looking back with wonder at the trouble to which people would go to actually stop by a liquor store—in the days before guests took to pulling out their wallets at the end of a party and asking their hosts what they owed.

Fortunately, we are not quite there yet. You could empty out your bank account and still not be socially quits. Here is what is Miss Manners finds on the debit sheet:

After having enjoyed someone's hospitality, you owe that person return hospitality and, in the case of dinner parties and overnight stays, written expressions of thanks. Bringing wine—or any other little present—is fine but not required for dinners, although necessary for house visits, either upon arrival or after one has cased the place to see what is needed. Even presents and letters do not cancel the obligation to reciprocate.

When someone with whom you have a personal tie has an important milestone, you are also obliged to express pleasure in spoken or written words. A present is not strictly necessary if one declines an invitation to a wedding, birthday party or anniversary celebration, but is mandated by custom if one does.

Sending money kills the opportunity of thinking how one can please the person concerned (however relieved that person may be at this admission of defeat), so gifts of money should at least be accompanied by a letter suggesting possible uses, however vague.

It seems to Miss Manners that office collections are an imposition requiring people to fake friendship with their colleagues. Whether they are held or not, congratulations ought to be spoken by anyone who would recognize the honoree if they fell over each other in the cafeteria.

Deaths require either paying calls on the bereaved, when it is customary to acknowledge the disruption of the household by bringing cooked food, or writing letters expressing sympathy with them. These obligations cannot be canceled, even with a well-meaning check. Miss Manners realizes that money may be a joy to the happy and a consolation to the afflicted. It is still not quite as valuable—or rare and coveted—a commodity as human attention.

Working for Hosts

Is being invited out to dinner getting to be too much work?

An increasing number of people are reporting to Miss Manners that the one certainty of an invitation to dinner—that the guest wouldn't have to cook that night—no longer holds true. Accepting an invitation is likely to be tantamount to accepting a cooking assignment. Typically, a Gentle Reader reports that a few days after receiving an invitation to a birthday party, "the hostess called again to suggest that I bake the birthday cake, to serve thirty, and perhaps bring a liter of wine as well." Others complain of accepting dinner invitations and then being told to make the main course, or at least a salad. The thoughtful host has come to be the one who offers the guest—not dinner but a choice of what to bring for dinner.

Miss Manners' correspondent asks if it is possible to "choose politely to decline to bring something other than good cheer and a host/hostess gift of my own volition? I was reared with the belief that when one hosts a social affair, however simple or lavish, one ought in fact to host it. To treat one's guests as contributing caterers would be unthinkable."

The new practice is known—when the hosts even take care to issue warnings, rather than springing assignments after what seems like an ordinary invitation to dinner—as the potluck supper. A potluck supper traditionally meant that guests would be treated as family, in the sense of being served whatever happened to be in the pot that night. Now it means that they will be treated as help.

Miss Manners acknowledges that a practice known as the covered dish supper, to which everyone brings a contribution to a joint meal, has an honorable history under certain circumstances. These include such cooperative events as church suppers, picnics and book clubs, where no one is really a host, although someone may be in charge of organizing. Occasionally, such meals are also held in private homes, among friends who gather regularly and rotate where they meet, or among those who do not do full-scale housekeeping, such as students or others on their own for the first time.

What is new and offensive is the idea that one can "give" a dinner, in the sense of offering hospitality and deciding the arrangements, by putting the guests to work. Miss Manners understands that entertaining has come to seem a burden for those with multiple responsibilities, and is as anxious as anyone that the prospect of added chores and expenses not kill off social life. Many people do, in fact, skip entertaining when they have young children and fledgling careers, only to find that when the time comes that they could enjoy—and even need—friends, they don't have any. The solution, it seems to her, is simpler forms of entertainment—non-mealtime parties or non-taxing menus. Restaurant dining, even if cost is not a problem, does not provide the same warm atmosphere as visiting, but carry-out meals can be dished up with the same élan as home-cooked ones.

The cooperative meal does not seem to Miss Manners to be an altogether satisfactory solution because it merely divides the work on a given evening, rather than distributing it the traditional way by reciprocal entertainment. It is true that it is work to have a number of people over to dinner, but that occasion should be followed by several evenings of no work at all, as the hosts dine at those people's houses. (Miss Manners suspects that lack of faith in guests' performing their duty has led to hosts' desire to even up the social debts on the spot, instead of extending social credit.)

For those who nevertheless wish to participate in the so-called potluck supper, Miss Manners insists that the terms reflect the spirit of cooperation. The invitation is not "Would you come to dinner?" but "I thought we might have a joint party over at my place, everybody doing some of the cooking—I'd be very pleased if you'd like to join us." The assignment is not "You're making beef Wellington for fifty" but "Is there anything special you'd like to bring?" with the suggestion that those who don't want to cook could instead bring the wine.

The thanks for the evening should be extended in both directions—everyone of course thanking the person at whose house the party was held, and that person taking care to thank each of the sub-hosts who helped put on the party.

Overworking Guests

DEAR MISS MANNERS — When I was invited to a potluck dinner, the hostess said she would drop off a recipe for me to prepare. It consisted of half a page of exotic ingredients and directions for frying, marinating, roasting and crushing, which would have required me to spend most of the day in the kitchen. I didn't have the presence of mind to refuse the invitation, but I can afford neither the time nor the money.

I realize that most people who write to you are simply asking for corroboration of their own opinions, and I am no different. Is this lady nervy, or what?

Is there any polite way to accept without accepting the conditions of the invitation—in other words, can I show up with a meatloaf? Realistically, can I show up with a tasty dish along similar lines, which is less costly and time consuming? I would very much like to go to the dinner because, for one thing, I like her husband. I suppose I would really like some way to put her in her place without incurring her ill-will. Is this beyond the limits of human nature?

GENTLE READER—Well, it's not easy. People who are put in their place tend not to like it there. They get miffed at the person who put them there. Still, Miss Manners thinks she can manage. Like you, she despises the bait-and-switch ploy by which people first offer hospitality and then demand that their unwitting guests provide it. An honest cooperative dinner must be announced as such, and those who agree to contribute must be asked what they would like to contribute.

If you bring a substitute dish, your hostess will assume that you are at fault, not she. If you prefer to call attention to her failure, the polite way to do it is to telephone her and say, "I'm afraid I can't manage the cooking assignment you gave me. Do you want me to attend anyway?"

Refusing to Hire Guests

DEAR MISS MANNERS—I'm in my late 20's, newly married, and as time allows, my husband and I enjoy having dinner guests. I am simply looking for their company, and have no intention of asking them to bring part of the meal. Our gatherings are rarely formal, but it is still my instinct to think that if I am inviting someone to my house, it is impolite to assume that the guest should have to help with the meal. Sometimes, the wife offers to bring something and I usually graciously decline.

When other couples invite us, my husband will ask what I offered to bring. My answer is usually nothing. I don't recall having heard my mom offer to bring food when invited to dinner. Is this a custom I have been unaware of? Is it fair to believe that if we are invited to someone's home we shouldn't feel obligated to bring a side-dish or something?

GENTLE READER — It is increasingly customary for people to treat all meals as cooperative ventures, but that doesn't mean Miss Manners likes it any more than you do. When hosts do it—"Please come to dinner—and bring dinner around the back"—it is clearly rude. When guests offer to bring something, it is kind; but it is still rude for the hosts to be too quick to take them up on it, or to do it with such frequency that they might as well announce that they expect it.

Yes, friends should share the cooking—but unless a group of people has agreed to a truly cooperative meal, in which the person who offers the house is not the host but the organizer who gains other people's consent, the proper way is by issuing reciprocal invitations.

As you do your full share of entertaining, Miss Manners absolves you of the task of cooking for other people's dinner parties.

Ordering Supplies from Guests

DEAR MISS MANNERS — Due to circumstances beyond my control, I am currently "purchasing" my food with USDA food coupons. Would it exceed the bounds of etiquette to request that my dinner guests bring soap, napkins and other amenities? A good neighbor, who still has a paying job, is always bringing food. I am not starving, and have been giving food away so it won't spoil.

GENTLE READER — Considering the number of well-to-do people who invite people to dinner and then assign them to bring food, or who place orders with people who might be expected to give them presents, Miss Manners would like to go easy with you. You are offering hospitality under difficult circumstances, and she doesn't want to discourage you.

Yet the rules about not making demands on guests still apply. Should people ask the increasingly common question "Is there something I can bring?" you can ask if they would mind picking up napkins or soap. Spontaneous presents of food must be graciously accepted, whether you need them or not. As you have realized, they give you the opportunity to help people even less fortunate than yourself.

FULFILLING THE TERMS

"Casual" used to be a happy-go-lucky sort of term, merrily announcing a brief holiday from the usual formalities. The catch was that formality had to be usual for it to be a pleasant relief, once in a while, to indulge in a bit of laxness. So when laxness became the general standard, the idea of things being casual should have disappeared. Miss Manners might not have been thrilled, but she would have understood.

Instead, Casual became a religion. It must now be one of the most zealously overused terms we have. One hears all the time of Casual clothes, Casual meals, Casual entertaining, Casual attitudes and even dedicated Casual people, as in "I'm a Casual sort of guy." Miss Manners gathers from the fervor with which such allegiance is declared that if there is one thing that is no longer casual, it is aspiring to being Casual. People seem to work so hard at it.

Furthermore, Casual is perceived as a moral state. From the tone in which people talk of being Casual, it is hard to avoid noticing that they are bragging. Miss Manners has never been big on negative virtues. She would prefer to admire people for what they do, not what they fail to do. It seems to her that more effort is involved. She especially doesn't like this particular failure. From careful observation, she gathers that Casual has now come to mean "the state of not giving a hoot." Or whatever it is that people don't give when they haven't the least interest in pleasing others.

Casual meals are those in which there is nothing to wash afterwards because everything can be thrown away, including the carpet where the food soaked through the paper plate and wasn't noticed because people wandered about aimlessly on top of it.

Casual clothing means it feels better than it looks—unless it is Faux-Casual, in observance of the new religious holiday, Casual Friday, in which case it only costs more than it looks.

Casual entertaining is where neither host nor guest has the responsibility for making things go, so after hanging around unattended for a while, the people do.

Casual people are those who take pride in their unfailing unwillingness to exert themselves.

The Casual attitude means that none of this much matters. Miss Manners thinks it does. Far from wanting to abolish casualness, she wants to restore it to its former dignity. Properly speaking, Casual was supposed to be easygoing, not hard on everyone but oneself. It therefore requires certain amenities.

Casual meals may consist of simple food, which may be simply delivered, but they should be served with and on things that do not simply give up in the middle—platters rather than cartons, metal rather than plastic, earthenware or cloth rather than paper.

Casual clothes are still supposed to be clean, reasonably attractive and fit for the occasion.

A Casual occasion can derive charm from being spontaneous, informal and low-key, but not from being indifferent to the convenience and pleasure of those involved.

Miss Manners knows perfectly well that one reason people rhapsodize about being Casual is that they think this frees them from etiquette. On the contrary—formality has well-known rules built into its forms, so that one doesn't really need to think much about them. It's when the forms are abandoned that well-meaning people have to pay attention to figure out how to be polite.

So watch out for any self-declared Casual Sort of Person. It is a warning that this person isn't going to do anything he or she doesn't feel like doing, regardless of the consequences to you.

Making an Effort (Hosts)

DEAR MISS MANNERS — Lately, it seems that friends and relatives who invite us for dinner often remark, "We are having something simple," or "Do not expect anything fancy." They are by no means poor. We were recently served a five-month-old frozen meatloaf! Why do they make a point of informing us of this? It makes me feel as though we are not very important guests.

GENTLE READER — The meatloaf is not the problem. Graciously offered (which is to say, without announcing how long it has been mouldering in the freezer), humble hospitality can be charming. So might possibly be a very small apology suggesting that the fare, whatever it is, is not worthy of one's guests.

Your friends sound more as if they are bragging. No doubt they believe they are practicing the Cult of Informality, a currently common form of social confusion, in which lack of consideration and hospitality is supposed to glow with the warmth of intimacy.

Why not bothering on behalf of one's guests should be considered a virtue, Miss Manners cannot figure out. Like you, she has a great deal of trouble distinguishing this from the Cult of Not Giving a Hoot.

Not Making an Effort (Hosts)

DEAR MISS MANNERS — I'm hosting a bonfire in my backyard. I have invited 30 guests and requested that they bring Coke or chips or ketchup and mustard. I feel slightly uncomfortable, but I don't feel that I should pay for everything. After all, I am providing the location, wood and hot dogs and buns. Is this appropriate?

GENTLE READER — You are hosting a bonfire? Miss Manners realizes that you are not Smokey Bear (note to editor: It's not Smokey the Bear, any more than it is Miss the Manners), but even so, this seems like a strange idea. Surely you mean that you are giving a cookout, or a picnic.

Let us consider whether you really wish to be a host at all, as opposed to merely allowing a group of people to use your premises for a cooperative event. Anyone who aspires to that gracious title is expected to provide for the comfort of his guests, including refreshments, as well as location. He may, if necessary, beg close friends to help out as a favor, but he does not congratulate himself on providing some sustenance, with the implication that those freeloading ingrates ought to be contributing to their own keep.

Making an Effort (Guests)

DEAR MISS MANNERS — We recently went to an informal party at a friend's house. There were about 20 people there. I had debated whether to go or not, since I had a headache. I had told the host earlier in the day I was coming, so I decided to go, but to only stay a little while. After about a half hour I left with my sister. My husband said leaving so early was rude, and it would have been better not to have come at all. My sister and I believe that it is better to make an appearance, say hi to everyone, and chat for a few minutes, than not to go at all. I'm told the host did make some comments, after we left, about our leaving early. For future reference, could you tell me whether there is a minimum amount of time one should stay at an informal party?

GENTLE READER — By "informal," do you mean that the invitation was for cocktails or tea and specified a range of time ("five to seven" or "six to eight") during which people were expected to drop in? If so, the answer is that you must stay at least an hour. Or do you mean that you considered it one at which manners were not important?

If that is your idea, Miss Manners is obliged to tell you that there is no such thing. If the invitation was for the whole evening, the only way to leave after half an hour would have been to announce convincingly that you had been stricken ill on the spot, preferably with something more demonstrably an emergency than an ordinary headache. At the risk of sounding like your mother when you tried to claim that you were too sick to go to school but well enough to go out with your friends after school, either you are sick and may cancel your duties to convalesce, or you are well and must perform them.

Not Making an Effort (Guests of Honor)

DEAR MISS MANNERS — When friends of ours returned from a six-month vacation, my husband and I decided to give them a welcome back party, and invited about 50 couples, many who came from long distances. A few minutes after the guests of honor arrived, they and another couple proceeded to play cards. At no time during the party did they take a break and socialize with other guests. In fact, they would ask passing guests to get them plates of food from the buffet line and bring it back to them. Some guests complained and quietly left the party.

When the subject was brought up a few days later, my guest of honor emphatically stated that it was her party and she could do anything she wanted, and I should not have expected her to hold my hand, or any of the other guests' hands, for that matter. Though I replied I didn't expect that, I did think it would have been nice for them to take an occasional break and socialize.

Of course my idea of etiquette is wrong, in her opinion. Since then, she has brought it up numerous times in front of others and has had a good laugh at my expense. Our friendship has never been the same since.

I am not one to press who is right and who is wrong, especially with one who exudes etiquette. But I am tired of being made to look the fool because my etiquette is not always as proper as hers. If you say I'm wrong, I will apologize to her and bear the laughter.

GENTLE READER — Oh, so that phrase, and that idea, have spread, have they? It used to be just brides who stamped their little satin-shod feet and unbecomingly declared, "It's my day and I can do anything I want," at the expense of their guests. That would be mean enough, if they didn't all then go and declare themselves etiquette experts. Etiquette!—the most devout guardian of the sacred notion of hospitality!

Miss Manners assures you that you need not worry about being rude, but you should worry about such rude people being your friends (as she worries about their claiming to be her followers). That is not etiquette which this person exudes. Nobody should attend, much less give, a party for someone—or marry someone—with such an attitude. Miss Manners' advice is that when you hear that statement about "I can do anything I want"—run.

Ending the Effort

DEAR MISS MANNERS — One of the happiest moments of my life was when I stopped operating a restaurant without a license and hung up my apron. For years, I was the host with the most, wining and dining people, carefully cooking fresh ingredients, asking people what they liked and disliked, telling them the menu in advance, not ever wanting anything contributed to the meal from guests—and what did I get for it?

Nothing in return. For years we entertained friends and relatives and hardly ever were asked over for dinner or even an evening of entertainment. Once a friend said she could not possibly have me over for dinner as her cooking and entertaining could not compare with mine. I replied that a pizza ordered would do just as well. She did not get the hint and afterwards was cut off from hog heaven.

Joking aside, I am disgusted. What bothers me is to have people sit at your dinner table and tell you about restaurants they have gone to and described the meals in detail while feasting at our table. They eat, burp, push away. Rather than comparing it to casting pearls before swine it's more like casting grub to the pigs.

People eat out more today. Anyone can go to a restaurant, it doesn't take any talent. It takes care, thoughtfulness, and consideration plus skill to put on a good meal for 8 to 10 people. It became such that people thought it was a regular duty on my part and one day I took a look at the china, sterling silver, linen napkins, tablecloths, candlesticks and flower vases and thought that if I wanted to, I would have gone into the restaurant business legally years ago and would have made a success of it.

I did not want to continue being a lawbreaker by operating a restaurant without the proper permit so I gave it all up and am no worse off for it. Tell my friends that it is too late—it's all over with, you get what you pay for. You did not even pay us with a sincere thank you therefore the slop shop is closed. Fend for yourself!!!!

GENTLE READER — Now, now. Please calm yourself. Allow Miss Manners to offer you a bit of refreshment, if not comfort. Sadly, she cannot disagree with the cause of your disillusionment. Entertainment requires that the guests do their share, which includes gratitude and reciprocation, as well as answering and following the terms of invitations, and putting themselves out to be charming.

The failure to do so is why restaurant-going has largely replaced private entertaining, as you note. It's not just that many people feel it is too much work to be proper hosts, but that those who enjoy it are discouraged by doing so for people who feel it is too much work to be proper guests.

Enjoyable as going to restaurants might be, it means that something important is missing from life. Giving and receiving hospitality is one of the most fundamental and satisfying experiences one can have. Miss Manners hopes you will not be permanently discouraged. There are people who appreciate this, and she hopes you and they will find one another.

Being Deserted

DEAR MISS MANNERS — One of my closest friends assured me, the morning of my Hallowe'en party, that she and her husband would be there. Not only did she not attend, she did not call me beforehand to say she could not make it; nor has she called me since to apologize for not coming, or at least to explain why they chose not to attend.

Am I supposed to call her and ask what happened, or am I to wait until she contacts me? I do not know what to say, and am somewhat angry and more than somewhat hurt at her lack of communication. She is very etiquette-oriented, and would raise a royal fuss if I did this to her.

GENTLE READER — What is your friend's idea of etiquette? "You have to treat me with consideration, but I am exempt from inconvenient rules"?

Miss Manners does not wish her any ill but feels obliged to point out that only tragedy would save her reputation for being polite. If she calls eventually to say "I feel dreadful about having missed your party, but my uncle-in-law had a heart attack that very afternoon, and we rushed off to the airport to get to him as quickly as possible," Miss Manners will allow her to continue to consider herself "etiquette-oriented."

You might want to speed or suggest this solution by calling her and saying, "I've been frantic with worry about you. What happened? I expected you and had no word at all—so I had to assume the worst. I know you wouldn't have disappeared like that without an explanation unless something dreadful had happened." Then let her try to say "No, I just didn't feel like attending your silly party."

Being Utterly Deserted

DEAR MISS MANNERS — I'm a married man, and my wife was out of town for two weeks with her mother. I invited over several male friends, men mostly in the same line of work. All requests were made in person or by phone, for Monday night, six o'clock, for a cook-out, some pool in the pool room, some poker, maybe a video. I laid in steaks, deli food, beer, wine, the works.

Six o'clock comes and goes. Likewise seven, then eight. The dog and I eat steak and watch TV. No one shows. I don't have B.O., so that's not it. A couple of days later, one of my best friends said, "Oh, you never called back." Am I supposed to re-confirm? Am I missing something?

GENTLE READER — You seem to have missed the demise of guest manners; the mere offer of hospitality no longer suggests to people that they are under any obligation to cooperate. As this outrageously selfish notion has been around for some time now—making havoc out of social life and disgusting many otherwise sociable people to the point of refusing to do any non-business-sponsored entertaining—Miss Manners is intrigued that you had been hitherto protected from it. Is it possible that in your circle, the wives, retaining the once-prevalent idea that social life was their special obligation, had been covering for the husbands' bad manners?

Notice how someone you call a best friend has neatly managed to blame you for this failure. He is trying to suggest that all the obligations are on the host's side, including that of nagging the guests into attending.

Others may tell you that the event sounded so "casual" that they didn't think you would care if they showed up or not. This is a bogus argument. Miss Manners assures you that if the event had been anything but casual—had it been your daughter's wedding—the same people would have argued that it was so grand an event that they figured you never would have noticed if they had attended or not.

Do not allow yourself to be bullied into accepting this callousness as a standard. Anybody who tries to tell you that nobody cares about such essential points of etiquette nowadays is discounting the feelings of a kind gentleman left with a free evening, an empty house and a lot of steaks.

The Cost of Being Deserted

DEAR MISS MANNERS — A friend of mine regularly receives theater tickets from her employer and invites friends to attend with her and her spouse. However, on more than one occasion, they have called at the last minute to advise that the invitation is off, due to their securing a more desirable social function for that evening.

When one friend mentioned that she was a bit put off by this, the couple's astonished response was, "Why would you be mad when you aren't even paying for the tickets?" While we enjoy this couple's company and are appreciative to be asked to be their guests, I am having difficulty recognizing as acceptable the premise that an invitation stands only unless something or someone better comes along.

GENTLE READER — Miss Manners is having worse difficulty with people who see money as the only factor in life, even in social life. Does having a planned evening ruined, or being told that something more important than one's company has come up, not count as long as one is not actually out of pocket?

If these people wanted to be polite, as well as generous, they would offer the tickets saying, at the time of the invitation, "We're not sure if we will be able to join you, but anyway, we hope you enjoy the show."

Timing Being Deserted

DEAR MISS MANNERS — I am a single professional woman, and when I entertain, I usually spend a long hard day getting everything ready, including a meal that can be served buffet-style so I am free to spend time with my guests. By the afternoon, I am exhausted and try to get in a quick nap so I am fresh for the party. About the time I lie down, the phone starts ringing with the regret telephone calls. This pattern is unchanged whether I have specified R.S.V.P. on the invitation or not: Invited friends will call as late as 30 minutes prior to the planned party to cancel out! The fact that my much-needed nap is disturbed is bad enough (I have an answering machine, but think it is very rude to leave a ringing phone unanswered when I am home), but that I am given so little forewarning by those who will not be coming is what steams me so much I really can't rest.

To the last party, I invited 20 people, estimated about 16 would come, had six regrets in the last three hours, and ended up with a party of eight. As a hostess, I give up, unless you have suggestions to avoid this recurring problem.

GENTLE READER—Obviously your problem is caused by your prospective guests' failure to observe social decency, in which acceptances of invitations are binding. They are rude. It is compounded by your false notion that guests must be allowed to come and go, by telephone, whenever they please. That is foolish. With a total open line policy, you will never get a nap in peace. Solving one problem may help solve the other.

Miss Manners doesn't guarantee that people so callous as to cancel social engagements in the last half hour might realize that not being able to cancel means that they ought to go, but it might give them pause. When you next see them, try showing extreme concern at the emergency that must have befallen them to necessitate their standing you up. If they are shameless, the nap should at least leave you fresh to entertain your polite guests. Miss Manners regrets that there seem to be so few of that type left.

Replacing the Deserter

DEAR MISS MANNERS—I invited a colleague to a really nice event, a private performance of the symphony, several weeks prior to the event. He responded by saying that he would go with me if his schedule permitted. I gave him my phone number, and we agreed that he would call when he knew his schedule for that week. Well, the concert has come and gone, and I never heard from him. Tempted as I am to label him a complete boor, I would like to assume that he has some valid reason why he could not so much as make his regrets.

Nonetheless, this complete lack of acknowledgement has me puzzled. At what point would it have been appropriate to invite another guest? Three hours before the concert? One day? One week? I will soon return to his work location after several months working elsewhere. I do not wish to be rude or unprofessional, but neither do I wish to belittle the situation with "It was no big deal." After all, it was a big deal.

GENTLE READER — It certainly was. Miss Manners is more often in the position of calming down the overly snippy, rather than revving up the overly tolerant, but totally ignoring an invitation is about as rude as you can get without hitting someone.

There was no valid reason for him to string you along. Had his schedule shown another engagement, he could have called you immediately. Had an emergency arisen that very minute—had his mother been on Call Waiting, to tell him that she had just been run over and required him to take her to the hospital—he could have found someone to inform you, or called with apologies after he had turned her over to a doctor.

The point at which you could have invited another person to the concert was the one in which your colleague claimed not to know his schedule, without volunteering to call you back that very day. "Oh, well, then, perhaps I'd better catch you at another time" would have been the polite response. Now the tone to take is strictly professional plus an ice cube—that is, with not the slightest indication that you had any social relationship with him or could ever do so.

Retaliating

Seldom does retribution for a violation of etiquette come so swiftly. Miss Manners cannot resist telling you a story with a severe moral (although she will try to resist telling it gleefully):

An old-fashioned lady was giving one of her old-fashioned dinner parties, the kind that called for open salt cellars instead of shakers, and fruit knives and forks for the extra course before the sweet dessert. Being of the old school, she had assembled her guest list not only for conversational compatibility but so that the table would be surrounded by neatly alternating ladies and gentlemen. She was just shaking out the damask on the day of the dinner, when, to her surprise, one of the guests called to say that she wouldn't be able to make it but would stop in afterwards for coffee.

Not able to make it? As the hostess well knew, the only proper excuse for canceling a commitment to go to a dinner party is sudden death. Lingering death won't do. This guest didn't sound dead at all. Her health was confirmed by the cheerful tone in which she explained that she had been invited to a rather fancy dinner given by someone quite important, and that she believed it would be useful to her career to go. She added that the other half of the couple in which she was invited to the first dinner party, the gentleman with whom she resided, would keep the original engagement, as he was not included in the later invitation.

Remember that Miss Manners told you that the hostess was a very old-fashioned lady. So old-fashioned that she had no trouble whatsoever with unmarried couples living together—her old-fashionedness making her believe that that aspect of their life was none of her business. But to have someone frankly confess canceling a dinner date because a more advantageous opportunity arose shocked her into near immobility.

It wasn't total immobility, because she was strict enough not to consider social catastrophe to be an excuse for letting down her guests. They could perhaps have survived without a full table, but this lady, the sort of perfectionist who measured the distance between place settings (which she called covers) when setting the table, believed it her duty to fill in all the blanks.

"Extra lady, extra lady," she thought desperately. "Whom do I know well enough to ask such a favor?" (She knew, of course, that while it is a compliment to a guest to issue an invitation at the proper time, it is an intimate favor to ask someone to come at the last minute. Proper reciprocation is not only a subsequent invitation, made far in advance, but the silent acknowledgment that the hostess must make every effort to be available for last-minute duty at that person's parties.) Then she thought of someone perfect—someone who would not only even out the dinner table but grace it with beauty and wit.

Indeed, that is what happened. You may be pleased to know—if Miss Manners has been able to stretch your imagination enough to engage your sympathies for a lady who still believes in dinner tables that are meticulously set and surrounded—that the party was a success.

Even the gentleman who had been left behind to fill an ordinary engagement, while his lady had moved up to something grander, seemed to be enjoying himself. In fact, he especially seemed to be enjoying himself. When the lady with whom he resided showed up as promised, for coffee—prompting her hostess to believe that her coffee must be better than the other host's, for surely the social honor system could not have been a factor—she found him sitting on a drawing room sofa, next to the replacement guest.

They were merely sipping coffee, chatting quietly, and looking at each other as proper guests do after a proper meal. The old-fashioned hostess thought their behavior impeccable. The latecomer didn't. She took one look at them and understood, with piercing accuracy as it turned out, what had happened. As a desperate last-minute move to salvage her private life, she attempted to insert herself into the nonexistent space on the sofa between them.

It was too late. The gentleman escorted the latecomer to their mutual home, and the other lady thanked her hostess, who pressed her hand warmly in a silent gesture of return thanks for saving the evening. Miss Manners is happy to report that some time after the dinner party, the gentleman and the so-called extra lady were married. This is a true story, and she invites her readers to supply the moral.

Mixing

It isn't as though people aren't open to making new friends nowadays, as those who feel left out have complained to Miss Manners. Sure they are. They easily plunge right into intimate conversation with strangers and chat for hours. It's just that the chief requirement for friendship has become the likelihood of never having to see that person ever again—or at all.

In cyberspace and traveling around conventional space in airplanes and trains, people freely exchange life stories and medical symptoms, and compare opinions and tastes. It's only when they're out socially that they freeze.

"My husband and I attended the wedding reception of a friend's son and were assigned to a table with the bride's co-workers," a Gentle Reader reports. "Being the newcomers, we attempted introductions and pleasant conversation—the key word being "attempted." If we spoke to them, they answered. Otherwise, they spoke around us above us and about us—but not to us. When the wife of the company's vice president looked at me and said to someone else that she thought all that dark hair with the gray streak was attractive, I was glued to my chair! They were talking about me as though I was a piece of furniture!"

Another Gentle Reader has found that at public receptions—"non-political and not dedicated to the goal of meeting powerful people"—such as the opera's opening gala, most people "stand in twos and threes, glassy-eyed, with drinks, appetizers or desserts in hand, and talk only to those they already know." She reports: "To a man I found myself next to, I said as humorously as possible, 'I don't know a soul here,' and his icy response was, 'Why did you come, then?' I introduced myself to someone else, who said cynically, 'Why are you here?'—he turned out to be one of the event's organizers. Couldn't he have said, 'Thank you for coming?' "

A "transplant from another state" eager to make friends writes that when she and her husband both approach a group: "He can speak successfully to the men present, and I will only receive scornful looks from the women. This has happened on several occasions and is very upsetting to someone who has never had a shortage of people to socialize with. Are women so territorial that they are unwilling to let other unknown women become a part of their circle?"

A gentleman newly moved to a retirement community reports going to events, meals and the pool to socialize: "I laughed and talked with a number of residents, but became friendly with a few," whom he invited to meals—only to have them fail to show up. "I wasn't overbearing, pompous or boring," he promises; "I was neither self-centered nor opinionated. I believe that I showed genuine interest in those I talked to. I expect a certain amount of imprudence from the younger generation, but not from my elderly peers who should know better."

Miss Manners cannot imagine being so socially overstuffed—or so tired of the world—as to be immune to the possibility of finding an interesting new friend. Even more baffling is plentiful evidence that even those who particularly want to meet new people (Miss Manners is trying to avoid the word "singles") panic at the idea of going to a party or wedding alone. They drum up someone to bring along, rather than take their chances on new people. Or they stay home and write advertisements about themselves in the hope of attracting total strangers rather than the friends of their friends.

This is, after all, a society that prides itself on openness and friendliness. And then spends its time complaining of loneliness. What does Miss Manners have to do to teach people to extend themselves socially at social events? Charter airplanes for them?

Criticizing

DEAR MISS MANNERS—What do you think of dinner guests who critique and criticize the food they are served? I spent an entire day preparing a delicious five-course meal and did not receive one compliment or thank you. In fact, they left in the middle of the meal, after they overheard me telling my husband in the kitchen that I was getting upset over their insulting comments.

I was taught that you always say thank you and compliment anyone who is gracious enough to invite you into their home for a meal, no matter what is served. I was also taught that you should take the host/hostess a small gift, such as wine, flowers, candy, as a token of your appreciation. These people have eaten at our home several times and have never brought me anything or sent a thank you note.

GENTLE READER — What you describe—guests insulting the hosts in the dining room, and the hosts insulting the guests sotto voce in the kitchen—sounds like a social nightmare, a screenplay or both. In neither case does it seem quite fair to Miss Manners not to supply her with the essential details.

Were your friends insulting you by actually making disparaging comments about the dinner you offered them, or by not offering thanks and compliments between bites? Were you overheard to complain about their failure to bring presents? Did they behave this way before? Or has the situation been building slowly to the point where they sit around the table saying what a lousy meal they're eating, and you broadcast from the kitchen your desire that they would shut up and go home? Who was retaliating against whom? If they have never before thanked you, why do you keep inviting them back?

You won't have to worry about that now. Miss Manners declares this a social disaster area, and suggests you start again with a new set of friends and a soundproof kitchen door.

Complaining

You must never break bread with people and speak ill of them afterwards.

This rule of etiquette, designed to discourage guests from the tempting treachery of accepting hospitality and then making fun of their hosts, is an ancient and venerable one. Miss Manners is not claiming that it was always as scrupulously observed as it was widely known. She remembers an instance when she arrived at a social event of such stupefying pretension that its nature was apparent at the entrance. A lady who arrived simultaneously took one look at the overpowering arrangements and whispered, "I don't think I'm going to eat my roll at dinner." That was all she needed to say. Miss Manners understood (which is not to say that she approved).

She is therefore more saddened than surprised that this rule is now so often neglected, perhaps even forgotten entirely. One hears people critically describing hospitality that they have enjoyed—or rather, not enjoyed, as they take pains to make clear, but only endured. It is as if they regard the entertainment that they are offered by friends as the same as that which they purchase, and feel as free to rate dinners and parties as they do restaurant meals and shows.

The old rule is still on the books, Miss Manners wants everyone to know. Participating in a social event and then going around complaining about it remains horribly rude. Still worse is that it is not uncommon now to hear people criticizing a social event while they are still attending it.

Here are the kind of remarks one is apt to hear among guests milling around at a party:

"Is this all we're going to get to eat?"
"They ought to sue their decorator."
"Watch out for those people over there—they're awful."
"Want to go some place more interesting?"

Perhaps it is just as well that some of these guests also commit the rudeness of simply leaving large gatherings when they have had enough, without actually seeking out the hosts to say good-bye. Considering their ideas of freedom and frankness, who knows what they might say instead of the traditional thanks?

"I've had better evenings."
"I know you tried, but it didn't really come off."
"Sorry I have to leave early, but I can't take it any longer."

It is hardly less rude to attempt to improve the terms of an invitation by negotiation beforehand. Inquiring who the other guests are to be, announcing what one would like to eat and declaring that one will attend only part of the event are not acceptable social maneuvers.

The only proper way to avoid a social event you think you might not like is to decline the invitation with thanks—and with alacrity. There should be no thinking it over, no probing to find out its attractiveness and no offer of party hints that might make it more to your taste. The basis on which a guest has to decide is knowledge and previous experience of the hosts, the basic definition of the event, and the date. Take it or leave it.

Every once in a while, this means that someone may be trapped at a disagreeable social event. Well, so be it. Not every party is a success, any more than any other evening, and one that may be pleasant for some guests may not be for others. This does not strike Miss Manners as the greatest tragedy in the world. It is certainly no excuse for vilifying people whose crime, after all, is only to provide food, drink and company for those they suppose to be friends rather than rotten ingrates.

RECIPROCATING

Halting the Cycle

"What a shame it is that nobody gives dinner parties any more," many people are given to saying. Miss Manners always clucks sympathetically. (Clucking is a lost art, which saves the work of saying "Oh, how true, how true." Remind Miss Manners to demonstrate it for you sometime.)

The truth is that some people do still give dinner parties, and the ones who are complaining probably went to them, had a wonderful time and then failed to reciprocate. What they really mean is that they don't give dinner parties any more, and that they are helping discourage those who do.

Goodness knows there are enough reasons to be discouraged, even before the hosts check their answering machines in vain for return invitations. More and more of them are reporting that from their first overtures, the guests act as if they would be doing the hosts a favor by attending.

First, they ignore the invitation. If caught, they try to renegotiate the terms: The married people want to come without their spouses, and the single people want to come with them (that is, their sub-spouses, other people's spouses, their children or their dogs). They demand to know who the other guests are. They order their own menus. They stack engagements on the same night so that they don't fully attend any one of the events. They may or may not show up, as likely as not late and dressed for some other activity.

To round it all off, they show no gratitude. Etiquette demands that those who have been entertained at dinner express their thanks not only at the door but again in a letter or telephone call. But, then, etiquette doesn't always get what she demands.

Etiquette also demands that people who have been entertained reciprocate in kind, but Miss Manners has always been most reasonable about how this is done. She discourages friends from counting exactly how many times each entertained the other, so long as there is some rough form of taking turns. Nor does she require that the return invitations be as elaborate as the original ones—each according to his own style and ability is the rule in social life.

Nevertheless, there is resistance. Those who accept hospitality but do not dispense it argue that:

They have no time.

They don't have the equipment—the setting, spoons, whatever.

They haven't enough money.

They are too young to be expected to entertain people who have been at it for years.

They are too old to be expected to entertain people who ought to take up the burden.

They are single and cannot manage it alone.

They are married and haven't enough time with their spouses.

They have children and are therefore exclusively concerned with their needs.

They don't have children, and other people who do won't want to socialize with them because they are exclusively taken up by the children; besides, these children make unpleasant guests.

As you can figure, there aren't too many people left. Yet Miss Manners would like to point out that some people, even those who could claim one of these categories, do nevertheless entertain—at least until they get bitter about not being invited back.

Miss Manners' interest in keeping the custom of home entertainment alive is not just sentiment. She believes home entertaining to be a cornerstone of civilization, the cultivation of disinterested friendship being one of the joys and comforts of life. Money, time, age and family life are not valid excuses for not doing one's share. Breakfasts and teas, with little work and less cost, count as returns. There is no perfect stage of life that makes entertaining effortless, and waiting for one would consume a—friendless—lifetime. Children and adults can be entertained separately but simultaneously. People who entertain flawlessly nevertheless appreciate being invited to leave their perfect settings now and then.

Bartering

DEAR MISS MANNERS—I love to entertain at home for lunch or afternoon tea, but would also like to be asked back to the homes of friends and acquaintances who frequently attend. Some do, of course, but several ladies have—instead—brought a small hostess gift. Does this discharge any obligation on their part to reciprocate?

GENTLE READER— Have we gone on the barter system? Had we done so— over Miss Manners' dead body—would these people think that a box of candy or a bottle of wine is a fair trade for a home-cooked meal?

It is not the meal they are expected to reciprocate, it is an act of hospitality and friendship. These, being priceless, can only be repaid in kind, or a rough equivalent, such as taking you out. Hostess presents are all very well, but they do not wipe out the debt.

Reciprocating Wholesale

DEAR MISS MANNERS— We have been graciously entertained by many people in our community. Our home is not large enough to accommodate one hundred or so guests. Is it proper to separate our parties into a few weekends? Have you any suggestions how my invitations should be worded?

GENTLE READER— It occurs to Miss Manners that what may be troubling you is the suspicion that the guests will all find out about not only the parties to which you invite them, but the others. They will then assume that any party to which they were not invited must be the A list party.

Well, so be it. You can't invite everyone to everything. Indeed, these one hundred or so people did not all entertain you together at one gathering. To do so yourself would be to make it obvious that this was a payoff party, not an occasion on which you could see your dear hosts again.

The invitation for a medium-sized informal gathering—Miss Manners is not asking you to entertain them individually, for a hundred weekends—is usually "cocktails, 5 to 7 P.M." or whatever time you set. A more formal gathering is called a reception.

The Day After

DEAR MISS MANNERS — I gave a cocktail party, and the day after, starting at 8:15 A.M., if you can believe that, my guests began calling to say what a lovely party it had been and how they enjoyed themselves. Now, they'd all thanked me upon their departure the previous evening. And as I live alone and had a heavy schedule the next day, it was truly an interruption to have to answer the phone and listen all over again to "thank you so much, we enjoyed it all, etc., etc." I know it was courtesy and thoughtfulness that prompted their calls, but honestly, I wish they had not bothered!

Perhaps a hundred years ago, ladies drove by in their carriages and "left a card on" the hostess the day following a festivity. Perhaps 50 years ago, ladies might have sent around a very brief handwritten line or two, mailing it if not within a short neighborhood walk. Perhaps these telephoned thanks have taken the place of those earlier niceties. And perhaps, even, you approve, and won't want to discourage the practice. However, I think it ought to be pointed out delicately that often it becomes a genuine nuisance and really is not necessary!

GENTLE READER — Did you have too good a time at your own party, and are you feeling a bit ill-disposed today?

Miss Manners is very sorry, but do you really expect her to join your little crusade of discouraging people from offering thanks? Would you like to expand it and tell children not to trouble their grandparents with thanks for presents? Do you have any idea how many people accept hospitality nowadays, with no thought as to performing any of the duties of guests, such as answering invitations, thanking their hosts, and later reciprocating by inviting them to parties?

As you say, telephoned thanks, when they are offered, do often take the place of practices of the past—although the last time Miss Manners checked, the mail was still available for the transmission of more properly expressed written thanks.

Each custom blessedly comes with protection for the exhausted hostess. When cards were left, it was upon people who had a servant to accept them, with the conventional, not literal, explanation that Madam was not at home. With the telephone, we have the answering machine, which similarly takes the message without bothering the hostess. You are in sore need of that answering machine. Miss Manners is sure that you will be delighted to listen to the accumulated praise for your kindness once your head clears.

Chapter Eight

ENTERTAINING:
THE SOCIAL EVENT

CHOOSING THE FORM

Entertaining at home is the perfect hobby for a society where everybody is in show business. Everyone already knows the format, and having people sit on your very own sofa talking directly to you is ever so much more fun than eavesdropping on the conversation of talk show guests, who remain oblivious to all the clever comments you throw their way. As a live host, you get to be both director and star, although you are required to observe union demands (from the etiquette union) to attend to the well-being of others. You get to pick the style and arrange the lighting in the setting you designed.

You get to throw people together in combinations of your own devising and watch what happens. To top it off, everybody is obliged to keep telling you how perfectly marvelous you are.

Miss Manners isn't fooled by all those claims that we are much too casual (read charmingly folksy and modest) for that kind of thing. Then who are all those people who devote years to planning and restaging their elaborate weddings, freaking out if anyone questions their orders? How come civic activities, from politics to philanthropy, only attract people when they are packaged as fancy parties? Why should carefully arranged seating plans be considered silly at dinner parties but meaningful at fashion openings?

Of all social scripts, the best is for small, seated dinner parties, because nobody gets left out and everybody gets to sit down. If family dinner is the root of civilization (or whatever other metaphors Miss Manners may use in her tireless effort to promote the outrageous concept of nightly gatherings with other people who happen to live in the same house), the sit-down dinner party is its flower.

Formal or informal—or the in-between style that has become the standard for modern dinner parties—the basic procedure is the same. A half dozen to a dozen carefully chosen people gather at a specific hour (or up to eight minutes after), freshly turned out and primed for the pleasures of talk and table. They are given a drink, a nibble and a chance to become acquainted or catch up before being led to their places at a candlelit table and fed.

For the host or hostess to serve guests from platters at the table is both the modern informal and the ancient formal way of offering food. The modern formal way is to have footmen carry around platters of food from which guests help themselves while pretending not to recognize the footmen as their own party help or the hosts' children.

If this is too elaborate, there are other charming scripts for entertaining at home. Meals by daylight are lighter, even formal luncheons, where bouillon and salad and sherbet are considered filling, if not actually lavish; or brunches where heating the breads from the bakery and making pretty patterns of the goodies from the delicatessen is considered the mark of a fine cook.

To serve even less food, you invite people who already have dinner plans—offering a cold supper after the theater, or late evening dessert; or you invite people between meals—for morning coffee or afternoon tea. Although the former is the least formal of invitations, and often the coziest, the latter is now thought immensely grand.

However, if you serve cocktails and hors d'oeuvres in the late afternoon, once the sophisticated way to entertain, your guests will descend into fuzzy shock as, one by one, they realize that they have to go elsewhere to forage for dinner. The way to entertain a lot of people at once is still to make them stand up—indoors, if you don't mind risking your rug, and outdoors during those eleven days a year when it isn't too hot or too cold—but whether you bill it as a buffet dinner or a cocktail buffet, it amounts to the same thing. Whatever its form, there is so little such live entertainment being done that you will soon have a full house, with others clamoring to be admitted.

Paying Attention

DEAR MISS MANNERS — My husband and I entertain quite often, our favorite being small dinners with friends. We do all the work equally, and they always go off well.

My only problem is that my husband is a sports nut. Our large dining room connects to the living room, and if a big game is on, he insists on leaving the television on so he can glimpse it during the meal. It can only be seen by half the table, and the sound is off, but I still think it is wrong. He says he just glances at it, and that just about everyone watches television while eating, these days.

GENTLE READER — Miss Manners refuses to rescind the absolute rule against television during dinner, much less dinner parties, other than for events specifically planned around a particular television broadcast. For goodness' sake, can't you invite people over when there is no game on, or record it for viewing later?

Shifting the Work

Suppose you are really unable, ever, to reciprocate hospitality? Must you then vow social celibacy? Mindful of Miss Manners' admonition that hospitality has to be returned by hospitality—that it cannot be paid for, event by event; that someone who brings a present or a dish to a host has not thus canceled his or her social indebtedness—a Gentle Reader pleads extenuating circumstances.

"Consider, please, those associates who will never reciprocate in kind because they cannot," she writes. "They are bright and fun, they will bring gourmet dishes, money, love, and brilliant party decor 35 miles. But their house is not my house because of a sour spouse, a sour house, a kid just out of jail, and other embarrassments they cannot cover up because they work 50 hours a week and commute another 20.

"Also, they are convinced that nobody would show up if asked. People are sometimes sensitive enough to detect this situation. So some arrange a fair contribution by everyone concerned, so as to have a celebration. Someone who may not have gourmet dishes, money, love or decor may have a decent place not more than 50 miles from everyone. Where does fair sharing end, and taking advantage begin? That line, that line, it must be somewhere . . . snuffle, snuffle, sniff, sniff. Please be plain."

Yes, yes, yes, but please stop crying. Miss Manners cannot bear it. Here, have a lavender-scented handkerchief.

Miss Manners never meant to be so harsh as to outlaw the cooperative party, or to advise those who entertain to keep strict accounts of return invitations in order to drop delinquents. However, there have been so many abuses of hospitality on the part of both hosts and guests that she really must set strict limits on exceptions to the principle of social reciprocity. Not only has it become common first to invite people and then to inform them that they must cook or pay, but a shocking number of such events are in honor of the hosts—to celebrate a birthday, an anniversary, or even a wedding. That is not a cooperative party. It is a mockery of hospitality, in which someone pretending to entertain is actually tricking others into doing the work and meeting the expenses of entertaining.

A legitimate cooperative party is one in which several people decide to entertain themselves, sharing the responsibilities. Consent is sought ahead of time, because everyone concerned is a host as well as a guest. Such an event can be done in someone's honor, if that person is excluded from being a host, but it cannot be done in honor of oneself.

"Shall we all get together and put on a party for me?" is not a proper invitation. Nor is a proper social attitude "You can always be the host, and I'll always be the guest," no matter how generous a guest one may be.

Miss Manners has a great deal of sympathy for those who find it impossible to entertain and is happy to carry them through such a period. She does notice that some of them have too much sympathy for themselves, and not enough for those who entertain them.

Simply being busy, or not having fancy equipment, is not an excuse for not bearing one's share of the social burden. Neither is being young or poor or having small children. All these circumstances legitimately influence the way one entertains. People should entertain in a style they can manage, not in imitation of other

THE GRAND DINNER: *The table is properly set, but, as so often happens, the guests are out of control. The great dinner party problem is not the cliché about which fork to use. (Obviously the spoon is intended for the soup, after which one has only to go from outside the plate to in to find the fish knife and fork, meat knife and fork, and salad knife and fork in the order of those courses, while the dessert silver will arrive with the dessert.) Rather it is the rudeness of using a dinner party to take telephone calls, smoke, apply makeup, collect silver, hit on one's dinner partner and commit other rudenesses. And this is just before they've started serious drinking (the glasses, right to left, are for sherry with the soup, white wine with the fish, red wine with the meat, water when desperately needed and champagne in back to go with the dessert), although the lady down front still has an iron grip, in an improperly gloved fist, on her pre-dinner drink.*

people's standards. A family-style hamburger supper is a perfectly respectable return on a formal dinner.

Those who cannot invite people to their homes should entertain out. If the expense of a restaurant meal is impossible, they could thoughtfully arrange a much cheaper excursion, such as a nature walk or museum trek with a stop for coffee or ice cream. The point is to initiate and plan entertainment for other people. Even those who have the resources to give frequent elaborate parties are grateful if someone else thinks of doing the inviting and arranging, for a change. It makes them feel appreciated in a way that no present, no matter how thoughtful, can do.

TABLE MANNERS

Fear of Forks

For nearly a thousand years, the same ghastly fear has been gripping humanity. Death? Disease? Starvation? Annihilation?

No, forks. Well, sure, those other things too. But when there is no imminent danger, the fear of choice is forks.

When Miss Manners first heard this, she was stunned. Those nice forks that only want to nourish people and keep their clothes clean? How can anyone be reduced to cowering by a common household item? Nevertheless, the confession of Fear of Forks—more specifically, the deadly fear of using the wrong fork—is made so boldly and so often that she cannot imagine that everybody who claims to be suffering from it is making this up just to tweak her.

Miss Manners understands that few people who announce that they are flummoxed by this complicated and sinister instrument are admitting ineptitude. The rest are bragging. The declaration of not knowing which fork to use is intended to prove how sensitive one is, on the grounds that only a heartless snob would know how to eat.

Some form of this fear has been rampant at least since the 11th century, when it was uncharitably suggested that the folly of using a fork when the fingers would do would be sure to provoke God's wrath. Nowadays, it isn't the mere fact of using a fork that puts the fear of God into people so much as the idea of being given a multiple-choice test at the table. As they always put it: "I see five forks all lined up, and I'm terrified because I don't know which is the one I'm supposed to use."

The interesting thing about this problem is that it doesn't exist in real life. It never happened and it couldn't happen, not even to people who believe it has happened to them. Miss Manners always inquires politely where exactly it was that those five forks were laid out, and she always gets the sort of puzzled-and-panicked look that was supposedly directed at the flatware. The fact is that nowhere, not even at the White House, would a place be properly set with more than three forks. Formal dinners are rarely more than four courses nowadays (and one is usually soup, which has no truck with forks), but even if more forks were needed, it would be incorrect to place them on the table. Any fourth or fifth fork would have to be brought in with the course for which it was needed.

The rule for choosing among the original three is ridiculously simple: Always take the one farthest from the plate. If you make a mistake, it's the fault of the person who set the table wrong. If you still manage to choose the wrong one, you can rest assured that this is the least detectable social crime you can commit. Polite people are, by definition, barred from monitoring how others are eating, much less sniffing at them. Furthermore, anyone who ate the fish with the meat fork ought to have the fish fork left with which to eat the meat. (If not, there's a more serious crime being committed than simply misusing a fork.)

Yet Miss Manners does understand the historical reason why Fear of Forks persists as a fantasy nightmare. A variety of highly specialized forks existed only for a few decades, until about World War I, when life got streamlined—and it became profitable to melt them down for the silver. Nobody except Miss Manners still has bacon forks or strawberry forks or ramekin forks or terrapin forks, but during the Industrial Revolution, the fork business had gone wild, probably because name-brand sneakers hadn't been invented yet, and people who became suddenly rich needed ways to spend their money and show off to their poorer friends.

This made no impression on the fading upper classes, whose inherited silver didn't include these newly invented specialized forks. (The actual fortunes of this "kind of people" did make an impression on them, which they demonstrated by marrying their sons to the new heiresses.) They continued to use plain forks and spoke witheringly of "the kind of people who buy their silver." It made an indelible impression, however, on the not-so-rich, who were dazzled by the outlay of dedicated forks, confused about which was which, and intimidated into believing that this branded them as inferior. Generations later, they are still frightened. Miss Manners hereby absolves them—not of the necessity of eating properly but of the notion that they need fear being tested on defunct details.

No Table, No Manners

DEAR MISS MANNERS — My husband is a wonderful barbecue chef, and one of his requested specialties at our frequent pool parties is a marinated, crispy-skinned chicken. I was appalled to see one of our guests sitting casually in front of a platter of smoking-hot chicken, stripping the crispy skin from every piece and eating it, licking her fingers as she did so. She then returned each denuded piece to the platter, presumably for the other guests to enjoy.

Miss Manners, this is not an ignorant woman. She is a graduate of a fine Eastern college for women and has an MBA degree. She is a well-regarded financial planner for a prestigious brokerage. I am amazed that she indulged such a porcine habit so publicly. More to the point, is there a polite way to res-cue future barbecued chicken for our guests who prefer their food unskinned—and unfingered?

I thought of snatching the greasy hand and giving it a quick minatory slap, along with the admonition, "No! That's nasty!" This seems appropriate to the immaturity of the offense, but I know Miss Manners wouldn't allow it, and I would like to stay on speaking terms with the offender. I also thought of packing up the stripped meat in a plastic container and presenting it to the lady as she left, saying, "We weren't able to use this, but we thought perhaps you might." Again, I think this measure fails the Miss Manners test, though more subtly.

Our dog, Mitzi, thought the chicken was delicious and had no fault to find with its skinned condition. Possibly I need to cultivate her attitude of noncha-lance, but I just can't.

GENTLE READER — As you so admirably demonstrate, a polite hostess does not embarrass her guests, even porcine ones. In this case, you protected the offending guest by controlling yourself, which could not have been easy, and you protected your other guests by finding them something else to eat, which couldn't have been easy, either. Miss Manners congratulates you on both your manners and your larder.

The way to protect future guests is to spare them being invited with someone who is so thoroughly out of civilized control. The way to protect that person is to invite her only with those who will find her manners agreeable. The candidate who springs to Miss Manners' mind is Mitzi.

Anti-Manners Snobbery

The following anecdote about a grand etiquetteer of the past was told to Miss Manners by a prominent national politician:

It seems that many administrations ago, this great lady was dining at the White House, where she was seated next to a well-known Washington figure of the time (who told the story to the gentleman who told it to Miss Manners). The original storyteller reported that he had inquired of the lady whether she was indeed the great authority on behavior, and upon her confirming this, retorted, "Well, you're eating my salad."

Tee-hee.

Miss Manners is not amused. It's not only because she has heard this story before and with a variety of people cast in the roles of Pretentious Lady and Man-of-Good-Sense-and-of-the-People. Nor does she fail to roll on the floor with uncontrollable merriment because she took offense at the affront to an august colleague in the noble field of etiquette (cheeky as that is).

The story flops because it is just not plausible. It didn't happen, not to that lady nor to any of the others about whom it is told.

How can Miss Manners be sure of that when she was not present? Because at formal dinners, salad is served as a separate course, after the main course. It is unthinkable that dinner partners would have gone most of the way through the meal without introducing themselves. Their salad plates would be placed right in front of them, not to each person's left, as when salad is informally served to the side of the main course.

Furthermore, until the current administration, food was properly offered to the guests from platters, not slapped down in ready-filled plates, so the lady would have had to put her own salad on her plate. To eat her dinner partner's salad would have involved ignoring what she had just put in front of herself and leaning over to eat from the plate directly in front of him.

Etiquette is peculiarly blessed in having this sneaky control on those who delight in demeaning etiquette without being versed in it. By the same test, it is obvious that people who gleefully report that some highly proper person looked at them aghast for making a trivial error—almost always "choosing the wrong fork"—are faking. By definition, no proper person would register that someone else had made a mistake.

Other noble callings are not so fortunate as to have all this built-in protection. For example, you could probably say just about anything about a politician and be believed.

Miss Manners understands that there is no point in meeting people of reputation unless one can come away with an anecdote that illustrates one of the following premises:

1. This person is exactly what you would expect, only more so. (Example of looking aghast, usually accompanied by the additional offense of chastising the offender.)
2. This person is exactly the opposite of what you would expect. (Salad example.)

She also sympathizes with the fact that as most such people prefer not to make spectacles of themselves, their behavior is reasonably ordinary and there is not much dramatic material available in routine encounters. She can hardly expect anyone to report having met someone interesting and yet reply to the inevitable question "What is he like?" by saying "Pleasant enough, I suppose, I don't really know." So she supposes that all she can ask in the name of good manners is that gossipers try, if at all possible, to be kind. And if they can't be kind, they should at least be truthful.

SEATING ARRANGEMENTS

Ranking Guests

DEAR MISS MANNERS — At dinners in the homes of acquaintances (very special evenings: formal dinners, semi formal attire expected, where we go prepared with gifts for the couple in anticipation of a great evening) there were separate tables to accommodate the guests. Some were seated in the dining room with the finest china, stemware, silver and fabulous decorations and others at a table in either the kitchen with clearly the everyday ware or, in my humble opinion, worse yet, in hallways or some other room of the house.

While I understand that the intent of the hosts may be to include many of their friends at one time for such an evening, I think the practice is demeaning to those relegated to other areas of the house than the dining room with the hosts. Whether I am seated in the main room with the hosts or relegated elsewhere, jokes are always made about being at the "B" table. I am left feeling uncomfortable no matter what. My husband and I are in disagreement as to the correctness of this practice. Am I being overly sensitive and formal on this issue and should I just be gracious in accepting further invitations, or is this practice lacking in manners?

GENTLE READER — Would you both be satisfied if Miss Manners condones the practice but condemns the way your hosts managed it? Probably not. Miss Manners feels like being even-handed, anyway, because that is what it takes to manage A and B tables without insulting the guests.

    The rule is that if they can tell which is A and which is B, you've been rude. Clearly, the dining room outranks the kitchen, the hosts' table outranks a hostless one, and the good stuff outranks the everyday table things. But what would you say if the kitchen table were set with the best things and the hostess presided over it? Suppose you were put in the dining room and your husband in the kitchen, and other couples were similarly split between the two rooms? And the hosts went around whispering such things as "I've put you near me so we can have a good talk" or "We consider you such an intimate of the house that I'm going to ask you to sit in the middle next to someone who is dying to meet you"?

Honoring Guests

DEAR MISS MANNERS — I know the guests of honor sit at the right hand of the host and hostess, but at a little dinner party I am planning, two couples are equally important to me and they are also in the same age bracket. How do I seat them so that the one will not feel less important than the other?

GENTLE READER — If there is no obvious difference of age, rank (such as one person's being a member of the clergy or Miss Manners) or intimacy (people you know better yield the place of honor to newer guests) you must befuddle these couples so they can't figure out how you ranked them. This is done by seating the wife of one couple at the host's right, and the husband of the other couple at the hostess's right. Even the pickiest guests can only argue afterwards about whether you like her better than him, which—whatever it does to the marriage—at least leaves you in the clear.

Separating Couples

DEAR MISS MANNERS — Over the years, I have hosted many dinner parties, and have occasionally been confronted by a couple who have taken umbrage that I have not seated them next to each other. Couples have even changed their place cards without telling me.

I recently had an experience that tested the limits of my social conscience. It was a birthday party for 60 people. It took me two and a half hours to complete the seating arrangement. When I was confronted by three couples—and heard about two others—who complained about not being seated together, I adamantly (but politely, of course) refused to change the seating.

GENTLE READER — You are, of course, correct that married couples should never be seated together at dinner parties. This is for their own good. Separating them gives each a chance to tell shared stories without fear of contradiction.

Perhaps because this is a time when many marriages are of little more duration than dinner parties, there are those who try to seize every moment. Your guests are doing so rudely, by attempting to take your seating arrangement into their own hands. You can't separate them by force on the spot, but you should take note of their wanting to spend the evening talking to each other and not trouble them by suggesting they again leave the conjugal harmony of their very own dinner table for yours.

Miss Manners also has some misgivings about your spending two and a half hours doing a seating chart. It is easy to become more devoted to one's own masterpiece than to the social good it is intended to create. Take that as just a little cautionary note. Miss Manners would be relieved to hear that you are putting an equal effort into introducing the guests to one another once they arrive, and helping them kick off mutually satisfying conversations.

SOME TROUBLESOME DETAILS

Napkin Rings

At the Miss Manners' family dinner table, when guests are not present, napkin rings are used in the traditional way. That is to say, each member of the family has a different napkin ring (in this case, the designs are different, but it is also customary to have similar rings with identifying names or initials), replaces it on the napkin after a meal and thus is able to receive the same napkin for use at the next meal.

"Do you mean to say," she has been asked incredulously, "that you don't have fresh napkins at every meal?"

Well, yes, that is what Miss Manners means, if not what she had necessarily meant to reveal. Just as ordinary households have the sheets and towels changed once a week (not twice a day, as fastidious tycoons with full-time laundresses are said to demand, since tycoons require afternoon naps on fresh sheets to soften the stress of all that money), ordinary households have the napkins changed every few days, barring accidents or finger food orgies.

Or so Miss Manners had thought until she encountered this reaction. Are other people doing a load of napkins every day, one for each meal that each member of the family takes at home? Since Miss Manners agrees that in an ideal world, there would be no recycling of used napkins, ought she to be spending her time attending to the home question rather than the world's etiquette problems?

Not really. The world of etiquette is not unfamiliar with compromise and trade-offs, and Miss Manners can live with recycled napkins in order to have time for doing anything else, and in order not to create a water shortage. It was only later that Miss Manners discovered the real meaning of those questions. It seems that she has survived into a world where people believe that napkin rings are useless but decorative items to be put out on the company table.

Of course there are always fresh napkins out for company, which is why napkin rings were strictly an informal, family device that would be considered ludicrous at a dinner party. But it seems that there are also now fresh napkins out for each family meal—not because household laundry has increased but because the definition of napkin has come to mean something made out of paper. Cloth napkins are thought to be too much trouble in a busy modern household.

Miss Manners urges a revival of daily cloth napkins, along with the labor-saving napkin rings. Contrary to anti-etiquette propaganda, various prematurely abandoned tableware devices were not invented in order to put sensible people to unnecessary expense and trouble. On the contrary. For example, finger bowls have survived only where they are least needed—at formal dinners, where there is little likelihood of finger food being served. The effete versions on doilies, floating rose petals, to be put to one side untouched by the diner, disguise the fact that finger bowls properly serve the purpose of a moist towelette in a package. Salad knives have pretty much passed out of use (but not at Miss Manners' table), but it continues to be impossible to cut a wedge of lettuce or tomato with the side of a fork.

In regard to napkin ring usage, Miss Manners has been asked whether it isn't disgusting to reuse a napkin one has used before. Not if you also use another quaint old tradition that has also fallen into disuse. Table manners.

Napkins

DEAR MISS MANNERS — I'm having an on-going disagreement with my club members concerning the placement of large cloth napkins when giving a formal luncheon or dinner. I was taught that napkins are to be folded and placed on the left of the silverware or stuffed in the water goblet, but never forced into the smaller wine goblet where they flop over most ungracefully—but which my friends say is proper.

GENTLE READER — Miss Manners is about to make a lot of enemies—perhaps even you among them—by taking your side. Well, sort of taking your side.

The fact is that Miss Manners loathes napkins stuffed into drinking glasses. They remind her of handkerchiefs stuffed into jacket breast pockets, which, in turn, makes her worry what will happen if the gentleman sneezes and he doesn't want to use his show handkerchief, and there goes her appetite. However, she is well aware that stating these prejudices infuriates otherwise polite people, who never think to rebel when she only tells them how to run the world or their lives.

Miss Manners apologizes that she cannot interest herself in whether the silly thing is hanging out of the water glass or the wine glass. Napkins belong on the service plate or to the left of the forks.

Soup Spoons

DEAR MISS MANNERS — My mother taught me (although she was mistaken about some things and may have been mistaken in this case) that the choice of bowls and spoons for soup is determined by the type of soup one is serving: Round spoons and bowls or two-handled cups for cream soup, and soup plates and oval spoons for clear soup. I have been busy trying to remember which of my guests I may have served incorrectly, and hoping that they either overlooked or were unaware of my gaffe.

GENTLE READER — The mistaken notion here is that mothers make mistakes. Yours didn't. In fact, she spared you an additional complication: Bowls and cups are appropriate for luncheon, but only soup plates should be used at formal dinners. This makes it difficult to serve cream soup at night, which is a shame. (Miss Manners happens to prefer light soups at luncheon, which works because bouillon may be served in a cup with a small round bouillon spoon, but where does that leave the cream soup? Out in the cold, so to speak.)

Never mind. Fortunately for you, Miss Manners and your mother are the only people who remember these rules. Being gracious ladies, they make generous assumptions about extenuating circumstances, such as menu or cupboard considerations.

Finger Bowls

DEAR MISS MANNERS — I understand that I place the dessert fork to the left of the dessert plate on which it arrives, and that I place the dessert spoon to the right of the dessert plate. But what about the finger bowl, which I'm all for—how many fingers may be placed in it, and which fingers, if any? Do I place my fingers in the bowl before or after I place it, with its hand crocheted doily, where the bread-and-butter plate used to be?

How do I use the dessert fork and dessert spoon at the same time? Which goes in which hand, and which brings the dessert to your mouth? What is the other piece of silver doing in the meantime: lying on the plate, or remaining in the hand? And in what position are the fork and spoon left when dessert is over? What position are they left in if I pause to take a sip of champagne? Tines/bowl up or down?

If there are no rules concerning these details, it is certainly time there were.

GENTLE READER — All right, sure. There already are. But by the time dessert rolls around, even the nosiest people are too tired to police one another. Probably any crimes you could commit would pass unnoticed, except possibly drinking up your finger bowl, and even that might pass as late night humor to perk up a flagging party.

When a formal dessert service arrives, consisting of a finger bowl on a doily, fork on the left and spoon on the right, you put the fork on the table, to the left of the remaining dessert plate, the spoon on the right, and pick up bowl and doily and place it to your left, just as you said. There should have been no bread-and-butter place there before, as they are not present in formal dinner service, but yes, that's the position. (The necessity for doing this should not baffle the uninitiated. Any fool can see that something has to be moved if the dessert itself is not to be plopped down in the middle of a puddle of lukewarm water.)

At this point you may, if you must, dip your fingertips (all of them—except that most people miss the little finger, because it's too short—but not the thumb) into the water, and wipe them on your napkin. Frankly, you haven't been eating with your hands at a formal dinner, so most people consider the finger bowl purely symbolic and skip the actual washing.

It is not absolutely required that you use both fork and spoon, and if you pick one, it should be the fork unless there is an obvious reason—a runny dessert—to use the spoon. An unused utensil is left on the table. In using both, the fork remains in the left hand and the spoon in the right. This means that the fork is of little practical use, except possibly as a discreet pusher, but it is held on to nevertheless.

During pauses, the utensils are placed crossways, so the waiter won't snatch away yummies you haven't finished. For those who envision the plate as a clock, this is approximately 7:30, although the hands (which is to say, the tools you use to avoid using your hands) should meet somewhat below the center. Fork prongs down, spoon bowl up. When you are finished and they are left together, crosswise, the tines go up as well. Those who believe that European manners are snazzier than American, and encourage otherwise stalwart patriots to eat with their forks in their left hands through the meal, will argue that the tines should be left down. Don't listen to them.

Glasses

DEAR MISS MANNERS — My husband and I have a dear friend (I'll call her Mrs. Frigg) who believes that the labels should be left on her crystal stemware. We have dined in some of the finest restaurants in the world, and have never noticed labeled stemware before. Mrs. Frigg is so adamant that the labels should never be removed from stemware, that I thought I would appeal to your judgment. Since a great deal of time has been absorbed debating this issue, we have agreed to abide by your answer.

GENTLE READER — Baffled about what could have propelled Mrs. Frigg so far from the basic tenets of taste and sense, Miss Manners has come up with the following hypothesis: Mrs. Frigg has been trying for years now to get those pesky stickers off, and hasn't succeeded. She kept breaking her fingernails trying to pick them off. She tried soaking the glasses, only to find that the labels slid somewhat, but were as tenacious in their new locations as in the old. In desperation, she tried scraping one off with a knife, only to break the glass. Thoroughly fed up, she decided that it would be easier to convince gullible people, who already live in a society where it is customary to pay good money to wear T-shirts with advertising on them, that the labels belong there. As sorry as Miss Manners feels for Mrs. Frigg, she advises you not to fall for it.

Bottles

DEAR MISS MANNERS — When dining casually with friends, white wine hides discreetly in its ice bucket, but a red wine bottle seems at home on the table. Is there any exception to the general prohibition of commercial containers from civilized tables? Somehow a bottle of wine seems different from a bottle of catsup or milk.

GENTLE READER — The wine is hiding in the bucket when dining out casually with its friends? Miss Manners thought it was one of the more playful guests.

Wine sure is different from catsup or milk. No doubt about it. Among the less obvious differences is the fact that wine is properly placed on the table in its original container. All right, not the barrel, but the bottle (or the truly original container—the grape). You may use a wine coaster, or one of those thingamabobs that attach a handle to the bottle, if you wish. You may even decant it, if you have an excess of large crystal containers. But it happens that while putting a milk carton or catsup bottle on the table is a high etiquette crime, disguising the wine bottle is considered excessively genteel. Go figure.

FOOD

Menu Order

DEAR MISS MANNERS — At a dinner party, I was surprised to see the hostess serve the soup first and then a delicious salad before the main course. I may be wrong, but I always served the salad first and then the soup. I'm sure it really makes no difference, but I would appreciate your opinion.

GENTLE READER — What happened to the oysters? Oysters are supposed to be the first course. Or terrapin. Then the soup, then the fish, then the mushrooms or asparagus, then the roast, then the frozen punch, then the game, then the salad, then the creamed dessert, then the frozen dessert, then the cheese, then the fruit, and then hungry guests can get into the candy and nuts.

At least this was the traditional order of dinner back when meals were meals. A lot of funny notions about nutrition and health have come up since then, which is why Miss Manners no longer insists on that order (as if she could stand up against the fierceness of the food fanatics, if she tried). Most of these courses have been eliminated, and the standard formal meal is soup, fish or meat (but occasionally still both, as separate courses in that order), salad, dessert and/or fruit.

Often, nowadays, people will start with the salad because they have picked up the habit from restaurants, where formal service has been altered for the practical consideration of staving off hunger while the main course is cooked. Others start with salad for health reasons. Miss Manners does not object, provided she doesn't have to listen to the lecture about why.

Pushing Food

"Have something more to eat," the genial host urges the reluctant guest. "Have another drink. Because if you don't, I will badger and humiliate you until you'll wish you had."

That last remark is not actually spoken. But Miss Manners can perceive an implied threat from a certain tone and persistence, and so can those who find themselves the hapless victims of forced hospitality.

Against their judgment and their desires, supposedly pampered guests consume items they don't like, want or believe are good for them, and in quantities not of their own choosing. They will do this, mistakenly, in the name of etiquette.

Actually, etiquette has no interest whatsoever in making people turn green and rush out of the room. On the contrary. It is puzzled that guests, as well as hosts, harbor the strange notion that force-feeding people more refreshment than they seem to want constitutes politeness, and that holding out against this campaign is rude.

Miss Manners has no brief for the modern adult version of the food fuss.

Those who go around telling their hosts not only their own likes and dislikes, which is bad enough, but their beliefs—that this or that food will damage either your body or your soul—don't even pretend to be polite. They believe that a good cause always justifies making everybody miserable. Perhaps this creates a desire to find a non-criminal way to stuff their cheeks so that they are unable to talk.

Nevertheless, Miss Manners staunchly defends the right of grown-up people to choose what they eat and drink and what they don't, and if they base their choices on health, moral or religious choices, rather than mere prejudices, all the better. It is no etiquette violation to be selective, as long as one doesn't make extra demands on one's host's patience, energy or dignity. Exercising this right is not easy when the food pushers are at work. Their endless patter of coercion—"Oh, come on, one won't hurt you, I made this especially for you, it doesn't have any calories, you're too thin anyway, it's good for you, you're not going to make me eat leftovers tomorrow"—often succeeds in driving people to drink and chocolate.

What do these hosts have in mind? Do they really measure social success by intake? Do they believe that guests are terminally shy people who would starve to death for fear of seeming enthusiastic? Do they overestimate the amount of food that even hearty eaters could possibly consume?

Whatever the reason, Miss Manners asks them to cut it out. Politeness consists of offering food and drink without cajoling or embarrassing people into taking it. (It is a nice point of etiquette that reofferings never include a count: One does not say, "Oh, have another helping," but, "Would you like some pie?" Such offers, if accepted, may be repeated as long as the pie and the guest hold out, but the wording is the same.) So is the wording of refusal. The phrase is "No, thank you," and no guest should have to defend his or her choice. If a host is so rude as to argue, the guest should just keep repeating the polite refusal until the host is discouraged or Lent has arrived, whichever comes first.

Reheating Food

DEAR MISS MANNERS — When dining at the home of a friend, is it rude to ask to warm up your dinner briefly in the microwave? I like food to be hotter than most people do, and I do this myself at home, but am reluctant to inflict this preference on a hostess, even under very informal circumstances.

GENTLE READER — One of the hardships of social life is that people who eat out at one another's houses don't always get exactly what they want to eat, exactly the way they want to eat it.

The trade-off is supposed to be that they get to be with their dear friends, who have tried to please them, even if they haven't succeeded. Miss Manners is dismayed that an increasing number of people don't seem to think that this is worth it. They can eat at home, but they cannot make special orders, and they cannot go into the kitchen to make adjustments. So no, you cannot zap your food when you dine out. Your reluctance was your own good sense of manners kicking in.

Etiquette has gone quite far enough in requiring hosts to provide salt and pepper so that guests may season the food to their own taste. Some of them turn unreasonably morose when they see the salt and pepper used, interpreting it as a reflection on their cooking. Miss Manners appreciates your help in not encouraging such tendencies. You really don't want your hosts running around grabbing everybody's filled plate back saying "Is yours cold, too?"

Dessert

DEAR MISS MANNERS — My son-in-law says the hostess is supposed to take the first bite of a dessert. I say (coming from my grandmother from the South, who was rigid on manners and protocol) that the hostess always takes the first bite at the beginning of the meal, as well as dessert. I must say, I find the people here very short on manners.

GENTLE READER — Evidently, if you would rather quarrel than sit down quietly and consider that both of you could be right. So are any relatives you have who maintain that the hostess takes the first sip of soup, the first taste of spaghetti, salad, and so on.

Miss Manners doesn't doubt that people can spin all kinds of stories about waiting for the first taste in case the hostess keels over from poisoning, but the present purpose of the custom is to indicate that it is now time to dig in to that particular course. If she is delayed from eating, or does intend to poison her guests, saying "Oh, please go ahead" will do just as well.

No Dessert

DEAR MISS MANNERS — For a casual supper with three other couples who meet on weekends to play cards, I baked an apple pie and brought it along. I had just started a diet program and did not intend to have any dessert myself. When my husband and I walked into their kitchen and the hostess saw my pie, she said, "Oh, you're not going to have any pie, but it's all right for the rest of us to eat it!" Meaning we can gain weight, but not you.

I was shocked at her lack of graciousness, and blurted out that she could throw the pie out instead of eating it. I might add that everyone ate some pie and complimented me greatly on how wonderful it was—including the hostess's husband, but not her. She never did say a thing. What would have been a better response to her callous remark?

GENTLE READER — Neither you nor your hostess distinguished herself in this encounter, and Miss Manners is only relieved that it ended without a food fight. Had you wanted to make the point graciously, you could have replied, "I wanted to give you some pleasure, even if I couldn't share it. Surely you don't have my weight problems."

After-Dinner Coffee

DEAR MISS MANNERS — I love giving dinner parties—special parties, about twice a year, with great food, live music and entertainers. But as soon as the guests have had their dinner, they thank me with a nice smile and say bye-bye.

I've noticed that when we are invited to other dinner parties, guests tend to do the same. As soon as their bellies are full, they all retreat. Don't you think that this is abominable behavior? I believe that to stay a little longer after eating and meet other guests is a polite way to show their appreciation to the hosts for being invited.

GENTLE READER — Yes, yes, it's abominable, but it's the coffee.

Oops. Miss Manners did not mean to suggest that your coffee was abominable. Excuse her while she thanks you with a nice smile and rushes out the door and off the face of the earth. What she meant was that the nice old-fashioned habit of serving after-dinner coffee in the living room gave guests somewhere to go to continue the socializing after they left the table. If you, like many hosts, have dropped that custom in favor of serving coffee at the table, there is no signal that guests may stay once they have finished the meal.

After dessert, ask "Shall we go into the other room for coffee?" and Miss Manners is sure everyone will follow you and settle down for more cozy chatting. You will be writing back, not only to express your gratitude, but to ask her how you can now get them to go home so you can go to bed.

PARTIES

Young Adults' Parties

Young people's parties are too dark, too noisy and too loosely organized.

Is this the complaint of a curmudgeon whose own idea of socializing is scandalously tame? Well, yes. Personally, Miss Manners tends to favor mild encounters where even the glow of candlelight is tempered by silken shades, voices are modulated (often in obverse proportion to the explosiveness of the conversation) and guests are never allowed to outnumber the available soft chairs.

But far from grudging the socially restless their pleasures, Miss Manners worries that their parties do not adequately serve the intended purposes, let alone the wider objectives of their social life. It is not that the form is offensive—but that it is counterproductive.

As Miss Manners understands it, a typical such party has no fixed times, no fixed guest list and no fixed refreshments. People wander in throughout the evening, in pre-formed couples and groups that do not necessarily correspond to the acquaintance of the hosts, and these guests are accompanied by at least part of what they expect to eat or drink, or to trade for sustenance. Hosting duties are therefore minimal, especially since they no longer even require opening the front door and saying hello. That is done by anyone who happens to be passing by when the doorbell rings, if, indeed, the door has not been left invitingly open.

Announcing the date, providing a table on which offerings can be set and sweeping up the breakage is about it. Guests, too, have minimal obligations. Without advance commitment, they can drift in—or skip the whole thing—as they choose, and use it to entertain their own friends.

Here we have no-fault hospitality. Even Miss Manners could not work up the energy to insist that thank you letters are due when participants and hosts may never actually meet, at least so as to be able to recognize one another in broad daylight.

If the purpose of partying were to find inexpensive venues where pairs or groups of friends could enjoy themselves without regard to others, Miss Manners would acknowledge that these parties work. As a sort of disco scene run on a cooperative basis, it certainly cuts down the cost when, instead of buying supplies at the necessarily inflated rate of a commercial establishment, the clients supply their own. But—as Miss Manners hears, in plaintive tones from those who attend such events—music, atmosphere and drinks are not all that they want. They want to meet people. There remains a vestigial social feeling that it is better to meet new people at the homes of people one already knows—or whose friends one already knows; or whose friends of friends—than to pick them up in a public accommodation.

That young people have a great need to encounter huge numbers of their contemporaries before they settle into domesticity is something of which society has never been unaware. One might say that society's existence is owed to this need. Certainly disposable-income parents have said so for years, as they were grudgingly yanked from the comforts of their own hearths to put on debutante balls and other devices to assist the young people in leaving their herds for couplehood. As the stiffest dragon running such an event realized, strangers must be able to meet. If they arrive in couples, or in their own groups, they have little chance of meeting anyone new. If no one performs the host function of making introductions, few self-introductions will be made.

Lights dim enough for romance should nevertheless be sufficient for people to be able to discern the facial lineaments of those they encounter. Music pervasive enough to cover awkward pauses must nevertheless allow for the understanding of introductions. If there is no order about taking food and drink in common, thirst and hunger may be satisfied without any incidental satisfaction of other appetites.

If young people want to meet new romantic possibilities, Miss Manners suggests that it may be well worth the trouble of organizing a party in which a goodly number of people attend alone, eat and drink together and can see and hear what they are doing.

Teenagers' Parties

Here is an invitation that many people receive from people they love (and believe they are loved by):

"I'm giving a party. If you feel you must put in an appearance, please make it brief. And for heaven's sake, don't say anything embarrassing. But can't you find something else to do that night? I'd really rather you weren't there at all."

Why the recipients of such invitations humbly refrain from noticing how rude they are, Miss Manners does not understand. The fact that the spurned guests happened to have brought up the hosts may have something to do with it. Still, she is astonished that many parents not only allow such an invitation to be issued to them but accept its terms.

Miss Manners admits that one has to admire the skills of teenagers who were able to resurrect that defunct adage "Children should be seen and not heard" and use it with equal force in the opposite direction. Even more impressive is the way the last few generations—including some who have now graduated to being parents—managed to establish the idea that teenagerhood is such a different culture from the adult society's that the very people who reared teenagers are the least capable of understanding them or evaluating their actions.

This does not, however, work the other way. Oddly enough, considering that the parents have all been children and none of the children have been parents, the children still seem to claim the right to judge their parents. It is just they who prefer to be ruled by their peers. The unsubstantiated argument that everyone else does something is considered a persuasive one.

Miss Manners thoroughly understands why such arguments are made. Finding that a child docilely accepts all limitations may not be immediate cause for calling the pediatrician, but it should be watched. Allowing this case to be developed as ingeniously as possible is excellent practice, especially for those who hope to rear lawyers.

She just doesn't understand why any parent would buy the idea that he or she has impaired judgment. It's a short way from there to being told that they dress funny. Once successful, the premise extends to parents being embarrassing by their very existence—nobody else has visible parents. Certainly not at a party.

Miss Manners is not suggesting that the parents actually join their teenaged children's parties—only that they not be run off the premises. "Putting in an appearance" doesn't even have to consist of helping the hosts greet their guests (and thereby frightening the guests into thinking it will be a mixed-generation party).

Ideally, the parents appear in the party room when most people are there, and greet them—well, as if they own the place. That is, they look like the same warm and confident selves they would be to their own guests. They may then retire, but at least once or twice during the evening, should stroll through again on a normal household errand—to get a book from downstairs, for example, or a snack from the party food—and have a few pleasant words with the guests. This is not only to police the activities, as their children will immediately charge and the parents will deny, although that is not out of the question. A pleasant police officer strolling his beat and greeting everyone by name may save himself or herself rougher duties later. Even the hosts may not be sorry to know that a parent is available to play the role of the heavy when they themselves cannot cope with uninvited or misbehaving guests.

The more presentable reason is that they actually like meeting their children's friends and want to make them welcome. Besides, it's their house. The pattern to use—and to ask the children to recall—is how they were treated when they were small and an adult party was being held. Although not invited to join the dinner party, the children were allowed to make an appearance at the beginning of the evening, before trotting off to bed, and one or two later trips downstairs were more or less tolerated. It's time to collect on that.

Graduation Parties

DEAR MISS MANNERS — It seems to be a state law here that the parents of each graduating high school senior hold an open house to which they invite every name in their Rolodex. I have been invited to open houses by people whose children I have never actually met. (Invitees can buy their way out with a congratulatory card enclosing a check for $25 or so. When the parents send out a couple of hundred invitations, these can add up to a tidy pile.)

When I am invited to a party for a child I have known and been fond of since birth, I go to commemorate the end of an era. Here is what happens:

I hand the card and enclosed check to the graduating honoree. He accepts it with a grunt, looking away so as not to make eye contact, and deposits it in a basket. He then eases off to rejoin his friends, and for the rest of the party will studiously avoid social contact with any of the adults present. I have never seen an adult at one of these affairs who looked as if he or she were having a good time. After a couple of hours, one is allowed to leave, unless one is a grandparent, in which case one must stay the entire time and chat up the procession of total strangers.

I am determined not to put people through this. Would it be all right if I gave a party for my son's friends only? I don't want to be remiss in meeting my social obligations, but I will be very happy if Miss Manners allows me to skip this one.

GENTLE READER—From your description, it sounds as if you will not be the only happy person. To resolve not to invite people to have a bad time is a good idea.

Miss Manners questions why these parties are so awful. In theory, multigenerational celebrations ought to be a lot of fun. Those who don't think so need only send their congratulations—there is no charge for declining an invitation.

From your description, these parties falter from a shocking lack of manners on the part of the hosts and the guest of honor. It's not only a matter of the child's showing gratitude. He and his parents have an obligation to socialize with all their guests and introduce them around.

So, while Miss Manners is willing to let you off the hook, she would like you to reconsider. As great a contribution to the social happiness of the community as it would be not to give the party, you could make more of a contribution by giving a good one. This would require involving your son in the planning, and teaching him how to be a good host—training that will be valuable to him throughout life. You cannot hope to bring this off without his enthusiastic participation, but you might be able to prod him into showing some imaginative interest.

Children's Birthday Parties

The first rule of children's birthday parties is that they shouldn't scare the daylights out of the children. Miss Manners would have thought this obvious to all parents of small children, and parents of small children happen to be practically the only people mad enough to attempt to give parties for small children. Apparently it is not obvious. Violating this rule seems to be the first object of those who can afford it. The now popular adult fantasy about the ideal children's party—with an army of entertainers, trained animals, electronic wizardry, fancy catering and crowds of guests creating avalanches of presents—does a thorough job of terrorizing both nominative hosts and their guests.

Miss Manners is afraid that grown-ups forget what (besides alcohol) makes them enjoy huge bashes: It is the thought that they are getting fed and entertained for free. As people who are used to being fed and entertained for free, young children prefer to be the agents of noise and confusion, rather than merely its victims.

The classic children's birthday party, with its rule about the number of guests being the same as the age of the birthday child, and its cake-and-games routine of highly-supervised bedlam, tends to be more successful with the guests than the big-and-scary parties that so impress their parents. This brings Miss Manners to her real interest in the matter, which concerns the second—one would also think obvious—rule about children's birthday parties: that one must never allow the child to expect to be, even for a day, the center of the universe.

Mind you, Miss Manners is all for pleasing one's children and giving them special treatment on their birthdays. That their wishes should be studied and, when reasonable and possible, indulged is not what disturbs her. It is the notion that this glory momentarily cancels the necessity of their considering others' feelings and suspends the etiquette rules connected with this. Miss Manners considers this illusion worse for them even than the foodstuffs they picked out for the day's menus. As expectations of total control can never be realized, believing that one deserves this leads to a lifetime of birthday grudges. Relatives and friends who may try to divine and fulfill all birthday wishes are bound to encounter resentment when they happen to guess wrong or not do enough.

This is an attitude that gets decidedly uglier with age. The weddings of people brought up on this expectation of perfection are a public menace. Schooled in birthday selfishness, they go around screaming "But it's our wedding and we can do whatever we want!" as an excuse for spending other people's money, manipulating their behavior, ignoring their wishes and generally abandoning the obligations human beings must have to one another if we are to live in relative peace.

So rather than using a birthday party as an occasion for promoting piggy behavior, proper parents use it to teach the extra duties that a host has for the welfare of his guests. That being the center of attention creates responsibilities to others is a hard lesson, but a crucial one.

It starts with the guest list. Any thinking child sees this as an opportunity to settle scores, rather than obligations. A polite parent insists that guests must include those who might reasonably expect to be invited (because the guest attended their parties, or because the entire rest of the class is), not only people who happen to be in favor at the moment.

Guests must be greeted at the door, included in whatever activities take place, offered refreshment and shown gratitude for their generosity, even if they are trying not to let go of the presents they have brought. Contrary to all juvenile power of reasoning, present-giving must be handled so that it gratifies the giver as well as the receiver. Teaching someone to thank everyone enthusiastically, without regard to one's actual personal opinion of the item given, is another of those unreasonable but essential lessons of civilization.

The most horrifying of innovations Miss Manners has heard is the idea that the guest of honor—the birthday child, but later in life, the bride-to-be at the shower—gets a kickback on any prizes won. Favors and prizes are intended for guests. They are there to be shown a good time, not to kowtow to the host. Children who learn that are going to have a better chance of getting from one birthday to the next.

The Ritual of Opening Presents

DEAR MISS MANNERS—Children's birthday parties have changed a great deal since I was a child. Professional entertainment has replaced musical chairs, expensive goodie bags have replaced hats and streamers, and elaborate theme cakes rival those at weddings.

This is all well and good for those who can afford it. But one change troubles me deeply: No longer does the birthday child open his or her gifts with their guests present, oohing and ahhing over each acquisition. Am I old fashioned (I am only 35) to think that this is not only rude but unfair to all of those who participate in the party?

My children, ages 3 and 6, go to a great deal of trouble to pick out their friends' birthday gifts. My oldest child cruises the aisles looking for the perfect gift for Betty Birthday ("she loves horses, but she can't read yet, but she likes to play games, but only those kind of games where more than two can play, and her favorite color is pink, but not hot pink, and oh yeah, she really wants only Barbie stuff, but no hot pink Barbie stuff . . ."). Even my three-year-old wants to find the perfect gift for her friend, the one that will make the birthday child happiest. They both understand, as most children I believe do, the spirit of the old adage "'tis better to give than to receive."

But here's what happens: They arrive at the party and the proffered gift is snatched out of their hands as if it's admission to an event. Two hours later the party is over, the guests are ushered out the door, goodie bags in hand as the brightly wrapped gifts are gathered up into large plastic garbage bags to be spirited away.

My children are disappointed because they didn't get to see the reaction on the child's face on opening the gift so carefully chosen. And what about the gifts from other children? They want to see those too. Then there's the birthday child, denied his chance to be the center of attention (particularly since the clown kind of overshadowed the singing of "Happy Birthday").

Later, we do get a "thank-you note," usually written by the parent but totally illegible and therefore not very meaningful to a three-year-old. (On the other hand, an exuberant "It's exactly what I wanted!" from the birthday child is worth millions.) Sometimes the cards get separated from the gifts in those big plastic garbage bags and we never receive an acknowledgment.

The arguments for this practice that has become so prevalent include:

1. Not wanting to make the guests feel bad because they didn't receive all those gifts (how does one learn the joy of giving if their only experience is receiving?),

2. Saving the parents from embarrassment when their beloved Betty Birthday announces how much she hates a certain gift (how else are children to learn to be gracious?) and

3. It's easier to return unwanted items if they are not paraded in front of twenty kids.

What do you think? I miss those days when the opening of the presents was the highlight of the party.

GENTLE READER—The very ritual you miss is responsible for souring Miss Manners on children's birthday parties in recent years. She has seen the concept that one can gather people for the purpose of showily receiving their offerings turn into the defining event of people's lives.

People who experienced it and liked it, those who experienced it and felt shortchanged, and those who never experienced it all want to re-create this moment. That is a lot of people giving themselves birthday parties all their lives and demanding similar treatment on every other occasion they can dream up.

But she has always believed, as you do, that what legitimizes children's birthday parties is the opportunity to teach unreasonable social skills, such as letting go of a present one has brought, or pretending to like something one already has. For that alone, she is willing to support the present-opening ritual.

Children's Adult Birthday Parties

DEAR MISS MANNERS—Our social circle includes friends and acquaintances with small children and recently we have been invited to a number of birthday parties for children as young as two and three years old. These are not just small gatherings for the family and closest friends. For example, my husband's former colleague called to invite us to his two-year-old daughter's birthday.

We opted not to attend, but weren't sure what to do. Do we send a card with best wishes to a toddler? Are we being too cynical, or is it indeed perfectly acceptable to organize such events?

GENTLE READER — Do you do business with these two-year-olds? Not that Miss Manners would justify toddlers' entertaining their professional acquaintances at their birthday parties. She is only inquiring because you do not seem to fit any of the proper categories of birthday party guests—the celebrant's friends, relatives and others (who may include parents' friends) who have demonstrated that they dote upon the honored one.

So why were you invited? While Miss Manners can guess at the nature of your cynical speculation, she does not really think that parents go after you in order to secure yet another stuffed animal. Rather, she suspects that they classify the entire world as people who dote upon their children. Many parents require remarkably little encouragement to do this. Think back—did you once say "My, what a nice baby"? That could have done it.

There is also a less charming possibility. A great many people do not think of their guests as people to be given a good time, but as supernumeraries in their own, or their children's, pageantry. So they may have assumed that offering you food and drink was enticement enough, without their having to create an occasion that would also interest you. In either case, you need only decline the invitation with thanks and your best birthday wishes.

Self-Surprise Parties

DEAR MISS MANNERS — One of my closest friends, who is a wonderful hostess and enjoys throwing her own parties, birthday and otherwise, has informed me that she planned to do the same this year. Then, two days ago, a friend of hers approached me with the idea of rounding up several of her friends to plan and give her a surprise birthday. I liked the idea, so I discussed it with a mutual friend, and we devised a plan that, with enough care, could be successfully executed.

My excitement quickly fizzled when I discovered that the guest of honor had "suggested" to the friend who approached me that he get some of her friends to throw a "surprise" party. She has since mentioned this (a hint perhaps?) to my co-planner who is as confused as I am as to why someone would intentionally plant the idea for her own surprise birthday party, instead of being straightforward and saying, "Will you, in lieu of a gift, help me throw my birthday party"?

I am more than willing to help her organize and execute her gala buying and preparing food, contacting guests, etc., but do not appreciate being encouraged to give a party that clearly will not be a surprise, as it is the guest of honor's idea. If I am approached by her, however directly or indirectly, how should I tactfully respond?

GENTLE READER — Has your friend the great hostess ever given you a birthday party, surprise or otherwise? It is not that she was obligated to do so—Miss Manners is just hoping to eke out one little bit of pity for this pitiful person, and needs all the help she can get.

More likely, your friend is one of a growing number of people who refuse to leave the possibility of kindness in their friends to chance. So they are willing to undertake the burden of deciding how to pamper themselves, and of instructing others in how to carry it out. Thus the practice of adults giving birthday parties for themselves has spread wildly, along with the number of brides who direct their bridesmaids to give them showers, and graduates who instruct their relatives what presents to give them.

Your friend's idea, of giving herself a surprise party, takes this to a whole new level. If she wants to leap out of hiding and shout "Surprise!" at herself, why does she need to involve so many intermediaries? Still, she is one of your closest friends and, you attest, a wonderful hostess. So Miss Manners will try to think of her as someone who is gallantly trying to make up for being slighted by life, and whose friends are willing to make up for that perceived neglect.

May she suggest just a gentle way of reminding your friend that she would be better off trusting her friends' affection than attempting to pre-empt it? You could just run to her and say in a devastated tone, "Oh, we wanted so much to give you a surprise party—but I hear you knew all about it. We're so disappointed. Now we want you to forget I said anything, so that some other year we can go ahead and really take you by surprise."

The Gift-Gathering Party

DEAR MISS MANNERS — Do I set up a table for gifts at our 25th anniversary (we will be reciting our vows and have a reception afterwards)? Do they bring gifts for this occasion? Or would it be proper to put "cards and gifts optional" on the invitation?

GENTLE READER — Optional, as opposed to what? As opposed to "Cards and gifts are mandatory, and steps will be taken to collect from those who do not contribute"?

Presents are always optional, and it is not the place of people who happen to be celebrating an anniversary, or any other occasion, to expect them—not even by attempts to discourage them. If "No gifts" gives people the idea that their hosts are pointedly dwelling on the idea (and it does, it does), Miss Manners can only imagine what your wording would suggest.

Some people will probably bring presents and some not. It is your obligation to lessen any embarrassment on the part of the latter, as well as to show appreciation to the former. This would best be done by setting aside whatever presents are brought, ideally with the unobtrusive assistance of a close friend or relative who can discreetly write the giver's name on each package, in case cards are missing. After the festivities, you can then write them letters of thanks. If you have a table to store them, please make it inconspicuous, so that it doesn't seem to serve the purpose of a ticket-taker's booth.

The Testimonial Party

DEAR MISS MANNERS — My parents will soon be hosting their 50th wedding anniversary party for about 150 guests, most of whom their children do not know. They have planned, as the entertainment, that each of their children, as well as their children's spouses, provide a few remarks on what it's like to be a member of the family.

My brothers and sisters and I do not feel this is a good idea for several reasons. This might not be very entertaining for those assembled (as it might be for an all-family gathering), but, more importantly, our immediate family hasn't gotten together in almost 20 years (we each live in different cities) and thus our shared memories in recent decades are non-existent.

Do you think it a good idea? Is there some other form of acceptable entertainment at these events? The only anniversary party I've been to with entertainment was when a couple who were professional performers sang several sweet songs in honor of the anniversary couple. This was sweet and light and well received.

GENTLE READER — Miss Manners agrees that it is a terrible idea to put the children on the spot and bore the guests. She also begs you to consider the state of mind of people—your very own parents—who would go to the extreme of coercing their children into making public testimonials to them.

The fact that the family hasn't gotten together in twenty years only makes it the more poignant. Your parents are rather in the position of children who want to force divorced parents to pretend to be a couple, just for the occasion of their own wedding. They want to nudge you to behave like united and devoted children in front of their friends.

Anniversary parties do not need special entertainment; the guests are supposed to be sufficiently entertained by enjoying sociability with the couple and others who care for them. Yet toasts would be in order. Miss Manners suggests that you children interpret the parental wish by offering several brief but effusive toasts to your parents. It might also be a good idea for you to supplement these individually with letters of reminiscence and affection. If your parents choose to share these later with their friends, at least you won't have to be a party to watching the display.

The Repeat Party

DEAR MISS MANNERS — Our seven children gave us a beautiful catered 40th anniversary party, and all our relatives—my husband has three brothers and I have five sisters and one brother—came. Now they want to give us a 50th party. I say it is in bad taste to have two such parties and have all the same people show up. Not one of our nieces or nephews have given anyone else a party, although they are grown and have the money.

GENTLE READER — Have the party. Miss Manners' rule is that adults get three all-out parties per half century—say the 60th and 75th birthdays, or the 50th and 60th anniversaries—and as many smaller gatherings for which their intimates have the enthusiasm. She's going to count your 40th and 50th anniversaries for your first half century, so you can have a 60th and a 75th as well.

Whether this seems to show up your siblings' children is not for you to ponder. Miss Manners prefers to believe that they enjoy these family gatherings all the more because they are the only ones.

ADMISSION-FEE PARTIES

The Shower

DEAR MISS MANNERS — We are an international family on assignment from France to this great country for the past three years. We have come to appreciate American hospitality, and really enjoy the informality of backyard barbecues, play groups for children, yard sales, open houses, or just the good neighborly "come and drop by for a cup of coffee" event. However, there is one thing called SHOWERS that has me utterly confused, if not frustrated. Here is the scenario as I see it:

A young couple plans to get married. Friends, colleagues and (or) relatives give a bridal shower. I bring a gift or contribute to a collective gift coordinated by the host.

The same young couple gets married. I attend the wedding and bring or send a gift.

The same young couple buys a new home. Friends, colleagues and (or) relatives give a housewarming shower. I contribute same as above.

The same young couple moves into their new home in our neighborhood. We visit and bring a housewarming gift.

The same young couple is going to have a baby. Friends, colleagues and (or) relatives give a baby shower. I contribute exactly the same as above.

The new baby is born. We go and visit the young family and bring a gift.

Word is out that the same couple (not so young any more) is not getting along so well, and has filed for divorce. Friends, colleagues and (or) relatives give a divorce shower. I contribute the same way as described before.

Of course, I haven't been to a divorce shower yet. But if they are not already invented, I am sure somebody will.

Exaggeratedly speaking, I could carry this on until the bitter end (i.e., funeral shower), but I think I made my point.

GENTLE READER — It is a point well taken. Americans, as well as their gracious visitors, are being drenched by unusually prevalent showers. (Please don't make jokes about divorce or funeral showers. Every time Miss Manners recklessly exaggerates an already ludicrous situation, she is deluged with mail indicating that reality is way ahead of any joke one can make.)

In proper American etiquette, a shower is a lighthearted event among intimate friends, properly given only before a wedding and the birth of a first baby. Relatives should never issue invitations. If friends give them, they do so of their own free will—it is not mandatory for bridesmaids, for example, to throw showers. No one should be invited to more than one such event for the occasion. Presents should be mere tokens. Housewarming parties are given by the owners themselves, but the traditional good luck present is bread and salt.

However, we live in an age of greed and entitlement. The shower has been perceived as one more opportunity to turn a milestone to consumer advantage, and all these rules are being violated right and left. This should not discourage you from abiding by the rules of etiquette available to guests: You may decline the invitation, sending nothing more than your good wishes. Some of us used to think that that in itself was quite valuable.

The Divorce Solicitation

DEAR MISS MANNERS—I am in the process of getting a divorce. I want to make a new beginning for myself and my five-year-old daughter. Since we will be moving into a new apartment and will be buying everything new, a friend suggested that I have a "divorce reception" (as opposed to a wedding reception) and register at department stores.

Is this proper, and if so, how would I let my guests know that I'm registered? Personally, I think I should have a house warming party.

I must add, I did not have the traditional wedding with reception, and most of everything we had belonged to my soon-to-be-ex-husband. Please help me out on this. I really try to go by "the book" on things like this.

GENTLE READER—The book says you don't parody weddings by celebrating a divorce. Never mind that you might consider it a joyous event. You can hardly expect your daughter to witness your glee at having gotten rid of her father.

By all means have a housewarming party. First Miss Manners asks you to rid yourself of that sneaking feeling that you are entitled to be deluged with presents you forgot to collect upon your now-defunct marriage.

The Frank Solicitation

DEAR MISS MANNERS — A flyer was placed in my mailbox last week, which reads, "Julie and Dean invite you to a housewarming. Bring a covered dish and a lawn chair. Cash donations accepted." It then lists their address and phone number and the date of the get-together.

I have never seen these people. I saw a moving van at the house one day when I drove by. I think these are neighbors I want to avoid at all times. My husband says that at least we know what kind of people they are.

I have never heard of anyone giving themselves a party, inviting strangers to come, and then asking for a cash donation. Are we wrong to find this offensive? Is this a normal thing now for people to do? Someone told me the latest thing going on is to have a birthday party and ask the guests to bring food. The hostess will furnish the cake and ice cream, and the guests bring the rest of the food. This is happening at children's parties.

My first reaction was to pick up the phone to tell them how I felt, but after thinking it over, I decided to just ignore the whole thing.

GENTLE READER — Once upon a time, etiquetteers were able to squelch something distasteful by the phrase "It is simply not done." Nowadays, Miss Manners finds it more prudent to make a distinction between what ought to be done and what is done.

Social fund-raising is an increasing practice. Bridal and anniversary couples urge everyone they know to indulge them in pre-chosen luxuries. Birthdays and Christmas are considered opportunities for writing out your own shopping list and then expecting other people to do the shopping. Those calling themselves hosts are, as you have noticed, requesting their guests to supply the hospitality. So while Miss Manners is shocked, she is not that surprised that some enterprising people should wonder why this extortion should be limited to their friends, and begin to extend it to strangers.

That there are vulgar, greedy people in the world, Miss Manners has always known. What puzzles her is how there can be so many dupes who go along with these practices. Of course you will not dignify this appeal with an answer. But if you were to slither around on the day of the event, Miss Manners would be curious to know whether anyone actually responded to this appeal.

A Surprise Solicitation

DEAR MISS MANNERS — Our long-time friend's husband invited us to what he called a surprise 30th birthday party for her to be held at a restaurant. I was amazed that he chose such an expensive place; however, they are extremely well off. The party of ten had a great time and our dear friend was lavished with many gifts. When the bill came, her husband announced that each person owed $30.

Faces dropped. Most of us had to charge it, because we didn't have that much cash. Times are so tough for us right now that we'll be paying interest on this for a long time. He did not even buy any drinks while she opened presents at the bar, and when he ordered one appetizer, he didn't pass it around. He did pass around two slices of pie with ten spoons, which was repulsive. I have yet to receive a thank you note. Do you think someone should say something to this cheapskate?

GENTLE READER — My, that was a surprise party, wasn't it? Unfortunately, the bait-and-switch ploy of inviting guests and then charging them is no longer a surprise to Miss Manners, who is daily bombarded with reports from others who have been caught.

Alas, she does not condone denouncing one's host, if you can call him that. Just be warned about future solicitations disguised as invitations. She also suggests you not hold your breath waiting for a letter of thanks for your birthday present. People who don't see why they should feed their own guests also have a hard time seeing why they should express gratitude.

A Profit-Making Venture

DEAR MISS MANNERS — In order to celebrate her 50th anniversary, a friend of mine put a notice in the local newspaper. The affair was held in a local hall on a Saturday night. She supplied food, disk jockey and a cash bar. She told me she received $900 from 90 people. I suppose that each person paid or donated $10 for the event. Is this in good taste?

GENTLE READER — Why do you ask? Has the suspicion been raised in your mind that there is something questionable about turning one's wedding anniversary into a profit-making event aimed at the general public? Perhaps you feel that the personal milestones of life should be celebrated with people whom one actually knows personally, and whom one, in fact, selects, through personal invitations, to receive hospitality. Perhaps you feel that hospitality consists of entertaining guests at one's own expense. Perhaps you feel that any material show of warmth on the part of one's guests should be left to their discretion.

As a matter of fact, Miss Manners feels that way, too. That makes two of us against 92—the guests and the happy couple—of them.

A More Gracious Party

DEAR MISS MANNERS — We are planning to add on to our house, and do most of the work ourselves. Many family members have said they'll help out when they can. We deeply appreciate this, and plan to have a "thank you" party after it's done for all those who helped.

Would it be appropriate to invite only the workers, or do we include their entire families? These other people are our extended family, but it could add up to 50 people or more.

GENTLE READER — As you are obviously not speaking of two helpers who have immediate families of 25 each, Miss Manners gathers that you were lucky enough to have a great deal of help. Thus, the thank you party would naturally include many people.

Among them should be the spouses and children of your workers. It is their presence that will make it clear that you are throwing a party, not another work session. Up until now, when your relatives were welcomed without their families, they were accompanied by their toolboxes. Asking people to bring their spouses, rather than their hammers, is what will make this a festive occasion.

Chapter Nine

ENTERTAINING:
THE RELATIVES

FAMILY TRADITIONS

Here's how to create a family holiday tradition all your own: 1. You start with an inherited pattern of celebrations that you have never quite liked. Typically, at every Thanksgiving dinner or Fourth of July picnic, there is at least one cherub coldly appraising the scene in all its homely detail and thinking. "This is stupid. I have to put up with it now, but when I'm grown up, things are going to be different." 2. You grow up to preside over your own household. Visiting obligations aside, you are in a position to decide how holidays should be celebrated. Childhood vows being sacred to the child who made them, you do things your way.

3. You sense something is missing.

4. After a while, you restore the inherited elements you didn't like, because otherwise it doesn't feel quite right.

5. You try to impress the charm of the result upon your own children, in the hope that they will continue your way of doing things when no longer obliged to do so.

At the risk of stating the obvious, Miss Manners will point out that this is why it is called tradition. Whooping things up in your own way, jolly as it may be, is something else. It may all be very well, but it doesn't carry the same emotional weight—which is why people are never as moved by wedding ceremonies written by the participants, however much feeling they contain, as they are to hear the time-honored service. There is no such thing as spontaneous tradition. The point of tradition is its history.

Sure, it gets altered along the way. Technological and social changes are incorporated. The invention of electric light took the candles off the Christmas tree until the invention of nostalgia brought them back. Families are no longer divided by gender after dinner, between the kitchen and the living room. Now they are divided more or less by gender according to who wants to watch the game on television and who would just as soon do the dishes while talking everyone else over.

This process would be relatively simple if it were not for the custom by which new families are made—and, for that matter, old families are unmade. Marriage and divorce are what complicate tradition (and a lot of other elements of life).

In the best of circumstances, the first holiday celebrated by a couple together involves competing traditions. Many a person was brought to a new appreciation of parental tradition by the shock of having married someone who has the effrontery to prefer a competing tradition. Otherwise happy couples have been known to work themselves up to a frenzy over such details as whether the holiday dinner is served in the afternoon or evening or whether a birthday celebrant gets to choose the menu for the whole day. Miss Manners attributes this reaction to the fact that it really is peculiar to turn a perfect stranger into a relative, however alluring that stranger may be. Eventually, compromises are made—a bit from one person's family, a bit from the other's, with some ideas that just floated in from nowhere. Tradition is passed on sort of in the way that a message is passed on—slightly garbled but still recognizable.

That's only when things are going well. When a family breaks apart, there develops a reaction against its traditions, even above the difficulties in continuing it caused by changed conditions, such as moving and custody arrangements. Even under such difficult circumstances, it is well to remember that traditions are better altered to fit new needs than rejected outright. Children ought to be able to enjoy Step 1 rather than to find themselves thrust prematurely into Step 3.

Holiday Memories

DEAR MISS MANNERS — Frankly, my most memorable Thanksgiving Day dinners were 35 years ago, when my mother's three sisters, their husbands and families gathered at Grandma's house for a three to five day Annual Civil War (strange name for a war under any circumstances).

I recall the holidays as a huge harangue with each personality well-defined. Corrections and instructions were flung with ruthless abandon; discipline meted out with immediacy; favorite recipes were brought in case "someone" forgot; and authority was everyone's responsibility. The men spoke of their businesses, with a sense of status seeking on behalf of the female siblings, creating a slightly competitive undercurrent.

Once the table was "set," it may as well have been a checkerboard. Gram placed names at each place setting, and they were promptly repositioned to accommodate the "lefties," preferences for particular glasses or dinnerware, or to reflect a certain level of tolerance for someone else's eating habits. This prevented serving delays due to protests over unexpected or unacceptable seating arrangements.

Children often had a separate table where "seating" was a euphemism for foxhole—each seat became a cover from flying food. Any adult within arm's reach had swatting privileges.

The only story that repeatedly made it to the dinner table was Gram's medical history update, which substantiated why "This will probably be my last Thanksgiving." The threat of her immediate demise due to high blood pressure was always minimized by the mimicking of her by her huge, humorous son-in-law, which everyone joined in.

There was a moment of silence when grace was announced—but chairs squeaked and shifted with impatience. Irreverent imaginings would start: Thanksgiving prayers became "prey-ers," people in from the hunt and harvest. Grateful for not becoming the prey of the elements and animals themselves, they gazed at their offerings saying, as thanks, "But for the grace of God go I." And so Christianity came under criticism, much to the concern of the more committed members of the family.

Multiple marriages accounted for the absence of certain children after the main meal, when fathers had visitation rights. With our father, we made the rounds to his eight brothers and sisters who had upwards of eight children each. All of them circulated to welcome in the holiday season with the over-90 members, whose stamina may not have seen them through the excitement. The same atmosphere prevailed in this parade from house to house: Advice and wisdom flowed freely in the relaxed holiday atmosphere, absorbing any shocks that daily routines intensify.

It was apparent that manners were practiced at home, but only performed in public! Practice permits errors and allows for leniency that performance doesn't.

The smaller groups who gather now tend to be courteous and low-key, making for a kind of unmemorable season. Gifts tend to reflect less knowing of one another, less dynamics, and more obligations or—courtesy. It seems that when all goes courteously, less is remembered. It's the outrageous claims and calamities that made each holiday unique and unforgettable.

In the old days, we separated as we greeted—with tears and hugs, and spent the year ruminating over and recovering from things that were said and done—always anticipating the next year's celebration.

GENTLE READER— Miss Manners congratulates you on making an etiquette-free tradition sound warm and charming. You only lose her when you suggest that polite get-togethers are inevitably boring.

The difference between family members and less intimate company is supposed to be that the family members are aware of one another's toleration limits. Thus, while they may appear to be doing and saying outrageous things, they may in fact be observing unspoken rules. It's all right to tease Cindy about her boyfriend but not about her weight, for example, while her brother likes to be teased about his muscles but not about his sexual orientation. If relatives treat one another as casual acquaintances, it will indeed be meaningless, even if—not because—manners are present.

The Divided-Family Tradition

Sometimes it seems to Miss Manners as if all that old-fashioned families worry about at holiday time is how to avoid seeing one another. New-style families worry about how to get to see everyone.

Perhaps this is not clear. Miss Manners will try again. Let us say we have a conventional, or what used to be conventional, three-generation family. Christmas dinner has always been at the grandparents' house, with all the grown-up children and grandchildren of different ages expected.

What do these people want to know from Miss Manners at this time of year? How best to please their relatives? How to share the burden of entertaining while according the elders their proper authority? How to delight the children while instructing them in the spiritual nature of the holiday?

No. They want to know how they can get out of going. They want to be with their friends. They are tired of hearing the same questions and comments about the way they live. It's too much trouble to get there. They can get better food at a restaurant.

Let us say that we have a family in which Grandmother has cashiered Grandfather for someone else, and Grandfather is being amply consoled elsewhere. In the middle generation are not only the children and their current spouses but a few former spouses who have kept up the attachment or who must be invited with their children, and assorted, ah, spouse equivalents, some with their own children. The youngest have been dividing their time all year between rival parental households, without managing to get to the splintered households of the other relatives, whom they now hardly know. In addition to all the other problems, the families have scattered geographically.

Do these people share that yearning to have Christmas dinner by themselves, or in compatible subgroups, or in a restaurant, or with people to whom they are not related? Oh, no. They cherish the notion of a big traditional family gathering, with all the trimmings and everyone present—except, of course, the particular former relative or prospective relative whom they want everyone to leave out in the cold. Granny doesn't want anyone to go to Grandpa's. Papa doesn't want anyone to go to Mamma's. And everybody has called for barring at least one child's or parent's current love interest. But otherwise, each wants an all-inclusive family holiday.

Among those who want to keep the peace appropriate to the season, there has therefore grown up the custom of having multiple celebrations. Instead of going caroling from house to house, those who are on good terms with everyone go feasting from house to house. Perhaps Papa and his wife give Christmas Eve dinner, and Mamma and her husband give Christmas Day dinner. Or perhaps they have both decided that Christmas Day is the only proper day to celebrate, so Mamma gives a midday meal and Papa the evening meal. Of course, both give presents, and both may lead the same rituals, such as tree trimming. This makes things hard on the double-duty relatives. Children who have no natural trouble expressing delight at one round of festivities find themselves strained at the second. There is such a thing as too much of a good thing.

Miss Manners suggests a Christmas truce. Christmas is not the time to start barring relatives' attachments, whether they are romantic partners or stepchildren. The answer to "If she comes I won't" is, except in extreme cases, "I hope you'll change your mind, because we would miss you very much."

In irrevocably split families, there has to be some understanding about dividing holiday rituals. Making the same people repeat rituals, other than kisses and present-exchanging, is using the holiday for a weapon, not a celebration. And requiring anyone to eat two traditional Christmas meals is dangerous cruelty.

Alternating holiday dinners, say with one person doing Thanksgiving and the other Christmas, is one way; celebrating Twelfth Night as the second round is another. If the households are nearby, a Christmas call on the one who is not serving Christmas dinner should be made. Such lessons in tact should not be lost on those who have only one such celebration to get through.

Family Stories

DEAR MISS MANNERS — Because my parents are "alone" (do not live together), I invited them as guests for Thanksgiving and Christmas. We had gifts for them, and were sitting at dinner when they got into a loud conversation. To their surprise, I asked them to take their coffee and go to another part of the house to complete the discussion. They always talk about the Depression and how hard it was washing diapers in the bathtub, even cleaning a chicken! We were ready to barf.

What to do? Keep inviting them, as I have for 25 years, and put up with bad manners and the same conversation? What happened to party manners?

GENTLE READER — Miss Manners supposes you will just have to learn to develop them. For a host to insult guests and banish them from the table on the grounds that their conversation is boring is rudeness of truly startling dimensions. Even more amazing is that your objection arises because your separated parents, when thrown together on family occasions, use the opportunity to reminisce peaceably. Miss Manners invites you to look in her mailbox to discover what most people's estranged parents say when they find themselves under the same roof.

An Etiquette Checklist

Like everyone else, Miss Manners thinks of the holidays in terms of nice treats that others might give her. In her case, it is not a list of dry goods she wants to own but wants other people to find and pay for. She is not one of those thoughtful souls whose greatest wish is to spare others the pain of guessing what to buy them.

What Miss Manners wants every winter is a pleasant holiday. This is not some vaguely sentimental wish for peace on earth, although she wouldn't reject that if offered. Her immediate wish is to be spared the usual dreadful holiday week she annually spends mediating between relatives, lovers and intimate friends who have hideously offended one another by way of celebration. She is therefore supplying a checklist of simple etiquette rules designed to head off the most common forms of holiday provocation.

1. There are a number of standard holiday greetings, but "I see you've put on some weight!" or "Are your parents still supporting you?" are not among them.
2. Everybody should make the effort to dress up for holiday dinners, although in some households this means suits and dresses, while in others it means the once-a-year opportunity to wear red and green socks with bells sewn on them.
3. When presents are brought for some children, they must be brought for all who will be there, including the visiting playmates of the family's children and the children of the family's visiting playmates.
4. As peculiar as it is to be invited to a heavy meal in the middle of the afternoon, it is unconscionable for visitors to arrive, or for dinner to be served, long past the hour set.
5. It does not enhance a present to tell the person who is opening it, "You probably won't like this," "I had a lot of trouble finding this," "I didn't

know what to get you" or "I was going to get you . . ." followed by the description of a different, perhaps better, present.

6. Bones of contention should not be on the menu, which excludes evaluating the food nutritionally or philosophically and checking on what is or is not disappearing into the mouths of anyone over the age of ten.

7. Although one of the pleasures of intimacy is being allowed to pick up a drumstick, the general requirement of eating in a civilized fashion so as not to disgust everyone at the table is not suspended for the holiday.

8. Unreserved thanks must be given for all presents, including the ugly, the inappropriate and the ill-fitting.

9. All parents are responsible for checking that their children do not damage other children, other children's presents or the spirit of the occasion. Other adults should confine themselves to drawing such problems to the parents' attention in sympathetic ways: "Brooke seems to be overtired," "Perhaps you'd better see what Shannon's problem is," "I'm afraid if Justinian keeps banging like that, he might hurt himself."

10. Correcting of children's manners should be confined to parental looks, whispers or the sort of reminder designed to pass itself off as a cheerfully idle observation: "Children, wait—the grown-ups haven't gotten their plates yet."

11. People who are engaged or pregnant will volunteer this information, so it is neither useful nor polite to prompt them by expressing impatience, however coyly or humorously.

12. The tradition being to give the footmen the day off, it is incumbent on everyone to offer to help with the cleaning up, although requests to leave everything or to stay out of the kitchen should—if delivered with raised eyebrows and firm voice—be taken seriously.

THE FAMILY AS GUESTS

Including the Difficult

"Do we have to invite him? You know how he gets."

"What's the use of all this planning when they always find a way to spoil everything?"

"It doesn't matter what she promises—you know what she's going to be like once she gets there. It never fails."

"Remember last time? And the time before that?"

If any of this sounds familiar, Miss Manners has an idea that you might belong to a family. And that this family sometimes entertains at events, such as ceremonial celebrations or holiday meals, where all the relatives are expected to be included, along with guests who have been chosen with more discrimination. And that perhaps not everybody in the family is presentable. Or bearable. Or predictable.

It doesn't require a lot of provocation to be embarrassed about relatives in front of friends. Parents routinely shame their school-age children simply by being a generation older than they.

For that matter, all relatives are potentially dangerous. They know too much.

But some go out of their way. They make bigoted remarks or they tell obscene jokes. They pick fights or their noses. They turn morose or silly. They denounce the food or they get into the liquor. They snub the other guests or they try to borrow money from them. They never stop complaining or they never stop bragging. They corner people who are trying desperately to get away, and bore them or proposition them.

Nobody would put up with them who didn't have to, and those who do have to are losing their patience. Hence the forlorn pleas of whether—just this once—it wouldn't be possible to have an event where nobody had to keep rescuing the guests from Aunt Snarly or Uncle Nuisance, and various cousins and in-laws from their own instincts and appetites. Sometimes one of the awful relatives manages to go so far below the minimum level of human decency as to be banished, at least for a while.

Most good-hearted families find a way to refer to objectionable behavior within the family as an eccentricity or illness, and to come down on the side of consideration and respect for those who haven't shown any themselves. Miss Manners admires this and wants to help. She will even go over and listen to your grandmother's analysis of what is wrong with the government, the generation and the dinner, although she draws the line at dancing with your brother-in-law.

You will still need the Family Phalanx. In a well-coordinated family, the Family Phalanx—a damage-control team that moves in at the first hint of trouble—is not always explicitly organized, but everybody understands the signal. Someone with a firm voice may announce to the troublemaker, "Oh, you know you don't mean that," less as a warning to that person than as a general call to arms.

Wordless sympathy and encouragement for patience are flashed around a table or a room. Eyebrows are raised so that voices don't have to be.

Various members of the family spring into action: They change the conversation, whisk away the perpetrator or the intended victim, or move everybody on to the next stage of the event—playing softball, cleaning up, going home. Even babies are expected to do their part; this is a good time for them to make anguished demands.

It might be necessary to make a statement on the spot, in protection of an individual or in opposition to a repugnant declaration. Someone who has a commanding presence and/or senior position in the family does this for the record, in such a way that it does not open an argument or discussion.

When the crisis is past, some deal with it by pretending it didn't happen and rising above it. Others offer apologies or explanations. Parents take the children aside to teach them the complicated morality involved in putting up with people of whose behavior one does not approve. Another family event is brought off in spite of the family burdens. The problem has not been solved, of course, but it has been successfully surrounded one more time.

Excluding the Impossible

DEAR MISS MANNERS — My father was, and is, a violent, boorish drunk. When he has had one too many (a daily occurrence), he slurs his speech, bumps into walls and speaks very loudly. He is prone to pontificating on everything from "those damn liberals" to "the coloreds." I am terrified that he will get drunk and embarrass everyone at my wedding. We do not propose to serve liquor, but that will not stop my father from bringing his own, as he did at my cousin's wedding.

He physically abused me as a child, as well. I have no desire to have him involved, or even in attendance at, our wedding. Should I exclude him? If so, should I explain why? My mother and my brother may refuse to attend if this is done. Although I would not miss my brother, I would really like for my mother to attend.

From friends, I have received two basic sets of advice:

1. Exclude him as it is our wedding and we should be comfortable with all the arrangements.
2. "Do the right thing" by including him and just pray that he behaves.

Please help me in this momentous decision.

GENTLE READER — Your father does not sound like a good prospect for a wedding guest, but Miss Manners does not care for either of these statements. The first attitude is selfish, and the second foolhardy.

Weddings are for families and friends, not just for the bridal couple concerned, and Miss Manners deplores the attitude that the couple's wishes are the only concern. Although your father sounds like that extreme case of a relative who has excluded himself from consideration, your mother and brother's feelings ought to be a factor in your decision. You also owe something to the solemnity of the event and the feelings of others who are likely to be the butt of your father's probable misbehavior.

Instead of fighting your mother and brother on this issue, Miss Manners suggests that you enlist their help. They must be only too aware of the dangers involved. Ask them whether, if they agree to police your father's behavior, it is likely that the wedding may proceed smoothly. If they admit that this wouldn't work, or are unwilling to assist, at least they ought to be able to understand better why it would then be necessary to keep him from attending.

The Choosey Host

DEAR MISS MANNERS — My husband has a rather large family with several siblings, spouses, children and so on, and on major holidays, his mother has hosted a family dinner that includes everyone. For the last year or so, "Mama" has not been physically able to host this event and I am wondering, is it appropriate to invite only the siblings and their spouses and children that we would enjoy eating and spending the day with or not? I am able to host this event in my home but there are some of his siblings that my husband does not care to be around and I feel the same.

GENTLE READER — Miss Manners is afraid that you have confused two distinct social events. One is the dinner party, to which the hosts invite people they happen to like and who they hope will get along well with one another. The other is the family gathering, to which hosts invite the people to whom they are related and hope for the best.

If you want to entertain relatives you like, go right ahead. But if you do this on holidays, both Miss Manners and your mother-in-law will interpret it as splitting, rather than gathering, the family.

Choosey Junior Hosts

DEAR MISS MANNERS — At some of our family holiday functions, there are other children whose ages are closely matched with my children's, including the offspring of the host and hostess. Is it reasonable of me to expect these "junior" hosts and hostesses to play a part in entertaining the other junior guests? Is it appropriate for the children of the host and hostess to leave the party, leaving the junior guests to stare at the wall while they go off with friends they brought to what was supposed to be strictly a family gathering, or sequester themselves in their rooms with stereos blaring while the cousins make small talk with Aunt Bess and Uncle Homer?

Also, could you clarify the rules for seating arrangements at large family dinners, where there is more than one table—the other being the dreaded dinner in the kitchen. Who is to be seated at the main table? Certainly the patriarch and matriarch of the family. Host and hostess? Their off-spring? The oldest of each family, until capacity is reached, and then seating at the alternate site? The guests, even if it means seating your oldest son, who is of voting age, with children in highchairs? This situation always brings arguments and complaints.

GENTLE READER — Indeed, young people do have responsibilities as junior hosts for guests of their age in their homes—regardless of whether they invited these people, or even like them. They may offer activities as a sub-entertainment while the adults are talking, or include these guests with their own friends, but they cannot leave them to their own devices.

Miss Manners believes that your relatives are doing their children a disservice by not using these occasions to train them in the ways of consideration and hospitality. They will be anxious if they don't know these techniques when they are old enough to engage in business entertaining, Miss Manners promises you. At that point, it will be harder for them to learn how to be gracious to people with whom they don't have much in common.

For the very reason that the younger generation is supposed to play host to its peers, the usual table division—and precedence, when it comes to the dining room over the kitchen—is by age, with the eldest children given the choice of being grown-ups or lording it over the younger ones. Babies are excepted; it is well known that babies who have trouble aiming their food into their mouths want to be near a napkin-wielding parent.

Other People's Children

DEAR MISS MANNERS—Our family has not been a close one. Both emotionally and geographically, we are separated. However, recently, we organized our first family reunion. Almost everyone came, and it seemed to go reasonably well on the surface.

One of my sisters brought along a friend for her 12-year old daughter. Although I felt this was completely out-of-place, I said nothing, as we were unaware of her intention earlier. The girl was accepted by all. When I took some pictures, it became awkward. I sensed the unfortunate situation, but felt these pictures were memories of a once-in-a-lifetime occasion. I was as polite as I could be, but I excluded her. I am now the victim of a fault-finding frenzy. I am accused of being rude and insensitive. This new "excuse" is causing a rift in our family.

I feel hurt and unjustly judged. I feel the lack of understanding of customary practices is what created the situation—not me. A note concerning the proper manners on inviting strangers to a family reunion or similar occasion would be appreciated.

GENTLE READER—The etiquette of any invitation is that one does not bring uninvited guests, or, if the event is cooperatively planned, one asks in advance what policy about other guests will be satisfactory to everyone. Miss Manners is sure you will like to hear that.

Right now, she is less concerned with that general rule than she is with the particular case of being nice to a guest, especially a child, however the guest happened to be there. There you will not like what Miss Manners has to say.

Making it clear to a child at a party that she is an outsider, if not actually an intruder, is rude and cruel. Miss Manners can think of no justification for it. The child herself was innocent of the arrangements, and yet she would bear the brunt of the embarrassment.

Anyway, pictures are supposed to reflect the occasion at which they were taken. This occasion happened to include your niece's friend. Why could the guest not be included and identified as such in your albums? That is not to say that you could not have gotten pictures that omitted her, either by posing a few of, for example, your generation only; or even by asking her to take one of the group pictures for you, which would put her out of camera range by being in a position of trust and honor behind it.

To do this in a way that made it clear to the child that she did not belong at the event is a greater transgression of etiquette than the one of bringing an uninvited guest. As your family was, by your account, not close to begin with and quick to take what you consider to be an "excuse" for feuding, it is perhaps well that your niece should cultivate friends. She will need them.

Other People's Relatives

DEAR MISS MANNERS — Close friends have long had the generous habit of inviting my husband and me to celebrate certain family holidays like Thanksgiving with them and their children, a tradition we enjoy and appreciate very much. We are childless and live thousands of miles from our families of origin.

Last year, however, they invited us to share Thanksgiving with the rest of the husband's large extended family at his parents' house. His parents and siblings all live close by and we know them quite well, so we didn't hesitate to accept.

Once we arrived, it became clear that while our friends were glad we were there, the rest of the clan (albeit polite) regarded us more or less as intruders on a family gathering. Our friend seemed to deliberately ignore these "vibes" from his siblings and acted as if all was well, when in truth we felt quite uncomfortable.

I had hoped we could simply resume our old pattern of celebrating holidays at his house, but he recently invited us to another family occasion at his parents', and I'm in a quandary. If we decline or make excuses (now or on future occasions), I know he'll be offended, but I daren't accept for fear of alienating his family. Nor do I wish to embarrass him by explaining that we felt out of place last time and would rather not intrude. Can you suggest a graceful way out?

GENTLE READER — Certainly. Invite him and his family to a holiday dinner.

It is lovely to be the beneficiary of a hospitable tradition, and Miss Manners is sure you are good about expressing gratitude, helping out and bringing presents. Even the most hospitable people maintaining traditions may get to the point where they require something more—someone else to take over. This may be the reason that Thanksgiving moved to the parents' house.

It would be even nicer if you invited the extended family, as you do know them and have accepted their hospitality, lukewarm as it was. They may well decline, preferring their family gathering, but Miss Manners assures you that they will feel more kindly about including you. They won't be able to be hurt if you decline on the grounds of doing your own entertaining, at which you had hoped to include them.

THE STYLE

Making Things Festive

Why use a tablecloth when it's sure to get stains on it? A plastic cover only requires wiping.

Why use real napkins, when they would only need to be washed and ironed afterwards? Paper can be thrown away.

Why use the silver, when it would have to be polished first? There's enough of the everyday stuff if the children use the picnic things.

Why use the good china, when it probably shouldn't go in the dishwasher and will have to be done by hand? With paper plates, you don't even have to scrape off the garbage.

Why use the good glasses when someone is bound to break one? With plastic glasses, no one has to be nervous.

Why get flowers for the table when they're so expensive and they don't last? Nobody notices, anyway.

Why set the table at all, when things can be put out buffet-style for people to take what they want? That way, you don't have to serve them and they can fight among themselves over the drumsticks.

Why use platters, when it would just mean getting something else dirty? Today's pots are made to go from the oven to the table.

Why plan on having everyone sit down together, when they always wander in at different times and get up from the table whenever they feel like it? They would probably prefer watching television during dinner to making conversation, anyway.

Why dress up, when jeans and running clothes are more comfortable? It's only going to be family and friends.

Ah, yes. Welcome to modern festivity, where the theme of the day is: Why bother?

Mind you, Miss Manners is not indifferent to the fact that it takes work and money to put on a festive dinner. She is aware that gracious celebrations are often put on by people whose only collection of silver is kept in their change purses; she never looks up from her dessert to inquire "Did you make this yourself?"; and she has an ingenious argument about the charm of worn-looking patterns on china, designed to justify putting the good stuff in the dishwasher. It's not the dry goods that bother her; it's the attitude.

No, wait. Miss Manners doesn't quite mean that. It's the dry goods too. Let's not have any of that nonsense along the lines of "What's the difference how I dish out the food as long as I have a good heart?" What she means is that ceremony requires caring, and deciding that the best household possessions are too good to be used for the family and friends who sent them as wedding presents in the first place is not what she would call the proper spirit.

It is entirely possible that if Miss Manners knew your relatives, she might not like them any more than you do. Nevertheless, the effort to set a pretty table is good for the soul, flattering to the guests, and a good investment in promoting holiday harmony. For all those hoity-toity, pathetic and wicked relatives, Miss Manners would scour the cupboards and bring out the hoity-toity stuff (menu card holders, nut picks, knife rests and finger bowls—which have a snobbish reputation now that they go almost exclusively to formal dinners, where they are less than useless because sloppy food isn't served, but would be great at family dinners where it is); the pathetic stuff (inherited or yard sale dishes, cups or candlesticks that have long since lost their old buddies); and the wicked stuff (cigarette urns—horrors!—but filled with candy or nuts).

"If you have good things, you should use them" used to be a byword of mothers regardless of where they were on the financial scale. Only once did Miss Manners blanch at use of this familiar injunction. A gentleman who had been the guest of a zillionaire on a yachting trip told her that he had inquired whether the sea air wouldn't hurt his host's Rembrandt, and that gentleman had replied thoughtfully, "Perhaps, but I always believe that if you have good things, you should enjoy them."

It is the concept of hospitality, much more than the silver, that has become tarnished and ugly when hosts take the cynical approach of asking why they should bother. Admittedly encouraged in this by guests who won't do their share—who won't show up when asked, dress for the occasion, stay through the meal, or make themselves charming to others—they refuse to put themselves out for a bunch of ingrates. The result is a lot of families who assemble for the holidays with the determination to do as little as possible to put themselves out for one another. Miss Manners wonders why they bother.

Dampening Festivity

Grousing is not allowed at the Thanksgiving dinner table. Nobody wants to hear which foods you don't like, much less why. For that matter, Miss Manners doesn't want to hear the traditional Thanksgiving Day dinner table compliment: "I'm so stuffed that if I have one more bite I'm going to throw up. Well, all right, but just one bite." However much the intent is to praise the cook, this remark does not suggest a pretty picture.

Family conversation is another traditional danger. What an opportunity holidays are for relatives to catch up on one another's lives and offer constructive criticism (Miss Manners has never heard tell of any other kind). Yet such good-natured ribbing as "Yes, but when are you going to get a real job?" and "Again? Hasn't anybody explained to you where these babies are coming from?" seldom leads to conviviality.

Miss Manners believes in heading all this off by suggesting a topic. Under her Thanksgiving system, each person is requested in turn to name the things for which he or she is grateful. The suggestion shocks newcomers because of its apparent irrelevance to a day consecrated to food and football.

There is to be no sneering at the simplest statements with which all but the incorrigible smart alecks begin—"For my children's good health," "That we are all able to be here today" and "Well, nobody's dropping nuclear bombs on us at the moment." Sentiments can be profound without being original, Miss Manners has noticed.

Encouraged to build from there, people often warm to the subject and produce expressions of gratitude they didn't know they had. We are all so used to focusing on what is wrong that it is startling to be forced to take an opposite approach. Miss Manners herself is, by the nature of her work, kept on the alert to uncover ever new manners atrocities. Her Gentle Readers also keep her posted on all the newest appalling developments. (Fortunately, they never commit violations themselves, but they are in a constant state of suffering from disgraceful behavior on the part of their colleagues, friends, neighbors, acquaintances and perfect strangers.)

Because of her vigilance in the cause of improving public behavior, Miss Manners is sometimes taxed with believing that things are constantly getting worse—that the modern era is a sad falling-off from the good old days when she and Queen Victoria and the rest of the pitiless etiquette cabal had everybody under perfect control. The truth is that etiquette improvements of the second half of the 20th century are so extraordinary that Miss Manners would not for the world return to a period before they went into effect. No more than she would return to a world without air-conditioning, no matter how pretty the fans she could flutter, or a world in which looking a word up in the *Oxford English Dictionary* required heavy lifting instead of sliding in a CD-ROM.

The first etiquette development for which Miss Manners gives thanks on Thanksgiving is that nobody is throwing the turkey bones on the floor. (Are they? You pick that up right now, you hear?) The Victorian era is remembered unkindly for its proliferation of table utensils—but that was only in the mid-to-late Victorian period. Early in the era, landed aristocrats were still eating with only their knives in ways that would get them thrown out of a high school cafeteria. Miss Manners is thankful that for all the lip people give her about forks nowadays, she doesn't have to explain what forks are. She doesn't have to remind people not to blow their noses in the tablecloth, a rule that needed repeating to our forebears.

The mannerly concept of egalitarianism has grown dramatically since their day, and etiquette rules for showing respect for everyone have proliferated. Miss Manners is extremely grateful to be no longer alone in suggesting that no one is above having to be polite, and no one is below having to be treated politely. There are those who complain that it isn't safe to insult anyone nowadays, but she doesn't have a great deal of sympathy for them.

The new respect—perhaps not yet fully in effect, but at least everybody knows that it is expected—extends to the workplace. Miss Manners is thankful that the asymmetry of small politenesses on the job—the old system by which the bosses were addressed respectfully but the underlings were called by their first names as if they were children—is gone. She wishes it had been resolved with dignity extended to all, instead of to no one, but she is grateful for what she got.

Nor does she complain, as many do, that a lot of modern talk about helping the unfortunate is hypocritical lip service. Given the choice between lip service and service, she, too, would prefer the latter. But a society that feels obliged to articulate humane concerns is better than one in which people air their selfishness frankly (not that we don't have some of that, too), and for that, Miss Manners is grateful.

Sabotaging Festivity

DEAR MISS MANNERS — We always have holiday dinners at my brother's house because it is convenient for the elderly relatives, and we always have the same problems. My brother, who is a designer and a perfectionist, seems to expect us to get all excited about a table covered with lace, china, candles and floral arrangements. How can we tell them to have a more casual event? How do we get them to lighten up? How do we convey to him and his wife that it is more important to value their young relatives rather than their material belongings?

He puts slipcovers on the chairs for the children (there are a lot, ages 3–10) and serves their food on decorated plastic "kid" dishes instead of on china. When my little girl asks why her place is different, he tells her something like, "Because you're a princess for the day." My daughter is too smart to be fooled by this. I end up smoothing things over by apologizing to her because the hosts disappointed her (a regular occurrence). Just because our child is a mere five years of age doesn't mean she should be treated like a second-class citizen.

The children sometimes don't like "grown-up" food and we parents make trips to the kitchen for cereal, sandwiches, etc. Also, the children sometimes cry or complain, as little children are wont to do. After dinner, the hostess tries to make someone feel guilty enough to help her with the dishes. Everyone usually brings a dish for the dinner, so the hosts are responsible mostly for set-up and clean-up. If she would use everyday dishes instead of china, she could use the dishwasher. Even though we are family, we would like to be properly treated like guests and be allowed to chat after dinner. We are usually busy tending to the children as well.

Right in front of the parents, my brother will say to the children, rather self-righteously, "Johnny, please don't play with the china cabinet door" or "Please don't touch the stereo." They expect the children never to run in the house (ostensibly for the "children's safety," though we think it is for the safety of the hosts' priceless lamps and furniture). It is not a large house and the children understandably become rambunctious after being inside all day when it is too cold to go out.

The hosts sometimes look to us to enforce their "house rules." The "entertainment" provided by the hosts is not of interest to the children (for example, puzzles that are old and too difficult, a few tired crayons and dull coloring books, etc.). We have let the hosts know that some age-appropriate toys might keep the children occupied, but they have ignored our suggestion.

We do not have the time or the dining room space to host the dinner. We don't want to decline to come, even though we find the atmosphere to be too formal and too restrictive. It is not relaxing. It is, however, the only way to see all of the relatives. After talking to other parents at the preschool and at work, these situations seem to occur in many, many households on the holidays. Many people recall the same treatment from their grandparents, that is, "children should be seen and not heard."

GENTLE READER— Miss Manners must have missed the "not heard" part. Does your brother not allow the children to join the conversation? Snubbing the children would indeed be dreadful evidence of your accusation that he only cares about material things.

All you reported was that he does not want them to break things, run wild or demand special meals. And that he and his wife go all out to make things nice for the entire extended family (as no one else seems to be willing to do), thus giving these children their only exposure to the kind of festive holiday that used to be a treasured feature of family life at all economic levels.

Couldn't you help just a little? Suggesting that they dumb down their hospitality and buy more up-to-date toys does not count. Teaching your children simple childhood manners—don't race through the house, watch out for fragile things, don't tell hosts you hate their food—and issuing reminders on the spot would be more helpful.

If Miss Manners sympathizes with your brother, it is not against your children, but on their behalf. You do them no favor in encouraging them to think only of how others treat them, and not of how they should treat others.

Sabotaging the Spirit

DEAR MISS MANNERS— My mother-in-law is a lady who prides herself on her adherence to etiquette, and relishes nothing so much as a formal affair in which she can expect things to be done in a specific manner—i.e., by the book. The holidays provide her with the perfect backdrop on which to gather her large family for a nice Victorian-style dinner, replete with china and exquisite dinners, over which she labors for hours, if not days. Her expectations are rarely met, and the meal (and day) always ends with hard feelings all around. The friction occurs over several issues:

1. She wears herself out preparing the meal and gets little help from the family because some are just arriving from long journeys, most have not seen each other in over a year and are becoming reacquainted, young grandchildren must be entertained and/or watched, and she doesn't ask for assistance—in fact occasionally turns down offers for help on things she says she needs to do herself.

2. She gets little help in clearing the meal because she starts clearing when a few people are still chewing the last bite or contemplating another serving of the excellent food, dinner conversation is just becoming animated as people catch up

on a year's worth of news and debates, those who have finished are relishing a glass of wine or coffee and don't realize that she needs assistance, she starts cleaning and washing a few items without asking for help or even announcing her intentions, and young grandchildren get restless by then and need their share of attention.

3. Her criticisms and complaints come in the form of hints, parables, deep sighs, clanking dishes, vacuumed feet and even, once, an underlined advice column left at the breakfast table the next day. These are difficult to respond to.

4. Her criticisms are directed much more at her daughters-in-law because such household chores should be done by women. She might ask her sons to clear the snow or fix the plumbing, but these are tasks that rarely need to be accomplished during the dinner hour or the conversation which follows.

Could you please suggest an ideal solution and perhaps also a more realistic alternative that would give us all the best chance for a harmonious and happy holiday? Some of us travel 700 miles, and an alternative location at smaller residences does not seem possible.

GENTLE READER — Your mother-in-law goes by the book? Which book is that? One of those cozy books that suggest that families make up their very own traditions, thus encouraging your mother-in-law to enshrine her traditional grump session?

This lady may have mastered the mechanics of giving a formal dinner, but she seems to have missed more essential points of etiquette. Two absolute imperatives for hosts are:

Don't rush your guests when they're still eating or drinking, and don't interrupt animated conversation.

Don't sulk at or around the dinner table.

Still, we tend to go easy on mothers at holiday time. This is not only, as you say, because we want a harmonious gathering, but because we owe them respect as matriarchs, because we appreciate how hard they've worked, and because a fat lot of good it would do to try to change them.

Miss Manners recommends a pre-dinner huddle, at which the grown-up children agree to tell (not ask) Mamma that they are going to do all the cleaning up, and that they have it all worked out among them who is to do what and at what time. (This may necessitate pre-huddle huddles, at which the sons are told by their wives that they are cheerfully to insist on doing their share as if it were their own idea.)

This will of course not prevent your mother-in-law from popping up from the table. She will still do everything she can to work up some lather, not only for the dishes but for her tradition of feeling aggrieved. You must replace this with a new tradition. Each time you discover her getting up, you must set up a chorus in which you all good-naturedly tease her about taking away your job and insist that she return to the table. The grandchildren will be especially good at this. Assign them to keep an eye on her and report whenever she leaves the table. (Well, perhaps you'd better say when she leaves the table for the kitchen. We don't want the poor lady embarrassed more than necessary.) Send them after her with instructions to bring her back.

All of this must be interlaced with appreciation for the meal and inquiries that draw her into the conversation. Between that and the game of "Oops, Grandma's escaped again," she will be receiving far too much attention to be able to go off and be morose.

THE ULTIMATE TEST

The Family Trip

"I had no trouble understanding the dynamics of revolution," a college student of Miss Manners' acquaintance told her. "I'd learned it when I was little, on a family trip." Reassured that there was no cause for retroactive alarm—the family had not been caught in actual warfare—Miss Manners was pleased to hear of such an educational vacation. Surely, learning history is one of the great delights of travel, ranking right up there with beautiful views and afternoon naps.

The young lady's parents had taken advantage of an on-the-spot opportunity, even though it appears that the lesson was unrelated to the history of the place they happened to be visiting.

"We had rented a car," the student explained, "and my father wanted to get to the next city before nightfall. It was a long way and traffic was bad, so he refused to stop for food or bathroom breaks. My brother and I tried to protest, but he said we could wait. Mother admitted she was hungry, but he wouldn't listen to her, either.

"We were all in our corners of the car being sullen, so we hardly noticed when he did pull up and stop. He needed gas. But Mother sprang out and opened the back door and we went tearing out after her. When we'd all been to the bathroom, we hit the snack bar, madly grabbing sandwiches and candy bars. Father was already in there, announcing, 'All right, we're leaving now,' and then arguing, 'Look at that line—we'd be here all night,' and finally pleading, 'You can hold out—I promise we'll get a real dinner when we get there.' But we wouldn't budge. What's more, we declared we wouldn't get back into the car until he promised we could have another bathroom break if we needed it.

"So here's what we learned: When people are deprived of the basic necessities, they can be cowed. It doesn't even occur to them that they have numbers on their side. It is only when there is a slight improvement in their condition—when a few human wants have been satisfied—that they start plotting revolution."

Miss Manners noticed another lesson in here about human nature: that perfectly nice families who may live together in loving harmony can find themselves at war when they travel.

It is said that people who can travel together successfully can surely live happily together, because they are thrown closely together and obliged to resolve conflicts and meet emergencies. Perhaps so, although Miss Manners suspects that this argument is left over from when parents still had the energy to be horrified that their children proposed to go on the wedding trip before the wedding.

She also knows people who live happily together, dealing with conflicts and emergencies that are likely to be more serious than restaurant choices or canceled flights, who find it difficult to travel together. Some like to cover territory, while others like to find a good spot and loll around. Being in charge of the arrangements can turn kindly people into tyrants, while having someone else in charge can turn responsible people into laggards. Some people like to see every sight, not leaving anything in case they return, while others like to go through every shop, not leaving anything in case they return.

Miss Manners believes that a daily mix—of movement and rest, museums and street life, education and entertainment—makes a more satisfying holiday than pursuit of any one of these. Yet she is cheerfully willing to admit this as a preference that she need not inflict on others. Separate vacations are a solution to family differences, but Miss Manners doesn't know why so few families try a less drastic solution: the same vacation, but separate daily vacation activities, to be talked over at dinner (if they can agree upon a restaurant). As always, she prefers negotiation, compromise, concessions and constitutional amendments to revolution.

Chapter Ten

─────────■■■■■■■─────────

THE COMMUNITY

THE NEIGHBORHOOD

The Good Neighbor

A good neighbor is rich, taciturn and childless; desires neither pets nor guests; and is fanatic about keeping the property neat and clean but horrified at the idea of making any creative changes in it. This is not Miss Manners' definition. Personally, she prefers to be surrounded by people who are alive. It seems to be the ideal of neighborhood associations and boards of cooperative buildings. When their members convene to evaluate would-be neighbors or chastise the ones with whom they are already stuck, this is the standard by which they measure. It's not what they get, of course. Hermits tend not to play around with real estate.

Even if buildings and neighborhoods could be filled with such types, Miss Manners is not convinced that they would improve the neighborhood. She understands that the old-style model neighbor—friendly, helpful and hospitable—is capable of driving everybody on the block or floor crazy, and therefore maintaining some distance is desirable. You don't want to have to keep explaining your life to people who are well situated for conducting surveillance. Even neighbors who become friends are supposed to pretend they don't see one another giving parties to which they are not invited or taking in the paper in their nightclothes.

A chatty neighbor can waste your time and destroy your patience; a nosy one has an unfair advantage in keeping track of who is coming and going. Children are sure to wail, play pranks, toss balls into windows or drive tricycles into hallway walls—and that's only until they are old enough to develop a taste for what they euphemistically call music. The neighbors' guests have the notion that they've also been invited to park their cars.

However, you probably do want your neighbors to notice who is coming into your house by unscrewing the iron grille on a window. You probably want to be trusted with the neighbors' keys so you can get in when they are away and the wind sets off their alarm. The children who cut across your lawn or push all the elevator buttons may be useful when you're both older and you need them to shovel your walk or pick you up off of it when you break your hip. The neighbors who keep asking you to take in packages because you work at home can be asked in return to pick up things for you on their way home.

Anyway, Miss Manners is afraid that much of the annoyance of living near living people has to be tolerated for the sake of harmony, heavily backed by the fear of retaliation. At the very least, problems have to be handled with tremendous tact. They all know where you live. It is a mistake to make a fuss about guests' parking, only to have the painters show up for work at your house the next day with very long trucks. Or to keep carping about children until you suddenly find you are expecting children or visits from grandchildren. Or to establish the principle of zero tolerance for minor infractions if you're planning to lead a normal life.

Miss Manners keeps hearing about recalcitrant neighbors who are impervious to the comforts and complaints of others. She has no doubt that some such exist, and that it may take the power of landlords, building superintendents, neighborhood associations, police officers, zoning boards and the court system to make them behave. It is also possible that some of them are being trained to be hostile. How else does one expect people to reply to angry threats invoking rights and insults about invasions of space? That they're terribly sorry, didn't realize they were causing a disturbance and will never do it again?

Miss Manners recommends using old-style neighborliness—an aura of good will, mixed with regret at having to call a problem to the attention of someone also presumed to be of good will—before resorting to lawsuits. It is quicker and cheaper. It is also easier than finding neighbors who are never visually, aurally or personally intrusive.

Complaining About Nosy Neighbors

DEAR MISS MANNERS — Due to a relationship break-up and my financial circumstances, I was forced to move back home with my mother at the age of 45. She lives in a senior citizen condominium complex. Obviously, I feel out of place living amongst the elderly residents. I try to tell myself that I should just go about my business, and a simple "Good morning" or "Hello" is enough if I happen to pass someone. I feel that neighbors are of no real significance in one's life, chances being that we would never see them again if they move away.

Am I wrong? These neighbors don't feel the same way. They all know each other and much about everyone's lives. One of them even had the nerve to ask me how much I paid for my earrings, and if they were gold. I was so taken aback, I was lost for a good answer. How can one live in a place like this and still have privacy from these meddlesome, rude and invasive neighbors? How can one make these types understand that I don't want to be bothered with or by them, without appearing rude or aloof? What makes them so nosy and curious about each other's lives, anyway?

GENTLE READER — What makes people curious about each other's lives is our common humanity. What makes people express this humanity by asking nosy questions is rudeness.

Miss Manners is troubled by your equating such rudeness with any sort of neighborliness. She can tell you how to fend off nosy questions, and she can even tell you how to fend off all sociability, but she would consider the latter to be a mistake.

To have friendly neighbors is a tremendous boon. Neighbors can do one another all sorts of favors that even intimate friends and relations cannot do if they live at a distance. It can also be lovely to make friends that one will then have close at hand. Miss Manners urges you not only to stop being a snob about age, but to remember that elderly people often have descendants, and all of those are younger than they are. You might want to meet them.

To discourage nosy questions, one should have a firm policy of not answering them. A polite way to do it is to fail to understand the question. For example, the answer to "How much did you pay for your earrings? Are they real gold?" is "Oh, I'm so glad you like them."

To discourage all conversation, you must cultivate an air of preoccupied bewilderment, when anybody addresses you, and keep apologizing that you have to run off. Just don't come complaining to Miss Manners when you hear that one of these people you snubbed is being visited by the very person you have always wanted to meet.

Complaining About Discreet Neighbors

DEAR MISS MANNERS — When we moved into this neighborhood six months ago and the couple next door invited us for dinner, we were pleased to accept their invitation. The evening was not an unpleasant one. We stayed until nearly midnight, and the conversation ranged over a number of subject areas: either about the other couple and their doings, or a few topics of mutual interest.

But during the entire time we were in their home, neither my wife nor I was asked a single question about ourselves: not what we do for a living, how we've come to be in this city, our educational backgrounds, our children, etc. There were several openings during the course of the dinner for them to "pick up" on topics of this sort, but it simply did not happen.

We are not angry so much as puzzled, Miss Manners. These folks are apparently in their own world and happy to be there. But do we owe them a reciprocal invitation? The idea makes us uncomfortable if such an evening were to be a repeat of the one described; we'd feel even more sensitive about subjecting a third (innocent!) couple to punishment of this sort. On the other hand, they are neighbors and we expect to live here for a while. Is there a gracious alternative that we don't see here?

GENTLE READER — Miss Manners could weep. She has spent so much energy in trying to persuade people not to ask prying questions, and here you are, having stayed up to midnight discussing topics of mutual interest with new people, complaining that they are self-centered for not having quizzed you about your personal life.

It is possible that the last couple whose occupations and schools they asked got huffy because they felt they were being investigated to see if they were important. The one before that burst into tears upon being asked about their children because they have been unable to have any.

This was a first time get-together, after all. Polite people make general conversation before investigating one another's histories. Yet these people made a step toward closer acquaintanceship by volunteering information about themselves; surely, you could have done that, as well. At least promise Miss Manners you will try. If they reply "Who cares?" and go on talking about themselves, she will concede that you were right and can confine your neighborliness to an occasional over the fence greeting.

Peeping In

DEAR MISS MANNERS — Our kitchen window is directly across from the kitchen window of a neighbor's house, which is only a few feet away. When I am doing dishes, I can see into their kitchen, and occasionally I will catch my neighbor's eye. At first, we exchanged a wave or a smile. I guess the novelty has worn off, because lately the neighbor seems to pretend that I am not there. We hardly ever see them outside, but when we do, we exchange only hellos; they do not seem interested in conversation.

When I was a child, we knew almost everyone on the block. Do most people just want to be left to themselves these days? The current state of affairs has left me feeling uncomfortable and lonely.

GENTLE READER — Neighborliness is a wonderful thing, and Miss Manners would be delighted to help you revive it. First, she has to explain that ignoring its limits is as much to blame for destroying it as is any modern self-centered aloofness.

The poor lady next door does not want to feel that you are forever in her kitchen, keeping a friendly eye on her as she attempts to live her own life in her own house. Perhaps that is why she is limiting herself to polite greetings. If you are frankly peeking in now, she may well be wondering what you might do if she encouraged you. Call out that what she's cooking needs more salt? Or that she shouldn't be licking the pot?

Urban life requires a balance of sociability with privacy. For this reason, certain conventions are necessary, enabling people to ignore one another at times without being rude. These can include not only hurrying by with a quick greeting, rather than treating each encounter as a visit, but sometimes actually pretending you do not see someone when you obviously do. Modern folk are not good at this sort of subtlety, but without it, genuine feelings of neighborliness would be stretched beyond reasonable endurance. The mere accident of your being able to see in someone's window does not entitle you to free entrance through it.

By all means, continue to greet your neighbors on the street, but learn to pretend that you do not, in fact, see inside their houses. Miss Manners does not want to discourage your being sociable with your neighbors, but no friendship can flourish when one of the parties feels cornered, especially on her very own turf.

Dropping In

DEAR MISS MANNERS — About 18 months ago, I moved from the city to a small community in the north woods, where I have been thoroughly enjoying the solitude, climate and beauty. Everything is going well, except that I am a bit vexed about how to adapt to a peculiar local custom. Folks here love to drop in for a visit without giving any notice. It's not that I'm phoneless—when I did have one, they never called to announce their imminent arrivals. This might not pose a problem if only I had the option of simply refusing to answer the door. But up in this territory, people knock briskly and enter, then begin to snoop about like hounds on a fresh trail.

There is a certain amount of community pride invested in maintaining a liberal standard of trust and openness. To lock my door, if I had a lock, would be tantamount to declaring that not only do I not trust my country neighbors, but also that I have something to hide. Should I dash upstairs and cower under the bedsheets till they leave? The custom seems to allow visitors free run of the ground floor, but I think there is sort of an unwritten taboo preventing them from going up steps in their investigations. Why should I have to take flight, or make myself presentable at the drop of a latch?

I suppose I could fake a burglary on my own home and then use it as an excuse to secure the premises. However, this would send shock waves of fear and suspicion through this innocent little burg. This is, after all, a benign nuisance. I'm grateful to be living in a crime-free zone. These are good, honest, friendly, well meaning people (with robust curiosity!). I don't want to hurt their feelings. I've found it helpful to view this as a sort of anthropological project. It's as if I'm living in a remote tribal village, enjoying friendship with the natives, while attempting to garner respect for my own folkways, too. Is it that I'm attempting to have it both ways?

GENTLE READER — Sure, but why shouldn't you? Miss Manners hardly thinks it too much to want to live in peace and privacy and yet to get on with one's neighbors.

She advises you to get the word out that you are busy working (or napping) most of the time, but would love to receive anyone who wants to visit, say from four to six on most weekends. Then lock up. Should anyone complain, you can apologize with the statement that this was not done because of that person or any other neighbor, because they all know that you don't do visiting during the day. It was done in case strangers who don't know your ways happened by. This not only reinforces your bond to the community, but establishes you as the town eccentric, which is not a bad thing to be.

Dressing Up

DEAR MISS MANNERS — You told us it was all right not to get fully dressed to go out on the front porch to get the morning paper. Is there a further dispensation for subscribers to papers whose carriers do not consider the front porch within their jurisdiction? May we go out to the sidewalk in nightclothes to get the paper?

GENTLE READER — Surely you meant to address this letter to the circulation department. Two questions of decency are involved here—doing a job properly and ensuring that the populace not stray too far in its nightclothes—and the former, at least, comes within that department's jurisdiction. If that were solved, the latter problem would not exist. However, it does, doesn't it? Miss Manners can't get out of it that easily.

Her answer depends on your definition of nightclothes, and on the cooperation of your neighbors. Revealing clothing may not be worn beyond the threshold.

Opaque robes may be, provided that your neighbors understand that in case you do not appear to advantage at that hour, they have not officially observed you in the act of fetching the paper.

Running Into

DEAR MISS MANNERS — I love to walk for exercise, and many times would run into a neighbor also out for her walk. About a year and a half ago, we started walking together. At first, it was nice to have a partner, so you'd tend not to skip, but I'm finding myself hating to walk now, because I'm tied in to walking with her.

She doesn't work outside the home and I do, so I'm having to call every time, to see if my free time will work for her (which it always does). We don't have much in common, and I find her problems minor compared to the serious ones I'm dealing with. With all the stress in my life, this scheduled walking time with her has added to my stress level, instead of helping. I want to go back to walking alone. I meditate and pray when I walk alone, and it's a great stress reducer. I know if I tell her, she will be hurt and I will feel guilty every time I step out the door. I need to be freed of this!

GENTLE READER — Tied to her? At a time when people consider marriage vows to be temporary commitment, valid only when mutually satisfactory, Miss Manners is amazed that you consider an agreement to go walking as a permanent bond precluding not just other partners but solitude.

While the neighbor may enjoy walking with you, Miss Manners doubts that knowing that you take other walks will be a major blow to her. She may even be glad to have the same freedom herself. Just go ahead and take your solos, right out there in the open, waving at your neighbor cheerfully if you should happen to pass. Every once in a while, you could also propose a joint walk, to show that your new habit is not a criticism of the old one.

Reasonable Curiosity

DEAR MISS MANNERS — As soon as the For Sale sign goes up on the front lawn, one can almost feel the buzz of speculation take hold of the neighbors. They seem to feel that they have a vested interest in your property, i.e., if you do well, so will they. If your property does not sell, self-congratulatory back pats all around—"Weren't we smart not to list right now?"

One begins to feel awkward about stepping out the front door, as it is impossible to avoid being grilled on "how the open-house went," or "Haven't you sold yet?" If we had, the sign on the lawn would indicate that. Well-meaning concern feels like gloating in disguise. And the details of your transaction seem not to be private, either. Without my disclosing any information, they have nevertheless become privy to where we are going, how much we paid, etc. If details are not forthcoming from the adults, children are there to satisfy the need to know. Am I wrong in assuming that the rule of etiquette about not asking others about their financial affairs should also apply to selling the home?

GENTLE READER—Just a minute, here. Miss Manners is a national leader in the battle against nosiness, but the fact is that the neighbors do have a vested interest in neighborhood real estate prices. What is more, the sale price will eventually be a matter of public record, which any of them considering selling a house will undoubtedly consult.

It is true that "Haven't you sold yet?" is a dumb question, and that grilling children is dreadful. A little chitchat about a deeply mutual interest is not out of place. Such questions are rude only when there is no legitimate motive for asking. When one's house is for sale, many people who would normally cut out their tongues rather than ask the price of anything owned by anyone else might inquire for the sake of telling possible buyers they know. Anyway, this is hardly the time to worry about getting on cozier terms with the neighbors. The ultimate solution to the neighbors problem is always moving away—provided you can get a good deal on your house, of course.

Unreasonable Criticism

DEAR MISS MANNERS—My wife, who has an art degree, hung several of her large, non-representational paintings in the den and living room of the house we just finished decorating. Personally, I love these paintings. To me, they make dramatic statements about color and texture, and seem to make the house come to life. I wouldn't want to take them down for anything, and neither does my wife.

But in the past two months, we have entertained three different couples—and all have frequently and directly told us that if we really wanted to make more friends in the community, it would be advisable for us to remove my wife's paintings and replace them with more traditional and "less insulting" imagery. A visitor asking us to join her church has merely made the comment that the paintings are rather upsetting, but has kept quiet after that remark.

Are we violating any standards of manners that we don't know about? I thought it was okay to have your own paintings, no matter what they were, up in your own house. My wife's work is really no more harmful or upsetting than Robert Rauschenberg's work back in the 70s.

It's not that we expect anyone to become art majors. It's that we wonder whether we should keep our home the way we want it, or, as in the days we were children, conform to our parents' rules about the house. Or are there rules we are not aware of?

GENTLE READER — Where do you live? There must be legions of artists whose ambition it is to shock people, but who find it difficult to get a rise out of anyone any more, and utterly impossible to do so with nonrepresentational art. They might want to move next door, which would at least solve your problem.

There are people in this situation who do seem to be unaware of rules of etiquette, but the people are your visitors, and the rules of which they are unaware are: "Mind your own business" and "Do not insult your hosts" (on two counts: their talents and their decor). Miss Manners cannot believe that there is an entire community of such rude people. Perhaps you should express your regret that they do not approve of your taste and your wife's talents, and look farther afield for polite companionship.

NEIGHBORHOOD PARTIES

The Commercial Welcome

What a charming idea, the neighbors thought when they received housewarming invitations from the stranger who bought the house they had all been wondering about. (They hadn't been wondering who would move into it, but how much it would fetch and whether they could then jack up the price of their own houses, but never mind.)

Miss Manners hopes that some of the established residents also had a small twinge, remembering that it was their duty to welcome newcomers, and not the newcomers' to announce themselves. No matter whose idea it was, the thought of meeting new neighbors other than over a discussion of whose-dog-did-what-where was an appealing one.

Actually, it wasn't the new neighbors' idea. Closer inspection of the invitation showed that the party to meet the neighbors in their new house was being given by the real estate agent who sold it to them. Although the party would serve the new-neighbor purpose, the intention behind it had to be a desire to make new clients.

Miss Manners sniffs a trend here. As people neglect their social duties, commercial ventures take over. Added to conventional business entertaining, fund-raising events put on by nonprofit enterprises and publicity-raising events put on by profit enterprises (Miss Manners sometimes wonders when the definition of society became people who attend parties thrown by perfume companies to launch new smells) are these more simple events.

She does not, however, sniff at the effort. Indeed, she is indebted to the bookstore for taking up Madame de Staël's burden of providing a salon where people of literary inclinations could meet. With the decline of private entertaining, it is as well that someone is taking up the slack.

What worries her is that all this will administer the death blow to the already feeble notion of private social duty. Look what the burgeoning popularity of the restaurant has done to the private dinner party. Restaurant manners allow deciding at the last minute if one wants to eat out, bringing along whoever one wishes, ignoring everybody else present and, above all, declaring one's dietary preferences. So why can't one do that when invited for dinner by a friend? Any host could explain why not, and the rude ones sometimes do. Using restaurant manners in private homes has ruined private entertaining.

Conversely, look what using home manners for watching television—talking, eating, walking in and out, stopping for telephone calls—has done to movie-going, theater-going and other such activities. If the situation becomes even more confused, how will anyone know which manners are required?

Even strict Miss Manners cannot pretend that parties given for commercial purposes incur the same obligations as does pure hospitality. For example, you don't have to invite the department store back. Nor to remember to send it something at Christmas, because it gave you a bag full of samples to take home.

Superficially, there is little difference between the open house that a real estate agent might give to show a house on the market to prospective buyers and the party to show the buyer to the neighbors. People are already used to the etiquette appropriate to viewing a house for sale. Miss Manners is only afraid that they will traipse through the new neighbor's house, complaining about its deficiencies, inquiring about its cost and commenting about how its looks could be improved by upgrading the taste of the furnishings. She would also hate to see anyone still inclined to perform such a personal duty as calling on a new neighbor decide to wait until someone with a financial motive makes the effort instead.

The Charming Welcome

DEAR MISS MANNERS — Our next door neighbors, with whom we were pretty close, sold their house to a couple who will be moving in next week. My family and I would like to get to know our new neighbors, and help them move in—but not in a nosy manner. How can we approach them so we do not seem to be intruding?

GENTLE READER — Have we come to this? That the fine old tradition of welcoming new neighbors is in danger of appearing to be an affront?

Unfortunately, Miss Manners knows how this has happened. There is so much genuine nosiness going about shamelessly rooting for gossip, that fastidious people may be wary of any interest. So it is not unreasonable to worry that your desire to be helpful may be misinterpreted.

If your previous neighbors have not moved out of town, you might suggest that they introduce you; at the least, they could introduce you by mail. Still, it will be your place to make the first move. Just hanging around as they move in may not be a good idea. People tend to feel at their worst then, and to take offers of help as disguised license for scrutinizing their possessions. The charming way is to leave the traditional bread and salt, or a little basket of flowers or fruit, with a note offering to tell them about the neighborhood and your telephone number.

The Nude Welcome

DEAR MISS MANNERS — In our new neighborhood, the neighbors couldn't be more friendly. Our next door neighbor had a welcome-to-the-neighborhood party for us, and told us to bring towels if we wanted to relax and converse in their spa after dinner. The problem was, we were the only ones wearing bathing suits. Everyone else was totally naked, even one couple who are Mormon.

While no one commented on our wearing bathing suits, we felt very uncomfortable, but didn't want to be rude and leave, particularly since these were the nicest people we have met in ages. They accepted us as we were, yet we couldn't accept their nudity. What should we have done? What should we do in the future?

GENTLE READER—They do sound like nice people, although of course Miss Manners hasn't seen as much of them as you have. Giving a welcoming party and failing to notice that you were differently attired from everyone else are both polite acts. So surely you do not want Miss Manners to chastise them for setting the dress standard in their own house. (They might properly have warned you of it, but perhaps they consider it a well-known local custom.)

Rather, you have the choice of (1) accepting similar invitations after asking if they mind if you wear your bathing suits and after having practiced looking everybody straight in the eye, and (2) declining invitations to their spa but encouraging their friendship otherwise by issuing other invitations to them.

In the latter case, you might want to borrow the phrase people used to use when the custom of wearing evening clothes in the evening could unfortunately no longer be taken for granted. People who still observed the amenities would say to their guests, "We'll be dressing for dinner."

The Commercial Housewarming

DEAR MISS MANNERS—There are two problems with the housewarming party I am having: One, that I have a lot of things, such as knickknacks, glassware, books and expensive furniture. And two, that I have a huge, two-story colonial that looks like a mansion.

What it boils down to is that I am afraid that people might feel there is nothing they can get me, because it may look to them as if I have everything, which I don't. Also, they might get very jealous when they walk into my home and leave and finally that they may feel their present is not good enough. What should I do? Should I send a list of things I need along with the invitation, or simply send the invitation and hope things work out?

GENTLE READER—Miss Manners understands your fear that people might find this occasion confusing. By calling it a housewarming, you are only too likely to give the unfortunate impression that the purpose is to offer hospitality, rather than to solicit contributions.

The ritual you have in mind is not the party, but the charity drive. Miss Manners is not super-confident that you will encounter many people who prefer to devote their philanthropy to the owners of colonial "mansions" than to the homeless, but at least they will have been warned what you expect.

Are Parties Included in the Rent?

DEAR MISS MANNERS—I am a single woman who rents the ground floor apartment in a large house otherwise occupied by my landlord and his family. I have enjoyed a cordial relationship with them, exchanging pleasantries when we meet, but something bothers me. My landlords give several outdoor barbecues in the backyard for many of their friends on warm weekends, and I never even once received a courtesy invitation to join them. This despite the fact that the barbecue was set right in front of my living room window, my door is always open in summer, and barbecue odors inevitably waft through my apartment. These people knew I was home, they could see me inside, but merely waved hello and went on cooking and eating no more than six feet away.

I am not needy. Nor do I desperately need food. But I've had tenants of my own in the past, and always invited them and my neighbors to any backyard barbecues. I do not remember anyone who did not appreciate the courtesy, much less decline to come. Now I am the tenant and I feel my landlords are rude and insensitive. Surely inviting one more guest would not be a burden when they are entertaining a dozen others. I am considering moving out. What do you say?

GENTLE READER—That you should move out.

It is not that Miss Manners shares your indignation. People who feel that social privileges go with the real estate should simply not be living with those who are understandably wary of setting such precedents. The problem with landlord-tenant socializing is that each can plainly see what the other is doing. It is obvious when a party is being given, and it may also be obvious whether someone who declines an invitation is really otherwise busy.

Warmly as etiquette promotes friendliness and hospitality, it also discourages intrusiveness. Thus we have the convention of pretending not to notice—a widely useful social fiction by which people seem unaware of what is happening under their noses (or in the case of the barbecue odors, right up their noses). If this were not invoked, neighbors would never be free from one another's company or interest. Without even trying, near-neighbors simply have too much information about one another for comfort. You don't want them to tell you what they think of the gentleman who comes calling or to ask why a nice young lady like you is so often home alone on weekends.

The accident of geography has no relation to whether those dozen friends of theirs would like you or you would like them. You might soon find yourself hiding under your bed, or they might be reduced to sneaking people in and cautioning them not to sound as if they are having too good a time.

Provided that everyone understands and practices a general policy of not noticing what is going on, Miss Manners would see no harm, and perhaps some good, in making a very occasional exception. As one can no longer count on anyone's being able to handle any behavior more complicated than blurting out the obvious, your landlords may not want to raise your expectations. As you already have social expectations of them, Miss Manners cannot help thinking that they may be right.

The Neighborhood Holiday

DEAR MISS MANNERS — Teenagers who arrive without a costume, cigarettes aglow, hanging all over their latest squeeze, with a pillowcase as a trick or treat sack, have made many of my neighbors consider turning off the lights and locking the door on Halloween. My next door neighbor was literally cursed for having run out of candy!

I personally spend what I consider a generous amount (over $100) on candy to give to young children. I do it because when I was a child, the people in our community did it for us. It was a magical time of make-believe.

So every year, I drag out all my decorations, buy candy, put on my costume and wait to hear the joyous sound of little children shouting, "Trick or treat!" I always enjoy the sense of merriment I experience through the children.

I resent, however, giving candy to people who are bigger than I am, and should be looking for a job instead of a handout of candy.

I find it more than a little discouraging that parents haven't shown or explained to their youngsters appropriate behavior for this activity, but clearly they have not. I would have been whipped for some of the rudeness I have encountered when my parents got wind of it—and they would have certainly heard from the offended party. I would like to propose some guidelines for those taking part that would make it a pleasant experience for all involved.

1. Children under 13 only (unless you are escorting a younger brother or sister).
2. Limit yourself from 6:00 to 8:00 P.M. (before six you interrupt dinner; after eight, you interrupt rest).
3. While elaborate costumes are unnecessary, any attempt at dressing up is appreciated by those of us who spend our money on the trick or treaters.
4. Say, "Trick or treat!" once the door is opened to you.
5. Once the treat has been given do not:
   a. Make remarks about the amount or nature of the treat (remember they do not have to give you anything)
   b. Ask for seconds for your "sick little sister" (just share what you get with her)
6. Then say "thank you," for heaven's sake!

I truly think that everyone would enjoy Halloween more. I plan to have fun no matter how inconsiderate others may be and I hope that the children that come to my door all have a safe and fun Halloween.

GENTLE READER—Miss Manners welcomes you to the etiquette business. Instead of shutting your doors and blaming the children, you understand that the problem is ignorance of the rules, and you have taken the trouble to supply them. She might question you about some details: What about children who are too shy to make the required announcement? Is an age cutoff that important if the people are in costume and in the spirit of the occasion? (And how can you tell nowadays whether a teenager is in costume?) Shouldn't you alert people to respond to excessive demands by saying gently "Please wait until everybody has had firsts" or "I'm saving these for the little ones"?

That should not obscure her hearty basic agreement with you. Without its rules and traditions, Trick or Treating is indistinguishable from mugging. Why would anyone willingly open the doors to that?

NEIGHBORHOOD NUISANCES

Noise

All right, we've solved the smoking problem. Now let's move on to the noise problem.

What's that? We haven't solved the smoking problem? Why? Because the citizens are battling one another on the streets? Because friendships have been destroyed through banishment and boycotts? Because families haven't been so torn down the middle by a single issue since the Civil War? Miss Manners, who tries to operate at a lofty level above that squabbling, only meant that we have solved the smoking problem in principle. The practice takes somewhat longer. Much longer. All right, a lot longer.

The principle is that people who enjoy themselves in potentially intrusive ways ought—preferably without being asked, but most certainly if they are asked (politely, one hopes)—to restrain themselves in the presence of those on whom such activities have an unpleasant effect. Is that a sufficiently nonprovocative way of putting it?

It is not that we want to spoil anybody's fun—only that we want to take reasonable precautions against spoiling the pleasure of others. (That neither part of this statement is true does not disturb Miss Manners; decent people must act as if they were.) It is not an even contest: The wish not to be disturbed has precedence over the desire to do something generally recognized as disturbing.

In a society that has emphasized individual rights at the expense of community preferences, the idea that one shouldn't exercise one's right to annoy people is a hard-won principle. It ought to be more widely applied, and noise would be a good place to start. There is nothing inherently wrong in talking, laughing, playing music, playing really loud music, snapping chewing gum, whistling, whispering or receiving telephone calls, but there are wrong places to do each of these things, and people should not have to bop one another on the head to establish where they are.

Yet we seem condemned to attack the noise issue separately, each instance with its own drawn-out warfare. Miss Manners is afraid that this is because we didn't really learn from the smoking wars. Instead of accepting the etiquette principle, we recast the problem as being entirely a health issue, giving it enough dignity to be removed from the jurisdiction of etiquette and turned over to the law.

Miss Manners is not disputing that smoking is also a health issue. Please go away with all those intrusive statistics. But by making health the only issue involved, we have managed to avoid dealing with the annoyance issue, which keeps popping up. It has become illegal to smoke in many places, but it is not illegal to annoy others if you can find ways to do so without causing cancer. By hounding them for smoking where they are permitted to do so, for example.

Miss Manners hastens to say that she does not want annoyance to be declared illegal, however much her own life would be improved by making the police deal with the rapidly rising annoyance rate. The number of laws that would have to be passed would bring the society—not to mention the cause of freedom—to a screeching halt, although screeching itself would doubtless be outlawed. That is why she is not going to make self-righteous claims about noise being a health hazard, however tempting that might be. She is not even going to advance everybody's currently favorite argument—that whatever is disagreeable causes serious damage to mental health.

Noise annoys the neighbors. People shouldn't annoy one another because it's annoying.

Not Shouting Back

DEAR MISS MANNERS — Every morning, between 6:30 and 6:45, my neighbor says good-bye to her family by honking the horn two to four times as she drives up the street. This is also their way of saying hello and good-bye throughout the day. My bedroom faces the street, and because of inadequate sound-proofing (which would be cost prohibitive right now), along with a sleeping problem I'm having, I hear this even with the windows closed. Custom-made earplugs don't work for me. Since the sleeping problem is mine, not theirs, and I have not heard of any other complaints, do I have a right to politely ask them to refrain from honking so early? I don't want to create hard feelings.

GENTLE READER — Hard feelings do not generally arise from neighborly requests along the lines of "I'm so sorry, but I'm afraid I have a sleeping problem, and although I've tried closing the windows and wearing earplugs, I still wake up when you honk the horn in the morning. I wonder if you would mind not using the horn unless it's an emergency."

Hard feelings arise when people say nothing until they can't stand it another minute and then lean out the window screaming, "Will you idiots shut up—it's 6:30 in the morning, and normal people are trying to sleep! Keep it up and I'm coming out there after you and you'd better believe it'll be to shut you up permanently."

Miss Manners has always wondered why so many people try the second method without even giving the first one a chance. When she inquires, she is told that it is unwise nowadays to venture any criticism at all, however politely, because there are so many crazy people around. So they hold off as long as they can—which is not forever. Oddly enough, the one point on which they and the neighbors are sure to agree is that there are crazy people in the neighborhood.

Not Stabbing Back

DEAR MISS MANNERS — How is an apartment dweller to deal gently but convincingly with neighbors who tread heavily overhead? The cleanliness of my criminal record is in your hands.

When Mr. Clydesdale moved in and started making my light fixtures sway, I tried telling him that, surely unbeknownst to him, his traffic was all too apparent. Mystified, he said that he was not often home and when he was, he never wore shoes. I begged him nevertheless to keep the issue in mind, as it was causing me discomfort. Clearly, he thought I had lost my mind. Perhaps, he suggested, I wanted him not to walk about his apartment whatsoever. My assurances that I sought mere sensitivity fell on deaf ears, and I withdrew. His eventual departure brought—gasp—worse still. Miss Mastodon is petite, but she packs a bigger thud. She took my entreaty in good cheer, but one still expects feet to come though the ceiling—my guests glance distractedly skyward.

Can Miss Manners provide this reader with a bit of fortitude with which to try polite channels again, when homicide is foremost on his mind? These low-frequency sounds cannot be covered up with, say, background music. I need to convey the idea that one can moderate one's gait.

GENTLE READER — Miss Manners is trying very hard to be on your side, not only to keep the homicide rate down, but because you seem so reasonable. Also, she sympathizes with sensitivity to noise. So she was somewhat dismayed to find herself slipping over to the point of view of the gentleman who already removes his shoes and is nervous about what you expect him to do next. Neighbors should not be disturbed by noise, but it is a bit much to ask people to remove their feet when they come home.

How can Miss Manners protect you, while keeping your complaint at its present gentle level, when it is not working? She noticed that the situation was not peculiar to one neighbor, as the next tenant was a problem as well. Nor was it peculiar to you (forgive Miss Manners, but the possibility occurred to her), as your guests also hear it.

Suddenly, she realized that you could complain just as reasonably, but with a more reasonable solution to propose, if you were to redirect your complaint to your landlord. To keep this polite while making it effective, you should enlist the other residents in declaring that the construction of the building is such that only by installing heavy carpeting can the noise problem be solved.

Shaming Back

DEAR MISS MANNERS — We have a neighbor who plays his stereo so loudly that everyone in the neighborhood has to hear it all weekend every weekend. I can't ever spend a Sunday afternoon reading on the deck, for example, because he dominates the atmosphere. Whenever I ask him to turn it down, he grumbles and does so, but soon the volume's up again. It's like he wants to prove to us all that he rules the neighborhood. Any ideas? The police are uninterested.

GENTLE READER — The police refuse to enforce your noise ordinances, so you want Miss Manners to march in there and turn that thing off? Or perhaps pitch it out the window and your neighbor along with it?

Grateful as she is for your faith, Miss Manners regrets to tell you that etiquette does not use force. It uses people's good will, if they have any, and if that doesn't work, it uses shame. You have already tried the good will, so let us move on.

Shame would work best if it involved the offender's reputation with the whole neighborhood, not just with one person whom he can dismiss as a fussbudget. You could send a letter with a number of signatures on it, or you could organize a group of people to go with you next time he blasts the neighborhood. In either case, the complaint should be made politely as well as firmly. Nevertheless, confronting a group of unhappy people who live all around him may turn out to be just as frightening as opening the door to police or to Miss Manners brandishing a fork.

CHILDREN

The necessity of warning children against predatory adults—not only in the streets but now also on the information highway that cuts right through the household—has left families in a state of etiquette bewilderment. Here is the way most parents handle it:

1. Teach children that they must always be polite, helpful, friendly, truthful and respectful to adults.
2. Teach children that some adults are wicked and should be snubbed, spurned and reported to the authorities.

Is that clear, children?

No, you can't report the man next door, even though he is so mean when your ball goes into his yard or you play the radio with the windows open. Yes, you have to help your great-aunt find her glasses, although it's true that she never says please; and yes, you have to answer Grandpa's nosy questions about your grades and be polite when he lectures you about things that are not your fault.

Well, then who is it who is bad and doesn't need to be treated politely?

Oh. It's grown-ups who try especially hard to be friendly and helpful to children. If one of those approaches you—run.

All of this makes perfect sense to Miss Manners, but not to the parents who say it, much less to the children. The parents leave themselves so confused and weakened by their own lessons that they come down with a severe case of paradox.

They end up telling themselves that the first lesson—which they had taken so much trouble to impress upon the children when they were too young to venture about by themselves—represents an etiquette ideal which would be nice in a perfect world, while the second is necessary for survival in the real world. The more foolish among them may even offer the children this explanation—basically that etiquette is for suckers. Miss Manners could offer them relief. But it would require taking another heavy dose of etiquette rather than swearing off it.

The problem is that for more than a generation now, idealists have worked to erase the differences between strangers and friends or intimates. The guideposts by which one could distinguish the progression from one stage to another—introductions, the long-term changes in the way people address one another, the gradual growth of confidentiality—have been systematically abolished as stuffy and snobbish. There are no strangers. Only new friends. Some people went further than that and taught the idea that there was a special bond among strangers. Friends may not have one's best interests at heart, relatives are presumed psychological enemies, but there was supposed to be something pure about confidences exchanged among strangers. It was no longer necessary to purchase an airplane ticket to find new people to whom to tell one's life story and troubles.

Finally, with the advent of cyberspace communities, strangers were free even of material clues. Looks, after all, offer some information, even though much can be faked. How old the person is, whether his or her demeanor seems restrained, and the symbolic messages in clothing choice can at least be roughly guessed. But age, gender and identity can be instantly and successfully disguised on-line.

Miss Manners realizes that she is sounding colossally stuffy again. Many people enjoy and benefit from the freedom of association thus offered. That is all very well as long as participants understand that the foundation of friendship—trust—cannot be present. It is impossible to judge the sincerity or intentions of someone you don't know and can't see.

Children who have not been taught that properly behaved people maintain a certain distance from those they do not know are going to have a hard time keeping this in mind when they are immediately invited to address adults as intimately as they address their relatives and instructed by their pastors to hug strangers sitting next to them. Thus, the difficulty lies with the etiquette lessons that have not been given, rather than with the ones that have. Children must be taught to recognize when people—not just strangers but people they know—are claiming privileges they don't deserve. This is because the being-totally-open-to-everyone idea is a false, if flattering, conception of etiquette. Polite behavior actually permits a far greater amount of privacy and autonomy than is endorsed by the society at large, where the mandate for universal friendliness (perhaps spurred on by the hope of meeting exciting strangers) negates that choice.

By the standards of good manners, strangers on the street properly ignore one another, except for quick requests for the time or directions that are obviously not conversation openers. People one meets on-line are stepping out of line if they attempt to ascertain personal information or make arrangements to meet off-line. Any overture beyond what is warranted by the conventions of the situation—"taking liberties" is the haughty phrase for it—should be considered a danger signal from which it is proper, as well as prudent, to withdraw. There is nothing improper about rejecting improper advances.

Causing Disturbances

DEAR MISS MANNERS — Our neighbors have a four-year-old son who has become rude, uncontrolled and seemingly without the guidance needed from parents. They choose to ignore his impolite behavior, name-calling and disobedient actions. We very much like our neighbors, but we find their son's behavior intolerable. Several other neighbors are reluctant to allow the lad to play with their children of a similar age. The parents seem oblivious to this fact. The boy is about one year away from going to school and will experience a variety of problems unless his behavior changes drastically in the near future. Should we say anything on this topic to the parents?

GENTLE READER — Such as "Everybody in this neighborhood finds your son intolerable"? To which they can reply, "Really? We hadn't noticed, but we are grateful to you for bringing this to our attention; he is rather intolerable, isn't he? Perhaps we should upgrade."

One does not make negative generalizations about other people's children or child-rearing. For one thing, it is rude, and for another, you may be unaware of what the problems are and how the parents may be working on them. For a third, it doesn't help. Their first loyalties are to him, however misguided their methods, and you will simply anger and upset them.

Miss Manners does allow you to complain about specific things that affect you. If you promise to speak with a sorrowful air of understanding the waywardness of children and difficulty of a parent's job, you can say "I'm sorry to have to tell on him, but I thought you'd want to know that Clarence has been screaming obscenities around the neighborhood again."

Causing Damage

DEAR MISS MANNERS — When my family and I returned home from vacation, we found that our house had been "wrapped." About 40 or 50 rolls of toilet paper were used. They had entered our gate and had strewn toilet paper over our hammock, our barbecue pit, our hot-tub, the porch, and, of course, the bushes, trees and rooftops. They did a thorough job. It had been raining, so all the paper turned to soggy mush.

The next day, a "friend" at church informed us that he had driven his daughter and her friends to our home. He was making sure the girls were "safe," and he posted look-outs in the front of our house as the girls wrapped it. I was speechless and devastated. I took it very personally. Adults—would-be friends—were encouraging their children, even helping them, to vandalize our home while they knew we were on vacation and defenseless.

I told our good neighbors exactly what I thought of our wonderful welcome home surprise. Am I over-reacting? Is this really an OK thing to do to a neighbor? My husband thinks I'm silly. I think it is terribly rude and I do not feel comfortable around people who would do such a thing without offering to help clean up the mess or uttering one word of apology.

GENTLE READER — Miss Manners is not amused, and does not require you to be so. An action that created trouble and mess—not to mention the fact that it probably alerted potential burglars to the fact that your house was uninhabited—cannot be classified as a harmless prank. However, she understands that your husband does not want to start a feud with the neighbors.

The way to get around this difficulty is to appeal to them as responsible parents (in the face of proof that they are not). As they expressed concern over the safety of their children, you might assume that they are also worried about the children's character. Tell them that you suppose they want to teach their children responsibility for their actions, and that you would be glad to supervise, and perhaps even provide light refreshments, for the day on which the children will clean up the mess. An unwrapping party, as it were.

The hospitable phrasing of this is not just to make palatable your highly justified indignation. Miss Manners believes it would be a genuine contribution to civility for you to show the children that you are not a disembodied target for their amusement, but a person who cares about her neighbors, as well as about her property.

Playing Rough

DEAR MISS MANNERS — My husband and I live in a middle class neighborhood, have no children and take a great pride in our yard, specifically our beautiful flower garden and grass. We have neighbors with teenage boys who play basketball all the time, breaking our flowers and knocking down our shrubs. It's awful. The worst of it all is that the parents instigate the situation, join in and call us foul names and continually harass us. I have called the sheriff one night when one teenage boy was playing basketball with a friend and ran over my newly planted blue spruce tree. The teenager called me nasty names and when the father came home, he told us not to touch his grass. Is there no discipline for children any more?

GENTLE READER — No, but there is not much among neighbors, either. Your neighbors, who are adults, are calling you names, and you are calling in the law to deal with a careless game of basketball. Miss Manners' advice to all of you is to calm down and build a fence.

Hanging Out

DEAR MISS MANNERS — Our home has become the neighborhood center for a large group of my son's friends. They are all very nice boys, about twelve years old, and we are happy to host them. Some of the children, however, arrive early in the morning and leave only well after dinner. During the school year, they come to our house instead of going home after school. Our suggestions to these boys that their parents might sometimes take the initiative to host the group have been to no avail. In three years, there are parents we have never met or seen only in passing. We are now worried about losing our temper when we finally do see these parents. Is there a way to get these parents involved without making them mad?

GENTLE READER — Probably not. They don't sound as if they are involved with their own children so why would they want to be involved with other people's?

Miss Manners asks you to stifle your anger and reflect how much luckier your son is for having parents who care and a home where he knows his friends are welcome. You might even reflect on how lucky you are. You know where your son is. You have the chance to get to know his friends and to offer them some badly needed warmth and supervision. If their parents were just overburdened and grateful that their children had somewhere to go when they work—as no doubt they will argue if you confront them—you would have heard them overflowing with gratitude to you long ago.

ANIMALS

Pets

DEAR MISS MANNERS—I live in a community of town homes in which we share yard space. Certain of my neighbors allow their leashed dogs to relieve themselves daily on the grass in this common space. How can I ask them to pick up after their pets? I find it embarrassing.

GENTLE READER—Embarrassing because of the nature of the matter in question? Or embarrassing because of the nature of your neighbors?

Miss Manners is guessing it's the latter. People don't seem to be shy about mentioning the unmentionable nowadays. They only shy away from mentioning their legitimate grievances to the people who caused them.

The way to avoid offending offensive people is to assume that they never meant to offend you and will be grateful for the chance to make amends for an inadvertent error. Something along the lines of "I don't know if you realize that some of us use the park to play Frisbee. So we're asking pet owners to clean up after their dogs." As if you couldn't have expected anyone to know that the entire outdoors is not a public bathroom.

Miss Manners knows that this probably does not represent what you feel. But if you scream "How'd you like it if I did this on your front steps?" you are not likely to have a peaceful neighborhood. She cast her suggested statement in the plural in order to generalize the problem and thus lessen the embarrassment of the person addressed. The fact that it also suggests that a neighborhood posse might be formed by the huge number of people who share your complaint is incidental.

Service Dogs

DEAR MISS MANNERS—I am hearing-impaired, and last year acquired a wonderful hearing assistance dog who listens for sounds I do not hear and accompanies me everywhere.

As I was walking through the beautiful wooded campus of my apartment complex last week, a woman I had never seen before came up to me and told me I should not walk the dog in her neighborhood. Assuming that she was concerned about the dog's natural activities, I showed her the scooper I always carry with me and assured her I always picked up. No, she said, she didn't want to always be washing the grass with soap and water where the dog had gone! Well, I had no answer to that, but explained that my dog was a service dog and by law allowed to go wherever I went.

"We'll see about that," she said. "I've lived here for 30 years and we've never had a service dog."

Today I saw this same woman coming toward me, so I kept on walking, choosing not to stop. She followed me for a bit, shouting something, but thankfully I could not hear what she said. What is the proper way to deal with this situation, as it is sure to arise again? I do not wish to defend myself constantly, but I do need to take the dog for her walk.

GENTLE READER — Oh, nice. Miss Manners was aware of the increasingly widespread belief that consideration for other people is an optional virtue, dispensable if one has other concerns, but even she didn't think it would come to this. Your tormentor is probably all puffed up with the virtue of protecting the cleanliness of the grass.

You have tried etiquette's Step One, which politely assumes good will on the part of someone who hasn't demonstrated any, and attempts to appeal to her sense of human decency. This person demonstrated that she doesn't have any. So you proceeded to Step Two, etiquette's strongest weapon of refusing to acknowledge the existence of someone not fit for human society. She proved that you were right by behaving even worse.

Miss Manners is afraid that it is time to call in the reserves. She hates it when etiquette fails, and has to turn things over to civic authorities, but that is the way deliberate and unrepentant transgressors must be handled. If the neighbor continues to harass you, you should report this to the police.

PROPERTY

The Boundary

DEAR MISS MANNERS — We had an open argument with this neighbor three years ago about the driveway and narrow flowerbed which are the only division between our two urban homes. I ended up refusing to let him remove a tree on our property and pave over our flowerbed. I must admit I also lost my "cool" in the exchange and accused him of being a bully in front of several other neighbors and the work crew he'd already assembled, without consulting us, to cut the tree and lay the cement. Since then, there has been no verbal exchange, until recently.

My husband and I are usually open, friendly people and get along well with all our other neighbors. When we are working in our yard facing his and he comes out of the house only a few feet away, we smile, almost without thinking, and even occasionally say hello. He always responds with a glare. Recently, when my husband greeted him by name, he gave his usual frown and said, "I don't want to talk to you, and you make damned sure you stay on your side of the property line."

My major problem with this man has always been not how he conducts his own life but his insistence that we do likewise (the tree he wanted to cut, for instance, shades our bathroom window and provides privacy, both of which we cherish). A part of me is reacting again to his demand that we not smile and say hello. According to the rules of etiquette, should I: (1) Say, "Hello, Richard," when I spontaneously feel the urge; (2) say, "Hello, Mr. ———" instead; (3) scowl back; (4) never weed my garden facing in that direction, which would entail exposing my backside to his occasional view, something I'm not comfortable with either.

GENTLE READER — Did you really have to throw in that fourth example? Miss Manners would so much rather not have that picture in mind as she asks you to make one more attempt to disarm your irascible neighbor.

She realizes this may not be possible. With someone that unreasonable, you would be justified in withdrawing to a state of silence and vigilance. But that is not a nice way to live and, as you are clever enough to recognize, it would mean that you had allowed him to dictate your behavior. Miss Manners recommends that you continue to recognize his presence with a friendly smile, if not an actual "Hello." If it doesn't soften him, you will still have the satisfaction of knowing— and knowing that he knows—that he was unable to change you.

The Lawn

DEAR MISS MANNERS — I have some neighbors who I feel lack in manners and consideration when they cut their grass early in the morning during the week and also on weekends. What is the proper etiquette regarding mowing your lawn?

GENTLE READER—According to your neighbors, it is refraining from mowing lawns during working hours, when they are trying to work at home, and evenings, when they are trying to talk to one another. Miss Manners mentions this to point out that the hours you find bothersome are not inherently less reasonable than obvious alternatives. These people are probably just trying to avoid the midday sun by mowing early, and they mow on weekends because it is hard to run home and mow during the working week.

   This is not to say that you have to be bothered; only that you may not fuel this feeling with righteous wrath. The polite and neighborly thing to do is to mention apologetically that the hours they choose are bad for you, and to ask them very nicely if there are not other times on which you could both agree.

The Leaves

DEAR MISS MANNERS—One of my neighbors purchased a leaf blower and blows all of her leaves against the fence surrounding her backyard. It is a short chain link fence, so most of the leaves go through and over, into the surrounding neighbors' yards. We had just cleaned up our yard and I wish I had not seen what she was doing, as she seemed quite happy to see her leaves vanish from her yard. It makes me wonder if she has considered anyone but herself. Should we get a leaf blower and blow them back?

GENTLE READER—Oh, a leaf-blowing contest. What a good idea for a neighborhood get-together. You could all get blowers and then fight about whose leaves are in whose yards. Of course, you would not only turn your home turf into a battleground, but all the yards would end up, after a hard day's yard work, covered with leaves.

   Miss Manners has a less dramatic idea. Why don't you give your neighbor the benefit of the doubt? Allowing the fun of a new toy to blind one to the consequences for others is not the most evil form of selfishness on record. You could say, in a neighborly way, "I've been admiring your leaf blower, and I was thinking of getting one. But then your leaves ended up in my yard—so if I got one, they'd just end up back in your yard. Is there a way to use it which would actually get rid of the leaves?"

The Leaf Blowing Contest

BLOWING OFF THE NEIGHBORS: *Pride in property, prowess and noisy equipment may be among the joys of civilized life, but antagonizing the neighbors is self-defeating, not to mention highly unwise. They know where you live.*

The Garbage

DEAR MISS MANNERS — Along with all our neighbors, we have always placed our refuse in front of our home. However, our new next door neighbors insist on putting their garbage in front of our house. They even went as far as to place an old toilet in our driveway. They don't seem to like the appearance of garbage in front of their home. If this behavior is improper, how should we approach them?

GENTLE READER — With the toilet seat in hand, a concerned look on your faces, and the question "Did you lose this?" Miss Manners does not, however, recommend doing this with a bag full of garbage. Whatever subtlety there was (which she admits isn't much) would be lost. A polite note, along the lines of "We hate to bother you with such a petty matter, but for some reason, your garbage seems to be drifting down to our house, and we're afraid the collectors might think we're exceeding our amount," would be better.

Yes, Miss Manners knows that the offense, probably in more senses than one, is theirs. Nevertheless, neighbor-to-neighbor challenges never lead to any good. Especially not when they are already skilled at transporting their garbage.

Recycling

DEAR MISS MANNERS — I know this is really dumb, but I want to know what consideration one might expect from the sanitation department and from one's neighbors in the age of recycling. I love recycling, but I think the process needs more thinking through.

I have two large grocery bags a week of mixed paper, small cardboard items and magazines. I don't want to take them out to the curb early, because they look messy and it might rain. Also, that's my personal mail among the discards. If a bag gets kicked and broken by kids, I don't want my personal mail blowing up and down the block, so I close these bags with staples. I'm sure the city hates that, so they had better think of a better system than the open boxes they provide.

When I entertain, I have two bags of recycle paper lying around with no place to store them out of sight. When they were garbage, it was simple to carry them to the trash can.

Cans and bottles I find easy. If they're too messy to rinse fairly clean with one swipe under the faucet, I put them in the dishwasher. If a can is really gunked up, I toss it in the garbage. They go under the sink in a bag, then get transferred to the street at the last minute.

My neighbors are not as compulsive as I am. One keeps a recycle box in our shared carport area and throws all tins in there until it's full, which can be a month. Nothing is rinsed and old chili and spaghetti sauce are open to the heat and flies. This used to be against the sanitation laws. Actually, I think it probably still is. But mostly I hate it because I'm compulsively tidy.

GENTLE READER — If you don't mind, Miss Manners will leave the rethinking about recycling to you, who are better qualified than she to do it, and confine herself to dealing with the etiquette aspect of the situation. That requires recognizing—both on your part, in dealing with your neighbors, and on the part of your local authorities, to whom you should appeal—that the recycling you feel necessary puts a burden on the citizens.

That is not to say that this may not be worth it—but only that the concept of washing the garbage is a relatively new one, for which acceptance and compliance depends on attitude as well as law. Thus, you will be more successful with law enforcers if you suggest ways, such as better-sealed containers, to make things easier. Your neighbors will be more receptive to sympathy about their fly problem than to complaints about their sloppiness.

Your charm in attributing your compliance to excessive tidiness is a good start. Miss Manners doesn't for a moment believe that the opposite of messiness is compulsiveness, but she understands the value of self-deprecation in getting others up to one's standards.

The Pool

DEAR MISS MANNERS — My husband and I worked hard in order to afford to have a pool installed in our backyard, yet the neighbors talk as though we'll be running a community swim club. They are dropping subtle hints, such as "My children are so anxious to try out your new pool."

I barely know the mother's name, let alone the children's, but now we're to be the closest of friends. These same neighbors have rudely ignored my attempts to be friendly since we moved in three years ago, when I attempted to strike up conversations—instead making references to my youth and the fact that I work rather than stay home. Maybe I have some resentment because I feel this sudden friendliness is phony. How do I politely let them know that the pool was installed for my family's use and we don't intend to be lifeguards for their children all summer?

Why is it that neighbors would never dream of asking to borrow your new car for the weekend, but think nothing of inviting themselves over to use your new pool?

GENTLE READER — Why? Because they have cars, of course.

It is true that a swimming pool is a classic example of what Miss Manners believes is known as an attractive nuisance, which in this case means that it has attracted the local nuisances. Miss Manners defends your right not to have to entertain the neighborhood; you need only say, "I'm afraid we really can't have people using it when we're not there—insurance problems, you know—and usually when we are there, because my husband and I have so little time to relax alone."

Shall we be slightly more charitable? (Easy for Miss Manners to say, considering that it's your pool.) You did, after all, once think it desirable to be on friendly terms with your neighbors. What about throwing a neighborhood pool party in, say, midsummer? Don't do it at the beginning, or it will look as if you are opening the pool season. This way, you will have made a gesture, and you can reply to all self-invitations with "Yes, we're so looking forward to seeing you the second Saturday in August."

The Driveway

DEAR MISS MANNERS — I was taught to respect other people's property. How do you feel about next door neighbors using your driveway to turn around in— every day or night?! I consider it very rude, but then I thought maybe it was just the way I was raised.

GENTLE READER — Miss Manners must have an underdeveloped sense of property, but try as she will, she cannot imagine what harm is done you by your neighbors' turning around in your driveway. Is it wearing out the cement? She also has a different standard than you do of what is "very rude." Borrowing your car without your permission would be very rude. Running over your dog would be very rude. Driving into your driveway for the purpose of making rude gestures at you would be very rude.

Miss Manners notices that you do not ask how to get them to stop, but how she feels about it. She feels that this is a trivial technical trespass that could easily be overlooked in the interests of neighborliness.

The Neighborhood Nut

DEAR MISS MANNERS — Let me tell you a story about a self-appointed dictator: I have lived for almost 40 years on a street that is just off of a main street (to be referred to as M). There are 5 short streets that run off of M. Designating these short streets as 1, 2, 3, 4, and 5, with #1 being the northernmost street, I can take any of those 5 streets to get to my house. I live on street #4, and for years I have traveled any and all of streets #1 through #5. The one I take depends upon which direction I am traveling and the flow of traffic at the time.

I have a neighbor (designated as N for neighbor) that I met years ago, shortly after moving into this neighborhood. We were friends for many years, but that time has passed. She now behaves like a self-appointed authority determining what I can or can't do. She has, it seems, dictated that I cannot drive on Street No. 3 (the reason being that a male friend of her family has an apartment on Street No. 3 in which he spends a portion of each week). I have spotted two "spies" living on Street #3, watching to see where I drive. The "spy" apparently calls N's house to report that I am driving on the "forbidden" street. One day, I had driven from M street on Street #3, and I had watched a spy watching me. Just after turning the corner to get to my house on Street #4, I met N's husband, driving as fast as he could safely drive to get to Street #3. He looked terribly upset. Obviously, the spy had called N's house to report that I was driving on the "forbidden" street.

I went over to N's house to discuss the matter. She opened her front door, stood with the door partially opened, and said "Yes?"

I said to her, "As far as I know this is still a free country and we still have a Constitution. That Constitution guarantees and/or protects the individual rights of people who live in this country." (If they are U.S. citizens.) I went on to say, "I can drive my car on any street I want." She slammed the door—and I went home!

My opinion, Miss Manners, is that if a self-appointed dictator is attempting to tell you what you can or cannot do, use any legal means at your disposal to counteract the tyranny!

GENTLE READER— Even without paying strict attention to your formula with all those interesting numbers and letters, Miss Manners concludes that what you have there is a genuine Neighborhood Nut. An imaginative one at that. Dreadful as neighborhood bullies are, they usually confine themselves to criticizing lawns, children, parties and pets. Attempting to run you off the city streets is a new one.

You may be the immediate target—and forgive Miss Manners, but for all she knows, you may even be the N.N. yourself, to whom this is not really happening. In either case, everyone is bound to know about the Neighborhood Nut, who becomes the stuff of legend to children. When action must be taken, it is therefore possible to get together a group to complain, calmly and sympathetically but firmly, to a responsible person (a grown child, for example) or whatever local authority can help. What one does not do is to confront the Neighborhood Nut by yelling nuttily back—first, because it is, by definition, useless, and second, because it is nutty.

THE WIDER COMMUNITY

Doing Good

In theory, we treasure those good-hearted, generous souls who care about so much more than just their own personal welfare that they constantly devote themselves to causes that benefit others. So why do we all run when we see them coming?

Miss Manners has long been puzzling over the unpopularity of do-gooders. We ought to cherish, above all, those whose dedication to improving the world is not simply sporadic, but a major commitment. Yet we tend to find them tiresome, if not actually offensive. How can that be? Miss Manners has concluded that it is—surprise, surprise—a question of manners.

It is true that many socially active people are as devoted to the niceties of behavior that affect the feelings of the individuals they meet as they are to the larger issues that affect all humanity, not to mention the animal kingdom and the environment. A great many others believe that having morals relieves them of the need to have mere manners. No matter how many causes they are able to embrace, they only seem to have room for one virtue. And the practice of etiquette isn't it. In fact, Miss Manners is scandalized to find, they will often deny that practicing etiquette is a virtue. Rather, they would classify it as a sin—the dread sin of (shudder) hypocrisy.

When it comes to that, Miss Manners believes that the world could use a great deal more hypocrisy. People who pretend to care more about others than they actually do are a great deal easier to bear than those who fail to drop a gentle disguise over their most unpalatable thoughts and feelings.

Surely, people who actually do care about doing good in the world ought to recognize that there are instances in which the virtue of kindness ought to take precedence over the virtue of speaking one's mind.

Yet one-on-one kindness seems to strike certain do-gooders as too petty to be worthwhile. Pressed on having neglected such niceties as showing respect for others, honoring their privacy, and refraining from embarrassing or humiliating them, they will declare a state of emergency, in which looming tragedy has canceled prevailing etiquette.

The need for etiquette is not canceled so easily. Springing, as it does, from a commitment to honoring the feelings of others, the practice of etiquette is abandoned at some cost. What a rude person has to say about morality is easily dismissed, on the grounds that any claim to altruism is obviously spurious. (Besides, the reasoning is faulty. Emergencies are when etiquette is needed most. Heroism is the decision to maintain one's consideration for others in the face of danger to oneself.)

Acting for the general good does not excuse sacrificing any individuals who happen to get in one's way. Techniques of drawing good causes to the public attention through hurling insults, yelling at passersby on the street, subjecting them to public humiliation or throwing things at them cancel any claim to a true interest in doing good, Miss Manners maintains.

Besides, they never work. Miss Manners has seen many a person won over to a good cause through polite appeals to reason or compassion, under conditions ranging from drawing room discussion to picketing. She has never yet heard of anyone who was under rude attack killing the instinct for self-defense and saying: "Wait a minute—I believe you have a point there. It's a good thing you yelled and threw paint at me, because it made me realize that you are right and I was wrong. I appreciate your calling this to my attention."

Doing Damage

DEAR MISS MANNERS — A few years ago, I was involved in a city-wide ministry that matched people who had problems with people who had been through the same problem.

After I gave birth to a child with Down's Syndrome, I was helped immeasurably by a woman who called me up out of the blue and talked about her own daughter. She told me a nurse at the hospital had mentioned I might need some help, and we talked for two hours. I am naturally reticent, but I later signed up for the ministry with the intention of giving back what I had been given—namely hope and sanity.

My first call was fine. I went to a hospital to see a new mother and left her feeling better, I believe. My next call was a nightmare. The woman who answered refused to let me speak with the new mother and demanded to know how I got her name, refusing to believe that I had no idea who turned it in. She was extremely rude and told me not to call again. This crushed me, and I resigned from the ministry. Lately, I have begun to wonder if maybe the whole concept had been—well, invasive. Where is the line between invading and helping?

GENTLE READER — You meant so well that Miss Manners would like to make you feel better by sharing a similar experience. But she hasn't had any. Here's why:

She shares your belief that an essential way to repay kindness is to pass it on to others. At the same time, she has always remembered what so many people forget in the throes of a commendable desire to help—that morality never cancels the need for mannerliness. When the sharing technique you describe swept the country, enthusiasts forgot that charity must be tempered with respect for the sovereignty of others. Many believed so strongly in its benefits that they forced confidences on and from others, in the belief that any resistance should be overcome for the other person's own good.

It is wrong, as you were jarred to discover, to invade the privacy of others, particularly when they are suffering. Not everybody finds it comforting to talk with strangers. This should not discourage you from offering help—only from skipping the step of inquiring delicately whether it would be welcome. It would be best if someone from the hospital staff told patients that this counseling is available. You could also help your ministry by drawing up a letter explaining what it offers. Strangers should not be telephoning around to offer their services—even the medical profession considers that wrong.

Sleazy Tactics

A new social form is replacing those great staples of fund-raising, the bake sale and the car wash. It's called the "celebrity auction," and every organization that wants to help a school or fight a disease is holding one (and referring to it, in announcements and invitations, as their own "creative idea").

Instead of making brownies or spending a day washing cars, the community-minded put their efforts into petitioning celebrities to donate "something personal," on which the citizenry will be inspired to spend vast sums that it would not otherwise have considered donating to charity. The acquisitive desires of groupies are thus painlessly channeled into philanthropy.

It struck Miss Manners as rather unseemly that respectable causes with high-minded goals should be supported by public eagerness to obtain the cast-off undergarments of rock stars. Even now that she has found out that it is only auto-graphed pictures, T-shirts and doodles from people whose claim to celebrity often has to be explained to the potential bidders, the idea still bothers her.

She realizes that she is out of her mind to say so. It will bring some highly in-dignant reactions from people who are only trying to help others. First, there will be the genuinely heartrending explanation of how worthy and needy the cause is, and how much suffering is alleviated by the money thus raised. Then, there will be the equally valid description of the demands life makes on the people involved in the organization. That will come laced with the insinuation that asking them to do the old tasks is tantamount to saying that mothers should be home baking in-stead of out earning a living to feed their children, and that fathers should be cur-tailing the pitifully small amount of free time that they are able to spend with their children. Finally, there will be the assertion that the celebrity auction has been shown to work, attracting money to good causes in a way that the efforts of real people cannot. To top it off, the undisputed need for such money will be restated.

Miss Manners does not deny any of these assertions. Nor does she stint on her admiration and appreciation of people who work on behalf of others. She just doesn't totally understand why the fact that these causes are good, and that the efforts made on their behalf are selfless and valuable, precludes a discussion of the methods involved.

This is a problem she has had with worse tactics routinely employed in fund-raising drives. There is hardly a worthy cause around that does not instruct its vol-unteers on how to use humiliation and guilt to bludgeon others to give or increase donations. The person who responds generously may be sure that hardly are the perfunctory thanks out when a notation is made to pressure him or her into feel-ing obliged to donate more the following year.

Compared to such standard fund-raising methods as snooping into the income and spending habits of potential donors, and sending their colleagues or bosses to put embarrassing pressure on them, Miss Manners admits that offering fan paraphernalia for sale is harmless. Yet something is lost by the admission that the ordinary person's contribution of ability and hard work is of less value than junk collected from celebrities. People who might have taken pride in doing some-thing for a local organization are instead assigned to write wheedling letters, mix-ing flattery, suggestions of career benefits and a bit of guilt-inspiring pressure, to strangers outside the community.

"The success of our auction depends on items from noteworthy people such as yourself" is a typical plea.

"Something personal from you would attract the highest bid and provide the greatest resources for our young people."

"You know so well that every successful person has received help from others."

"Donations have enabled us to continue our good work along with providing tremendous publicity for generous celebrities."

"This is a wonderful opportunity to be recognized locally and become involved in a good cause. Your name will appear prominently in our event program, and in our donor acknowledgment materials."

"CELEBRITIES HAVE SHOWN THEY CARE!"

"Please feel good about the fact that your donation will help to generate funds for the fight against a terrible disease."

Miss Manners cannot help wondering about those who aren't eligible to feel good about what they could do because they are not celebrities. They don't have the time anyway, she is told.

No, nobody does. Miss Manners is far from suggesting that the burdens of parents be increased. One of the advantages of bake sales and car washes is that they harness the energies of teenagers in the service of others. Some auctions do use children as volunteers, but Miss Manners can hardly imagine that the satisfaction they get from begging from celebrities is equivalent to that of producing a genuinely salable article or service.

That brings Miss Manners back to the question of what actually does appeal to people who have discretionary money to spend, and might spend it more freely if they could feel that it went to support a worthy cause. Do they really value the castoffs of entertainment people over a home-baked brownie or a clean car?

Unseemly Tactics

DEAR MISS MANNERS — My best friend's 9-year-old son called last night and asked me to contribute on behalf of his karate club to his local children's hospital. Caught off guard and feeling extremely awkward—but not wanting his mother to think I was a cheapskate—I said I would contribute $20, after being forced to name a sum. When his mother got on the phone and I attempted to express my dissatisfaction, she laughed it off and said, "He's quite a little salesman, isn't he?" We spoke for a few more minutes, and then he implored her to get off the phone so he could call some more of her friends and relatives.

Still offended the next day, I wanted to let her know I was upset so the same scenario wouldn't happen again. When I told her my feelings, she replied that she felt I would be interested in her son's events—I am, but certainly not to this extent—and it was improper for him to call me. She said that if I ever had children, I'd better get used to this kind of thing. I said I still wouldn't donate to something in which I have no real interest. She then started to cry, said she'd rip up my check, that this wasn't a good time, and hung up. Was I wrong to feel offended? Was I wrong to express my feelings to her?

GENTLE READER — Surely people who feel for the plight of others should not be proud of themselves for deliberately causing embarrassment to their friends. Yet what you experienced is now a standard fund-raising technique. Perfectly good charities will deliberately choose someone—a friend, neighbor, colleague or supervisor—to make the pitch whom the person being approached would be embarrassed to turn down.

Children are considered particularly dexterous workers, much the way old-fashioned burglars used children to get into small spaces and then open the doors for them. Miss Manners strongly believes in teaching children to do charity work—but in a meaningful way, by donating time, money or possessions, not by embarrassing adults.

Now that she's got that off her chest, Miss Manners is going to turn on you for what you got off yours. To agree to make a donation and then to cancel the deal through the mother does not strike Miss Manners as honorable, either. You owed it to the child to stand by your word.

You needn't have given that word. Don't tell Miss Manners that you were "forced." As long as you were polite to the child, you could have said, "No, thank you, I'm not making a donation" and, if pressed, added firmly, "I'm sorry, dear, but I don't care to discuss it." If the mother wants the child trained as a salesman, you would indeed have shown a friendly interest in helping. Learning to accept a rebuff politely is an essential skill for salesmanship.

Counterproductive Support

That schools are in trouble unless the parents are interested in their children's progress and involved with their schools is something every schoolchild does not know. Schoolchildren are too busy being embarrassed—either because their parents show up at school or because their parents don't show up at school—to think about it. But everybody else knows it. Fortunate schools draw on valiant parents who not only keep up with what their children are studying and how well they are learning, but chaperone field trips and dances, give classroom talks, pitch in to spruce up the building and cheer the teams and applaud the plays, in addition to attending conferences and meetings, serving on committees and donating and raising money for various school projects.

Less well known is the paradox that schools are also in trouble when the parents are a little too interested in their children's progress and in running their school. Nobody wants to encourage child neglect, certainly not Miss Manners, so this possibility is rarely mentioned. As a result, there has developed—unchecked—a type of devoted and active parent who puts in a lot of time working on behalf of the child. This is the duty of every good parent, but it also involves working against the school. In reaction to the old alliance whereby the parent and school conspired to civilize the child, this parent is wholly allied with the child. The problem here is not with the devotion but with the direction it is given.

Schools are besieged by angry parents demanding what their children want: less work, higher grades than they have earned and more time off. The best positions on teams and the leads in plays, regardless of their own skills and the quality of the competition. Immunity from rules and suspension of punishments. Praise and honors, without a lot of tiresome quibbling about whether they are deserved. Protection from being treated rudely by other children without having to chafe under behavioral restrictions themselves. These do not strike Miss Manners as useful contributions to a child's education, although she supposes that depends on what kind of person the parent wants to educate the child to be.

She does notice that whether they work to support the school for their child or the child against the school, parents are doing an enormous amount of work. That's as it should be, of course, but at the risk of sounding as if she were one of those parents who argues for less schoolwork, Miss Manners believes that there is an easier way: That is for parents to do their homework. Not the children's, but their own, which is to teach the children manners.

School manners include respecting teachers, accepting responsibility for duties and transgressions, sitting still, giving others a chance to be heard, pretending to believe that competitions are held fairly even when one doesn't win, and not parking gum under desks. And that's just for starters. Parents who do this will still have to attend meetings and offer help, and they may still have to investigate complaints from their children and then protest deficiencies and injustices. But they will have given the school an enormous gift of time and money by freeing staff from doing remedial parenting and suffering the consequences of children who have been shielded from becoming civilized.

Giving Up

DEAR MISS MANNERS — From what I see happening in my community, the refusal to do favors without compensation is only going to increase. The public schools and many of the private schools require that community service hours be completed before a student may be graduated. I am involved in one of the community organizations certified by the school system to grant the time. We have not been overwhelmed with volunteers, and once the hours have been completed, the students are not seen again unless we offer a salary. In the surrounding areas without this "volunteer" requirement they are able to staff a similar program with a full volunteer staff.

Interestingly, our community also has an active community service program in place for juvenile offenders in lieu of jail time.

A related development is that service hours are also required for a variety of religious advancements. I was pleased when my child decided to volunteer for an activity involving 80 hours during the summer. Because he will be marking a religious milestone next school year, we checked on the documentation requirements for the service component. I was shocked and saddened to find that they would only let him use a small fraction of this time to meet the "volunteer" service requirements. The activities which are "mandated" for service are to my eye no more worthy or soul enhancing than those which have been freely selected. Now a child who was looking forward to cheerful volunteerism is dreading the enforced hours which will be needed to meet the requirements. Is it any wonder that people do not freely serve?

GENTLE READER — Like you, Miss Manners remembers when voluntary service was something for which people volunteered, rather than were sentenced to do. A lot has happened since then, notably the attitude that it is foolish to work for free. It is not only modern greed that created this, but a long-term general dismissal of the value of volunteer work because it was done by unsalaried women.

Surely the function of a mandatory educational system is to expose the young to ideas, fields, attitudes and information they might not otherwise encounter, or might even take pains to avoid. No doubt many of them do as little as possible for the service requirement and resolve never to return—but isn't that true of much else they are supposed to be learning?

Reverse psychology is all very well, but Miss Manners doubts that removing the algebra requirement, for example, would inspire otherwise dilatory students with an interest in algebra. She therefore hopes that in spite of your son's disillusionment, you will stop short of condemning the effort of schools and religious organizations to teach through requirements that one must donate services to the community.

The implementation of this may seem rigid, although Miss Manners can easily imagine why it might be unfeasible for young people to choose their own places of service—the problem of checking out the organization, for example, or the problem in checking out the child's idea of charity.

Miss Manners suggests you regard this practice charitably because of the worthiness of the idea. She assures you that in the etiquette business, we believe it is better for people to do the right thing because they feel coerced into doing it than to allow them to act only as they sincerely wish, and hope for the best.

Conclusion

The term "old-fashioned" is not quite the pejorative crusher it used to be, Miss Manners has noticed with some relief. Old-fashioned households, complete with children and cushions, are quite the latest thing.

For most of this century, the term "old-fashioned" (when applied to anything not containing liquor and even some folks who did) was a choice insult. The world was perceived as moving rapidly, churning out ever better ideas, products and ways of living, and stragglers were shot with scorn. Goodness knows this epithet was lobbed often enough at defenseless Miss Manners. She is a devotee of the Stopped Clock School of Fashion, by which one is madly chic twice every decade, when the clothing one prefers cycles around; and behind the times—or one can equally well say way, way ahead of them—the other years. She also admits to holding old-fashioned values, or at least she used to, until that became a code term for taking an unseemly interest in how other people pursue romance.

So you can imagine Miss Manners' alarm when, at the end of the 20th century, old-fashionedness became adorable. Even the Victorians, that beleaguered generation that promised to rival the Puritans for disrepute among its descendants, evolved into—cutie-pies. Miss Manners is afraid there is no other way to say it. She sometimes wonders whether global warming isn't the result of all of them spinning in their graves at once.

The most visible effect has been on households. After years of open space, geometrical shapes and bare surfaces, nooks and padding are everywhere. There is so much coziness and warmth that Miss Manners worries that the citizens must be having trouble finding their beds under their pillow collections. Handicrafts are booming; at least, taking instruction in handicrafts is booming. To perform household tasks the hardest way possible is considered a demonstration of loving care and personal attention. Why buy a bag of potato chips when you can spend the day making them?

Miss Manners could tell you why, possibly drawing in embarrassing reminders about how everyone claims to be too busy nowadays to perform the ordinary little politenesses of life. Not that she is opposed to charming hobbies or enhancing the home. Laces and tassels are quite to her overstuffed taste, and she reminds herself that lurching into the ludicrous, as demonstrated by the current enthusiasts with their crammed parlors and mincing manners, was an authentic plague of Victorian times.

There is something more deeply upsetting about this, however. It is all very well to turn one's home into a theme park at the expense of history, which isn't around to defend itself, but not if it does damage to the present. That happens when the artifacts take on so much weight that they crush the spirit—when the food receives more attention than the people who eat it, or when stylistic harmony inspires disharmony against those whose tastes and presents don't meet the standard.

Miss Manners is not so shallow as to say that surfaces don't matter. Nor is she after a period spirit to go with the bric-a-brac. We don't live Victorian lives, and a good thing that is, too. What bothers her is any sort of decoration piled on top of an unsound structure. The foundation of a civilized household is made with such qualities as respect, generosity, hospitality and shared time and resources. These things are not subject to going in and out of fashion.

The Source

DEAR MISS MANNERS—I have once again seen an ad on TV with an adult drinking juice from the family-sized container from the refrigerator. Would one dare to accept a drink of juice in anyone's home, after watching this happen over and over again?

GENTLE READER—Miss Manners has always hoped that people have more sense than to get their manners lessons from television commercials, in which case you wouldn't have to worry about this problem in real life. Please don't disillusion her.

Index